Reports of Cases Argued and Determined in the Court of Appeals of Virginia

— VOLUME I —

Bushrod Washington

HERITAGE BOOKS
2012

HERITAGE BOOKS
AN IMPRINT OF HERITAGE BOOKS, INC.

Books, CDs, and more—Worldwide

For our listing of thousands of titles see our website at
www.HeritageBooks.com

A Facsimile Reprint
Published 2012 by
HERITAGE BOOKS, INC.
Publishing Division
100 Railroad Ave. #104
Westminster, Maryland 21157

Copyright © 2000 Carol Chafin

Originally published
Richmond:
Printed by Thomas Nicolson,
1798

— Publisher's Notice —
In reprints such as this, it is often not possible to remove blemishes from the original. We feel the contents of this book warrant its reissue despite these blemishes and hope you will agree and read it with pleasure.

International Standard Book Numbers
Paperbound: 978-0-7884-1696-5
Clothbound: 978-0-7884-9138-2

TO

EDMUND PENDLETON, Esquire,

PRESIDENT

OF THE

COURT OF APPEALS,

THIS WORK

IS

RESPECTFULLY

DEDICATED,

AS A TESTIMONY

OF THE

VERY HIGH OPINION THE AUTHOR ENTERTAINS

OF HIS

DISTINGUISHED CHARACTER AND TALENTS.

DISTRICT OF VIRGINIA TO WIT:

BE it remembered, that on the 15th day of February in the 22d year of the Independence of the United States of America, BUSHROD WASHINGTON, of the said district, hath deposited in this office the title of a book, the right whereof he claims as author, in the words following, to wit: "Reports "of cases argued and determined in the Court of Appeals of Virginia," in conformity to the act of Congress of the United States entitled "An act for the encouragement of learning, by securing the copies of maps, charts and books to the authors and proprietors of such copies, during the times therein mentioned."

WILLIAM MARSHALL, Clk. of the District of Virginia.

TO THE
READER.

THE notes of the following cases commencing in the year 1792, were taken for my own use, without any view to a publication of them. I generally extended them into something like their present form, during the term in which the decisions were given, and whilst the impression which they made, were fresh upon my mind.

It was not until I despaired of some other gentleman of the bar undertaking a work of this kind, that I determined to revise the notes I had taken, and to publish them (with a few corrections) in the state in which I had originally written them, for I found that my professional engagements would deny me the opportunity of preparing them for public inspection in the manner I wished. The first volume has been printed during the spring term of the Superior Courts, which will account for many typographical errors.

That there should be many inaccuracies in the following reports I can easily believe. Engaged through the whole year either in attending the courts, or in preparing my suits for trial, I have had very little time to devote to a work which required much labor and attention. My sole aim has been to give a correct statement of the cases, and to make a true report of the arguments and decisions upon them. If I have succeeded in this, I shall be abundantly gratified; farther, I have never extended my views; I have not had time to polish.

The few cases which are reported prior to the year 1792, are taken from notes with which the President was so obliging as to furnish me. It is much to be wished that some gentleman who has taken notes of all the cases which have been decided since the present establishment of the Court of Appeals, may favor the public with reports of such of them as I have necessarily omitted.

It is with pleasure that I acknowledge the assistance I have received from many of the Judges of the Court of Appeals (and particularly from the President) from whose notes I have been enabled to correct those cases in which I had misconceived the opinions which had been delivered.

TABLE OF CASES REPORTED.

A.

Case	Page
Alberry &c. vs. Calloway.	72
Anderson vs Bernard.	186
Applebury & others vs. Anthony's Ex'r.	287
Armistead vs Marks, &c.	325

B.

Case	Page
Brown vs Belches, Braxton ex. of Claiborn vs Winslow &c.	9
Birch vs Alexander.	31
Butler vs Parks.	35
Bibb vs. Cauthorne.	76
Baird &c. vs. Blaigrove.	91
Banister's ex. vs Shore	170
Brown's adm'x. vs. Garland and others	173
Beckwith vs Butler &c.	221
Byrd vs Cocke.	224
Burwell vs Court.	232
Bentley, ex of Ronald, vs Harmanson's ex.	254
Buckner &c vs Smith &c.	273
Brown's ex. vs Putney.	296
Burnley vs Lambert.	302
Boswell &c. vs Jones.	308
Brewer vs Tarpley.	322
Barnett &c. vs Watson.	363
Braxton vs Morris.	372
	380

C.

Case	Page
Cockran vs Street.	79
Clayborn vs Hill.	177
Coleman vs Dick &c.	235
Carr vs Gooch.	260
Cole vs Clayborn.	262
Cooke vs Beale's ex.	312
Cosby ex. Loudon vs Hite.	365

D.

Case	Page
Downman vs Downman's executors.	26
Dade vs Alexander.	30
Daniel vs Robinson's ex.	154
Doe lessee of Murra vs. Northern.	282
Dandridge vs Harris.	326

E.

Case	Page
Evans vs Smith.	72
Eustace vs Gaskins ex. Eustace.	188

F.

Case	Page
Field's ex. vs Spotswood.	280

G.

Case	Page
Groves vs Graves.	1
Granberry's ex. vs Granberry, &c.	246

H.

Case	Page
Hudson vs Johnson.	10
Hooe & Harrison & others vs Oxley & Hancock.	19
Hubbard vs Blow and Barksdale.	70
Hudson vs Morris.	ibid
Hunters vs Haynes.	71
Hudson vs Ross & co.	74
Hill and Braxton vs. Southerland's ex.	128
Wm. Hunters ex. vs Spotswood.	145
Hoyle vs Young	150
Hawkin's ex. vs. Berkeley	204
Hooe &c. vs Mason.	207
Hooe &c. vs Pierce.	212
Hubbard vs Taylor.	259
Hewlett vs Chamberlayne	307
Hoomes &c. vs Smock.	389

I.

Case	Page
Johnson vs Macon.	4
Jones & Temple vs Logwood.	42
Jenkins vs Tom & others.	123
Irvin &c. vs Eldridge &c.	161
Johnson vs Bourn.	187
Jones vs Williams.	230

TABLE OF CASES REPORTED.

K.

Kennon vs M'Roberts & ux.	96
Keele and Roberts vs. Herbert's ex'rs.	138
Kennedy vs Baylor.	162
Kerr & Co. vs Love.	172
Keele and Roberts vs. Herbert	203
Keene vs Lee	239

L.

Lewis ex. of Thruston vs Norton	76
Leftwich & ux. vs. Stovall &c.	303
Lee ex. of Daniel vs. Cooke.	306

M.

M'Allister vs M'Allister.	193
M'Williams vs Willis.	199
Minnis &c. vs Aylett.	300
M'Guire vs Warder ex. of Parker.	368

N.

Nelson vs Nelson	136
Nicholas vs Fletcher.	330

P.

Pleasants vs Bibb.	8
Pleasants Shore & Co. &c. vs Ross.	156
Payne ex. Payne vs. Dudley ex. Fleet.	196
Peter vs Cocke.	257
Pleasants & co. vs Lewis.	273
Pendleton vs Vandevier.	381

R.

Ross vs Norvell.	14
Roane's ex. vs Hearne & ux.	47
Ross vs Gill & ux.	87
Ross vs Poythress.	120
Reynolds vs Waller's heir at law.	164

S.

Smith vs Harmanson.	6
Shermer vs Beale.	11
Seekright lessee of Mayo vs Paul Carrington & others.	45
David Shelton &c. vs John Shelton.	53
Scott vs Trent.	77
Scott's ex. vs Call.	115
Smith vs Walker ex. of Mickie.	135
Stevens vs Taliaferro.	155
Sallee vs Yates and ux.	226
Smith & Moreton vs Wallace.	254
Shermer vs Shermer's ex.	266
Smallwood vs Hansborough.	290
Stott & Donaldson vs Alexander & Co.	331
Southall vs M'Keand &c.	336

T.

Turpin vs Turpin.	75
Thornton vs Smith.	81
Taylor vs Dundass.	92
Thompson vs Davenport &c.	125
Thornton ex. of Champ, vs Jett.	138
Turner vs Turner.	139
Thornton ex. of Thompson &c. vs Spotswood.	142
Tarpley's adm. vs Dobyns.	185
Tomlin &c. vs Kelly.	190
Thweat &c. vs Finch.	217
Taylors admx. vs Peytons admx.	252
Turner vs Stip.	319

W.

Wilcox vs Calloway.	38
Wood vs Davis.	69

TABLE OF CASES REPORTED.

White vs Jones,	116	Wilson & M'Rae vs.	
Winslow vs Dawson.	118	Keeling.	194
Wilcox vs Rootes & others	140	Westfall vs Singleton.	227
Williams &c. ex. Corrie vs. Campbell.	153	Ward vs Webber & ux.	274
		Watson &c. vs. Alexander	340
White vs Johnson.	159	Wroe vs Washington &c.	357
White, Whittle & co. vs Banister's ex.	166		

JUDGES OF THE COURT OF APPEALS.

EDMUND PENDLETON, Esq. President.

PETER LYONS, Esq.

PAUL CARRINGTON, Esq.

WILLIAM FLEMING, Esq.

JAMES MERCER, Esq.

On the 12th of November 1793, HENRY TAZEWELL, Esq. qualified as a Judge of this Court in the room of James Mercer, Esq. who died during the term.

On the 13th of April 1795, SPENCER ROANE, Esq. qualified as a Judge of this Court in the room of HENRY TAZEWELL, Esq. resigned.

CASES DETERMINED
IN THE
COURT OF APPEALS,
IN
THE FALL TERM OF THE YEAR,
1790.

GROVES *against* GRAVES.

ON the 1st of October 1787, John Stockdell, and Francis Graves the appellee, made a writing to the appellant in the following words, viz," for value received we promise
" to pay John Groves, or order, on the 1st day of December
" next, the sum of £260 current money, in Pierce's final settle-
" ments at the rate of twenty shillings, such settlements, for
" each thirteen pence current money, the said John Groves
" agrees that the same may be discharged by the payment of
" a like sum in the said final settlements, at any time on or
" before the 1st day of November next ensuing the date hereof,
" at the rate of twenty shillings, of such final settlements,
" for each twenty six pence current money."

On the 3d of October 1787, the appellant received from Stockdell real security for the above debt, and gave him the following receipt, viz. I acknowledge to have received from Mr. John
" Stockdell an assignment of a tract of land containing 40,000
" acres, Ballard Smith to said Stockdell. The condition of which
" assignment is, that if the said Stockdell shall pay unto me the
" sum of eight thousand dollars in Pierce's final settlements, on
" or before the first day of November next, then the said deed
" to be returned him, otherwise to be sold at public sale to the
" highest bidder, and the balance, if any, after purchasing the
" said settlements, to be returned to the said Stockdell.

The Contract, of the 1st of October 1787, not being performed by Stockdell or Graves, the appellant instituted a suit at law upon it against both of the contractors.

B   The

The breach assigned in the declaration is, that the defendants did not deliver the final settlements equivalent to the said sum of £260 at the rate of twenty shillings, such settlements, for each twenty six pence current money contained in the said £260 on or before the 1st day of November, 1787, whereby a right accrued to demand the said final settlements, at the rate of 20 shillings of such settlements, for each thirteen pence current money contained in the said sum of £260.

The jury found a verdict for the plaintiff, and assessed his damages to £1200

The appellee filed his bill in the High Court of Chancery, praying an injunction to the judgment entered upon this verdict, that he might be relieved from so much of it as exceeded the sum of £260 with interest, and that the 40,000 acres of land might, in the first instance, be decreed to be sold to satisfy whatever sum the said Groves might be supposed entitled to. The equity stated in the bill is, that the plaintiff Graves was but a surety for Stockdell who was and is in needy circumstances, that the £260 was a mere loan to him from Groves, and that the payment of the final settlements, at thirteen pence in the pound, was intended either as a penalty, or for the purpose of procuring an usurious and unconscionable gain to the lender. An injunction 'till further order was granted. To this bill, the defendant John Groves filed his answer, denying that the £260 was loaned to the said Stockdell and stating that he agreed to purchase from the said Stockdell 8000 dollars in final settlement certificates, to be paid for immediately and to be delivered in future, and to guard against any possible loss, which might arise by a delivery at a future day, in consequence of the fluctuating and uncertain value of such paper, it was agreed, that, in consideration of a longer credit, the said sum of £260 paid in advance, should be repaid, by the delivery of certificates at the rate of 20 shillings thereof, for every 13 pence specie if delivered on the 1st of December following: and to stimulate Stockdell to an earlier delivery, the defendant agreed to accept the certificates at double that price, if delivered by the 1st of November preceding, that the writing was bottomed upon this agreement. The answer admits, (as the bill states,) that the jury in assessing the damages may have converted the £260 into final settlements at 13 pence to the pound, and then valued, the amount of the final

settlements

settlements thus produced, at five shillings in the pound, the then selling price of such papers.

The Chancellor, (being of opinion, that the plaintiff ought partly to be relieved against the judgment, because the writing, recited in the bill, appeared to have been designed to secure unconscionable profit to the said John Groves, and to have been obtained from one whom he had cause to believe at that time to be needy: and because the certificates which were secured to be paid, in default of payment of half the quantity on the first day of November, and the value of which was the damages assessed by the jury, were in nature of a penalty or forfeiture:) Decreed a perpetual injunction as to the plaintiff Graves, for so much of the judgment as exceeded £260 and interest thereon from the 1st of October 1787, after deducting the costs in the Court of Chancery.

From this decree Groves appealed.

THE PRESIDENT delivered the following as the opinion and decree of the Court. " The Contract between the parties
" ought to be taken as purporting the delivery of certificates
" on the 1st of November 1787, at twenty shillings, for
" every twenty six pence of the amount of the specie advanced,
" and, the payment in certificates at half the value in case
" of failure, only as a penalty; and, therefore, the contract
" was neither usurious, or so unconscionable as to be
" set aside in a Court of Equity, twenty sixpence being
" only the lowest rate of the market price of such certificates
" at the time. The verdict of the jury was not only wrong,
" as being for the penalty, but in the measure of damages,
" taking for that measure the value of certificates at the time
" of the trial when, under the peculiar circumstances of this
" case, the value at the time they should have been delivered,
" ought to be the rule. The decree, therefore, must be re-
" versed with costs, and an issue, ought to be made up, and
" tried by a jury between the parties, to ascertain what was
" the current market value of such certificates in specie, on
" the 1st day of November 1787, and so much specie as the
" £260 turned into certificates at 26 pence, and again changed
" into specie at the rate so to be settled by the jury, will
" amount to, with interest from the 1st of November 1787,
" and the costs at common law, ought to be paid to the appel-
" lant. But the parties waving the trial by a jury, and agree-
" ing, that the current market price of such certificates on the
said

"said 1st of November 1787, was twenty eight pence half-
"penny, and that £ 285 specie is the value thereof as ascer-
"tained according to the above opinion, it is decreed and or-
"dered that on payment by the appellee to the appellant of
"the said £ 285, with interest thereon, at the rate of 5 per
"cent. per annum, from the 1st of November 1787, 'till pay-
"ment, and all costs at common law, the injunction to the
"judgment be made perpetual, and that on such payment, the
"appellant shall deliver, and assign to the appellee the deed for
"the 40,000 acres of land, in the proceedings mentioned, and
"all papers relative thereto, or such as he received, to remain as
"a security to the appellee for his indemnification, and the sur-
"plus for the benefit of John Stockdell in the proceedings also
"mentioned, and, if payment, as aforesaid, be not made to the
"appellant within one month after making the final decree,
"that the said land be sold, by commissioners to be appointed
"by the High Court of Chancery, at public sale, for ready
"money, at a time and place to be previously advertised in
"one of the Gazettes. That this decree be satisfied out of
"the money arising from such sale, and that the surplus, after
"satisfying the appellee all his costs at law and in equity be
"paid to the said Stockdell."

JOHNSON *against* MACON.

THIS was an action on the case, brought by the appellant in the District Court of Richmond, against the appellee formerly sheriff of Hanover county, for the escape of Parke Smith committed at the suit of the appellant, upon a writ returned " executed and committed to jail" by William Bentley deputy sheriff.

The declaration sets forth the writ, service and return, that Macon kept an insufficient gaol; that he voluntarily and negligently suffered Smith to escape, and failed to take out an escape warrant against him, and to make fresh pursuit, by which the plaintiff had lost his debt, &c.

Upon not guilty pleaded, the jury found a verdict for the defendant, and on the next day the plaintiff moved for a new trial, upon the ground of a misdirection of the court, (at the trial,) who instructed the jury to find for the defendant, but the motion was over-ruled, the court being of opinion, that it was incumbent on the plaintiff to prove an actual escape by Smith from the custody, and by the consent or negligence of the defendant or his deputy, whereas the only evidence given by the plaintiff at the trial was the record of the suit against Smith, up to the judgment, and the oath of William Anderson the present high sheriff, that the said Smith was not at any time turned over to his custody by assignment from any former sheriff, together with the admission of the defendant, that when Smith was arrested, he the defendant was high sheriff of the county, and that Smith some years after resided in Charleston.

To the opinion of the court, over-ruling the motion for the reasons above mentioned, the plaintiff excepted, and tendered a bill, which though not appearing to have been sealed, is made part of the record.

Judgment for the defendant and appeal.

THE PRESIDENT delivered the opinion of the court. A motion for a new trial upon the ground of misdirection of the judge at nisi prius is never made to the same judge, but to the court of Kings Bench. To make the motion to the same judge who gave the direction is certainly irregular, and improper. The exception ought to have been stated to the direction itself.

But as the exception states the direction of the judge, and the ground of it, so as to enable this court to decide upon the propriety of the opinion, we shall pass over the form, and enquire into the grounds of that direction.

The opinion is in part right, since the actual escape, is the gift of the action and therefore ought to have been proved, and in part wrong, so far as it required the appellant to prove the escape to have been with the consent or through the negligence of the sheriff, since the consent or negligence, tho' made necessary by the act of Assembly, ought to be presumed, unless on the sheriffs part a tortious escape be shewn, and that fresh pursuit was made. But it is unnecessary to decide this point, since that part of the opinion which was clearly right, will justify the subsequent direction to the jury, there being no proof of an actual escape.

The parole proof is, that Macon was high sheriff when Smith was arrested, and that Smith resided in Charleston some years after, which is certainly no proof of an actual escape from the defendant or his deputy.

The record proves him to have been in custody in June 1778, when Macon could not have been sheriff, as he was so at the time of the arreſt in January 1775, more than two years before. But Anderſon ſwears, that Smith was not turned over to his cuſtody by aſſignment from any former ſheriff. Let it in the firſt place be remarked, that Anderſon was a very improper witneſs to exculpate himſelf.—But 2dly, Eſcapes which in England are fixed upon the ſheriff from legal deductions, ſeem to be done away in this country, by the act of Aſſembly, which ſubjects the ſheriff, only where the jury expreſsly find that the debtor eſcaped with the conſent, or through the negligence of the officer. This a jury would hardly find, when it appeared that the debtor was in the actual cuſtody of a ſucceeding ſheriff, altho' the formality of an aſſignment had been omitted.

Beſides, tho' no aſſignment were made, yet the other mode of transferring priſoners by entry on record might have been obſerved.

Judgment affirmed.

CASES ARGUED AND DETERMINED

IN THE

COURT OF APPEALS

IN THE SPRING TERM OF THE YEAR

1791.

SMITH *againſt* HARMANSON.

THIS was an action of debt brought upon a bond in the county court of Accomack by the appellant. Plea owe nothing, with leave to give the ſpecial matter in evidence; but oyer is not prayed. Verdict "that the defendant doth owe to the plaintiff £1147 18 4 parcel of the debt in the bill aforeſaid mentioned." Judgment is entered that the plaintiff recover againſt the defendant £2000 the debt in the declaration mentioned and his coſts, to be diſcharged by the payment of the ſaid £1147 18 4 and the coſts. The bond appears upon the record and is with a condition to pay £1000.

Upon

Upon appeal to the District court, this judgment was reversed, "the same having been entered for the aggregate sum of the principal and interest thereon to the day of the said judgment." The judgment of the District Court is for £2000 and costs, but to be discharged by the payment of £1000 with interest from the time it was payable and the costs.—From this judgment Smith appealed.

THE PRESIDENT.—The judgment of the District Court is more beneficial to the appellant than that of the County Court, (with which the defendant in that Court was discontented) because it entitled him to the continuing interest after the judgment. Yet he appeals to this Court; so that each party in his turn has complained of an error in judgment, which operated beneficially for himself.

The District Court have erred upon their own principles; for if the judgment of the County Court should have been for principal and continuing interest, yet as the £1147 18 8 found by the jury did not appear otherwise than by calculation to be the aggregate of principal and interest, they should in that case have reversed the judgment, and remanded the cause to the inferior court for a new trial, to ascertain the principal sum due which was to bear interest. This court considering that the judgment of the District Court must be reversed, the next question was, what judgment they should have pronounced.

Upon this, there was some difficulty and contrariety of opinion, whether we should pursue the principle of the District Court, and in doing so, direct a new trial in the County Court, or as their judgment attained the real justice of the case, and saved expence, it should be sustained? or whether the judgment of the County Court should be affirmed? a majority of the Court thinking the jury might make their verdict of the aggregate of principal and interest, which tending to the benefit of the defendant, he did not object to it at the time, and could not appeal or complain of it, are for affirming that judgment, pursuing in this, the judgment of the General Court in the Norfolk case mentioned at the bar, which was the same as this; except that here there was leave to give special matter in evidence, from whence the jury might have drawn some ingredients for compounding the £1147 18 4, besides the aggregate of principal and interest, either to increase or diminish that aggregate.

The judgment of the District Court must be reversed with costs, and that of the County Court affirmed with damages from the time of entering it, to that of the judgment of the District Court.

PLEASANTS *against* BIBB,

THIS was an action of debt brought in the County Court of Prince Edward by the appellant upon a bond bearing date the 1st of February 1780, with condition to pay £ 105 9 2½ on or before the 17th of December 1781, with interest thereon from the 16th of February 1779. Upon the plea of payment, the parties consented to submit the trial of the cause to the Court without a jury.

The Court upon a view of the bond, together with sundry exhibits (all made part of the record) were of opinion that the scale of depreciation ought to be fixed to the 16th of February 1776, and so the judgment was entered, from which Pleasants appealed.

This judgment was reversed in the District Court of Prince Edward, and entered for the debt in the declaration mentioned, to be discharged by the payment of £ 2 : 6 : 10½ specie, the value of the sum due, reduced according to law, with interest from the 16th of February 1779. From this judgment Pleasants appealed.

THE PRESIDENT delivered the opinion of the Court.

The single question upon this record is, at what period the scale of depreciation should be applied to the bond upon which the judgment was rendered.

The bond was dated on the 1st of February 1780 with condition for payment on the 17th of February 1781, *with interest from the* 16*th of February* 1779, thereby indicating, if not expressing, that the debt arose on the day last mentioned, though not reduced to a specialty until the year 1780. The record also contains letters from the obligor, shewing the debt to have arisen on account of money lent at different times in the year 1779.

Upon the bond and those circumstances, the County Court very properly decided that the debt arose in February 1779 and was to be scaled as of that period. The judgment of the District Court which considered the date of the bond as the proper period for scaling, is therefore erroneous, and must be reversed, and that of the County Court affirmed.

BROWN

OF THE YEAR 1791.

BROWN *against* BELCHES,

THIS was an action on the case, upon an *infimul computaſſet*, instituted in the Borough court of Williamsburg by Belches against Brown the appellant, and William Eaton. The declaration is against both, but an abatement of the suit was entered as to Eaton, upon the return of the writ, that he was no inhabitant of the city.—Plea, non assumpsit.—By consent of parties the cause was referred to arbitrators, whose award, it was agreed, should be the judgment of the court. This order was not discharged, but at a subsequent term a jury was impannelled, who found for the plaintiff.—A new trial being granted, a second verdict was found in favor of the plaintiff, and judgment being accordingly entered up in his favour, the defendant appealed to the District Court of Williamsburg where the judgment being affirmed, an appeal was taken to this court.

THE PRESIDENT.—The objection made to the judgment, is that it could not be entered against one partner only, upon a partnership transaction.

The case of *Rice vs. Shute,*—5 Burr. 2611 shews, that one partner may be sued alone, and that the plaintiff shall not be nonsuited at the trial upon proof that there are other partners. If the defendant would take advantage of that circumstance, he must plead in abatement, and point out the other partners.

The distinction between torts and contracts is over-ruled, and the principle seems to be established that the party contracted with may be sued alone.

In this case the plaintiff took out his writ against both; one could not be found, and, according to the act of assembly, the suit abated as to him.

The defendant, who was arrested, pleads that he did not assume—The jury have found that he did—The defendant, without assigning errors or taking any exceptions, appeals from a general verdict.

Though the declaration charges, that the defendant with another assumed, a fact which as to that other is not tried, yet, this does not vitiate the defendant's assumpsit, which is found against him.

Judgment affirmed.

HUDSON *against* JOHNSON.

This was an action of debt, instituted in the county court of Louisa by the appellant, against the appellee.—Plea, payment.

At the trial the plaintiff filed a demurrer to the evidence, stating, that the defendant offered in evidence to maintain the issue on his part, a receipt, bearing date long subsequent to this suit, given by John Lewis the attorney who prosecuted this action for the plaintiff, and amongst whose papers the bond on which the suit was brought, was found; as also, that prior to the payment made by the said defendant to the said Lewis, on which account the said receipt was given, the defendant applied to the plaintiff to know where the bond was, who replied that it was in the possession of the said Lewis.—The demurrer was not joined, but the jury were discharged, and at a subsequent term, the court, after argument, over-ruled the demurrer, and gave judgment for the defendant with full costs, from which the plaintiff appealed to the District Court of Charlottesville.

The District Court reversed the judgment, so far as costs were awarded the defendant *preceding the payment to Lewis*, and affirmed it as to the residue; and entered judgment for the appellee for the costs incurred up to the time of such payment, and damages for retarding the execution thereof with the costs of the appeal.

From this judgment Hudson appealed to this Court.

THE PRESIDENT.—In General, payment to an attorney at law, is good on the custom of the country, particularly if he have possession of the specialty. Under particular circumstances this rule might not apply, as if notice were given that no such power was vested in the attorney. But in this case, the circumstances support the general principle; for upon enquiry being made for the bond, the defendant was referred by the plaintiff to the attorney.

It was objected to the payment, that it was made *after the action was brought:*

It has always been the practice, and very properly so, to allow discounts up to the time of the trial, but not so as to destroy the plaintiffs action, and entitle the defendant to costs; in that case, it should be considered by analogy to the case of bringing the money into Court, so as to entitle the plaintiff to a

judgment

judgment for costs. Under the equity of the act, we think a payment to the plaintiff equivalent to bringing the money into court.

The judgment therefore of the District Court is right in reversing that of the County Court, giving costs to the defendant, and awarding the plaintiff his. But we cannot affirm this judgment, because it goes further, and awards damages on those costs.

It must therefore be reversed with costs for that error, as to the damages, and be affirmed as to the residue.

SHERMER *against* BEALE.

THE appellant having filed a bill in the High Court of Chancery against the appellee praying an account, an order was made by consent of parties, referring all matters in difference between them to the final determination of two arbitrators, indifferently chosen by them, and, in case of their disagreement, to such umpire as they should chuse, who are to proceed to determine the same, in conformity to bonds entered into by the parties on the 6th day May 1788.

The bond referred to, submits all suits, actions, litigations, and controversies to the final determination of the two arbitrators named in the above order, whose award was not to be made before the 1st of December following, that the parties might have time to procure their testimony. It stipulates that the above suit in chancery should, by a rule of Court be refered to the same arbitrators, to be proceeded in and determined according to the principles of this agreement; that all other suits depending in other Courts should also be referred to the same arbitrators; the arbitrators to name an umpire in case of their disagreement; the award or umpirage to be made the judgment or decree of the respective courts as far as they are applicable to the respective cases; they to be final, and no advantage to be taken of any informality or defect in the rules of reference, award, decree or judgment, nor an appeal to be prayed, or writ of error applied for, to such decree and judgment. The bond then proceeds to lay down certain rules and principles by which the reference is to be conducted, and stipulates that Shermer is to receive, in satisfaction of any sum which might
be

be awarded him, bonds or judgments if decided to be good, by the arbitrators, but to be guaranteed by Beale. The award to be made in writing, ready to be delivered on or before the 1ft of June 1789.

Upon this bond was endorfed an agreement figned by the parties, bearing date the 30th of May 1789, authorifing the arbitrators by endorfement on the above bond, to appoint any perfon they might chufe to affift them in forming and making up the award, fuch perfon to be paid by the parties for his trouble: the award to be ready to be delivered by the 20th of June 1789, and to have the fame effect, and be entered up in Court in the fame manner, as if it were made and delivered by the two arbitrators, on or before the day for that purpofe appointed. The parties then bind themfelves in the penalty of £ 10,000, each, to the other, to abide by this agreement, which is not to change or alter the bond in any refpect, except as is therein expreffed.

An endorfement, bearing date the 30th of May 1789, is made upon the bond by the two arbitrators, appointing a third perfon to unite with them, or one of them, in forming and making up the award.

An award was made and returned, figned by the three arbitrators, by which they award to the plaintiff £ 3022 to be paid conformably with the agreement in the conditions of the bonds refpectively fet forth; and further, that the defendant in 3 months from the date thereof give bond with good fecurity to the plaintiff, to indemnify him againft two bills of exchange for £ 600 fterling each, endorfed by the faid plaintiff. And on the defendant's complying with this award, each party to execute to the other a releafe of and concerning all matters and things by the faid order referred to the arbitrators :—the defendant to pay the cofts of this fuit.

On the motion of the plaintiff to enter up the award and bond as the decree of the High Court of Chancery, the judge of that Court refufed to admit the affidavit of the defendant, ftating certain exceptions to the award and umpirage, to be entered as part of the proceedings in the caufe, and ordered the bonds of fubmiffion, with the endorfements thereon, and the award and umpirage to be regiftered. But the Court refufed to make an abfolute decree in the terms, or according to the tenor, of the award and umpirage, left the defendant might poffibly be precluded from availing himfelf of any exception not appearing on the face of the award and umpirage, to which it might be liable.

It

It was therefore decreed and ordered, "that the defendant do perform the said award and umpirage, unless cause be shewn against it by the succeeding term."

Beale then filed a bill, making Shermer and the arbitrators parties, stating various objections to the justice and propriety of the award, and charging one of the arbitrators with partiality.

To this bill Shermer filed his answer, denying all the allegations in the bill: no replication was filed to this answer, nor did the arbitrators answer the bill. At the term succeeding that at which the interlocutory order before mentioned was made, Beale shewed cause against a final decree being entered up, "insisting that the Court's authority to make the said decree must be derived, either from the submission of the 6th May 1788, or that of the 30th of May 1789: that no such authority was derived from the former, because, though it was made a rule of Court, yet the award and umpirage was not made within the time limited by it: nor from the latter, because it was not made a rule of Court." The chancellor being satisfied with the cause shewn, set aside the former order and decree, from which Shermer appealed.

The PRESIDENT delivered the opinion of the Court.

Submissions were made rules of court, by consent, at common law, before the statute. *Sid.* 54. *T. Ray.* 35. and afterwards under the statute of 9 & 10 William III.

It seems to have been practiced on bonds of submission with condition that the submission should be made a rule of court, either to proceed to the award, and to have that entered as the judgment of the court, or to have the rule previously entered. The former was the case in Baily & Chefely, 1 *Salk.* 72. Since, on deciding the question about consent, the *award*, not the *submission*, was made the rule of the court.

Under the authority of this case, (the indorsement being considered as evidence of consent that the award should be made the judgment of the court,) the award might have been confirmed without a previous rule of submission.

In 2 *Atk.* 501. New rules of court were made to enlarge the times, but this does not prove that they were necessary. The court of chancery in England is always open, and it might have been a more convenient practice, than to enter into new agreements to extend the time,

The

The endorsement is to be considered as incorporated with, and part of the condition of the bond, so as to constitute one entire agreement, and to be taken by relation to the date of the bond, so as to bring it within the original rule. In this view of the case, the Chancellor erred in his decision upon the cause shewn, on the ground which he took.

We have examined this voluminous record, to see if there be any other ground more tenable. Reasons for obstructing or setting aside awards, according to the best construction of the statutes, are either for some illegality or injustice apparent on the face of them, or for misbehaviour in the arbitrators. Every argument, derived from the spirit of the statutes of Jeofails in favor of judgments, applies with increased force in favor of awards, since the judges in the latter case are of the parties own chusing.

The bill filed in this case, shewing cause against the award, not only goes over the whole subject of dispute, referring to former bills, answers and accounts, but contains a libel against one of the arbitrators, and all of them are made defendants.

This is a strange proceeding, first to chuse judges to decide a dispute, and then to make them defendants to a suit, in order to demand of them the reasons of their decision. The arbitrators might have demurred to the bill, not being obliged to answer.

The defendant Shermer has fully denied all the charges in the bill, and has done away the ground of suspicion (for it was only suspicion) of a partial attachment to him, in one of the arbitrators.

The causes therefore being fully done away in the mode chosen by the appellee, (like the case of an injunction which in such a case would have been dissolved,) there appears no reason to obstruct the decree directing the award to be performed.

DECREE reversed with costs.

ROSS *against* NORVELL.

THE appellee on the 5th of April 1779, filed his bill in the High court of Chancery, praying to redeem certain negroes which he states he had mortgaged to the appellant in the year 1765, to secure the payment of a debt due to him. The slaves were conveyed by an absolute bill of sale, bearing date the 18th of June 1765, with a warranty, and a receipt for the consideration stated in the deed, was endorsed thereon. The bill states, that

that the conveyance, though abſolute in form, was intended as a ſecurity, and that it was verbally agreed at the time, that the plaintiff might redeem at any time, upon payment of the principal and intereſt.

The anſwer admits the conveyance, but inſiſts that the ſale was abſolute, and was intended as a ſatisfaction of a prior debt due to the defendant.

Sundry depoſitions were taken in the cauſe, ſome of which fully eſtabliſh the allegations in the bill, but there is conſiderable contrariety in the evidence as to the real intention of the conveyance.

Upon a hearing of the cauſe, the Chancellor decreed the defendant, to deliver the ſlaves and their increaſe to the plaintiff, and to pay the profits of them, (after deducting therefrom the debt and intereſt to ſecure which they were conveyed,) to the plaintiff, for aſcertaining which profits an account was directed.

From this decree the defendant appealed.

The defendant Roſs, filed a croſs bill in the terms of his anſwer, and in addition thereto ſtated two promiſſory notes ſigned by Norvell, in the year 1767, the one for £ 5 : 8 : 6 for the hire of the above mentioned negroes, from the 18th of June 1765, until the 8th of June 1767, and the other for 13 s. 9 d. for their hire from the laſt mentioned date until the 10th of September following: and that at the hearing of the original ſuit he was unable to produce the above notes, which would have proved the ſale to be abſolute. The bill prays a ſuſpenſion of the original decree.

The anſwer to the croſs bill is a flat denial of all the allegations in it, and ſtates that the notes were given for the accruing intereſt of the debt due.

Upon a hearing of the croſs cauſe upon bill and anſwer, the bill was diſmiſſed, from which decree alſo, Roſs appealed.

THE PRESIDENT delivered the opinion of the Court.

It is objected in this caſe, that here is an abſolute deed, and that no parol proof is to be admitted to contradict it. This is a queſtion important in its conſequences, but which, in its full latitude, cannot be admitted either way, as the general rule. That is to ſay, we cannot determine that it *is not* to be admitted in *any caſe,* or, that it *is* to be admitted in *all caſes.*

To ſay that it ſhall be admitted in no caſe, would be to overturn all the deciſions in which relief has been granted againſt

deeds

deeds, upon the ground of fraud, mistake, oppression or imposition; or that they were made upon a secret trust between the parties. In all which cases, the fact which is the ground of relief, is established by the testimony of witnesses. Of the first class, the books abound with instances which are stated in the case of lord Irnham *vs.* Child. *Brow. Ch. Rep.* 92. Of the latter there are also many. The case of Gascoin *vs.* Thwing. 1 *Vern.* 366, is a strong one. A purchases in the name of B, to whom the conveyance is made. A was admitted to prove that he paid the purchase money, so as to make it a resulting trust to himself. So in the case of Hill & wife, *vs.* Wizgett. 2 Vern. 547, a surrender of a feme covert, and the admission upon the roll, were of a moiety only of her estate. Yet an entry on the stewards book, and parol proof by the foreman of the jury, were admitted as good evidence to prove that she surrendered the whole.

But against the current of authorities is cited the case of lord Irnham *vs.* Child, *Brow.* Ch. rep. 92. Child as agent for Mr. Lutterel son of lord Irnham, (but that circumstance not known to the father) treated with lord Irnham for the purchase of an annuity. The terms being settled, it was agreed that the annuity should be redeemable, but both parties consented that it should not be inserted in the grant, on a supposition that it would make the contract usurious and void. The annuity was assigned by Mr. Lutterel to others, and then lord Irnham brought his bill to redeem on the ground of the private agreement. Parol proof was offered to prove it, and in support of its admissibility a string of cases are cited. Does the chancellor over-rule their authority? By no means; he affirms them. Having stated the rule of law, that a deed in writing will admit of no contract that is not part of the deed whether it adds to, or takes, from the contract, he comes to the chancery cases, and says, " It is contended to be the general authority of a court of equity to relieve in cases of fraud, trust, accident or mistake, which applies to agreements as well as to other subjects. This must always clash with the argument drawn from the statute. It is admitted, that if there be no fraud the deed will bind. But objected, that when fraud interferes, *there the evidence may be introduced.*" Does he over-rule the objection in the cases on which it is founded? On the contrary, he says, " it is founded on a great deal of wisdom and good sense. But the question is, if it were to be admitted in all cases, whether it would not be subversive of justice: The court have held that it would."

He

He then puts the queſtion of fraud; if there were proof of that, the rule of evidence would not be ſubverted in admitting it. Then, the caſe of miſtake; he ſays, the court would not overturn the rule of evidence by varying the deed, but that it would be an equity dehors the deed. He then proceeds to ſtate the circumſtances of that caſe, and concludes thus: " I have " no idea of this being notice to the aſſignee of the annuities, that " they were redeemable. It is argued ſeveral ways; that they " had *notice perſonally*; that they had notice by their agent, and " that it was neceſſary for them to apply to lord Irnham: this " might have place, if they were bringing a bill againſt lord " Irnham, but here it has no place, for the deed was ſhewn to " them by which he conveyed abſolutely. I am not able to con-- " ceive, that they were obliged to recur to him, any more than " if it had been a dormant equity:" and ſo diſmiſſed the bill.

I think this caſe turns principally upon the equity of the aſſignees, who purchaſed on the faith of the abſolute deed, and would have applied ſtrongly in favor of a purchaſer from Mr. Roſs without notice. The general principles of the caſe prove, that parole evidence, when there is a deed, is not to be admitted in *all caſes*, nor refuſed *in all*, every caſe muſt depend on its own circumſtances. In that juſt noticed, the Chancellor admitted the proofs to be read, to diſcover if there were ground for relief on a new head of equity, and on the teſtimony, determined there was not.

The court have the leſs difficulty in admitting the proofs on the preſent occaſion, ſince Norvell was ſuffered to remain in poſſeſſion of the ſlaves, two years, as appears from the written papers; and this being contrary to the ordinary effect of a ſale, gives an impreſſion of a truſt of ſome kind, between the parties, and admits the introduction of evidence to explain that truſt.

The next objection is to the length of time. It is contended that after 20 years, the Chancellor will not admit a redemption of lands, where the mortgagee is in poſſeſſion, becauſe by that poſſeſſion the entry is taken away, and an ejectment barred. From hence it is argued, that, by analogy to this principle, the redemption of mortgaged ſlaves after 5 years would be refuſed, that being the length of time allowed for commencing an action of detinue or trover.

The firſt anſwer to this argument is, that if this were the caſe of an action of detinue upon a legal title, it would not be barred by the act of limitations.

Mr. Johnson proves, that in 1770 or 1772, Mr. Ross acknowledged to him, that Mr. Norvell had a right to redeem, on payment of principal and interest at any time. This acknowledgment of title in Norvell, was sufficient to discharge the case from the preceding lapse of time. The tender was in 1778.—Now take both extremes,—the conveyance in 1770, and the tender in 1778, is eight years; from which deduct the four years disallowed in the computation of time by the act of 1777, and the party will come within the 5 years.—Again, take one extreme and reject the other, and he will have brought his suit within a time far short of it.

It is laid down in Ld. Ray. 289 that the act of limitations is not to be taken by construction, but the possession must be clearly stated, to shew a party entitled to it.

But 2dly we doubt, whether the time mentioned in the statute having occurred, is the true rule of barring the redemption. As to lands, 20 years possession takes away the entry, and of course bars an ejectment. But what then? It does not bar other remedies to recover the land, since longer periods are allowed to commence various writs of right. It would seem therefore, that this is not the true ground upon which to adopt the rule which has been mentioned.

A more correct principle would seem to be, that after 20 years, a dereliction of the right of redeeming ought to be presumed, as a debt due by bond or even a judgment is presumed paid if that length of time has elapsed without payment of interest, or some acknowledgment which may repel the presumption. If this be the proper principle, it extends as well to slaves as to lands, and the Court of Chancery adopted that as the rule in the case of Rose and Dade, and allowed a redemption of slaves after five, but within twenty years. This I understood was approved of by the bar.

However, the period of twenty years, tho' generally fixed upon as that within which a redemption may be permitted, is sometimes departed from, and a redemption allowed upon equitable circumstances, after a much longer time: for

3dly, We are taught by the language of Chancellors, that no time for redemption can be limited. It is a case, not within the act of limitations, because there is a trust supposed between the parties; and a creditor can never be injured if he gets his principal and interest; a debtor may, if he loose his estate at perhaps half its value. Stale redemptions have however been denied after forty years.— 2 *Ventr.* 340.

A.

A demurrer was over-ruled as to a mortgage of 60 years old, upon the allegation of an agreement, that the mortgagee should enter and hold 'till he was satisfied, which was compared to a Welsh mortgage. *Vern.* 418. However the general rule was 20 years.

In recurring to the principles and nature of mortgages, we are told, they were borrowed from the civil law. They had their *pignus*, where the pledge was delivered into the possession of the creditor; and their *hypotheca*, where the debtor remained in possession; but no time for redemption appears in either case to have been limited. But in the former case, the creditor might bring his *actio pignoritia*, and in the latter, his *actio hypothecaria*, and on sentence, he was permitted to sell or use the pledge as his own property, answering to our bills of foreclosure.

This is mentioned in answer to the objection, on the part of Mr. Ross, that he was risking the lives of those slaves, whilst he was at the expence of raising and improving the issue of them for another. This risk and inconvenience, he might have put an end to, at any time, by a bill to compel a redemption of foreclosure; this case is a common one, and in most others, more slaves have been raised, and decreed to be delivered after a much longer time.

The decree must be affirmed, and remitted to the Court of Chancery to have the account of the profits taken, wherein a liberal allowance will no doubt be made, for the expences incurred in improving the slaves, which certainly ought to be done.

HOOE & HARRISON & others
against
OXLEY & HANCOCK.

IN the year 1783, Oxley and Hancock merchants in Great Britain, appointed Richard Ponsonby their agent in this Country, authorising him to purchase tobacco for them on Potowmack river, and to draw bills of exchange upon them to enable him to make the purchases. On the 31st of December 1783, they write to Ponsonby as follows, " we will take care " to give due honor to thy bills as they appear"—in their letter of the 9th February 1784 they write " thy bills on us are ma-
" ny

"ny of them now in courfe of payment, and we have received no tobacco but what came by the Peace and Plenty, &c. the being in advance, befides payment of the duties, makes it inconvenient. We muft beg of thee in future to avoid, if poffible drawing bills 'till the fhip with the tobacco is ready, as we may then have a better chance of being in cafh before they are due, but we do not mean to limit thee to any fixed plan, wifhing thee to act as nearly in conformity thereto as circumftances will admit." On the 21ft of February 1784, they write him thus, "we duly honored thy bills as they have appeared, many of which are paid, and we have made nothing of the tobacco as there has been no demand for that article lately, for which reafon we requeft that thou wilt endeavour in future not to draw any bills till the fhip is ready to fail." In their letter to him of the 19th of March 1784 they point out the neceffity of his being cautious in advancing money for tobacco and conclude with faying "and the bills becoming due before the arrival of tobacco muft be obviated if poffible. We think no money fhould be paid, till the fhip is ready to fail, which would be the means of expediting the lading of her, we juft drop thefe hints for thy government, having no doubt of thy acting in the beft manner for our intereft—on the 18th of May 1784, they fay, "the feveral bills mentioned in your letters of the 20th and 22d of March will meet due honor."—In their letter of the 27th of March 1784, they write, that they fhall endeavour to charter a fhip of 400 or 500 hogfheads to be in the Chefapeake about Auguft, and wifhing that Ponfonby may by that time have a full cargo for her. On the 15th of April following, they inform Ponfonby that they had chartered the Snow Lady Johnfon, then ready to fail for Quebeck, and to be at St. Mary's by the 1ft of September, "if fhe fails, it is to be at the option of us or our agents to accept or refufe her; from this early notice we hope the tobacco will be ready to load her." On the 29th of September 1784, they write, "we hope the Lady Johnfon will get loaded and have no doubt of thy beft endeavours—all thy bills as advifed will be regularly paid;" this is again repeated in October and November. Ponfonby not having a cargo engaged for the Lady Johnfon, and without any expectation of being able to procure one on confignment, by the time of her arrival, determined to *purchafe*, and did actually purchafe about 500 hogfheads in order to load her. To enable him to raife money for this purpofe, he drew bills on Oxley and Hancock, which
were

were either paid away for the tobacco or fold for cash, and that applied to the purchase of this commodity.

The Lady Johnson did arrive about the 10th of September 1784, was taken up and loaded by Ponsonby with the tobacco thus purchased, consigned to Oxley and Hancock, but chiefly *shipped on his own account.*

The bills drawn on account of this cargo which bore date between the 11th of October, and the 4th of December 1784, were protested.

In their letter to Ponsonby of the 30th of November 1784, they say, " we are sorry to observe that the Lady Johnson was " taken up, as it will lay thee under the necessity of purchasing " a large quantity of tobacco to compleat her loading; this is a " plan we do not approve, as we never intended to be purcha-" sers on our own account, so we by no means wish thee to " adventure largely, or, indeed in any degree (especially when " it must be attended with a certain loss) to promote our inter-" est; our original intention when we accepted thy agency was " solely for thee to procure us consignments from the planters " and not for either of us to be concerned on our own accounts. " This must be highly disadvantageous in the present state of the " trade, and though in this instance the loss whatever it may " be, will fall upon thyself, yet it will give us pain, &c." they add that there was no necessity of taking up the vessel, as the captain would have taken in any quantity which was ready to be put on board, and conclude thus " what we are now " saying is not by way of blame, for we are well satisfied of " thy acting intentionally for the best; but we wish our senti-" ments to be rightly understood, for thy government in future; " that is, we are unwilling thee should ship any tobacco either " on our account, or thy own, except in the latter case a few " hogsheads now and then. We wish not to have any tobacco " shipped, except such as may be consigned to our address, nor " is it our intention to honor any bills, but on their account." In a letter dated December the 1st, 1784, they express themselves dissatisfied with his present mode of doing business, and inform him, that they have authorised Haxall and Welt to investigate his transactions, and either to put them in such a train as in future to be consistent with their intentions, or finally to close them; that they are pleased with his diligence, but wish to prevent his becoming a purchaser and speculator, to so large an amount.

On the 14th of January 1785, after expressing their surprise to find the cargo of the Lady Johnson (except a few hogsheads) shipped on his, the said Ponsonby's own account. They write thus, "notwithstanding thou hast acted in this strange manner, "we shall use every exertion in our power to make the matter as "little injurious to thee as possible, and hope we shall be enabled "to pay a great part of thy bills; we shall accept no more of thy "drawing, and desire a state of thy account, that all transacti-"ons between us may cease. We shall guard our correspon-"dents against any dependence they may have in our accepting "thy bills; we must however, confess, that except this strange "mode of procedure we were perfectly satisfied with thy ma-"nagement, we will do every thing we can to prevent any of "thy bills going back, under a persuasion that there will no "more appear."

To recover the amount of the bills drawn by Ponsonby on Oxley and Hancock and which they had protested, the holders of them filed their bill in equity in the county Court of Fairfax against the said Oxley and Hancock, Ponsonby, and sundry others who were indebted to Oxley and Hancock, in this state, praying to condemn in the hands of the latter so much of the debts due from them, as would satisfy the amount of the bills so protested.

The defendants Oxley and Hancock filed their answer, and alledged that Ponsonby had been employed early in the year 1783, by Roberts their partner, to procure consignments for Roberts, Oxley and Hancock. That the letters of Roberts, as well as of these defendants after Roberts retired from the co-partnery (which happened sometime in Autumn 1783) were never intended to confer on him greater powers than those of *soliciting* and *procuring consignments* from the planters, and of advancing to them certain sums of money for tobacco *actually consigned*. That to enable him to make those advances he usually drew bills upon them, which, whenever they appeared to be drawn *for those purposes*, they accepted, notwithstanding Ponsonby was never authorised to draw them. That the above quotations from their letters were written in answer to letters from Ponsonby specifying particular bills which he had drawn. That the bills in question were drawn to enable Ponsonby to pay for tobacco purchased on his own account.

The cause being removed by *certiorari* into the High Court of Chancery, sundry depositions were taken, many of which prove

prove that it was the general cuftom of the Englifh merchants, who folicited tobacco confignments, to appoint agents in this country for that purpofe, with power to make advances to the planters, and to draw bills on their principals to enable them to do this—that without fuch powers being vefted in their factors here, the bufinefs could not have been carried on. That Ponfonby was generally confidered as poffeffing thofe powers, and without the fanction of fuch an opinion, could not have fold his bills.—There are other witneffes who declare that they did not conceive that Ponfonby was authorifed to draw bills on Oxley and Hancock. Leake, one of their agents for foliciting tobacco confignments, fwears that he never conceived that he was cloathed with fuch a power.—It is ftated in the anfwer and proved by the depofition of Mr. Weft, that Weft and Haxall of Baltimore were the agents and attorneys in fact of Oxley and Hancock in the ftates of Maryland and Virginia, and had a power of general fuperintendance over their bufinefs in thofe ftates. Weft depofes that he never confidered Ponfonby as being authorifed to draw bills, and expreffed this opinion generally to others.

The court difmiffed the bill from which decree the plaintiffs appealed.

THE PRESIDENT delivered the opinion of the court.

Agents may be cloathed either with general, or fpecial powers.—1ft, A general agent may do every thing which the principal may. Powers of this fort are not ufually granted, and none fuch appear in the prefent cafe.

2d, Of the fecond fort are agents limited as to the objects, or the bufinefs to be done, and left at large as to the *mode* of tranfacting it. For example. Ponfonby was limited to the bufinefs of procuring confignments of tobacco to his principals, and of loading their fhips; but he might be left to his own difcretion as to the mode of conducting that bufinefs.

If a particular mode is not prefcribed by the original power, that which the agent may adopt, the principal may, by approving, fanctify, and give to it equal validity as if it had made a part of the original authority.

If in confequence of a notorious agency, the agent is in the habit of drawing bills, and the principal in the habit of paying them, this is fuch an affirmance of his power to draw, that a purchafer of his bills, has a right to expect payment of them by the principal, and if refufe, he may coerce it.

Thefe

These, I hold to be clear principles of law. They exclude however, the idea of collusion between the bill holder and the agent, to abuse the powers confided by the principal. Such a circumstance would defeat the bill holder in his attempt to charge the principal.

The great bulk of the trade between Great Britain and this country has been principally conducted by factorage. The ostensible object of that trade was *prima facie*, the barter of foreign merchandise for native commodities.

Experience, however, soon proved, that money must be advanced to the planters, and this necessity introduced a custom generally practised by the factors of drawing bills upon their principals, to enable them to make those advances. The mode of doing this was various; sometimes the factor prevailed upon the planter to wait until the meeting of the merchants, at which time he would draw for as much as was necessary for his purposes; others would procure a kind of banker, to advance the money as they wanted it, and take their bills at the meeting of the merchants: whilst others who could not succeed by either of those modes were obliged to draw bills at once to enable them, by sale of them, to make advances as the tobacco was purchased.

I never before heard it doubted, but that the principal was bound to accept and pay those bills; however the factor might have misapplied the money which they produced. If any case has been otherwise determined, it must have proceeded from some proof of notice of a revocation of the factor's power, or of some collusion between him and the bill holder.

Alarm of danger to the fortunes of all principals has been founded, if this doctrine should prevail. The answer is a short one. This danger should be contemplated at the time the power is given, and not when it has been exercised, and many innocent men thereby drawn in, to advance their money on the faith of an open and notorious agency.

In this case, it appears that the appellees were warned of the danger and consequences of the agency exercised by Ponsonby, so early as the fall of 1783, but they still went on.

It is unnecessary to travel over the particular correspondence between Ponsonby and his principals. Though in their answer they say that Ponsonby derived his power not from them but from Roberts their former partner, yet they not only confirm that appointment in a letter of the 12th of December 1783, but in their circular letter of May 31st preceding, they had fixed their signatures or firms to the letter of Roberts,

and

and thefe letters were tranfmitted to Ponfonby as their agent. The correfpondence between Smith and Oxley and Hancock is very ftrong evidence to prove the credit which they were difpofed to attach to Ponfonby's bills, for though Smith is an interefted witnefs, and therefore, as to facts which he may relate, is not to be regarded, yet the correfpondence to which, in his depofition, he refers, fpeaks for itfelf. In his letter of September 1783 he writes, that Ponfonby had applied to him to endorfe his bills on them to get money to advance to the fhippers, and that he had endorfed one. In anfwer to this letter, they thank Smith for his affiftance to Ponfonby, *whofe bills* on "them," they fay, " will meet due honor;" a general expreffion, not confined to the particular bill which Smith had endorfed, but to Ponfonby's bills generally. This too, was in the infancy of this agency, when Ponfonby's power to draw was not fo notorious, and an endorfer was required; but when this letter was received, and Ponfonby's bills were uniformly paid, he required a credit for them, which afterwards gave them currency without an endorfer. This continued without interruption till the fall of 1784, when the prefent bills were drawn.

It is faid, that Ponfonby, changed his agency from that of procuring confignments of tobacco from others, to that of purchafing this article for himfelf, and configning it to his principals; which not being authorifed by them, they were not bound to pay his bills drawn on that account.

This brings us to the affair of the Lady Johnfon. Let it be confidered as between Oxley and Hancock, and Ponfonby. On the 27th of March 1784 they apprize him of their intention to charter a fhip of 400 or 500 hogfheads, to be in the Chefapeak about Auguft, and wifh that a cargo may by that time be procured for her.—In April, they name the fhip in queftion, and fay, fhe is to be at St. Mary's by the 1ft of September; if fhe fail, to be at their option or that of *their agents*, to accept or refufe her. " From this early notice" (they fay) " We hope the tobacco *will be ready* to load her." From thefe letters it appears, that he was not to wait her arrival, but to procure her loading in the mean time, and that he was alfo entrufted with a difcretionary power of taking her up or not, in cafe fhe did not arrive in time. She arrived on the 10th of September. He did take her up, and loaded her with tobacco configned to them; but chiefly purchafed by himfelf, and fhipped on his own account.

Upon

Upon a correct view of this transaction, it would be doubtful, were this a question merely between them and Ponsonby, whether he was not strictly within the limits of his agency: the hazard of loss by the purchase was his, not theirs: the only difference being, that they thereby trusted *him* for their advance, instead of many; and lost the opportunity, which that advance would have afforded, of engaging many future correspondents. In their letter of November 30th 1784, with full information before them, of what he had done, they seem to confirm it, but forbid its being repeated.

But let the question, as between those parties, stand as it may, in what light is it to be viewed as it respects the bill-holders? They found him loading this ship, as he had before loaded others; selling bills as he had been accustomed to do, to raise money for the purposes of that business; they purchased his bills as usual, and were not concerned in the enquiry, whether he applied that money in making advances to others, or in purchasing tobacco to consign on his own account.

Upon the whole, we are of opinion, that Oxley and Hancock are liable to the plaintiffs, for the amount of the protested bills, with interest and such legal damages as they have been obliged to pay in consequence of such protest.

DOWNMAN

against

DOWNMAN'S Executors.

THIS was an action of debt, brought in the District Court of Northumberland, by the appellees against the appellant. A conditional judgment being confirmed at the rules held in the clerk's office, the appellant moved the court for leave to set it aside, and to file a plea in the following words, viz. " He de-
" fends the force, injury, and damages, when and where &c.
" and says the plaintiffs ought not to have or maintain their
" said action against him, because he says, that, he the said de-
" fendant, on the   day of May 1781, at the county
" &c. was ready and then and there offered to pay to the said
" John Chinn" (one of the executors) " the sum of £53, Vir-
" nia currency, the sum promised in the bill obligatory in the
" said

"said declaration, mentioned to be paid as a just and principal sum, together with all interest due thereon, and the said John Chinn then and there refused to receive the same, or any part thereof, in discharge of the said bill obligatory; and the said defendant on the same day and year last mentioned, was ready, and at all times after was ready, and yet is ready, to pay to the said plaintiffs, the said sum of money, in the said bill mentioned, as a principal sum assumed, with all interest on the same day and year last above mentioned due thereon, and the same here brings into Court ready to be paid to the said plaintiffs, if they will accept the same, and this &c."

On the motion of the plaintiffs, the Court refused to admit the defendant to plead such a plea, beause it was then too late, being after office-judgment confirmed: 2dly, because it appears to the Court, that the money, brought into court, is what was once paper money, but is not now money, under any description.

Judgment, for the debt in the declaration mentioned to be discharged by the payment of £53 with legal interest from the 24th of August 1769 till the 24th of August 1789 and costs.

From this judgment the defendant appealed.

THE PRESIDENT delivered the opinion of the Court.

There are two points to be considered in this case. 1st, whether an office-judgment can be set aside, in order to let in the plea of tender: & 2dly, Whether it ought to have been set aside upon this particular plea, in the form in which it was offered to the court?

The first point depends upon the correct exposition of the 28th section of the District Court law, which declares, that "every judgment entered in the office against a defendant and bail, or against a defendant and sheriff, shall be set aside, if the defendant at the succeeding court shall be allowed to appear without bail, put in good bail, being ruled so to do, or surrender himself in custody, and shall *plead to issue immediately*." These words, *plead to issue immediately*, are the same as were used in the old act of 1753, for establishing the General Court; under which, the practice of that court was very liberal, in allowing a defendant to plead that, which did not make an issue but required subsequent pleadings, provided the real justice of the case, and not an intended delay, was thereby promoted. This is unavoidable in cases of bonds with collateral condition, where the defendant cannot plead to issue. This is also agreeable to the principle laid down by lord Holt in 2 *Salk.*

622. "That tho' a judgment be ever so regularly entered, it shall be set aside at any time on payment of costs, so as the plaintiff does not lose a trial." The words of the new law, constituting the General Court, are the same as those used in the old law. What has been the practice under this law, I do not know.

A difficulty arises with respect to the plea of tender, not only from its not making an issue; but as that necessary part of it, *of having been always ready*, is said to be inconsistent with his taking an imparlance, and in this case with his failing to appear and plead.

I confess that I cannot discover any sound reason for this doctrine. An imparlance is intended to gain information of the real subject of the suit, which when the defendant finds to be for a debt which he had tendered, he may know he has always been ready to pay it. Nor do I see clearly what it meant by the plaintiff's granting an imparlance, which, the books say, shall preclude him from the objection.

However that may be, a judgment by default, since it may be entered for want of special bail under the act of Assembly, which the defendant may not have it in his power to give, does not imply a tardiness, as an imparlance does; nor make the reasoning, (such as it is) which rules in that case, apply in this.

I find in a book entitled "Practice in common pleas in the time of king William," page 134, this case. After a rule for time to plead an issuable plea, a plea of tender and refusal was offered, but the plaintiff signed judgment, which was held good, such a plea not being considered as an issuable plea. This is a strong and pointed case—but in *Stra.* 836 and 1 *Ld. Ray.* 254, a plea of tender and refusal is considered to be an issuable plea.

Considering the circumstances of this country, and the dispersed situation of the attornies and their clients, who can seldom communicate with each other but at court, justice seems to require a relaxation in these rules of practice. It would seem to me proper to allow a discretion in the judges to admit any plea which appears necessary for the defendants defence, and only to resort to the rigour of the rule where delay appears to be intended.

However, it is unnecessary to decide this point in the cause, since the court is of opinion that upon the second point, the plea was properly disallowed.

The plea is bad *in form* for the following reasons. 1st, That the day of the tender is left blank—2d, Instead of computing the intereft to that day, adding it to the principal, and faying, that he offered a fum certain—He pleads that he offered the principal £53, and all intereft due thereon.

3dly, The plea is, *always ready from the time of the tender*, which was 12 years after the day when the money was payable, inftead of pleading it from the time when payment fhould have been made. 1 *Ld. Ray.* 254. But the plaintiff might have demurred, for thefe caufes, and of courfe the want of form in the plea did not afford a fufficient caufe for rejecting it.

But the ground upon which the plea was refufed, we confider to be a proper one—it was, that the paper brought into court, *was not money then*.

A plea of tender offered at any time at rules or in court, ought not to be received, unlefs the money tendered accompanies it; if it do not, the plaintiff may fign judgment: 2 *Barn.* 296. it muft be money current at that time, otherwife it is not money at all. There was no paper current as money in April 1796, when this plea was offered.

This is a cafe, where a fort of money was declared by law to be a legal tender and which during the period of its legal exiftence was tendered, but its currency ceafed before the plea pleaded. In this refpect, the cafe ftruck me, upon the former argument, to be uncommon in its nature, and worthy of mature confideration; fince upon legal principles, fuch tender ought to be fupported, whether the law accorded with juftice and policy, or not. It occurred to me at that time, that the plea ought to ftate the *fort of money* tendered, that the defendant was always ready to pay *that very money*, which he brings into court. Then upon a demurrer, which would admit the fact, it might be decided upon the law at the time of the tender, independent of the fubfequent alteration in its nature and currency. Since the former argument, I have looked into the cafes upon this fubject, and found a quotation—in *Viners* abridgment, xx. 177, from Davis's *Rep.* 28, and *Dy.* 822, which feems appofite to that opinion.

In debt on a bond for £24 payable at two inftallments—Defendant pleads, that on the day when the firft inftallment became due, a certain money called Pollards was current in lieu of fterling, and that on that day he tendered a moiety of the debt in the faid money called Pollards which the plaintiff refufed to accept, and that he is *uncore prift* &c. and brings it into Court; and becaufe the plaintiff did not deny it, it was awarded that he recover one moiety in Pollards, and the other in pure fterling. So in the cafe of a fall in the value of shillings, a tender of them was specially pleaded, and the shillings were brought into Court, and the plaintiff obliged to accept them, at the value when tendered, without damages or costs. *Davis* 27.

Wades case 5 *Reps.* 114, does not apply, because the Spanish money was current by proclamation, and besides, when the tender was objected to, English money was procured and tendered.

The present plea makes no particular case, it alledges a tender of money generally, and that the defendant was always ready to pay *the said sum of money*, (not the said *kind* of money,) and brings it into Court. It was therefore incumbent upon the defendant to bring into Court that which was money at that time, which the paper bills were not.

The judgment therefore must be affirmed; it is entered wrong in stopping interest at the end of 20 years: but this is not material, since if it had been rightly entered, the defendant might pay the penalty and costs.

DADE *against* ALEXANDER.

IN this case, the following points were resolved by the court.
1st, That money, directed by will to be laid out in the purchase of slaves, and to be annexed to lands devised in tail by the same will, are to be considered as slaves, and will pass with the land in tail.

2d. A feme sole, being entitled to slaves in remainder or reversion, and afterwards marrying, and dying before the determination of the particular estate, the right vests in the husband.—The president stated, that this was the constant decision of the old General Court from the year 1753 to the revolution, and has since been confirmed in this Court in the cases of Sneed *vs.* Drummond, and Hord *vs.* Upshaw, that it had become a fixed and settled rule of property.

BRAXTON

BRAXTON, Executor of CLAIBORN,
against
WINSLOW &c. furviving Juftices of Spotfylvania County.

THIS was an action of debt, brought upon an executors bond againft the fecurities in the bond, under an act of aſſembly, to ſubject them to the payment of a bill of exchange. The bill of exchange was drawn by John Spotswood, for £344. ſterling, in favor of N. W. Dandridge, who endorſed it to Benjamin Waller, (the relator in the preſent action,) and was returned under proteſt. The drawer in the mean time had died, and appointed Bernard Moore his executor: and the ſuit was inſtituted upon the bond, at the inſtance of the endorſee, againſt Moore's ſecurities, without his having previouſly obtained a judgment againſt Moore the executor. It came into the Court of Appeals by writ of error, from the General Court. After oyer of the bond and condition, the defendants pleaded conditions performed. The replication traverſes the plea, and charges a breach in not having adminiſtered according to law, in this, that the ſaid John Spotswood had drawn a bill of exchange payable to N. W. Dandridge who had endorſed it to Waller; that it was proteſted, of which proteſt, Bernard Moore, the executor, had notice, but had not paid it; having paid debts of inferior dignity after ſuch notice, and waſted the aſſetts. Defendants rejoin by proteſtation, &c. and that Moore had not waſted the aſſetts. At the trial, one witneſs was examined, and the depoſition of another read, as to the fact in iſſue: to which evidence there was a demurrer, ſtating the whole facts which proved the waſte.

The jury found that there was £1114, due to Waller, the indorſee, upon the bill of exchange aforeſaid, and that Moore the executor had waſted the aſſetts; and aſſeſſed the plaintiff's damages to one penny: and upon argument, the demurrer was over-ruled by the court, and the judgment entered up for the penalty of the bond, to be diſcharged by the payment of £1114, according to the finding of the jury, as to this breach.

By the Court. In this caſe two queſtions are made at the bar, by the counſel for the plaintiff in error.

1ſt. Whether an action could be at all maintained upon the executors bond for the benefit of a creditor.

2d.

2d. Whether this action can be maintained before a judgment first had by the plaintiff againſt the repreſentatives of the debtor, and an execution and return of *Nulla bona?* The firſt is in truth no queſtion. This bond is taken by particular direction of the act of 1748. No leſs than ten ſections of that act are attentive to the teſtators eſtate, for the benefit of wives, legatees, next of kin, and creditors; and one of them declares in expreſs words, that this bond may be put in ſuit for their benefit. Of all thoſe, whoſe rights may be involved in a teſtators eſtate, a creditor is the moſt to be favored: his demand is *ex debito juſtitiæ*; and it would be ſtrange to ſay, that a ſection of an act, which gives a new remedy to this favored claſs by expreſs words, was inſerted in the act for no purpoſe. But an analogy is drawn from the St. 22 and 23 Charles 2. and authorities are cited to ſhew that the preſent action was in no wiſe maintainable. But moſt of theſe authorities are contradictory, and therefore deſerve no credit: though in truth the lateſt authority, that from Douglas, is expreſſly in point that ſuch an action is maintainable under that ſtatute. But beſides, our act of aſſembly differs from the Engliſh ſtatute. It was argued, that great inconvenience might ariſe from countenancing ſuch actions. That argument cuts both ways. Greater inconvenience would probably ariſe if ſuch an action could not be maintained. But ſuppoſe the inconvenience on both ſides equal; then inconvenience is no ground of deciſion. It is a rule of conſtruction, that where a ſtatute is ambiguouſly worded, Courts will be governed by arguments drawn from inconvenience: and will purſue the equity of the caſe ariſing under the ſtatute: but, in this act, there is not one ambiguous word. The true queſtion then is, has the relator Waller brought himſelf within the act? or in other words, does it appear from the record, that he is a party injured within the words and meaning of the act. A man who claims as a creditor, and means to take the benefit of this act, muſt ſhew himſelf to be a creditor; that the teſtator left aſſetts; that they came to the hands of the executor; that there was a ſufficiency to diſcharge his demand, or ſo much thereof after paying debts of a higher dignity; and that the executor has waſted the aſſetts. Without this concurrence, there is no injury done him.

An attempt was made at the bar to ſhew that the paying debts of an inferior dignity firſt, was of itſelf a *devaſtavit*; and that a *devaſtavit* for ever ſo trifling a ſum, renders the executor liable to the whole demand, although aſſetts to the twentieth

[part

part never came to his hands. But neither reason nor authorities warrant this doctrine: for surely if there be a sufficiency of assetts, it is of no consequence in what order they are paid. But the person who means to make use of this act, must shew himself to be a creditor in the usual course of law. It is not enough to produce a mere document of a debt; he must first institute a suit against the executor or administrator; because it is, in the first instance, a dispute between creditor and debtor whether, or no, a debt actually exist: a dispute, which the securities to such a bond, who are strangers to the contract, are by no means competent to manage. It is a principle of universal law that both parties shall be heard. Let us put this case: suppose A binds himself in a bond to pay B whatever sum C owes him (B) now before a forfeiture is incurred by A, must not B first prove by an action at law the sum that C actually owes him? Mr. Waller therefore ought to have shewn by an action brought against the executor that he was a creditor: he ought to have shewn by his action against Moore the executor, that he had committed a devastavit; a suggestion of a devastavit may be likened to a criminal prosecution: and an executor shall not be presumed guilty of a devastavit, till it is found against him by a verdict. It may be objected, 'that the act does not prescribe that a creditor shall not go against the securities in the first instance; and therefore this action was well brought; to which this answer presents itself, that it is an established principle of construction, that where a statute has given a new remedy, without pointing out the mode in which this remedy is to be attained, the rules of the common law, and the practice of the courts, founded upon the reason of the thing, shall be pursued. Therefore we are all of opinion that the judgment of the General Court must be reversed.

CASES DETERMINED
IN THE
COURT OF APPEALS
IN
THE FALL TERM OF THE YEAR,
1791.

BIRCH *against* ALEXANDER.

THIS was an appeal from the District Court of Dumfries, in an ejectment brought by the appellee. The jury found a special verdict, "that Sir William Berkley, Govern‑
"or of Virginia, granted to Robert Howsen, the lands con‑
"tained within a patent bearing date October 21st, 1669,
"whereof the lands in question are a part, lying within the
"proprietory of the Northern Neck, which patent they find
"in these words: to all &c." the patent is in the usual form, granting 6000 acres of land, in consideration of the transportation of a number of persons into the colony, and is abbreviated thus, " to have &c. yielding &c. provided &c."—They find the act of Assembly passed in the year 1736, entitled " An act for confirming and better securing the titles to lands in the Northern Neck, held under the right honorable Thomas Lord Fairfax, baron of Cameron, in that part of Great Britain called Scotland." Also the act passed in the year 1748, entitled " An act for confirming the grants made by his majesty, within the bounds of the Northern Neck, as they are now established."
" That on the 13th of October 1669, Howsen, being seized of
" the lands contained in the aforesaid patent, assigned and con‑
" veyed all the lands aforesaid therein contained, to John Alex‑
" ander, by deed poll, recorded in Stafford court which they
" also find in *hæc verba*.

" That John Alexander entered, and was seized and possessed
" as the law requires, and by a paper purporting to be his will,
" devised 500 acres of the said land to John Dry, 200 to Eli‑
" zabeth Hoomes, and the residue to his two sons, Robert and
" Philip, and their heirs."

" That

" That after the death of the said John Alexander, his son,
" and heir at law, Robert, by a deed executed in February
" 1690, confirmed to his brother, Philip, the lands left him
" by the said will, being a moiety of the land in question.—
" That in February 1693, the said Philip executed a deed to his
" brother Robert, of all his share and interest in the land con-
" tained in the above mentioned patent, with a reservation of
" 500 acres, which are no part of the lands in question, and
" neither Philip nor his heirs nor any claiming under him have
" since claimed any part of the land in question.

" That the said Robert Alexander, after the said conveyance
" from his brother, entered into the land in the declaration men-
" tioned, being part of the land contained in the aforesaid pa-
" tent, and was seized and possessed thereof as the law requires
" and so continued till his death, which happened before the
" 1st of June 1704, having previously thereto made his will,
" bearing date the 22d of December 1703, whereby he devised
" to his sons Robert and Charles the lands in question in fee
" simple equally to be divided, which will they find in *hæc verba*.

" That the said Robert left two sons, Robert his eldest, and
" Charles, who died intestate and without issue. That Robert
" after the death of his brother, was seized and possessed as the
" law requires, of all the land in question, and so continued
" until his death, which happened in the year 1735, leaving
" two sons, John his eldest, and Gerard—also two daughters,
" Sarah and Parthenia; that by his will dated in 1735, he de-
" vised several parcels of land to his said sons and daughters,
" and the lands in question, comprehended within the descrip-
" tion of the residue of his real estate, to his sons John and Gerard
" equally to be divided in tail," which will is also found.

" That the said John and Gerard entered into the lands in
" question, and were thereof seized and possessed as the law re-
" quires, and that John continued so seized and possessed until
" the time of his death."

" That they sued out a writ of *ad quod damnum*, in order to
" dock the intail of the said lands, and an inquisition being found
" thereupon, they, by a deed of bargain and sale conveyed the
" said land to T. Dade, who afterwards re-conveyed the same
" in fee simple:" Which writ, inquisition and deed are found.
" That there were other intailed lands adjoining, not included
" in the inquisition; that no lines were shewn to the jurors or
" surveyed in their presence—no consideration paid by the said
" Dade, and that the inquisition was fraudulent.

That

"That an act of Assembly was passed, and obtained the royal
"assent, for docking the intail of Gerard's part of the said land,
"which was an undivided moiety of the lands in question; that
"no partition of the said lands was ever made between the said
"John and Gerard, or any claiming under them."

"That John being so seized and possessed did in his life-time
"give to his son Charles his undivided moiety of the said land,
"and delivered him the possession thereof. That he died in
"1764, leaving issue six sons, of whom the said Charles (lessor
"of the plaintiff) was the eldest, and by his will made the
"16th of October 1763, devised to his said son Charles the
"lands in question by the following clause." "Also I give
"to my son Charles *all things already* given him, and which he
"has now in possession.

"That the said testator John, in his life-time conveyed to
"plaintiff's lessor so much of the land in question as lies to the
"westward of four mile run, laid down in the survey annexed."

They also find the act of Assembly for settling the titles and bounds of lands.

They find a grant from the proprietor of the Northern Neck, bearing date the 3d of March 1730, the bounds of which they ascertain, by reference to the survey, and is the land in question.

"That Robertson possessed the said land from the year 1733,
"to the year 1743, when an ejectment was served by John
"Alexander, for so much of the land as was included in How-
"fens patent, and he recovered a judgment in 1751, till which
"time Robertson continued in possession."

"That James Robertson recovered from Robert Alexander,
"and was put into possession of the lands contained within his
"grant by writ of possession in 1765."

"That Robertson died in 1768, leaving issue a daughter Jenet,
"wife of Birch the defendant, to whom, Robertson by his will
"devised the land contained within his patent."

"That the land in question is included within Howfens and
"Robertson's grants, and if &c."

The District Court gave judgment for the plaintiff from which the defendant appealed.

The PRESIDENT.—Many objections have been made at the bar to the insufficiency of this verdict. The first is, that the crown is not found to have been seized of the land in question, at the time of the grant to Howsen. According to the feudal system, the king was seized of all the lands in Virginia, as chief magistrate; and, whatever may have been the practice in England,

seizin

seizin in the crown is never found in this country, because that is the ultimate point, beyond which a party in tracing his title is not bound to go.

It was next contended, that by the patent to Howsen, only an estate for life passed, there being in it, no words of inheritance. That, for want of a seal to the patent, this grant was not embraced by the confirmation act of 1748, and of course, that the prior grant of the crown in 1668 to the proprietors of the Northern Neck, had deprived the crown of a right to make this grant to Howsen. That the assignment from Howsen to Alexander, "of all the land contained in *this patent,*" not appearing to have been endorsed on the patent, did not pass the land in question.—These and other objections were strongly insisted upon by the appellants counsel, and though they might all of them be controverted, yet they may be all safely admitted in this case, and then how will the cause stand?

In 1669 John Alexander entered, and was seized and possessed as the law requires. Not having title, he was a disseisor upon the proprietor of the Northern Neck, in whom the title was. The succession from him is continued regularly down, and each successor is found to have been seized and possessed as the law requires, and no entry of the proprietor's is stated, or claim by them to the land, till the grant to Robertson in 1730. So, that there is a clear seizin and possession of 61 years found under the disseisor, without any entry in the meantime to purge the disseisin. Here is a term, not only sufficient to give a title in ejectment, but to bar a writ of right, which alone would admit an enquiry into the mere right.

The counsel for the appellant observed, that the possession was not so found as to give a title; not being found to have been *uninterrupted.* But the ancestors of the appellee being stated to have been successively seized and possessed from 1669 to 1730, and no interruption found, their own maxim "that what appears not, is to be taken as not having existed," fixes the adverse possession to have been uninterrupted.

The justice of the maxim, *nullum tempus occurrit regi* has been questioned, or rather the application of it to a case like this, where it is resorted to, to support a new grant to one citizen, to the prejudice of an antient grantee and possessor, for some defect in his grant. But that either the reason of the rule extends, or that the rule itself was ever applied to preserve the title of a lord, we do not admit; and believe the appellants counsel was misinformed, as to the point having been otherwise decided in the old General Court.

On

On this point therefore, we affirm the judgment, without deciding on the other points. And we are happy in believing, that in establishing this ancient possession, we accord with the spirit, if not with the letter of the several laws passed since the year 1710, for the protection of such possessions, against attacks on the ground of legal defects.

Judgment affirmed.

WILCOX
against
CALLOWAY

THIS was an appeal from the High Court of Chancery. The case was this:

The appellee and Wilcox having purchased two entries for land, one of 400 and the other of 403 acres, obtained patents for each of them in June 1764.

In 1768 Wilcox agreed with Donaldson to sell him these two tracts of land for £125, but no conveyance was made, Wilcox being about to leave this state, sometime prior to 1769, placed in the hands of Donaldson as much money as would be sufficient to discharge the arrears of quitrents then due on the land, which Donaldson promised to apply to that purpose. John Cox in December 1767 petitioned the General Court for the above two tracts, as being lapsed for non-payment of quitrents, and want of cultivation; and in June 1772, judgment was rendered in his favor, and patents issued in July 1774 to Donaldson assignee of Cox.

On the 8th of August 1769, Donaldson informed Wilcox of the pendency of the above petitions, and recommended it to him, to attend the trial, and defend them. But on the 28th of July preceding, he, Donaldson had purchased the right of Cox, if he should succeed, at the price of £150, and took his bond for a conveyance. Of this purchase Donaldson takes no notice in his letter of August.

Cox not having pursued his judgment and obtained a patent within six months, Wilcox filed a caveat for this cause in August 1773, against a patent issuing upon Cox's judgments; in

April

April 1783, he obtained a judgment in his favor, which being certified, a patent issued to him for the two tracts.

In 1776, Calloway purchased the above land from Donaldson, received a conveyance for the same, and made valuable improvements on it.

Wilcox filed his bill against Calloway only, praying that he might be decreed to deliver to him the possession of the lands in question, and for general relief.

The defendant by his answer states himself to be a purchaser for valuable consideration actually paid; that he had no notice of any fraud or improper conduct in Cox or Donaldson, nor did he ever hear of any dispute respecting the title till the year 1782, long after his purchase.

There were many depositions taken in the cause, and on hearing, the bill was dismissed without prejudice; the Court being of opinion "that the defendant was a purchaser of the land in question for valuable consideration, not appearing to have been guilty of any fraud, or if any other was guilty of it, to have had notice thereof, or not being, or claiming under a like lite pendente purchaser."

From this decree Wilcox appealed.

The PRESIDENT—The first objection is, that Donaldson's purchase from Cox was void, as being contrary to the act to prevent the buying of pretensed titles. This law prohibits the purchasing of latent titles in order to disturb the possessions of others. But it was never intended to prevent a person in possession from confirming and strengthening that possession by purchasing the rights of others.

Donaldson having lawfully acquired the possession under his purchase from Wilcox, might without violating the statute make a contract with Cox for the securing of that possession. A man sued in an ejectment may defend the suit, and nevertheless agree to purchase the title of the plaintiff in case he should prove successful.

It was next contended, that the forfeiture made void all *mesne* sales by Wilcox or Cox. But if land be forfeited for non-payment of quitrents, or for want of cultivation, still, if those acts be performed before the land is petitioned for, it is saved. If Donaldson had purchased absolutely of Cox, he might have dismissed the petitions, taken conveyance from Wilcox, paid the quitrents, and improved the land, and would then have been safe under Wilcox's patents, though a forfeiture had been incurred. The rule applies thus. Cox recovers, and obtains a lapse patent. This shall relate to the date of the original patent, and avoid by priority all *mesne* grants from the crown, this has often been so adjudged, in disputes about priority, between two patents with interfering bounds.

In April 1772 the petitions were heard, and the lands were recovered. Although the evidence will not warrant us in charging Donaldson with fraud in this transaction, yet he was deceived in relying upon his own testimony, instead of the evidence of other witnesses, to prove payment of the quitrents, He was adjudged an interested witness, and in consequence of it, the land was lost. Had the facts, as they really existed, been proved, the decision would have been otherwise—being recovered in consequence of a mistake, Wilcox has a good ground of equity against Cox and Donaldson.

The effect of a petition and certificate is not to vest an absolute and indefeasible estate in the person who obtains it, but it gives him a right to purchase that particular piece of land, in preference to all other citizens, but upon condition of paying the consideration money within six months. The right then, which Cox acquired, was not absolute, but conditional: it was to depend upon his perfecting his title within a limited time. This right he assigned to Donaldson, and he might lawfully do so—but the condition passed with it, and Donaldson was bound to perform it—it is objected that the caveat was entered against Cox, instead of Donaldson, the purchaser. But the purchase was a matter in *pais*; and it does not appear that Wilcox had notice of it. The summons was served on Cox, who must be presumed to have given notice to Donaldson, the private purchaser. But what are the effects of a caveat? to prevent the emanation of a patent, not to set one aside. And if the General Court 1783 had been informed that the patent had issued, however improperly, they would not have heard the caveat, or given a decision which would have been vain in its effect, since a patent issued in consequence of their judgment, would not at law overreach the one to Donaldson in 1774. But this was denied at the bar.—It was contended, that the patent in 1784 has relation to those issued to Wilcox in 1764. But the counsel forgot, that Donaldson's patent in 1774 has relation to the same source, and priority of *title* will draw to it, priority of *relation*.

The remedy then was in Chancery to repeal the patent of 1774 as surreptitiously obtained whilst the caveat was depending, and to be relieved against the forfeiture adjudged in 1772, when, by mistake, the plaintiff was deprived of an opportunity of making that defence which ought to have saved his land.

On

On this ground, I should have no difficulty in decreeing the land to the plaintiff, if it remained in the hands of Donaldson, and had not been sold by the plaintiff; or in decreeing the purchase money and interest (the land having been sold by him) for which he should have a lien upon the land itself.

But this is upon a suppofition that he or his representatives were parties, and that the case appeared as it now does. But here is a train of examination, by which the moral character of a man long since in his grave is called in question, and the interest of his family affected, without affording to his family an opportunity of defending either—this can never be right, and either justifies the decree of difmiffion without prejudice, or suggests an opinion that the cause was not ripe for a hearing, until the bill had been amended and the representatives made parties: in which case the plaintiff must have begun *de novo*.

If Calloway had been such a purchaser, as that the land itself in his hands, was not bound to answer the purchase money, the difmiffion should have been final; since in that case, it would be unreasonable to keep him in Court merely to be a witness of a contest between others. If he be such a purchaser, as that the lien upon the land passed with it, and created an obligation upon him to pay the money in the stead of Donaldson, then Donaldson's representatives should have been made parties; because, being liable, either to Wilcox or Calloway, they ought to have had an opportunity of contesting the claim, or if not, it was proper that the bill should have been difmiffed without prejudice.

This brings us to the case of Mr. Calloway.

The rule, *caveat emptor*, applies only to purchasers of defective *legal* titles. A purchaser of the legal title is not to be affected by any latent equity, whether founded on truft, fraud or otherwife, of which he has not actual notice, or which does not appear in some deed neceffary in the deduction of the title, so as to amount to constructive notice. In these cases of notice, he will take the estate subject to the equity in the same manner as the person, from whom he purchased, had it.

Out of this principle has grown another rule, that a purchaser entitled to this protection, must be a *compleat* purchafer, by having a conveyance; and having also paid his purchase money before he has notice; for, if he receive that notice before either of these acts are perfected, he ought to stop, until the *equity* is enquired into, or he will be bound by it.

Calloway

Calloway states himself to have been a purchaser in 1776, for a valuable consideration, without notice of any claim of the plaintiff until the year 1782. This allegation is not disproved, nor is there any evidence of improper conduct on the part of Calloway. But in his answer, he neither ascertains what was the purchase money, nor at what time he paid it. Speaking of the purchase he says, " it was for *valuable consideration.*" He afterwards states, that the plaintiff did not bring his suit until Donaldson had removed away, (without saying when that was, and it might have been *after* 1782, when he had notice) with a good estate and £4000 received from him for the land—thereby conveying an idea that the money was then paid.—Whether this was really the fact, and that the removal was after notice; or that the payment was before the removal; or that removal before notice, and the inaccuracy was produced by inattention in drawing the answer, is doubtful; it might have been explained in his answer to an amended bill, if that mode had been adopted. In that way, the plaintiff must make a new case, founded on his claim to the purchase money and interest, and insist that he has a lien for that upon the lands in the possession of Calloway.

But this claim is disavowed by the present bill—the plaintiff denying the agreement to sell, for the sake of his claim to the land—that new case, he may make under the decree of dismission without prejudice and therefore this court approve the decree and
affirm it.

JONES & TEMPLE,
against
LOGWOOD.

THIS was an action of debt brought up by the appellee, in the District Court of King and Queen: the declaration is in common form, upon a bond—plea payment. At the trial, the defendants tendered a bill of exceptions, stating, that the plaintiff offered a writing to the jury as evidence in support of the declaration, to which there was no seal but a scroll: and the Court permitting this writing to go to the jury, the defendants excepted.

Also

Also the defendants offered in evidence, sundry receipts, to a greater amount than the debt in the declaration mentioned, and bearing date before the institution of this suit: but the plaintiff in opposition thereto, offered in evidence a bond of the defendants, dated on the same day with that mentioned in the declaration, but payable before it, and given for a larger quantity of tobacco; on which bond no suit had been instituted, and on this bond, some of the receipts were said to be credited: and the plaintiff insisting that not only those receipts, but such as were not endorsed thereon should be applied to the credit of that bond, the defendants objected to its going in evidence to the jury, urging that it was not their deed, and was given for an usurious consideration. But the Court after examining one of the attesting witnesses, who proved the execution of the bond, permitted it to go as evidence to the jury in opposition as well to the receipts which were not endorsed on the bond, as to those which were: to which opinion also the defendants excepted.

The endorsements on the bond, agree precisely with some of the receipts, as to their amount, and are stated to be in " part of this bond."

Verdict and judgment for the plaintiff and appeal.

The PRESIDENT delivered the opinion of the Court.

It is important that the Court should settle a question so interesting to the community as the following: whether a scroll used as a seal, constituted a good bond before the act of 1788, or whether to make it a seal, wax or something capable of impression, and impressed, was necessary. Acts of Parliament in England, and acts of Assembly in this country, frequently speak of seals; but none of them define what shall constitute a seal. Nor is there an adjudged case recollected, which determines that a seal must be necessarily something impressed on wax. To consider it upon the reason of the thing; a seal is required to give solemnity to the act; and I cannot perceive a difference, in point of solemnity, between the act of impressing wax and that of making a scroll.

Public corporate bodies have a known and fixed seal: and it is necessary that their acts should be under that common seal. In that instance an impression may be necessary, to shew that the act has been done in their corporate capacity.

But what is the private seal of an individual? Does an impression furnish any criterion by which to decide whether it

be

be his seal or not? it is true that some few gentlemen have seals which impress their family coats of arms; some have such as impress the initials of their names: but these are rare indeed when compared with the great body of the community who have no seals, and who use such as are placed on the writing for them, and make them their own by acknowledging them to be such. In truth and reality then, it is unimportant whether this adoption be of wax or a scroll. Lord Coke in his 2d institute, in a commentary upon a statute which speaks of a seal, says " a seal is wax with an impression." But there is neither an act of Parliament nor an adjudged case to bind the Court. It was his opinion only, founded probably on the practice of that day, and if that gives a binding rule, we may by going further back, discover a period of time, when the impression was made with the eye tooth. There was some utility in that custom, since the tooth impressed was the man's own, and furnished a test in case of forgery. But both are founded on the usage of the times. Scrolls have been long substituted for seals in this country. The party acknowledges the scroll to be his seal, and as such this court will consider it. If there had been a positive law to bind the court, we must have obeyed it, however inconvenient; but since none is shewn or recollected, we will not make a precedent, which would not only let loose great numbers of individuals from their engagements, but all or most of the executors, administrators, guardians and perhaps public collectors, from the force of their bonds: a decision which would dishonor government; relax public and private security, and convulse the state.

The late act, if it operates, is conclusive; if it does not, it is at least a legislative construction of the law in general; agreeable to, and adding strength to, that of the court.

On this point there is no error.

As to the other point, tho' notice of a set-off is given in England, it is not usually practised here: both parties seemed to have been prepared, the plaintiff to prove the execution of the bond first payable, and the defendant, his payments: as to the dispute which of those bonds the receipts ought to be applied to, the jury have decided it, and the court think properly.

Judgment affirmed.

BEEKRIGHT

SEEKRIGHT, Leſſee of Wm. MAYO,
againſt
PAUL CARRINGTON, and others.

THIS was an ejectment tried in the General Court. The parties argued a caſe, in effect as follows, viz. "That
" Joſeph Mayo being ſeized of the lands in queſtion at the time
" of making his will, as well as at the time of his death, did,
" on the 27th day of May 1780, duly make and publiſh his laſt
" will and teſtament, whereby, after ſundry ſpecific bequeſts of
" land and perſonal eſtate, he earneſtly requeſts his executors
" to petition the General Aſſembly for leave to emancipate all
" his ſlaves, and to uſe every exertion in their power to ſucceed
" in ſuch application. But provided it ſhould not be in the
" power of his executors to get this act of humanity effected,
" on that condition and no other, he gives and diſpoſes of the
" ſaid ſlaves, *and his other property*, which might remain after
" diſcharging his legacies and deviſes, in the following manner,
" viz. three of his ſlaves (by name) to John Tabb; all the re-
" ſidue of his ſlaves *and other property*, remaining after the diſ-
" charge of the above legacies and deviſes, he gives to be equal-
" ly divided between the ſons of Joſeph Mayo, William Mayo,
" ſon of Daniel, and Paul, George, Joſeph, Nathaniel, and
" Mayo Carrington, ſons of George Carrington, the ſame to
" be to them and their heirs for ever."

" That the teſtator departed this life in the year 1785, and
" that his will aforeſaid was duly proved and admitted to record."

" That the leſſor of the plaintiff, who is the ſon of Daniel
" in the will mentioned, is the heir at law of the ſaid teſtator."

" That an act of the General Aſſembly was, upon the petiti-
" on of the adminiſtrators with the will of the ſaid teſtator an-
" nexed, paſſed into a law authorizing the Chancellor to make
" all ſuch orders and decrees from time to time as might be ne-
" ceſſary for carrying into effect the bequeſt of the ſaid teſtator
" in favor of his ſlaves, having regard to the payment of all
" debts due by the ſaid teſtator, and ſuch legacies (if any) as
" ought to be paid prior to the emancipation; and alſo, to raiſe
" ſuch a ſum of money from the labor of the ſaid ſlaves, as
" might be ſufficient to provide for the maintenance and ſupport
" of the aged negroes and ſuch as were of tender years, ſo as to
" prevent them from becoming burthenſome to the community.

" That

"That so soon as these purposes were answered, it should be lawful for the High Court of Chancery to make such order or decree for emancipating the said slaves, as to the said court might seem proper: and that the slaves so decreed free should receive a certificate thereof, and be to all intents and purposes free.

"That a decree of the High Court of Chancery was made pursuant to the above law, whereby the said slaves were declared free.

"That after the personal estate was sold, the slaves were hired out for the purpose of paying the residue of the testators debts, and raising a fund for the maintenance of the aged, young and infirm; and that after paying the debts there will remain a surplus from the hires in the hands of the administrators, subject to the future decree of the High Court of Chancery.

"That the lands in question, and one other tract not specifically devised, were the most profitable parts of the testator's estate, from whence he drew his chief support: That he possessed three other considerable tracts of land."

"That the defendants are the residuary legatees of the said testator, and in equal degree of relationship to the testator, as the lessor of the plaintiff. And if upon the whole matter the law be for the plaintiff, &c."

Judgment for the defendants from which the plaintiff appealed.

THE PRESIDENT delivered the opinion of the Court.

The case may be at once discharged of the condition, which, it was contended, had prevented the devise of the residue from taking effect, inasmuch as the act of manumission had been obtained. The condition is clearly confined to the slaves, and not to the other part of the residuary estate.

The testator was anxious about the liberation of his slaves, which he considered as depending very much upon the zeal of his executors in their application for that purpose to the legislature. His executors are, with others, constituted his residuary legatees, and therefore, it never could have been in the contemplation of the testator to tempt his executors to withhold the ardor necessary to promote this his favorite wish, by punishing them with the loss of all the residue if they *succeeded*. He was under the necessity of confiding in them, so far as the slaves were

were concerned; and the event has proven that his confidence was not misplaced, or injudiciously given.

How then does this cause stand upon the principal question, throwing the slaves out of the question? It is admitted on all hands that the intention of the testator is to be sought for, and observed; but that intention is to be collected from the will itself. In questions which relate to the *subject* of the devise, or to the quantum of *interest* given, we find the judges labouring and catching at slight expressions of illiterate men, in order to effectuate their intentions. In the case of Hogan, lessee of Henry Wallace, *vs.* Rowland Jackson, *Cowp. Rep.* 299, the court are seen struggling to give to the words " wordly substance "— " all my effects &c." the same meaning as *property*.

That term is used in this case, and is as comprehensive as any which could have been thought of, for the purpose of embracing every thing. In the case of Huxtep *vs.* Brooman.—Brow. Ch. *Rep.* 437: The words; " all I am worth;" were adjudged sufficient to pass lands.

Upon the whole the court are unanimously of opinion that the judgment of the District Court is right and is to be affirmed.

ROANES Executors,

against

HERN & WIFE.

THIS was an appeal from the High Court of Chancery.

Upon the marriage of Mrs. Hern, formerly Mrs. Cook, with her former husband William Roane, an agreement was duly executed between them, which contained the following covenants;

1st. That the two parties should, during their coverture, hold, possess, and enjoy all such rights and privileges as belonged to them, in as full and ample a manner and form, as if the *agreement* had never been made.

2d. That if the said William should die before his said intended wife, she should immediately hold, possess, and enjoy during her life, the dwelling house, &c. with the appurtenances,

ces, together with 800 acres of land adjoining, and one third of a grift mill, in lieu of dower in the lands of the faid William.

3d. That fhe fhould poffefs and enjoy, immediately after his death, alfo 20 good negroes, including a full proportion of houfe fervants, fuch as fhe might choofe, and if the faid 20 negroes fhould not amount in value to a full third part of the negroes of which the faid William fhould die *poffeffed*, as many more to be allotted her, as will amount to a full third part of the whole of the negroes—all which, to be in lieu of dower of the flaves of the faid William, and to be fubject to the fame laws and regulations.

4th. That if his faid intended wife fhould furvive him, and have no child living at the time of his, or her, death, the negroes and their increafe that came into his eftate by this marriage, fhould be vefted in his faid wife in fuch abfolute manner as that fhe might difpofe of them to whom fhe pleafed; or otherwife to pafs and defcend to her heirs agreeably to the laws of the land: but if the faid William with the confent of his faid wife fhould fell any of thofe negroes, his eftate not be accountable for the fame.

5th. That at his death his faid wife fhould have the beft riding carriage and horfes *belonging to the fame* as her abfolute property, which fhould not be brought into account in the divifion of the perfonal eftate.

Laftly, that fhe fhould be entitled to receive one third part of the perfonal eftate, in the fame manner, and under the fame rules, cuftoms and laws, as if this agreement had never been made.

This agreement bears date, the 24th of October 1782; but was not executed until about the 14th of November, when the marriage took place.

About two or three days prior to the execution of the above marriage articles, William Roane conveyed to each of his two fons by a former wife 14 or 15 flaves.

William Roane died fometime in November 1785, leaving no iffue by his laft marriage; and by his will devifed, that, in addition to the houfehold furniture to which his wife was entitled by the marriage articles, his executors fhould allow and affign her as much more during her widowhood, as they fhould judge neceffary for her ufe.

After his death, an order of the county court, *upon the motion* of his executors, was made, appointing commiffioners to value the flaves of the faid decedent; and to allot to his widow, the

part

part thereof which she was entitled to by marriage contract; and to divide the residue amongst his children, according to his will.

In pursuance of this order, the commissioners at first allotted to the widow ten of the negroes originally belonging to William Roane, which, with those that came into the estate by his intermarriage with her, made the number twenty. But afterwards, finding that *one* of the negroes, which had belonged to the widow before marriage, had died since the death of William Roane, they allotted the widow only *nine* of the negroes properly belonging to his estate, but equal in value to the ten first mentioned; with this partition she acknowledged herself well pleased and satisfied. But afterwards, being advised that she was entitled to a greater number of the slaves, she filed her bill in the High Court of Chancery against the executors of William Roane, claiming as many more slaves as would make her proportion equal to one third of the whole number, including those conveyed to his sons, and excluding those to which she was entitled before marriage; the latter being claimed in absolute fee. The bill states that the executors had refused to deliver her more than two carriage horses, although four were accustomed to draw it, and had sold the whole of the personal estate, whereby the complainant had been compelled to purchase a considerable part of it, and was then actually sued by the executors for the amount of that purchase; to which suit she prays an injunction.

The executors answered, and insisted that the allottment of slaves was conformable to the sound construction of the articles. That the whole of the personal estate except slaves, would be exhausted in the payment of debts.—And lastly, that the carriage was usually drawn by two horses; a greater number having never been used, but when a journey was to be performed.

This suit having abated by the intermarriage of the plaintiff with Hern, was revived in their names, and the cause coming on to be heard, the court delivered the following opinion and decree, viz. " That in the slaves, to the possession of which
" the plaintiff Ann, by the marriage contract between her former husband William Roane the testator, and herself, was
" entitled in lieu of dower, those, which were her property
" at the time of their intermarriage, ought not to have been
" included; because the slaves which, by the contract, she
" should have and enjoy in the event of her surviving him,
" whether having a child by him or not, are supposed to be his
" proper slaves; since a power to settle them on her, in lieu of
dower

"dower or otherwise, implieth a property in *him*; and because the said slaves, to be in lieu of dower of his slaves were subject to the laws and regulations of dower slaves; whereas the slaves which the plaintiff Ann had at the time of the intermarriage, were not his, but remained her property when he died without having a child by her; and were not subject to the laws and regulations of dower slaves."

"That the plaintiffs ought not to be precluded by the order and decree of Essex County Court, and the division and assignment made in obedience thereto, from recovering, now, so many of the slaves, as the plaintiff Ann was entitled to, more than what were then assigned her; because the plaintiff Ann was not a party in the suit, if it can be called a suit, wherein that order and decree was made; nor does her present demand appear to have been discussed, or even stated at that time: that, whether the gifts by the testator to his sons Thomas and Spencer be fraudulent, is a question not proper to be decided in this cause, as it is now brought on, the donees not being made parties: And that the plaintiff Ann was entitled to the two horses *only* which she hath received, because only that pair having ordinarily drawn the carriage to which the horses were said to belong are understood to have been designated."

Ordered and decreed, "that of the surviving slaves, which were in possession of the testator at the time of his death, exclusive of the unprofitable from old age and infirmity, and also exclusive, as well of the plaintiffs now proper slaves, and the nine formerly received by the plaintiff Ann, as of those given by the deeds of gift to the testator's sons, although they might have been in his possession at his death, eleven, or so many more as with those nine will be equal to one third part, be assigned to the plaintiffs; together with the children of any females among those, so to be assigned, born since the testators death, the value of which slaves, so to be assigned, shall be in like proportion to the value of the flock whence they are to be taken, as one of the numbers is to the other; and that the defendants do account with the plantiffs for the profits of the slaves so to be assigned, from the end of the year in which the testator died."

An injunction, to stay further proceedings on the judgment at common law obtained by the defendants against the plaintiffs, was also awarded, on the usual terms, to continue until the account of administration of the testators estate should discover whether a surplus thereof would remain, the plaintiffs share of which might discharge, or be discounted out of, that debt.

From this decree the defendants appealed.

THE PRESIDENT delivered the opinion of the Court.

We will discharge the case from every thing connected with the division made under the order of Essex County Court. There was no suit commenced and the order was entirely *ex parte*.

It is the proper province of a court of equity to decree the specific execution of marriage articles, where the apparent intention of the parties will direct the decree without a strict scanning of the articles according to nice grammatical rules, or the technical meaning of the words.

It is objected, in the first place, that there are no parties to this statement. Mr. Roane and Mrs. Cook (the intended wife) are named as the contracting parties. All covenants refer to them, and the property spoken of refers to their property.—2d, It is objected, that there is no consideration. It is plain, that the intended marriage, was the consideration; and the motives expressed are, to make a provision for her, and to preserve peace in the family.

The first clause, tho' badly expressed, is easy to be understood: what were the respective maritial rights of the parties is not contemplated, or defined; but whatever they were, the settlement was not to meddle with them, but was to commence on the dissolution of the marriage. No provision is made for the case of his surviving, but in the case of her outliving him, her provision is fixed, as to the three classes of his property.

The 2d clause relates to the land, and describes what part she shall hold in lieu of dower; about this there is no dispute: one thing however might be remarked, that as *his* lands, and not *hers*, were the subject of this clause, it induces an opinion, that *his* slaves, and not *hers* were also the subject of the 3d clause. It is contended, that under this clause, the wife's slaves are to form a part of the 20 which are to be allotted to her; and that only so many of *his* are to be added, as will make up that number. This construction, it is said, is reasonable because the husband had but 40 slaves at the time of his death, and 20 would be half of that number, instead of a third, the proportion contemplated by the contract. But it is in proof that the estimate was made upon 70 slaves, of which he was possessed, at the time of the gifts of his sons.

It

It is also argued, that Mr. Roane was *possessed* of his wife's slaves at the time of his death, that they formed a part of the fund out of which the 20 were to be taken, and therefore that they should make a part of the number. The possession spoken of in this clause, means *property*, and not a mere *holding*. It means the same thing as is intended by the subsequent words, " of the slaves *of the said William.*" He had a right to hold her slaves during their joint lives, but the moment of his death put an end to his right. The contract operated upon, and gave them to another; and therefore they could not form any part of the stock out of which her dower was to be taken. Besides, the different degree of interest, which she had in her own slaves, from that which she would have in dower slaves, seems conclusive, that they were not intended to be coupled together. But if in this clause the question be doubted, the next fully explains it.

Hitherto the parties appear to have contemplated the husband's estate, and the wife's provision out of that. In the 4th clause, which in the settlement, is called the third, they take up the subject of the wife's slaves, and speak of them very inaccurately. It appears as if they had formed an intention for providing for the issue of the marriage, but no such provision is made, except by implication, and as there was no issue, it is immaterial.

Nor is any provision made for the case of the husband's surviving; in which event he would therefore have been entitled to her slaves; but neither did that event happen.

The event provided for did take place. She survived, and had no child living at his death, when she was to be vested with the slaves which came by her, and their increase, in such absolute manner, that she might dispose of them to whom she pleased, or they were to descend to her heirs. The child spoken of in this clause, means child of the marriage, since none other could be living at his death. Her death was probably mentioned in order to provide for the case of such a child living at his death, and dying before her.

Upon the whole of this point, the Court approve the decree, that the dower slaves shall be made up 20 in number out of Mr. Roane's slaves, independent of hers. They also approve the decree as to the chariot horses.

Decree affirmed with costs.

DAVID

DAVID SHELTON, WILLIAM SHELTON & SAMUEL SHELTON, Executors of JOSEPH SHELTON, deceased.

against

JOHN SHELTON.

THIS was an appeal from a decree of the High Court of Chancery. The case was this. Joseph Shelton by his will dated the 20th of September 1770, after directing his debts to be paid, devises as follows, viz: " to his brother David Shelton " all his land at Wild-Boarcreek, in fee, with all the cattle, " horses, cows, hogs and utensils and appurtenances thereto " belonging.

" To Samuel Shelton his brother, his tract of land on Lick-" ing Hole Creek, in fee, together with the cattle, &c. " *ut supra*, thereto belonging."

" To his brother William Shelton, his tract of land on Owens " Creek, (his manor plantation) with all the cattle, &c. there-" to belonging."

" To William Shelton, son of his brother John, his horse-" shoe tract in Louisa, in fee, with all the cattle &c. thereto " belonging, and £200.

" To John Shelton (the plaintiff) son of the said John after " the decease of Mary Trueheart, his tract of land on Totopo-" tomoy in Hanover, and all cattle &c. thereto belonging."

To Mary Trueheart his sister, he lends the Hanover plantation, for her life or widowhood, a limited number of cattle, hogs and horses, and some negroes by name; and, at her marriage or death, then immediately the land and cattle, horses, hogs and other appurtenances thereto belonging, to go to his nephew John.

He gives all his furniture equally to his brother William and nephew John. Then follows this clause: " *all* my negroes, " young and old, at *all* my plantations above named, to be " equally divided between my three brothers David, Samuel " and William, and those lent to sister Trueheart *also* after her " death or widowhood."

He next gives some trifling pecuniary legacies to others of his female relations, and then follows this clause: " It is my
" will

"will also, that in case my brothers sons, John and William, should either of them die before marriage or without issue, then the legacy above left to one, shall fall to the other brother; and should both die, without such lawful issue or marriage, then the legacy left them shall be equally divided between my brothers David, Samuel and William, and their heirs forever." There is no residuary clause in the will.

The appellees proved the will, and qualified as executors thereto.

The testator had, at the time of making his will, no lands but those devised, nor any slaves but what were upon those plantations. He lived till September 1784, and in the mean time purchased another tract of land, called *Williamsons*, and 8 or 9 slaves, three only of whom were at Williamsons at his death. The others were at the plantations devised, from whence others were removed to Williamsons, and two were out at nurse for their maintenance. There were at Williamsons at the time of the testators death about 19 slaves, young and old. The testator died in September 1784, without revoking, altering or republishing his will.

The appellee is the heir at law of the testator, and of his brother William; he having died in the life-time of the testator. He filed this bill against the executors of Joseph Shelton, claiming the £200 legacy devised to his brother, also the slaves purchased after the making of the will, and not belonging to any of the plantations in the will named, and a proportion of the undevised personal estate.

The High Court of Chancery was of opinion that the plaintiff was entitled to the £200 legacy with interest, from the end of one year after the testator's death, that the slaves, of which the testator was possessed at the time of his death, and which were not then settled on the land devised, nor, bequeathed to the testator's sister Mary Trueheart, descended to the plaintiff as heir at law of the testator, who was also entitled to their profits from the time when they should have been delivered. That the surplus of the testator's personal estate—excluding such of the sheep as were on the lands devised, and including emblements on the lands undevised, and also the crop made on such undevised lands, the year in which the testator died,—ought to be divided.

The decree being made final upon the report of the commissioner pursuant to the above opinion, the defendants appealed.

THE

THE PRESIDENT delivered the opinion of the court.

This was an appeal from the High Court of Chancery. It came on to be heard in June term 1791; but the questions being of consequence to the parties, and their decision important to the community, the court not having a library at hand, or leisure to digest the variety of adjudged cases relied on in argument, took time to consider of it, and directed the cause to be re-argued.

That has been done this term; and the court have derived much satisfaction from the laborious researches, and able reasonings of the gentlemen at the bar. They have now directed me to pronounce their final decree.

The case depends upon the will of Joseph Shelton, a rich old batchelor, which was dated and published September 20th 1770: but he living 14 years after, and in that time purchasing other lands called Williamsons, to which he removed part of the slaves from the plantations devised in his will, and purchasing other slaves, part of which were placed on those plantations; and there being three slaves (which may deserve a distinct consideration) which belonged to the plantations devised, but were occasionally absent at his death; and he dying in September 1784, without having revoked, republished or altered his will; great difficulty is occasioned in respect to the first and most important question in the cause, which is:

1st, Whether all the testators slaves shall pass by the generality of the words "all my slaves young and old," as would have been the case, had he died in 1770; since he had, then, no plantation but those devised, nor any slaves, but upon those plantations, to have made the words "on all my plantations above named," restrictive, if such he intended it.

If all did not pass, a second subordinate question has been made; whether the devise shall be confined to such slaves as the testator had at the publication of his will, in exclusion of those after purchased; or, whether the will shall speak at his death, and confine the bequest to such as were then upon the devised plantations, excluding such as were at Williamsons or elsewhere.

In discussing this question, it is agreed on all hands, that, the testators intention is to be the rule of decision; but the gentlemen at the bar have labored on the one side to enlarge, and on the other to narrow, the sources from whence we are to collect that intention.

It

It is said, 1st, we must collect it only from the written will, disregarding the parol proof and all other circumstances.

2d. That we must confine our contemplations either to the time of the publication of the will, or to the time of the testators death.

As to the first; It would be a strange waste of time to go over the string of decisions upon the admission of parol proof to explain, and even to contradict, written wills, more especially as they are in direct opposition to each other, and it is impossible to reconcile them. Indeed since the case of Selwin *vs.* Brown, cases Talbot 240 which was affirmed by the lords, the judgments have been more uniform, and the admission of parol proof less latitudinous; and if any rule upon the subject can be said to be fixed it seems to be this; That it is not to be admitted to *contradict* the common meaning or legal import of plain words in a will, but shall be allowed to *explain* a person or thing intended by doubtful words, or to correct mistakes in either discription. 3 Atk. 372.

But that, under the latter allowance, parol evidence of the estators circumstances, situation, connections with the legatees, and his transactions between the making of his will and death, are to be admitted to discover his intention. The Chancery books ancient and modern abound with instances.

As to the trite objection, that counsel would not know how to advise, if judges are to go out of the written will; I answer,

1st. That counsel in general would be very inattentive not to enquire (previous to giving an opinion) whether there were no change in the testators situation and circumstances subsequent to the making of the will, especially in a case like this, where the testator lived so long after; from whence revocations or ademptions of legacies from change of circumstances were, at least, to be suspected.

2d. That without such enquiry into extraneous circumstances, it would be difficult to discover from this will, any thing to restrain the generality of the words " all my slaves young and old on all my plantations" by the words, " above named," since it does not appear by the will that he had other plantations or slaves.

As to the second objection, " that we must confine our view of the will to circumstances, either at the date of the will or at the time of the testator's death, and not regard both;" I answer, that as we should frequently come short of the intention, by being confined to either, so I conceive we are not only authorised, lifed, but compelled, to view circumſtances at, and from the former period, to the latter, to difcover what was his original intention, and whether that continued to the time of his death, or was legally controuled by what happened in the mean time.

And this is proved: 1ſt, From the legal idea of a will, which we are told has its *inception* from the making, and its *confummation* by the death, ſhewing it to be one continued act. 1 *P. Williams*, 97.—*Salk*, 237.—2 *P. Williams*.

2d, From precedents.

In the cafe of after-purchafed lands, which will not pafs by a devife " of all the eſtate or lands I ſhall have at my death," you view the date of the will, and introduce the conveyance for the purchafe, to ſhew it to be fubfequent. This land will not pafs, not for want of intention, but from the controul of law upon that intention, for under the fame devife, after acquired chattels would pafs; this is one inſtance of looking to both periods, and an intervening act.

Another is, the known difputes about the ademption of legacies. You view the will, and find the legacy given, but at the teſtator's death the fubject is not found in his eſtate.

Whether this be an ademption or not, depends on the teſtators intention. *Ca. Temp. Talb.* 227. This is the general rule.

But an intention to revoke is not to be prefumed, 3 *Bac.* 470.

As to a fpecific thing devifed and afterwards fold by the teſtator: if merely voluntarily, it is an ademption, becaufe no other motive appears. But if compelled to pay debts, or to provide immediate neceſſaries, it is not fo, fince here is another motive, and his intention to revoke is not prefumed, and the money for which the thing was fold is to be paid out of the refidue, 3 *Bac.* 470. *Swinb.* 524. 3 *Bac.* 480.

As to a devife of a fpecific fum of money, due from, or in, a certain perfons hands: the teſtator receives the money; this is no ademption.

In *Gilb.* 32. 2 *Vern.* 681. 2 *P. Wms.* 165, a diſtinction is made where the payment is voluntary by the debtor in which cafe it is no ademption. If compelled by the creditor it is.—

But this diſtinction is exploded upon better reafoning. 1 *Abr. eq. Ca.* 32. 1 *P. Wms.* 464, 561. 2 *P. Wms.* 469. *Ca. Temp. Talbot* 227.

The great defideratum is in the teſtater's intention; but in equity it is important to confider how it affects the refiduary eſtate, which is difcharged of a debt by the fale of the fpecific thing, and augmented by the receipt of the fpecified debt.

This is another instance in which we must view the whole case to ascertain the intention of the testator: and as this depends on parol proof, it aids the answer to the first objection as to admitting parol proof.

We may reason as to the general rule from our act of wills in 1785, upon the subject of implied revocations, tho' it does not affect this case; and there that must be done, which both objections oppose.

Many other instances may occur, but these may suffice to shew, that we must consider the will upon its own words, and the parol proof as to the situation and circumstances of the testator when it was made, and at his death.

On a general view of this will, the testator appears to intend the disposition of his whole visible property.

His male relations were three surviving brothers, and two nephews, sons of his elder brother and heir, who was dead.

He had five plantations, and devised one to each of those five, with the stocks, plantation utensils and appurtenances to each belonging. Whether they were nearly equal, and that he meant to pursue the Jewish system of primogeniture, giving his eldest brothers sons a double share; or from what other motive he acted, does not appear, and is unimportant. However he makes provision out of his nephew John's land for his sister Mary Truehart for life or widowhood, and gives her for the same term, some slaves by name, and stocks by number; at her death the stocks with the land, were to go to John, and he gives to his nephew William £200.

He then devises all his household furniture to his brother William, and to his nephew John, equally to be divided.

Then comes the clause on which the dispute arises.—" *All* " my negroes *young and old* at *all my plantations* above named, " to be equally divided between my three brothers David, Sa- " muel and William, and those lent to sister Truehart, *also*, " after her death or widowhood."

He then gives £130, pecuniary legacies, and adds this clause: " If my nephews, John and William, should either of them " die before marriage or *without* issue, then the legacy above " left to one, shall fall to the other brother: and should both " die without such issue or marriage, then the legacy left to " them, shall be equally divided between the three brothers " David, Samuel and William:" and appoints them executors without any residuary clause.

If the teſtator had died at that time, there could have been no doubt but that all his ſlaves would have paſſed to his brothers, ſince whatever he might mean by the words, *on my plantations above named*, they could not then have operated reſtrictively, he having no other plantations, nor other ſlaves than were upon them.

It has been admitted, that the words " all my ſlaves" were ſufficient to paſs all he had, if he ſo intended; and it has been argued that the following words muſt have been added for ſome purpoſe, and that has been variouſly ſuppoſed to be, amplification, explanation, reſtriction, or that they had no meaning, and were thrown in by the writer *currente calamo*.

The words " all my ſlaves" were ſo plain and comprehenſive, as not to leave, in the ordinary underſtanding of men, any doubts of their meaning, ſo that he could not intend to amplify or explain: the conjecture, that he meant to ſhew he did not mean to paſs the ſlaves by the word *appurtenances*, uſed in the deviſe of lands and ſtocks, is ingenious but not found. That word *appurtenances*, was probably never in the teſtator's mind; it was the writers, and unluckily uſed by him for the purpoſe (as he declares) of expreſſing the teſtator's meaning.

" *Young and old*" was probably *his* alſo, and can have no effective meaning. " On all my plantations above named," could not in the teſtators view of things, at that time, act as a reſtriction, and therefore it ſtruck me at firſt, that he could not ſo intend it; but I accounted for their uſe by ſuppoſing that he reaſoned thus: " I have ſeverally diſpoſed of my lands and ſtocks by plantations, and now give all my ſlaves on all thoſe plantations as a ſtock, to be equally divided between my brothers:" differently from the diſpoſal of the lands and ſtocks. And the teſtator not meaning them reſtrictive at the time, they extended to *all*, *then*; and dying without altering his will, *all* at his death ought to paſs.

On more mature reflection, I diſcover an intention which he might have had in uſing thoſe words. He diſpoſed of all the lands and ſlaves he had *then*, but as he might live to acquire more, which he choſe ſhould depend on his future diſpoſition, he uſed ſpecific terms to confine the deviſes to the lands and ſlaves he then poſſeſſed. Whether this was really his intention or not, is immaterial; ſince if it be *poſſible* that it might have been his intention, it is ſufficient to prevent the Court's rejecting the words, as having no meaning.

This muſt be taken therefore as a ſpecific reſtrictive deviſe of the ſlaves on certain plantations, and not a deviſe of all his ſlaves. His

His intention afterwards is argued both ways: on one side it is said that intending to devise *all* when he made his will, and dying without altering that will; we must suppose he intended *all* should still pass.

On the other side it is contended that since we must suppose him to know how the devise was restrained, and finding him purchasing a plantation and making new arrangements of his slaves, fixing some on that, which would operate as an exclusion of those from the devise, and yet not altering his will, we ought to conclude he meant that those slaves as well as the land should be left to the disposition of the law.

Whatever might be his real intention, the latter supposition is what reason and precedent will impel the court to adopt.

In very many cases of local devises, the court discover a principle to influence their decision on this point; but to state a few is sufficient.

2 *Vern.* 747. was a hard case in itself, and I believe would not at this day be so determined under its particular circumstances. But the rule there laid down seems a good general one " that where goods in a house are devised, a voluntary removal of them in the testator's life time, without tort or fraud is a revocation.

2 *Vern.* 739. goods prepared and intended to be sent to the house, do not pass. 2 *Vern.* 688. What he had at *Wouston* at his death passed.

The after-purchased slaves are not to be distinguished from the others,

1st. The testator, as to lands, speaks from the date of the will; as to personals, at his death. And slaves from their nature, (from their being purchased without a conveyance recorded, and from the act of assembly where they are devised,) are to be ranked in the personal class.

2d. restriction and devise, is not of negroes by name but by the plantations: they were upon them, and those found there at his death will pass, whenever acquired.

Upon this point therefore the court decide the devise to be confined to the slaves in the devised plantations at the time of the testator's death, in exclusion of those at Williamsons; but are of opinion that their settled habitations as fixed by the testator ought to give the rule, and not any casual absence therefrom at his death, which could never be supposed to influence his intentions.

The

The proofs furnish an instance: All the working slaves from Williamson's were at work at the home-house, *Horse-Shoe,* the instant of the testator's death. Could that circumstance make them pass?

Many other instances occur: A servant sent on an errand: waggoners abroad on duty, and others.

The young negroes sent from the devised plantations to assist poor people, to remain there at will, or exchanged as Sampson was for Tom, furnish no proof of an intention to change their residence or to affect the devise. Such too is the case of the girl Rachel, and the boy Cudjo sent to Williamsons to work for a short time (not to reside there,) just before his death; so the negro Mark, sent from Williamsons in like manner to assist a poor family, is to be excluded from the above devise. The Chancellor's decree therefore as to this point, is to be varied so as to take from the heir the negroes Sampson, Cudjo and Rachel the spinner, and their profits: the negro Mark, as well as all the others belonging to Williamsons, descend to the appellee as heir at law.

The slaves, devised to Mary Trueheart, being specified by by name, passed in remainder to the three brothers wherever resident at the testator's death.

2d The next question respects the crops, whether they pass by the word " *appurtenances*" used in the devise of the lands and stocks, or go into the surplus as undisposed of.

Here we encounter an objection from the act of Assembly passed in 1748, *Ch.* 3, § 30, which declares " That where a " person dies between the 1st of March and 25th of December, " the servants and slaves he is possessed of shall be continued on " the plantations until the latter day, for making and finishing " a crop; which when made and finished, shall be *assets* in the " hands of executors and administrators. After the expence of " clothing and feeding them, of tools and utensils, quitrents of " the lands, levies, and other incidental charges are deducted." Which, it is said, is a legislative disposition of the crops, and restrains the power of testators to dispose of such crops.

But this construction does by no means accord with my idea of the spirit of the act.

This clause was clearly intended to suspend the devises of the lands and slaves, or their descent to heirs, until Christmas next after the testator or intestate's death, and to appropriate both to the purpose of finishing a growing crop, which would otherwise be lost to the family and community. As to the crops, the

primary

primary defign was to eafe the lands of quitrents and other charges of that year, and to provide food and clothing for the flaves, as a compenfation to their proprietors, for their having been employed in this beneficial work; but as to the furplus, it fays no more but generally, that it fhall be *affetts* in the hands of the *executors* or *adminiftrators*.

What is the confequence of the furplus being affetts? Does it belong to the executors? No gentleman thinks fo, but they fay it will go into the refiduum: this muft depend on the will, and feems to admit the ground of the opinion of the court, that the teftator has the fame power over this furplus of his crops, as he has over his other eftate.

Nay, I have no doubt but that a teftator might go further than the furplus, by devifing the crops entire, and directing the charges upon the lands, and the food and clothing for the flaves, to be paid out of his refiduary eftate; fince juftice, to the proprietors of the lands and flaves, is fully done, according to the intention of the act, and the teftator's power over that, which the law declares fhall be affetts in the hands of his executor, ought not to be reftrained.

It is yet affetts, and like all other perfonal legacies, muft pafs through executors hands, and is only perfected by his affent, that if neceffary, he may reftrain and apply it to the payment of debts; but if that be not neceffary, a court of equity will compel his affent according to the will of the teftator.

The cafe of lord Briftol *vs.* Hungerford *Chanc. prec.* 81, and 1 *cas.* in *eq. arb.* 244, is a devife of a furplus raifed by fale of lands, " to be deemed part of his perfonal eftate and go to his executors." This cafe is ftronger than our act, yet the furplus was diftributed as undifpofed of, tho' it conveys the fame idea.

Upon the whole of this point, we are clear that the teftator had power to difpofe of the furplus of the crops. And we come to the queftion, whether he has done fo in the devife of the lands and ftocks &c. which are alike, and one only need be noticed.

" I give my brother David Shelton all my lands at Wild-
" Boar Creek, in Goochland county, to him, and his heirs
" forever, with all the cattle, horfes, hogs and other utenfils,
" and *appurtenances* thereto belonging."

If the crops pafs at all, it muft be under the word *appurtenances*, which I am inclined to think fufficient for the purpofe, and that it was his intention the crops fhould pafs with every thing elfe on the plantations except the flaves, (a diftinct and important clafs of property,) which he afterwards particularly devifes, but is filent as to the crops.—

To

To admit the evidence of Mr. Todd, (the writer of the will) that he was directed to devife the crops, and thought he had done fo by this word, would be warranted by innumerable precedents in the Englifh Chancery.

However, I am not fond of this dangerous kind of evidence, fince, tho' Mr. Todd's function and character entitle him to credit, yet we muft adopt general rules. I am therefore inclined to take it upon the words of the will itfelf.

The determination in Trafford vs. Berrige 1 *Cas. eq. Abr.* 201. 14. and others of the fame kind, " that a devife of all his " goods, chattels, houfehold ftuff, furniture and *other things* " which fhould be in his houfe at his death, fhould be confined " to things of the fame nature and fpecies of thofe mentioned, " and not extend to £ 265 fpecie found in his houfe," does not feem to apply; fince that was founded on the words *other things* at the clofe of a ftring of *things* mentioned.

But in this will, after a devife of the lands, (as the principal,) it goes on with " all the cattle, horfes, hogs, utenfils, and appurtenances thereto belonging;" making each a diftinct relative defcription and devife, which has the land for its correlative; and the words *thereto belonging*, have the fame effect, as if inferted after each as " the cattle belonging to the faid lands &c." fo that we are to read the will " I give my lands with the appurtenances thereto belonging," which would include the crops *growing* according to the legal technical meaning of that term. For I take it that a grant of lands and appurtenances, would pafs growing crops to the purchafer if no refervation were made, which would not violate the principle " he that fows fhall reap," fince that right to reap, like all other property may be transferred.

The crop fevered indeed would not pafs by fuch a grant, and can only pafs by this will, on a fuppofition that the teftator intended to make no difference, and from the difficulty of diftinguifhing which was fevered.

The date of his will and his death happened in the fame month tho' 14 years diftant. It was in *September*, when corn is not fevered; perhaps the fodder was, and probably all or moft of the tobacco.

The cafe is doubtful, and tho' I am rather of opinion myfelf that he intended to devife the crops, I can without any reluctance yield to the opinion of my brethren, that they do not pafs, but muft go into the furplus, and it only remains to confider,—

What is to become of that surplus, whether it belongs to the executors, or is to be diſtributed to the next of kin? This is a queſtion of difficulty, requiring laborious reſearches, and in which we might find in the Chancery books, like Crokes law reports, precedents for almoſt any opinion we ſhould incline to give on the ſubject. Yet when we have labored thro' the various and contradictory deciſions, the *principles* which are to govern them, do not ſeem to be ſo very difficult to aſcertain.

As a precedent, our judgment may not perhaps be ſo important as I at firſt thought it, if I am not miſtaken in my conjecture, that our new ſtatute of diſtributions, has put an end to the diſpute as to all caſes ſubſequent to its paſſage, by directing diſtribution " where the perſon dies inteſtate as to his perſonal eſtate, *or any part thereof*: this however is juſt hinted at, without giving any opinion on it.

To ſtate the principles—there are two, which ſeem the ground work and are fixed.

1ſt. A legal one. " That the naming of an executor is a " diſpoſition to him of all the perſonal eſtate, and after pay-" ment of debts and legacies, the ſurplus belongs to him as a " recompence for his labor and trouble." 2 *Bac*. 423, *Wentw. off.* of executors 4. and if the ſpiritual court at this day are about to compel the executors to diſtribute the ſurplus to the next of kin, the Kings Bench will grant a prohibition 5. *Mod.* 247.

2d. A contending principle of equity, " that where there is " fraud in obtaining the executorſhip, or it manifeſtly appears " to have been the teſtator's intention the executor ſhould not " have the ſurplus, a Court of Equity will conſider the execu-" tor as a *truſtee* only as to the ſurplus, for the next of kin." 2 *Bac*. 423.

This we are told was firſt introduced about a century ago in Foſter *vs.* Munt, 1 *Vern*. 473, where an expreſs pecuniary legacy was given to the two executors of £10 each for their care and pains; which it was ſaid, was apparent evidence of his intention to exclude them from the ſurplus, ſince the legacy being to come out of the ſurplus, the teſtator could not intend to give them part and the whole. And to this apparent proof of the teſtator's intention in caſes of pecuniary deviſes, in conſideration of care and pains, and in a few other inſtances, was the rule confined at firſt, but ſoon branched into a variety of other conſiderations, which produced determinations not to be

reconciled

reconciled in principle to each other, and which muſt be reſolved into the different inclinations of the Chancellors to favor, ſome the legal, others the equitable rule, and endeavouring to make the favored rule apply to the caſe before them.

Thus ſome attack the rule of law and oppoſe to it the ſtatute of diſtributions, which they alledge gives the next of kin, a title to ſuch of the perſonal eſtate as is not diſpoſed of; ſimilar to that which the heir has to the real eſtate— 1 *P. Wms.* 554.— 2 *P. Wms.* 210.—3 *Atk.* 203: and that the office being in its nature fiduciary, and not beneficial; therefore the executor ought to take no more than is given him, and be a truſtee for the reſidue:—Whilſt others lament that ever the rule of equity was introduced, and will not interfere with the executor's title, but upon the moſt irreſiſtible proof appearing in the will of an intention to exclude him, 2 *Bac.* 423, to 426. *Brown* 330.

Sometimes a diſtinction is made between a ſpecific and a pecuniary deviſe to the executor, *Ch. Prec.* 231, 316. This again is exploded in others *Cas. Temp. Talb.* 3 *Atk.* 226.

Sometimes the circumſtance of the executor's being a near relation, or a ſtranger is thought important. In other inſtances that is denied, 1 *P. Wms.* 544.

And finally parol proof of the teſtator's intention is admitted in many caſes and denied in others.

From hence it may be concluded; that an enquirer after principles can derive very little ſatisfaction from thoſe caſes: thoſe who are curious, and have leiſure, may recur to them. I ſhall paſs them over, and confine myſelf to a few modern caſes, where moſt of the others are brought into review.

Farrington *vs.* Knightly 1 *P. Wms.* 544 was this, " the teſtator declared, as to his perſonal eſtate (if he ſhould leave any) " he gave £50 to his brother A, and £50 to his nephew B, whom " he made executors; gave 20ſ. each to others of his relations, ſe" veral of whom were his brothers, nephews and nieces, (and " as ſuch amongſt his next of kin entitled to diſtribution under " the ſtatute,) and then abruptly broke off without the uſual " concluſion, In witneſs &c. or making any diſpoſition of the " ſurplus which was £1200."

On a queſtion between the executors and next of kin, who ſhould have the ſurplus, lord Parker takes notice of the caſes on both ſides, which he endeavors to reconcile with the principle he affirms, viz. that where there is an expreſs legacy to the executor, or to the executors equally (if as in that caſe there be more than one) it shall exclude them from the surplus, even tho' there were legacies also to the next of kin.

As to the reason of the case he says: "it is most plain that "making a person executor, ought not to amount to a gift "of the personal estate; it is no more than making him a *trustee*; "the very word *executor* importing *ex vi termini*, that he was "only appointed to execute the will, and to have nothing but "the management of the personal estate. That he is a trustee "as well of the specific legacies, as of the surplus, since the "former passes to the legatee by his assent only."

He concludes for the equitable principle *pari ratione*, and decrees a distribution independant of the circumstance (which no doubt was weighty) of the will being unfinished, and a devise of the surplus, probably prevented. Except the labour of the case, it was plainly within the rule of equity, being a pecuniary legacy of equal sums to each of two executors, which in every instance since Foster and Munt, deprived the executor of the surplus, except when in the will itself, or from parol proof, it appears the testator intended to give it him, the contrary of which appeared in this case.

A distinction between equal and unequal bequests to a plurality of executors, was taken in Bachellor *vs.* Searle 2 *Vern.* 736; affirmed in Brasbridge *vs* Woodroffe 2. *Atk.* 68. and seems established in Bowker and al. *vs.* Hunter and Eaton Browns *Chan. Rep.* 328. first decreed by lord Thurlow, and on rehearing, that decree affirmed by lord Loughborough. The case was this, viz:

The testatrix devised £200 to Mr. Hunter, and after many intervening legacies to other persons, amongst whom were some (but not all) of her next of kin, she gave £50 to Mr. Eaton, added some charitable legacies, and made Hunter and Eaton executors, but made no disposition of the surplus.

Here was a case divested of all influence from parol proof, or the relation which subsisted between the testatrix and the executors on the one side, and the next of kin on the other: in short, no favorite wife to claim the assistance of the court: but it depended simply on the will, and whether the testator's intention to deprive the executor's of the surplus, was to be presumed from his having devised them *pecuniary* legacies.

It is obvious that lord Thurlow's general reasoning is opposed to lord Parker's in making the *legal* the *general rule*, and the *equitable* principle, only an exception from it. The consequence

each

each draws from thence, is materially different. Lord Thurlow's is, "that the rule "that the executor shall take the residue," must prevail, unless there be an irresistible inference "to the contrary." Lord Parker's is "that the next of kin "have the apparent right, and there must be a devise of the "surplus to the executors either expressly or unavoidably impli- "ed, to exclude the next of kin."

Lord Loughborough reasons with less appearance of bias than either; confesses there is great difficulty in the cases, but as neither the legal rule "that the appointment of an executor is a gift to him of the whole," nor the equitable one "that a legacy given to him excludes him from the surplus," can be shaken; he thinks a more certain principle cannot be laid down in the application of the equitable rule to particular wills, than was mentioned by lord Mansfield in Lawson *vs.* Lawson in the house of lords. 7 *Brown's par. cases* 511. "That where the legacies "to executors are consistent with their taking the residue, there "is no implication to exclude them," "tho' he confessed there "was great latitude in it." On that ground was the decree in the case then before the court made, because the devise to one of the executors being of £ 200, and to the other of £ 50, it was not inconsistent with their taking the surplus, since the latter was to be equally divided, and the former taken out in unequal portions. This being a very late case, and agreeable to those in 2 *Vern.* and 2 *Atk.* seems to give some rule by which to conduct ourselves in examining what was the testator's intention in the present will, and whether the bequests to the executors, be consistent with their taking the surplus?

The devise of lands to them separately, if equal would be unimportant, because with that species of property, executors have nothing to do, as executors.

The devise of the slaves I take to be on the same ground of reasoning as to the present question, since if undisposed of, they descend to the heir, and do not go into the surplus either for the executors or next of kin.

The excluding legacy must be of a personal thing, which if not devised would belong to the surplus, to bring it within the ground of objection *that the testator did not intend to give all and some;*

The bequests of personal things to the three brothers therefore are only to be viewed, laying aside the devises to them, of the lands and slaves.

To

To his brother David he gives "all his horses, cows, hogs and utensils, on his Goochland plantation."

To Samuel "all his horses, cows, hogs and utensils, at Licking Hole."

To William "all his horses, cows, hogs and utensils, at the home plantation, and half his houshold furniture, to be divided between him and his nephew William."

And having created crofs remainders between his nephews William and John, directs "that if both die unmarried, or without issue, the legacy to them should be equally divided between the three *brothers*.

I think the testator fo far from intending to exclude his executors by thefe legacies from the surplus, plainly intended it for them.

Having disposed of his visible property which he contemplated and described, he proceeds to give pecuniary legacies to the amount of £330, without making any provision for raising or directing who should pay either those or his debts which he had faid should be paid, or the expences of his funeral and administration. These he knew must be defrayed by his executors out of his money, certificates, and other things which conftitute the surplus; and not having made an exact estimate of the *fund* or the *charges*, he intended the *brothers* should take the one to answer the *other* without account to any person.

His having given all his slaves to his three brothers, and giving them all that was devised to his only other relations of his name, his nephews William and John, upon their dying without issue, creates a strong presumption that if he had made a residuary claufe, it would have been in their favor.

Then to take it upon the rule laid down by lord Mansfield, affirmed by lord Thurlow, and which lord Lougborough confiders as the best general one which can be adopted: I do not confider these devises as at all inconfiftent with their taking the surplus as executors.

1st It is not a devife to them jointly by the defcription of executors, but a separate *devife* to each as *brothers*, without mentioning the office or making any allufion to it,

2d But the principle point is, that the legacies are unequal; and if any point on this loofe queftion can be faid to be uniformly decided, this is, viz. that unequal legacies do not exclude the executors jointly from the surplus; we are therefore of opinion that the surplus go to the executors.

The

The decree muſt be reverſed. The plaintiff is entitled to the £ 200 deviſed to William with intereſt from a year after the teſtator's death, and to 16 ſlaves, undiſpoſed of, and their profits. The crops made the year the teſtator died, did not paſs to the deviſees of the plantations by the word "appurtenances," but after paying the ſeveral charges directed by the act of Aſſembly, the balance is to go into the ſurplus of the perſonal eſtate: and that ſurplus, after payment of debts, legacies, funeral and charges of adminiſtration, and the coſts of this ſuit on both ſides, belongs to the executors.

As to all other matters; the bill is to be diſmiſſed, and the coſts of both courts muſt be paid by the executors out of the ſurplus.

CASES DETERMINED
IN THE
COURT of APPEALS
IN
THE SPRING TERM OF THE YEAR,
1792.

WOOD *againſt* DAVIS.

THIS was an appeal from a judgment of the Diſtrict Court, obtained by the appellee againſt the appellant, upon a forthcoming bond, the condition of which is as follows, to wit: "The condition &c. is ſuch, that whereas Matt. Rodes deputy "ſheriff for Michael Thomas ſheriff for Albermarle county, "hath this day levied an execution on Fanny &c. negroes, the "property of the ſaid David and John Wood, taken at the ſuit "of J. Davis by a judgment of the Diſtrict Court of Char- "lottſville; for the ſum of 16,164lb of Tobacco, &c. now "if the ſaid D. and J. Wood, and Joſiah Wood ſhall deliver,

" or cause to be delivered, the aforesaid property, at David
" Woods barn, at his quarter, on the 14th of April next, then
" &c."

The objection to the judgment was, that the condition does not state that the 14th of April was *the day appointed, for the sale of the property.*

By the Court. It is not necessary that the time appointed for the delivery of the property should be stated to be that at which the sale is to take place. The law does not require it, nor can it produce any benefit whatever to the obligors, that it should be so stated.

Judgment affirmed.

HUBBARD
against
BLOW & BARKSDALE.

THIS was an action of debt, brought in the County Court, by the present appellees, upon a promissory note given for the payment of £319: 8: 7: *with interest from the date.* The declaration states the *principal sum* right, but takes no notice of the *interest.*

The defendant, without oyer, pleaded payment: afterwards withdrew the plea and suffered judgment by *non sum informatus*, which was entered for the principal *and interest* as expressed in the note. The defendant appealed to the district court, where the judgment was affirmed; and on appeal to this court, both judgments were reversed, and judgment entered according to the demand in the declaration, *without interest.*

HUDSON *against* MORRIS.

THIS was a motion made by the appellee against the appellant, and P. D. and I. L. in the County Court, for judgment on a replevy bond, given by the said Hudson P. D. and I. L. to Morris.

The court gave judgment for the plaintiff, and Hudson having filed a bill of exceptions, appealed to the District Court

of Charlottsville. The bill states " that the original suit was
" commenced against P. D for whom the said Hudson became
" appearance bail, but gave no bond; and a conditional judg-
" ment was entered and writ of enquiry thereupon executed
" against P. D. only. That a fi. fa. issued against the said P. D. *and*
" *the said Hudson* upon which this replevy bond was taken.
" That P. D. afterwards obtained an injunction, which was dif-
" solved for part of the sum, on which Morris afterwards
" sued out a ca. sa. against the body of P. D. only, which was
" returned " executed and imprisoned—the defendant Hudson
" therefore objected to a judgment being rendered against him
" on this motion, it appearing from the replevy bond that the
" fi. fa. issued against him, as well as P. D. though he, the
" said defendant, was no party to the original suit; and because
" it appeared by the return of the ca. fa. against P. D. that he
" was in custody."

The District Court affirmed the judgment of the County Court, from which an appeal was granted to this Court.

The appellant did not appear at the trial in this Court, and the Court having considered the record,

affirmed the judgment.

HUNTERS *against* HAYNES.

THIS was an ejectment, brought in the District Court of Suffolk by the lessee of the appellees against the appellants.

The parties agreed the following case, to wit.

" That William Hunter, the former proprietor of the land in
" question, by his will dated in 1764, devised the same to Eli-
" zabeth, his widow, during her natural life; and after her de-
" cease to his nephew, Thomas Haynes, and the heirs of his body
" lawfully begotten for ever; but in case his said nephew
" should die without such issue, then to Thomas Hunter brother
" of the testator, and his heirs for ever."

" That the said Thomas Haynes died in June 1780, under
" age, intestate and without issue."

" That Elizabeth the widow died on the 14th December 1786."

" That

"That the defendants are the widow and children of the said Thomas Hunter, the laft remainder-man."

"That the leffor of the plaintiff is the coufin of the whole blood, and heir at law to the faid Thomas Haynes, the firft remainder-man," and if &c.

The Diftrict Court gave judgment, upon this agreed cafe for the leffor of the plaintiff from which the defendants appealed to this Court.

The appellants being called, and not appearing the Court upon infpecting the record,

Affirmed the judgment.

EVANS *again* SMITH.

THIS was an action of debt, upon a bond brought by the appellee, in the Diftrict Court of King and Queen. A conditional judgment was obtained at rules; and fet afide in Court, the defendant pleading payment. An objection was taken, at the trial, to the giving of the bond in evidence, on account of a variance between it and the declaration in this, that the defendants are in the bond faid to be " of the County of Effex" which is omitted in the declaration; the objection being over-ruled by the court, the defendants excepted and appealed to this court where the judgment below was affirmed.

ASBERRY &c. *againft* CALLOWAY, &c.

THE defendants in error gave a notice in writing, to O. Trent and George Afberry, late deputy fheriffs under G. Scruggs, the adminiftrator of the faid defendant and to three others their fecurities, that a motion would be made againft them in the County Court of Bedford in November 1790, for the amount of the revenue tax, due for the year 1783, and the cofts and damages, which had been recovered by the commonwealth againft the faid Scruggs, in his life-time. O. Trent being ferved with a copy of the notice, appeared and put in a plea in writing, denying that the fheriff's bond, upon which the motion was made, was his deed; which he fwore to in court.

The

The court, on hearing the evidence, gave judgment, that the plaintiffs have execution against the said Trent, Afberry, and two of the securities, upon whom the notice was served, for the penalty of the bond, but to be discharged by the payment of £651 : 8 : 3½, with interest thereon, at the rate of 20 per cent. per annum from the first of November 1784, till payment and the costs.

From this judgment the two securities appealed, having filed a bill of exceptions to the opinion of the court, stating the reasons for which they appealed; which were: 1st, Because the bond upon which the judgment was given was joint, and that no testimony was adduced, on the part of the plaintiffs, to disprove the plea of O. Trent, except his acknowledgment in court that he had subscribed his name to the bond, and delivered it to the other defendant George Afberry, as a form, by which to draw such bond; but that he never acknowledged the same, or delivered it as obligatory upon him.

2d, Because the interlineations in the bond were not proved to have been made at the time of executing it.*

The District Court affirmed the judgment, as to George Afberry and the two securities; awarded severance as to O. Trent, and reversed the judgment against him: The court being of opinion, that the plea put in by him ought to have been tried by a jury; for which purpose they remanded the cause to the County Court.

The defendants George Afberry and the two securities, obtained a supersedeas to the judgment of the District Court from one of the judges of this court.

THE PRESIDENT.—The judgment of the District Court is erroneous and must be reversed, as must also that of the County Court. The errors in the latter judgment are:

1st, The evidence stated in the exceptions, is wholly insufficient to prove, that the writing obligatory, denied by the plea of Trent to be his act and deed, was such his deed; a fact which ought to be decided, prior to any judgment against the other obligors.

2d, The court erred, in awarding interest at the rate of twenty per centum per annum from the 1st of November 1784, till

---

* *This bill of exceptions is not sealed by the justices of the Court, but appears in the record, and none of the defendants appealed but the two securities.*

till payment upon the principal sum; because the act passed in 1780, which authorises judgments on motions by sheriffs against their deputies, justifies only a gross sum of *damages*, although called interest on the principal sum (stated in the act to be twenty per cent. the damages to which the sheriff was then liable, but which the court are of opinion ought to be changed to the damages to which the sheriff himself was liable according to the laws subsisting at the time of the transaction, and which in 1783 and ever since, were a gross sum of fifteen per cent. on the principal sum, and both sums to bear interest at five per cent. per annum till paid, with a power to the court to remit all or any part of the damages,) provided it appear that judgment has been obtained by the commonwealth against the sheriff for such damages.

3d, The law directs the judgment to be entered, for the principal sum with which the under sheriff is chargeable, and the damages; and not for the penalty, to be discharged by such payment; and this being a new law, introducing a new remedy contrary to the course of the common law, ought to be strictly pursued.

And as the record does not enable this court to determine what judgment the County Court ought to have given, the cause must be remanded to that court for further proceedings from the notice.

HUDSON *against* ROSS, & Co.

THE apellees brought an action of debt, in the County Court, against Christopher Hudson, who confessed a judgment, and then appealed. In November 1789, the death of the appellant being suggested upon the record, a *sci. fa.* issued, upon the motion of Charles Hudson the executor, to revive the appeal, and hear errors.

In April 1790, a *sci. fa.* to revive and hear errors, was awarded on the motion of the appellees, which was returned, *executed*

In April 1791 the District Court affirmed the judgment, and awarded the *damages and costs* of the appeal, against the appellant. From which judgment he appealed to this court

The PRESIDENT delivered the opinion of the Court.

There is no error in the proceedings in this cause, until we come to the judgment of the District Court, which is entered as if Christopher Hudson had been then living. The entry is: "that the judgment of the County Court be affirmed, and that the appellee recover, against the *apellant*, damages according to law &c. and costs &c."

The court take no notice of the death of Christopher, and yet that event had been regularly suggested upon the record, and the executor made a party by the service of the *sci. fa.*

In the case of Gordon *vs.* Bates where the executor was there stated as a party, this Court affirmed the judgment with damages and costs to be levied of the estate of the testator in the hands of the executor if so much he had, if not, then the damages and costs of the executor's proper goods.

The damages in that case being only one penny, they were not worth the attention of the court. On reviewing that subject we disapprove of that decision in awarding the damages against the proper estate of the executor, in case of deficiency in that of the testator, since the executor, in pursuit of his duty, only prosecuted an appeal entered by the testator himself.

The judgment of the District Court must be reversed, and that of the County Court affirmed, with damages from the time of entering the judgment in the County Court, to that of the affirmance in the District Court, and the costs in the latter Court, to be levied of the estate of the testator in the hands of the executor; &c.*

TURPIN *against* TURPIN.

THE only question in this case was, whether since the act respecting wills, (passed in 1785,) was in force; a man may devise lands which he should afterwards acquire?

---

* *A Motion was made, that the clerk might be permitted to give a certificate of the above judgment, to be entered in the District Court now sitting:—By the Court. This is a motion, which is never granted without strong reasons. In general it is not permitted, as we may change our opinions during the term. It is often granted, if the delay would endanger the debt. No sufficient reason appearing in this case, the motion is over-ruled.*

The

The court were of opinion he might; as that law in express terms permits the disposition, by last will, "of lands which the testator then hath, or *may have* at the time of his death." In this respect it is different from the law of England.

BUTLER *against* PARKS.

THIS was an action of detinue, in the County Court, for *five* negroes; and a verdict was rendered for *four*, without finding, either for plaintiff or defendant, as to the fifth. The judgment of the County Court was reversed in the District Court; from which the plaintiff below appealed to this court.

MARSHALL for the appellee contended, that only part of the issue having been found, the whole verdict must be set aside. He cited *Co. Lit.* 227. 3 *Leo.* 83. *Hard.* 166.

By the Court. The judgment of the County Court is certainly erroneous, in not finding the whole issue. The jury should have found that the defendant did, or did not, detain the fifth slave. This is exactly like the case of *Custice and Posey* in the old General Court; which was an action of detinue for three cows, and the jury having only found a verdict as to two, the verdict was set aside. But the judgment of the District Court, in this case is also erroneous, in not awarding a *Venire facias de novo*.

Both judgments therefore must be reversed, and the cause remanded to the County Court, to be tried anew.

LEWIS, Executor of Thruston, *against* NORTON.

THIS was an action on the case, brought by the appellee against the appellant in the District Court of Williamsburg, upon an assumpsit. On the general issue, the counsel for the appellee offered in evidence to prove his claim, his store books, which were proved to be in the hand writing of one of the appellee's book keepers, then dead. This was objected to by the appellant's counsel: but the court permitting it to go to the jury as evidence, connected with other testimony, such as a bill of exchange drawn by Thruston on the appellee, which they paid, as well as sundry letters from Thruston to the appellee, and invoices of goods in the hand writing of Thruston;—a bill of exceptions was filed by the appellant's counsel, and an appeal prayed and granted to this court. The letters, bill, invoices, and a note of hand given by Thruston to the appellee, are spread upon the record, which also states, that it was proved by a witness, that the books of the appellee were in general regularly kept.

THE PRESIDENT delivered the opinion of the Court.

Ever since the decision in lord Torrington case, the law has been settled, that a book of accounts in the hand writing of, and kept by, a clerk who is since dead, is proper evidence upon those facts being proved.

The District Court therefore did right in admitting those books, with the other evidence, to go to the jury, for them to weigh, and to produce on their minds such conviction, as such evidence might in their opinion deserve.

SCOTT

against

ALEXANDER & PETERFIELD TRENT,

THE appellees brought an action on the case, against the appellant in the District Court of Charlottsville; the declarations contains three counts; the first and second upon an *indebitatus assumpsit & quantum valebant* for goods sold and delivered, and the third for money lent. Plea *non assumpsit*.

At the trial, the defendant offered in evidence four receipts, signed by Peterfield Trent, as offsetts against the plaintiff's demand. One of the receipts is in the following words, to wit:

" Received

"Received of John Scott, per the hands of James Scott, £43: 14: which I shall return, when demanded—(Signed) Peterfield Trent"—The others are general and not differing essentially from the following viz: "Received of John Scott, thirty-five bushels of wheat—(Signed) Peterfield Trent." He also offered in evidence a receipt, signed by John Osborn, collector for Peterfield Trent, in the following words, to wit: "Received of John Scott, thirty-five bushels of wheat, on account of Peterfield Trent, (John Osborn.)" He also produced testimony, to prove, that before the commencement of this action, he paid to said P. Trent, twenty barrels of corn—and further offered to prove, that he presented to Peterfield Trent, the following account, to wit: "List of money &c. paid to P. Trent for payments of my debts, which you promised to pay, and the balance to my account that may arise with you, and your brother's stores." After which follows a number of items of payments &c.

The court refusing to admit the above receipts and list, as evidence of offsetts against the demand of the plaintiffs, the defendant filed a bill of exceptions, stating the above facts; and further, that it was proved, that when the said list of money &c. paid to P. Trent, was presented to him, he admitted all the items in it to be just, except one; and also that the said Trent had said, that the items, except the one objected to, had been taken from an account formerly rendered to the said Scott by him, but the defendant did not prove what the balance was after the payment of the said defendants debts, and it was admitted by the defendant, that the 35 bushels of wheat mentioned in one of the receipts was the same as charged in the list, and that the flour mentioned in another of the receipts, was only stored by the said P. Trent, for the defendant, and to be sent to Baker and Blowe for his use. The bill further states, that the defendant did not prove any otherwise, than as abovementioned, that the said payments were made to P. Trent, on account of the demand for which the present action was brought, and that it appeared, that a considerable private account subsisted between the said P. Trent, and the defendant; on which account the said P. Trent acknowledged himself to be the debtor of the defendant.

The jury found a verdict for the plaintiffs, and the defendant appealed.

The PRESIDENT delivered the opinion of the court.

It

It is undoubtedly true, that a debt due from an individual partner cannot be set off against a partnership demand. A payment indeed, to one partner, will be a payment to the company, and his receipt (unless perhaps, where such payment is forbidden by the company) will bind the whole. But in this case, the receipts do not specify, that the payments were made for the use of the company. The list does; but in that, the balance is not stated, and therefore being entirely unsettled, the court did right, in refusing to let it go in evidence to the jury.

If indeed, P. Trent has received the balance, and should be unable to pay it, Scott may obtain relief against the company by getting an injunction for so much.

Judgment affirmed.

COCHRAN *against* STREET.

THIS was an action of slander, brought by Street against Cochran, in the County Court; wherein a verdict was given in favor of the plaintiff for £150. Cochran having failed in a motion in arrest of judgment obtained an injunction on the chancery side of the same court, suggesting that the trial was unfair, and brought on by surprise, and also charging misbehavior in the jury.

The cause coming on for a hearing, the court (without setting aside the former verdict,) directed a new trial, and the verdict thereon to be reported in order to a final decree. The material facts, proved by the depositions taken in the suit in chancery, are, that this cause, and another of Cochran *vs* Street, were taken by consent, out of course, to be tried at November court; but that the latter coming on first employed the whole of the term; so that this was necessarily continued over until the succeeding term, when it was tried, tho' much objected to by Cochran. Four of the jurymen declared on oath, that they were of opinion upon the evidence that no damages ought to have been given against Cochran; but that being unacquainted with the duties of jurymen, and the nature of their office, and being told by others who were more experienced, that they must agree in any verdict which the majority should approve, they did not object to it.

From the decree of the County Court, Street appealed to the High Court of Chancery where it was reversed; and from that decree of reversal, an appeal was prayed to this court.

MARSHALL,

MARSHALL,—for appellant. The verdict in this case is the finding of only eight jurymen, and is in truth no verdict at all. If the circumstances, which attended it, had been known, it could not have been received by the County Court. Being afterwards discovered, there was no remedy but by the equitable interference of the court.

There are no better reasons for setting aside a verdict, than its having been unfairly procured, whether by surprize on the parties, or mistake in the jury.

I would also observe that the appeal in this case from the decree of the County Court was premature; for the court not having set aside the first verdict, but merely directed a new trial, the decree was interlocutory only.

DUVAL for appellee. If the court should affirm the decree of the County Court, much injustice may flow from it, as after so long a time since the former trial, witnesses may have died, or removed, by which the parties may not have so fair a trial as the former was. Besides, a new trial cannot be obtained at law after a motion in arrest of judgment; and therefore it ought not to be directed by a Court of Equity—5 Bac. 239, 242, 243.

Nothing can be productive of so much mischief, as a practice, once introduced, of permitting jurymen, by their after affidavits, to set aside their own verdicts. They are liable to be tampered with out of court, to defeat the fairest verdicts, and thus to produce endless vexation, and real injustice to the parties; particularly, where one of the parties may in the mean-time have lost his witnesses. The proof of misbehaviour should not come from the juryman but from some other person.—*Durnf* and *East, Rep.* 11.

This decree is as final, as one for negroes, where an account of the hires is directed; and yet there is no doubt but that an appeal may be taken from such a decree.

MARSHALL in reply. I grant that in the case stated by Mr. Duvall, it is the practice to appeal from such a decree; but the reason of it is, that as to the negroes it is final, and execution for them may issue immediately.

THE PRESIDENT delivered the opinion of the court.

We do not take into consideration the depositions, touching the merits of the cause, before the jury. They were the proper judges upon that subject. As to the unfairness of the trial on the score of surprise, there is no doubt, but that if it were proved, it would afford good ground for granting a new trial;

as if the caufe were tried out of its turn, without the previous confent of the party. But the court think the proof too flender to eftablifh the fact.

To meddle with the verdict of a jury, upon the evidence of fome of the jurors, is a delicate bufinefs, and fhould be proceeded in with caution, to prevent the mifchief of the jurymen being tampered with. Lord Mansfield very properly, in the cafe cited from *Durnf & Eaft*, refufed a new trial upon the affidavit of two of the jurors, that the caufe was decided by crofs and pile, becaufe it went, not only to prove *themfelves* guilty of mifbehaviour, but alfo ten others of the jury. But here, ten of the jurors are examined, and eight of them agree in the fact, that part of their body were oppofed to giving any damages at all, and that the verdict was found on the opinion of a majority. Four of them fwear that they did not incline to give any damages; that they did not diffent from the verdict, in confequence of a mifapprehenfion of the law, and a belief that the opinion of the majority was to prevail; that they did not previoufly agree to be bound, by the determination of a majority; and that, if they had known, that they could have prevented a verdict till their confciences were fatisfied, they would not have agreed to the verdict. There does not appear to have been any tampering with the jurors by any perfon, in order to obtain this information. It comes out upon examination as other teftimony does :—a great majority of the jury confirm the fact to which thefe four have fworn; and none of them contradict it. It is clear therefore that the verdict was found under a miftake, and that a new trial fhould be awarded.—The inconvenience which may happen from another trial, if real, is to be attributed to the party who complains of it.—It might, but for him, have been had at a much earlier day.

The decree of the chancellor muft be reverfed and that of the County Court affirmed.

THORNTON *againft* SMITH.

THIS was an action of flander brought by the plaintiff, in the Court of Huftings, for the city of Richmond. The declaration begins thus: " City of Richmond to wit:" It then proceeds to lay the words to have been fpoken " in the city aforefaid." After an imparlance the plea of not guilty was put in, in. Verdict for £55, and judgment thereupon, from which an appeal was prayed to the District Court, where the judgment was reversed: The cause came up, by writ of error, to this court.

THE PRESIDENT. The case of Medtard *vs.* Skipwith, was three times argued. That was an action of debt on a bond in the Borough Court of Richmond, which was stated in the declaration, to have been executed in the city of Richmond, without alledging it to be *within the jurisdiction of the court.* The judgment of the District Court, affirming that of the County Court rendered for the plaintiff, was affirmed in this.

There were various questions agitated by the court upon that occasion, and different opinions given upon them, most of which were by a bare majority. Among others was this: whether the words, *within the jurisdiction of the court* were indispensible in every declaration in a Corporation Court, or might be supplied by other words equivalent to them? That they might be so supplied, was the opinion of four judges. But a bare majority determined, that in that case, the words were not supplied, but that the omission was cured by the confession of judgment. The same majority also decided that the £5 damages laid in the declaration, were to be added to the £100 debt, which deprived that court of its jurisdiction. The judgment was at first reversed; but, on the third argument, a worthy judge changed his opinion, and it was finally affirmed.

At the time this writ of error was moved for, if that case remained as authority——the question would have been reduced to a single point, namely, whether a judgment upon a verdict were equal to one given upon the confession of the party?

But as there was a diversity of opinions, and various points agitated upon that occasion, the court were willing to hear the matter argued at large, as if that case had not been determined.

The case has been entered into much at length, and the subject having been maturely considered by the court, a bare majority are of opinion, that the judgment of the District Court is right in reversing that of the Borough Court, because the speaking of the words, tho' alledged to have been *in the city,* is not alledged to have been *within the jurisdiction of the court.* That according to uniform precedents, those precise words ought to be used, in all declarations in courts of inferior jurisdiction.

As the judgment of the court is founded upon precedents alone, and I feel a full conviction, that *they* if taken in a collective

lective view, prove the direct contrary, I am compelled, painful as it is, to differ in opinion from my worthy brethren, and to give my reasons for it.

Domestic precedents appear to me to stand thus:

It is said, that no case has been determined upon this point in the former General Court, nor do I recollect one.

In that court, since the revolution, one is mentioned; that of Pride *vs.* Hill, which was an ejectment in the Borough Court of Petersburg; for a lot in that town. The demise was laid to be made *in the town*, of a lot of ground situated there.— The plaintiff had a verdict and judgment; but, upon an appeal to the General Court, it was reversed; because it was not alledged, to be *within the jurisdiction*. This was said to be a leading case, in consequence of which, other cases were uniformly decided the same way; but the names or number of them was not stated: and if there were error in that case, which was a *local* action for a house in town, perhaps within the view of the court or jury, when trying the cause, there could be little doubt in a transitory action, where those words were omitted.

In the District Courts, where the same judges act separately, we find they are not uniform in their decisions upon the point; The judgment in Medard *vs* Skipwith being different. But how comes this court to be bound by precedents of the General Court, (however respectable they may be) whose judgments this court are authorised to controul? If so, and they have erred but once, we may correct it; but if they have repeated it, shall it cease to be error?

In Picket *vs.* Claiborn, this opinion did not prevail. The General Court reversed the judgment in that case, because there was no declaration, although there was a confession of judgment. This court, tho' forty similar precedents were mentioned, reversed their judgment.

This question is placed upon the authority of English precedents. I shall presently consider those cases at large, but let us first enquire how far we are bound by their authority. The ordinance of the convention in 1776, declares all the statutes of England prior to the 4th of James 1st, which were of a general nature, applicable to Virginia, and not local to that country, to be in force here.

Applying the principle of that ordinance to the force of precedents from thence, if it shall appear, that the rule now contended for (admit its existence) grew out of the local situation of the inferior courts in that country, and was grounded upon considerations in which ours totally differ from theirs, then the precedents cannot bind us.

The courts of inferior jurisdiction in that country are various, and differ much in the nature of their constitutions.

1st, The Spiritual Courts, limited by the *subject* in dispute, to matters of a spiritual nature.

2d, The Admiralty Courts, confined to cases arising upon the high seas—mariners may sue for their wages in the common law courts, their contracts being made on land; but they may and generally do sue in this court, because here they may all join, and charge the ship.

3d, The County and Sheriff's Courts, limited to the county, and to suits of the value of 40*s.*

4th, The Marshalsea Court, limited to residence within twelve miles of the palace.

5th, Corporation Courts, Royal Franchises, and Courts of Manors, all confined to residence within the jurisdiction.

6th, The Pie Powder Courts, limited as to time; the persons and subject of dispute which must arise during the fair between parties attending there.

These courts and many others, which it would be too tedious to enumerate, derive their existence from different sources—Prescription, Charters, and acts of Parliament, &c. Again, they differ as to the manner in which their judgments are controled, either before or after they are rendered.

Before:—As 1st by plea to the jurisdiction; or 2d, by a prohibition from a Superior Court.

After: 1st by writ of error; in cases where such writs lie:

2d By prohibition: where error does not lie, as to the admiralty and Ecclesiastical Courts.

3d By writ of false judgment to the *Base* Courts: but to what Courts they apply that *base* term, I cannot say with accuracy.

In this complex view of the inferior jurisdictions, it would have been difficult in declarations, to describe the various circumstances on which the jurisdiction depended. It therefore became a practice, founded in convenience and propriety, to alledge in the declaration, that the cause of action arose at such a place, *within the jurisdiction of the court.*

In Virginia, we have no Courts, deriving their origin from Prescription, or Charter. They are all created by the legislative acts, defining their powers, and their jurisdictions. The

true

true criterion of diſtinction between our ſuperior and inferior courts, ſeems to be the appellate juriſdiction: placing the Diſtrict Courts and all above them, in the firſt claſs; and in the latter the County and Corporation Courts; coupled together in principal; and referred to, as in the ſame predicament, in the laws allowing appeals, which ſometimes uſe the expreſſions " from the County and Corporation Courts" at other times " the county and other inferior courts."

Their juriſdictions are deſcribed in the ſame words, as to limits, tho' not as to extent. Theſe words " within the juriſdiction" have never been uſed, or conſidered as neceſſary, in the *former*.—It is ſufficient to alledge the cauſe to have ariſen in the county.—I cannot therefore conceive, why thoſe words ſhould be neceſſary, to bring the cauſe within the preſcribed juriſdiction of the *Corporation Courts*.

But let us now ſuppoſe that theſe courts are like to inferior Courts in England:—it will be found (I conceive) that the precedents are miſunderſtood. I have ſaid, that the form of the declarations there, were founded in convenience and propriety. But that ever a judgment was there reverſed, becauſe thoſe preciſe words were omitted, if a place was alledged, remains I think not only to be proved, but the contrary is to my mind evinced by the caſes produced, if the *principle* of them, inſtead of the *ſound of the reporters words* be attended to.

I ſtate this as a fact—that in all the caſes relied upon, no place was laid at which the *gift* (as they call it) of the action aroſe. And from hence, I infer, that the deciſions in thoſe caſes turned upon the want of a venue, which was not to be preſumed in inferior courts, nor did the ſtatute of Joefails, which cures the want of it, extend to thoſe courts. But do not thoſe ſtatutes extend to Corporation Courts here?

1 *Sand*. 73 is referred to as a leading caſe. But the error in that was, that no place was laid for the delivery of the goods. In 2 *Lev*. 87. no place was alledged as to the ſale and delivery, and the deciſion clearly turned upon the want of Venue. 1 *Ventr*. 2, is liable to the ſame obſervation—no place was laid—for tho' the demiſe was laid at Middle-row, the declaration did not ſtate, where Middle-row was. *Ib*. 72. Bernard and Bernard—it did not appear where Hull Bridge was. 2 *Ld. Ray*, 1310, the declaration does not alledge where the pond was. *Dwn.* and *Eaſt*. 151. It is not ſtated that the money was had and received *there*. In 2 *Wils.* 16, if it had been ſtated that the goods had been delivered at Ayleſbury, the judgment I think would

would have been different. But as to these cases my position that they turned upon the want of venue, is deduced by inference only.

Other cases plainly prove to my mind the solidity of the distinction.

Bernard *vs.* Bernard 1 *Vent.* 72, is no authority either way, as the cause finally went off, the court being divided. Waldock *vs* Cooper, 2 *Wils*. 16 before mentioned, produces in my mind unresistible conviction, that if the declaration had alledged the goods to have been delivered at Aylesbury, it would have been good, without expresly laying it, to have been *within the jurisdiction of the court.*

Lancaster *vs* Lovelace 12 *Mod.* 536, is directly in point, the declaration alledged the cause of action to have arisen at Canterbury.—On a writ of error it was objected, that it did not appear, that the jurisdiction was co-extensive with the city: an objection which could not be made here. But it was said, the defendant by coming in, and answering, had waved the advantage. This proves the principle I am endeavouring to support; that if a place be laid, and there be no plea to the jurisdiction, it is too late after judgment, to question the jurisdiction. In Hardwicks cases 116 there is one, in which the question was, whether the residence of the party, on which depended the jurisdiction, was defectively alledged (which is the most that can be urged in this case) so as to have been good on a demurrer. Yet after verdict, it was presumed to have been proved. Mr. MARSHALL in this case distinguished between the original judgment of amercement, and the action of debt upon the judgment. At the time, I thought there might be some weight in this argument, but it does not now appear to me a sound one. The words, *good on demurrer* and the proof presumed, must respect the new action, and not the amercement; from the conclusion of the judges, that without such proof, the amercement would have been *coram non judice,* and void: therefore no debt.

It is laid down in 2 *Ventr.* 333, that a party shall never be allowed to assign for error, that which he might have taken advantage of by pleading.

The modern cases all run in a train of presuming every thing after a verdict, according to the spirit of the statute of jeofails. They farther prove to me, that all the cases cited, turn upon the want of a venue, which the statutes of jeofails do not cure in proceedings in those inferior courts, and by no means upon the want of those particular words.

Since

Since then the precedents are founded on reasons applicable only to the nature of inferior courts in England, (in every respect unlike to our Corporation Courts,) to which our act of Jeofails does certainly extend, as well as to the County Courts, the principle of presuming every thing after verdict, which might have been proved, remains in cases of this sort, as in others, uninfluenced by those precedents.

Would it not be strange, that after a fair trial, where the defendant waved all exceptions not connected with the merits, when if they had been well founded, he might have availed himself of them; and after a jury has assessed the damages sustained by the injured party, a superior court shall declare, that for the want of a few cabalistical words, which, if inserted, every man of common sense would pronounce to be *tautologous*, the plaintiff shall not have the effect of his judgment? I say *tautologous*, because if the cause of action arose in the city, the law declares it to be within the jurisdiction of the court.

However, the other judges are impressed with a different view of the subject, and are of opinion that the judgment of the District Court is right. After having discharged my conscience, I shall acquiesce in the opinion and not stir the question again, unless the other judges should, on any future occasion, wish to reconsider it.*

Judgment of the District Court affirmed.

DAVID ROSS
against
ERASMUS GILL & SARAH his WIFE.

THIS was an action of debt determined in the District Court of Petersburg in favor of the appellees, the plaintiffs in that court. The declaration demands £490, and contains two counts. The first states that Lucy Newsum, the guardian of the female plaintiff, then an infant, and unmarried, did demise the premises for which the rent is claimed,

---

* In the fall term of 1792, the case of Winder vs. Eddy, was decided upon the same principles. The suit in that case was brought in the corporation court of Fredericksburg: The declaration was headed, "corporation court of Fredericksburg, to wit:" and laid the cause of action and assumpsit "at the corporation aforesaid," but the words *within the jurisdiction of the court* were omitted.

claimed, whereof the said Sarah at that time was siezed in her *demesne* as of fee to the said Ross, to hold from the first day of January 1776, till the said Sarah should marry or attain the age of 21 years which ever should first happen; yielding to the said Sarah £70 a year.—It states the entry thereupon and enjoyment for eleven years:—" that afterwards, to wit on the first of June 1786 the said Sarah being still an infant, intermarried with the said Erasmus, and £490, for the rent for 7 years ended the 1st of January 1787, to the said Erasmus, and Sarah, after the demise of the said premises to the said David, and after the espousals between the said Erasmus and the said Sarah celebrated,—were in arrear and yet are &c. whereby action accrued to the said plaintiff, &c Nevertheless the defendant hath not paid &c."

The second count states a demise made by the plaintiff Sarah who was then a feme sole, of other lands to the defendant, to hold so long as both parties should please, yielding the yearly rent of £70.—also the enjoyment thereof for eleven years by the defendant—the marriage of the plaintiff, and the same sum of £490 in arrear and unpaid " whereby action accrued to the plaintiffs, &c. nevertheless &c." the damages are laid at £800. Plea, owe nothing.

At the trial, a motion was made by the defendant, for a nonsuit; which the court refusing to direct, a bill of exceptions was filed, stating, that the plaintiffs gave in evidence a memorandum in writing, signed by Joseph Jones, in behalf of one Lucy Newsum, bearing date the 27th of January 1776, in these words to wit: " That David Ross shall occupy and possess the
" houses and plantations belonging to the estate of Peter Jones,
" from 1st of January 1776, until the *heir* shall marry, or come
" to age; but be at liberty to give it up, at the expiration of any
" of the years, giving three months previous notice; to pay £70
" per annum; to leave the plantation in tenantable repair; to com-
" mit no abuses in cutting fire-wood, nor get more rails than ne-
" cessary to repair the fences from time to time. Should the *heir*
" when of age, or married, want the said houses and plantation,
" to give the like notice of three months, before the expiration of
" the year; otherwise the said David to remain in possession, till
" the ensuing year, on the aforesaid terms:" That the plaintiffs also proved by a witness, as well as by letters of the defendant, that a verbal contract was entered into between the mother of the plaintiff with the defendant, as stated in the declaration, of which the defendant took the above memorandum, written by

himself

himself, and signed by Joseph Jones: That in pursuance of the agreement aforesaid, the defendant entered into, and was possessed of the demised premises, but that they produced no proof of any contract between the plaintiffs and the defendant, other than as above, or that the memorandum aforesaid was ever assigned to the plaintiffs, otherwise than as stated in the declaration: and this being the only evidence in the cause, to prove the terms on which the defendant held the lands, or to support the claim for rent; the defendant moved for a nonsuit, &c.

The jury find that the defendant "doth owe the debt in the declaration mentioned," and assess the damages to £130 : 6 : 3.

The judgment is, that the plaintiff recover against the defendant £490, the debt in the declaration mentioned, and their costs, but to be discharged by the payment of £420, together with the damages aforesaid and the costs.

THE PRESIDENT.—A doubt was started at the bar whether two counts could properly be laid in debt for rent; at least without demanding the amount of the two rents claimed in both counts. But a precedent of a similar kind was produced, and as the record states that no evidence was given on the second count, the court are satisfied that that count may be thrown out of the case as mere surplusage.

An objection was made, that the verdict finds that the defendant owes the debt in the declaration mentioned; and there being two counts for the same sum, there is nothing to guide the court in referring the finding to the one or the other.

The bill of exceptions furnishes an easy answer to this objection, by stating that no evidence was given upon the second count, and that full evidence was given upon the first. Of course the verdict obviously refers to that, to which the testimony applied, and considering each count as a distinct declaration, the expression is by no means doubtful or improper, particularly as the second count appears to have been abandoned by the parties.

The court were certainly right in rejecting the motion which was made; as we are of opinion that they had no power to direct a nonsuit, however destitute the plaintiff might be of a right to recover. They may advise it, and may direct the plaintiff to be called; but if he refuse to suffer a nonsuit, the court can no otherwise protect and enforce their opinion, but by awarding a new trial, in case the jury have found against their direction. Consequently a refusal in the court to direct a nonsuit, cannot be a ground of exception.

If the court admit improper evidence, an exception may be taken to their opinion; but if the queſtion depend upon the weight of teſtimony, the jury, and not the court, are excluſively, and uncontroulably the judges.

This queſtion then muſt turn upon the whole evidence, as well the parol as the written. The plea is *nil debet*; and it was inſiſted at the bar, that *nil habuit in tenementis* could not be given in evidence—This is a point which need not be now decided, ſince the leſſee having uninterruptedly occupied and enjoyed the land; he cannot avail himſelf of a want of title in the plaintiff, if the fact were, that ſhe had none; it would have been otherwiſe if *eviction* had been proved.

But the bill of exceptions, tho' it does not ſet forth the parol evidence at large, ſtates generally the weight of it, and that it proved a parol demiſe *as laid in the declaration*. This aided by the verdict, ſufficiently eſtabliſhes the title of Sarah, to the premiſes, and the demiſe of them, by her guardian, to the defendant.

There is no doubt but that a guardian may leaſe the lands of the ward during infancy, if the guardianſhip ſo long continue: and in this caſe, the demiſe being from year to year, if another guardian had been appointed, the term would have ceaſed. The reſervation of the rent to the infant was proper, and cannot be likened to the caſe of a reſervation to a ſtranger: for the inheritance being in the ward, there is a privity between her and the leſſee, and therefore there is no doubt of her right to maintain an action of debt, to recover the arrears of rent. It is true that the guardian may, by a leaſe in writing, reſerve the rent to himſelf to cover advances which he may make for the uſe of the ward; and in that caſe the action muſt be brought in his own name, unleſs he aſſign the leaſe to the ward. The reaſon why the ward cannot in ſuch a caſe maintain the action is, that, as he muſt declare upon the written leaſe, there would be a variance between the allegation, and the proof. But in either caſe, there is no doubt but that a payment of the rent to the guardian, during the continuance of the wardſhip, would be a good diſcharge of the tenant for ſo much.

We find no error therefore until we come to the entering up of the judgment. The verdict is for £490 the debt in the declaration mentioned and £130 : 16 : 3, damages and coſts. The judgment is for the ſame, but *to be diſcharged by the payment of* £420.

This latter part we do not consider as being any part of the judgment, but merely surplusage. For as there is no penalty in the case, the law does not warrant such an entry.

As the plantiffs do not complain of this reduction, we consider it as a release of so much by them, and as it is for the benefit of the defendant, he cannot object.

Judgment affirmed.

BIBB *against* CAUTHORNE.

THIS was an action of debt brought in the name of the commonwealth for the benefit of Mrs. Cauthorne, against William Bibb, Richard Bibb and John Watson, upon a bond executed by them, the former as sheriff, the two latter as his securities. The breach laid in the declaration is, that the said William Bibb did execute two writs of *fieri facias* issued from the County Court of Essex, upon judgments obtained there by A. R. against the said Cauthorne, notwithstanding two writs of supersedeas to the said judgments, had been obtained by the said Cauthorne directed to the said William Bibb, and which were tendered to, and refused by him before the service of the said execution; and for selling the goods of the said Cauthorne upon the said executions, in contempt of the said two writs of supersedeas, although there was manifest error in the said judgments, which the same would have reversed; whereby action accrued to the commonwealth for the benefit of the said Cauthorne to demand the penalty of the said bond.

The writ against William Bibb being returned "no inhabitant" the suit abated as to him, the other defendants plead conditions performed. A verdict was found, that the defendants had not performed, but had broken the condition of their bond, and assessed the damages for levying the executions in the declaration mentioned, in contempt of the said two writs of supersedeas to £260.

The judgment of the court is, "that the commonwealth reco-
"ver against the defendants for the benefit of the said Cauthorne
"£1000 (the penalty of the bond) and the costs, but to be dis-
"charged by the payment of the damages aforesaid, and such o-
"ther damages, as may be hereafter assessed, upon suing out a
"*scire facias* and assigning new breaches."

From this judgment the defendants appealed.

The PRESIDENT. It was objected by the defendant's counsel, that this action ought not to have been sustained, the bond having been made payable to the commonwealth, instead of the justices, as required by the ordinance of convention passed in 1776, *Ch.* 5. *Sec.* 8, which gives the remedy to individuals injured by a breach of it.

If the counsel had been correct in his premises, his conclusion would have been right; but there was at the time of passing this ordinance, a prior subsisting law of 1748 amended by another in 1753, which directed the giving of bonds of this sort, payable to the king, and pointing out the same remedy to individuals, injured by a breach of them. This law amongst others, was by the same ordinance of convention declared to be in force, and the legislature in 1782 considered it as being in force, by referring to and repealing part of it.

The bond in question, pursues the form of those laws, substituting the *commonwealth* for the *king*.

Upon the merits the plaintiff is right; but the court is of opinion that there is error in the judgment, in attaching the recovery to *Catharine Cauthorne* as to future injuries, excluding *all others*.

The judgment therefore must be reversed for this error, and entered, " that the commonwealth recover against the defendants " the said sum of £ 1000 and the costs, but to be discharged by the " payment of the damages by the jury assessed for the benefit of " Catharine Cauthorne, and the costs, and such other damages as " may be hereafter assessed upon suing out a *scire facias* and assign " ing new breaches by the said Catharine, *or by any other person " or persons injured.*"

TAYLOR

against

DUNDASS.

THE case was this: Dundass having obtained a judgment against Hendricks and Taylor, an execution was taken out at the request of Taylor, who was only a security, in order

that

that it might be levied upon the effects of Hendricks, who was about removing with his property from this state. It was issued without the knowledge or permission of Dundas, but with the consent of a gentleman, who had been counsel for him in the High Court of Chancery, upon an injunction, obtained by Hendricks, to the judgment at law. The execution was served upon the property of Hendricks, and a replevy bond taken. The security being entirely insufficient, Dundas sued out another execution with a direction to levy it upon the property of Taylor only; and upon a motion made by Taylor in the County Court, where the judgment was rendered, to quash the last execution, this question came on. The judgment of the County Court is, " that the execution be quashed, it appearing to have issued illegally."—Sundry exceptions being taken, the cause was carried by supersedeas before the District Court, where the judgment of the County Court, was reversed, from which an appeal was granted to this.

The PRESIDENT. The motion made in the County Court, as well as the grounds of the courts opinion, are imperfectly stated in the record; and had nothing else appeared, perhaps it might not have been sustainable. But, as the short entry of the motion and judgment was probably occasioned by the bill of exceptions stating the whole evidence, if from thence it appears, that a second execution issued, and was levied, after a former one had been issued on the same judgment against the same party, returned, " levied on slaves and a replevin bond taken"—the ground of the courts opinion will sufficiently appear, to enable a superior court to judge of its propriety.

The first execution is set forth, dated November 18th 1789, returnable to January court, and directed to the sheriff of Cumberland County. The return dated the 23d November 1789, is " levied on Peter, &c. and replevied for twelve months, J. " Hendricks security."

The second execution does not appear in the record, nor the date of it; except, that it is stated in the petition for the supersedeas, to have been issued April 29th 1790, against Hendricks and Taylor, and to have been served on Taylor's property only—and that this was the execution, which Taylor moved to quash, and which was quashed in June 1790.

The time of the first execution being returned (on which the question as to the propriety of issuing the second will turn) is no otherwise ascertained, than by the date of the return; which I suppose (as expressed) is the day on which it was levied.

It was for this purpose, I presume, that the execution book was referred to, where, I suppose, the clerk enters the time of the return; otherwise, I can see no reason for referring to it at all, as the first execution with the return on it, was before the court.

The bill of exceptions presents four questions, propounded to, and decided by the court. The first is a general one: Is the execution book a record, not to be contradicted by parol proof? The court decided in the affirmative. The nature, and tendency of the parol proof, not being stated, it is difficult to decide the question, as a general one either way. That the execution book, directed by law to be kept by the clerk, becomes part of the records, seems generally true. But, as in this instance, the time of returning an execution, is entered by the clerk in his office, without any writing to direct him, and as he might make a mistake in his entry, although *prima facie* it will be presumed right, it would seem too rigorous to preclude a party from denying the *truth* of the entry, if made out by clear proof.

Suppose a case of a motion to fine a sheriff for not returning an execution in time: the execution book might be received, as *prima facie* evidence, to prove the time of the return, liable to be contradicted by other proof. However, as no evidence is stated in this case to have been offered, to prove a mistake in the entry, I conclude that the question is stated as a general one, relative to the particular evidence spread upon the record.

The second question is: whether the defendant might be admitted to prove, by any evidence less than record, that the first execution was not issued by the order of Dundals, or his attorney? This is decided by the court in the negative.

The third point made, was: whether the defendant might be at liberty to prove, that Taylor undertook the management of the first execution, which was, by his agent, unduly served, and unfairly executed; so as to deprive the defendant of the benefit thereof? the court thought such evidence inadmissible, and not to be heard.

The fourth question was: whether the second execution ought to be quashed, being levied only on Taylor's estate, and it not appearing that Dundals had received any part of his judgment, or any satisfaction therefore, from the said Hendricks and Taylor, or from any other person? This was decided in the affirmative. Whether the evidence, offered to be given, was admissible or not, as contradicting a record, was

entirely

entirely immaterial, and did not tend to oppofe the motion for quafhing the fecond execution. It might have afforded good ground for quafhing the firft execution, or might have entitled Dundafs to a fuit againft Taylor for his conduct, but it could not warrant the iffuing of the fecond execution, where a former one had been returned *levied*, and continued at that time in force, unquafhed.

As to the fourth queftion, it is made a point: Whether the firft execution being returned levied, was a bar to the fecond, if no *actual fatisfaction* was made on the firft. The replevy bond is the fame as if the eftate had been fold to the amount of the debt; and though it is an indulgence given to the defendant, ftill the execution is confidered as levied, and the judgment difcharged.

According to the Englifh authorities, if a motion be made to quafh a fecond execution, or a writ of *fcire facias* iffue, to have execution, after fervice on one defendant; if the firft execution be *valuable*, as an *elegit*, *levari facias* or *fi. fa.* executed on the eftate of *one*, a new execution can never iffue on that judgment, whatever becomes of the eftate, unlefs the firft execution be quafhed; but it is otherwife in cafe of an execution againft the body; for that is not a fatisfaction, but only *tends to fatisfy*. But in that cafe, whilft the body is in cuftody, a new execution cannot iffue, and the queftion can only come on, when an efcape or death happens, or when the party is difcharged by taking the oath of an infolvent debtor. The diftinction is taken in Blumfield's cafe, 5 *Co. Rep.* and many others, and I believe no cafe lays it down, that a fecond *fi. fa.* can iffue on the fame judgment againft feveral defendants, if upon the firft, a fufficiency of goods had been taken, no matter to which of them they belonged.

In the cafe of Dykes againft Mercer, cited in 2 *Ld. Ray.* 1072. two were bound in a bond jointly and feverally, and judgment obtained in a feparate fuit againft *one*. A *fi. fa.* iffued, and a feifure to the value returned; but the property was not fold, nor the money paid. To a fecond action brought againft the other obligor, this matter was pleaded in bar; but determined againft him, nothing but actual fatisfaction by the other obligor being fufficient to difcharge him. In this cafe, both the obligors might have been fued feparately at the fame time, and judgments obtained againft each for the whole, but the plaintiff could receive but one actual fatisfaction.

The case of Hayling against Mullhall, 2 *Blac. Rep.* 1235, is decided upon the same principle: to wit, that the holder of a bill of exchange may sue a subsequent endorser, notwithstanding an ineffectual execution against a prior endorser. In that case, there was no doubt, as the execution was against the body, which was rendered ineffectual by being discharged by the plaintiff.

The court say in that case, that the remedy still remains in force (after the death or discharge of the defendant) against every other endorser, notwithstanding the ineffective *ca. sa.* in like manner, as if the plaintiff had sued out an *unproductive fi. fa.* I understand the court to mean by this expression, an execution on which no goods are taken.

Upon the whole, we are of opinion that the judgment of the District Court is erroneous; the evidence offered by the appellee, tending to prove that the first execution was issued and executed improperly, though if true, it would have been a good ground for quashing the first execution, if the appellee had made a motion for that purpose, yet it did not apply in opposition to the quashing of the second execution, which issued after the first was returned *executed*, and remained in that state: for we think, that under the act of Assembly, a bond to replevy, whilst the execution remains unquashed, is as complete an execution of the judgment, as if the estate had been sold to the full amount of the debt, and the party is left to pursue his new remedy upon the bond.

Judgment of the District Court reversed and that of the County Court affirmed.

KENNON

against

M'ROBERTS & WIFE.

THIS was an ejectment brought by the appellees to recover a tract of land called Ochaneachy island in which the following case was agreed.

That Robert Mumford was in his life-time seized in fee of the lands in dispute, called Ochaneachy island, of another tract called Finney wood, and of another called Cargills. That he was

was also seized and possessed of, and entitled to, the equity of redemption in a tract of land called Whitehall on Appamatox, containing 711 acres, which it is agreed was at his death of greater value than the Ochaneachy and Finney wood lands,—what other estate he possessed, or what debts he owed is not stated, except what was due on the mortgage of the Whitehall estate to Theophilus Field.

That being so seized and possessed, the said Robert Mumford made his last will bearing date the 8th of September 1743, and after the usual clauses respecting his soul and body, he adds "as touching my *temporal estate*, my will and desire is that it shall be employed and bestowed as hereafter, in this my will, is expressed."

"Item: I will that all my debts I owe in right or conscience, shall be paid by my executors, within convenient time after my death."

"Item: I will and bequeath to my son Robert Mumford (his heir at law) *all* my lands at the Ochaneachy island, also all my lands of Finny wood, with six negroes (by name) and ten horses and mares."

"Item: I will and bequeath to my son Theoderick *all* my lands at Cargills on Roanoke River, containing 690 acres, with two negroes; Sam at Roanoke, and Jack at Rowanty, also ten horses and mares."

"Item: to my well beloved wife, and only daughter Elizabeth, I will and bequeath *all the rest of my estate real and personal* saving one negro girl to my son Theoderick."

And appointed his wife, Theophilus Field, and Theoderick Bland his executors.

That he died in the year 1745 leaving his said widow and children beforementioned, and that the will was proved and admitted to record.

That Robert and Theoderick entered into the lands to them respectively devised, and they, and those claiming under them, continued in possession, till their several deaths.

That Theoderick died in 1772 and Robert in 1783, that the latter was aged about eight years at the time of his father's death.

That Ann the widow died in 1770; the daughter Elizabeth (now wife of the lessor of the plaintiff) surviving, and that no partition or severance was made between them.

The proceedings in a suit in chancery brought by the widow and daughter, to redeem the Whitehall estate is agreed, as also the payment of £830 : 16 : 4 on that account.

That the widow (who after her husbands death intermarried with ———— Currie) and daughter with their husbands, in 1770 conveyed the Whitehall estate to Theoderick Mumford in fee, for the consideration of £1000, reserving the use of a moiety of the land, with the houses thereon to Mr. Currie and his wife, and to the survivor for life, and afterwards half that moiety to Mrs. M'Roberts, during widowhood, upon the contingency of her becoming a widow.

The District Court of Brunswick gave judgment for the plaintiffs from which the defendant appealed.

THE PRESIDENT delivered the opinion of the Court.

The principal questions made in this cause were: 1st, what estate the sons Robert and Theoderick took in the lands devised to them; whether in fee simple or for life only? If the former, then the appellees have no title; if the latter, then

2d Whether the reversion in those lands passed under the residuary clause to the wife and daughter, or was undisposed of, and descended to the heir; and this latter supposition if true will be equally fatal to the title of the appellees.

For the appellant it is insisted that the fee passed to the sons.

1st Because the testator's debts are by the first clause in the will, charged upon the lands, and that this is sufficient to enlarge an estate, not given *expressly for life*, into a fee. That justice requiring, that all a man's property should be subject to the payment of his debts, slight words in a will, are sufficient to create a charge upon lands for this purpose, where the debts cannot otherwise be paid: cases cited *Cas. Temp. Talb.* 1 and *Prec. Ch.* 430.

If this were a case between creditors, and the devisees of the lands, I think that such a construction would be made.

But a charge which is by construction to give a fee in lands devised, seems to stand upon other ground. It must be a direct charge of a sum in gross, either upon the lands devised, or upon the person of the devisee, however small the sum may be; for life being precarious, it might end before any part of the money were raised, so as to render that onerous, which was intended to be beneficial to the devisee, 3 *Burr.* 1533—1618 *Cowp. Rep.* 352.

If the money charged be to be raised by rents and profits, or if the land be made liable only upon the event of the personal estate becoming deficient, a fee will not be created; because in neither case can the devisee be a loser by taking an estate for life. *Cowp. Rep.* 236.

The will now under confideration directs the teftator's debts to be paid by his executors, without prefcribing the mode, and contains no words exempting the legal fund, and charging them upon the lands or upon the perfons of the devifees—fo that the refiduary eftate is alone burthened with them, and the lands in queftion can only be reforted to, as an auxiliary fund, tomake up the deficiency—and as an application for that purpofe could only be made by the creditors, there feems to refult from confiderations of this fort no neceffity to create a fee in the devifees.

2d, It is infifted that a fee was intended to pafs, becaufe in the preamble of the will, the teftator declares an intention to difpofe of his whole eftate; and when he devifed lands to his fons generally, without limiting the duration of their tenure, he meant to give it abfolutely. That if fo, the court, rather than difappoint that intention, will carry the word *eftate*, from the preamble, to each devife, fo as to make the claufe in queftion read thus: " as to my *eftate* in the land at Ochaneachy, I give " it to my fon Robert," &c.

The counfel on the other fide admit, that the teftator's intention is to be the rule of decifion; but with this reftriction, that it is to be collected from the words of the will itfelf—and that it muft confift with the law and fettled rules of conftruction: that the rule, in common law conveyances " that where lands are conveyed without limiting any eftate, they only pafs for the life of the grantee," extends equally to wills, unlefs the teftator ufes fome words expreffing his intention to pafs a larger eftate: that none fuch are to be found in this will, unlefs it be the word *eftate*, in the preamble; which cannot have that effect, according to a late determination in the cafe of Wright and Wright &c. 3 *Wils.* 414.

To difcover what is comprehended in the refidue, we muft view and difcufs the preceding bequefts, to afcertain what he has difpofed of, and what remains undifpofed of, for the word *reft* to act upon. But I would firft premife, that we difclaim all legiflative power to change the law, and only affume our proper province of declaring what the law is: we difclaim all authority to mould teftator's wills into any form which fancy, whim, or worfe paffions might fuggeft; we regard his own words, and compare them with his circumftances, and the relative fituation of the devifees. So far we approve of Mr. Fearne's general reafoning, tho' we may not accord with him in another affertion: namely, " that legal rules of conftruction ought not to yield to the intention of *ignorant* teftators:" fince it is on account of that ignorance

norance, that their words are to be taken in the sense in which such men commonly use them, and not in that technical sense affixed to them by professional men. In Hodgson *vs.* Ambrose, *Dougl.* 323—a distinction is made which seems to be a sensible one, to wit: if the testator use legal phrazes, his intention should be construed by legal rules. If he use those that are common, his intention, according to the common understanding of the words he uses, shall be the rule.

The apparent clashing of the cases relied upon in this discussion, induced the court to trace the subject to its foundation, to see if they could discover a principle so certain, and uniform, as to direct a satisfactory decision either way.

When upon the adoption of the feudal system in England, an arrangement was made of the various tenures by which lands were to be holden, the mode and form of creating each of them was pointed out, and the power of each particular tenant over his estate settled: it was natural to suppose that their technical forms would not always be attended to, and therefore it became necessary to provide a rule for cases, where the duration of the estate was not described.

Common sense would have dictated, that an absolute estate should pass by a conveyance unlimited as to duration, and containing no provision for its return to the grantor, at a future period, or on a contingency. But reason was made to yield to the spirit of a system, unfriendly to alienations, or divisions of lands: and therefore, the rule that such conveyances passed only an estate for life, was established. The same spirit established the rights of primogeniture, and, (aided by the statute *de donis*,) permitted estates tail, and all lesser estates to be carved out of the fee simple; the residue ultimately continuing in the grantor, capable of being disposed of when the paticular estates should be ended. This disposition gave what was called a remainder in fee—but it often happened, that the fee was not disposed of; and generally in such cases, as this now before the court, when that fee rested in the donor as part of the old estate, it acquired the character of a reversion, and descended to the heir at law.

This spirit of the feud, is mentioned, as explanatory of those rules of construction, which, in favour to the heir at law, narrow as much as possible the operation of all conveyances, calculated to disinherit him.

By the American revolution, and some of our laws, we have happily got rid of the feudal system, and the rights

rights of primogeniture; so that the favour hitherto claimed by heirs at law in the construction of conveyances affecting their rights, will no longer be heard of, in cases happening after January 1787, when those laws took effect: but the intention of testators will become in *reality* the rule, which, though hitherto avowed to be such, hath been so refined away as in many instances to have been sacrificed to rigid technical terms.

However it may be as to such new cases, the present, as well as all others which may come before us, arising at a prior period, must be decided according to the law of that time, as far as we are enabled to discover it.

A general observation may here be made: that all the legal artillery now played off *against* the heir, was furnished by the above mentioned bias, to fortify his title; but if it may be thus turned against him by the rules of legal warfare, we cannot help it: we have only to enquire, if it do defeat him or not.

The feudal Rule " that where an estate was conveyed without limitation, no more than an estate for life passed, and the reversion descended to the heir," acted for a long time merely on feoffments and grants, the only conveyances then in use; and in such, the rule has constantly prevailed.

But it may be remarked, that as the personal wealth of the nation increased, a desire in the rich commoners, to realize their money, produced a new contending spirit, averse from perpetuities of land in the same families, and favorable to alienations.

It was this spirit which enabled Henry the 7th to gratify his wish of lessening the power of the Barons, by introducing the fictitious fine and recovery, as an effectual bar of estates tail, and all remainders and reversions depending upon them, and this became a new and common mode of conveyance.

The same spirit operated more powerfully in the next reign, producing the statute of uses, the parent of conveyances by lease and release and giving new vigor to covenants to stand seized to uses. This, and the statute of inrolments, gave rise to bargains and sales for money; and finally the statute of wills, enabled proprietors of lands to dispose of them, by their last wills at pleasure.

These new statutary conveyances received a much more liberal interpretation, to favor the intention of the parties, than were indulged to those at common law, but which need not now be mentioned.

In the construction of wills (more particularly,) an extensive latitude has been allowed, on account of the extremity, in which they are often made, not admitting of counsel being called in, but inducing the necessity of resorting to any person, however unskilful, who may be at hand. and it is not improbable, that the respect which all men have agreed to pay to the will of the dead, might have had considerable in fluence.

That the intention of the testator is to give the rule of construction, is declared by all the judges both ancient and modern. *Ld. Holt* and some others more modern, emphatically call that intention, the *Polar Star*, which is to guide our decision—and in a late case of Hodgson *vs*. Ambrose, *Dougl.* 323, the court say, that this is the governing rule, to which all other rules of construction must yield.

If this were a new question, I believe there would be no great difficulty in deciding, that the rule, which prescribes technical terms for the passing of different estates in common law conveyances, did not extend to wills at all; since no such terms were prescribed to testators, by the statute of wills, which enabled them to dispose of their lands at pleasure. But the judges, after laying down the true rule built upon intention, unfortunately admitted, that if there were no words of limitation, the common law rule must prevail; by which they tied a gordian knot, which they have since struggled to untie. It would have been better if they had cut it at once.

This rule however of construing wills according to intention, is laid down with some limitation, as 1st, The disposition, *intended* to be made, must not conflict with the rules of law: which I understand as applying to restraints upon the creation of perpetuities, devises in Mortman, and the like; and of course, it has no influence upon this question.

2d, The intention must be collected from the will itself.

This is true, if we admit those words to be explained by the relative situation of the parties, and the circumstances of the testator; which, a multiplicity of cases prove, ought to be considered. Thus explained, this limitation will be regarded.

3d, The intention is not to prevail against settled and fixed rules of construction.

If we could discover those *settled* rules of construction, we would pursue them. But, after all our researches, we are much inclined to affirm what is said by judge Wilmot in Baddeley *vs*. Leppingwell, 3 *Burn.* 1533. " that cases on wills serve rather

" to

"to obscure, than illuminate questions of this sort;" in which the present may be classed. So it is said by the court, in Jeffereys *vs.* Poyntz. 3 *W. ils.* 141. "That cases on wills may "guide as to general rules of construction, but, unless a case "cited be in every respect directly in point, and agree in "every circumstance, it will have little, or no weight with the "court, who always look upon the intention of the testator as "the polar star to direct them in the construction of wills."

The appellees, in applying this objection to the present case, insist upon it as a *settled* rule of construction, that where lands are devised without limitation, and no words are used to shew an intention to give a fee, the rule of law that only an estate for life passes, prevails. And this is laid down as a general position by most of the judges, who speak upon the subject: but from their manner of expression, and from their application of it to particular wills, it will appear to have but little influence upon their decisions.

In Bows *vs.* Blacket, *Cowp. Rep.* 236, a singular decision is made. It was a devise, "of all his freehold and leasehold lands, and *all his estate and interest therein* to his wife for life," remainder to two sisters as tenants in common, chargeable with the payment of debts and legacies; and it was determined that only an estate for life passed to the sisters.

In the case of Mudge *vs.* Blight, *Cowp. Rep.* 352. lord Mansfield says, "I really believe that every case determined upon the rule of law, directing an estate for life, if there be no limitation, defeats the intention of the testator."

To the same purpose is judge Buller, in Palmer *vs.* Richards, 3 *Durnf & East* 356. "There is hardly a case of this sort, "where only an estate for life is held to pass, but that it coun- "teracts the testator's intention: for where a testator uses gene- "ral words he means to dispose of every thing he has."

When therefore we find judges declaring that the intention of the testator is to be their guide, and that the rule of law now insisted on violates that intention, (as I believe all mankind will agree it does, for the reason given by judge Buller,) *it is no* wonder, that we find them constantly declaring, that tho' the rule must prevail if there be no words to controul it, yet no technical terms are necessary, but that they will lay hold of or (as some express themselves) will *catch* at any slight expressions, and make them answer the purpose.

At first indeed, they went no farther, than to supply the omission of the word *heirs*, necessary to give an inheritance in common-law conveyances, by other words tantamount to it. Such as to him and *his assigns*, to him and *his seed*, to him *for ever*, to him and his——and such like.

But in the progress of their struggle for the intention, against this rigid, unjust rule of law, they went further, and made various other words answer their purpose.

It was in this manner that the word *estate* was taken into the service, which in its vulgar and common meaning, is descriptive only, of the *quality* of things: as land &c. and not of the *interest* in them. Yet to serve this beneficial purpose, they have given it a more extensive signification, so as to make it comprehend as well the *thing* as the testator's *interest* in it; and so to pass a fee, which it would no more do in a common-law conveyance; than if there were no limitation whatever. For tho' lord Holt in the case of the countess of Bridgewater *vs.* the Duke of Bolton, 1 *Salk* 236, says " the word estate is *genus generalissimum*, and comprehends both the thing and the interest," yet that was in a case of a will; and lord Mansfield in Mudge and Blight before mentioned, expressly says, " It was on the ground of the judges laying hold of any expression to favor the intention, that a devise of *all one's estate*, or of *all his estate at* A, passed a fee." See also 2 *Ld. Ray.* 31—1 *Salk.* 234.

In the case before us, in the devises to his two sons, he gives to Robert all his lands at Ochaneachy island and Finneywood; and to Theoderick all his lands at Cargills, without any words of limitation whatever. The word *estate* is not used in the devise, nor are there any other expressions, indicating an intention to give a fee.

But it is insisted upon at the bar, 1st, That his intention is apparent from the relative situation of the testator, with the several devisees; since he could not intend to disinherit the grandsons who were to bear his name in favor of the issue of a wife and daughter.

It must be confessed, that such an intention would make the testator invert the order of every family provision; giving sons only an estate for life in lands, for whom perpetuities would generally be created, if not restrained by law, and instead of a *present provision* for a wife, give her a reversion after estates for life to her infant children; from which she could expect no benefit, tho' her issue by a second husband, might take the estate from the testator's grand-children.

To

To suppose such an intention in the testator is absurd in the extreme, and I am persuaded, that there is no person who believes he so intended it.

2d, The counsel then insisted that rather than disappoint this apparent intention, the court will carry the word *estate* from the preamble, to each clause in the will, so as to bring the case within the rule, that a devise of the *estate* passes a fee.

In opposition to this, Wright & Wright, 3 *Wils.* 414 is cited, and relied upon, as being not much unlike the present case.

In this case, the testator sets out thus, " As touching my tem-
" poral estate, I give and dispose thereof as followeth: my debts
" to be paid.—Item: I give to my nephews Henry and Nathan
" a house at Leeds, &c. Item: I give to my nephew William
" two houses at Seacroft," &c. After giving a number of
" small pecuniary legacies, he adds. " It is my will that none
" of the houses, &c. be entered into, 'till after the death of my
" executors,"—and makes his brother executor. It was determined, that only estates for life passed to the nephews in the houses; and chief judge De Grey declared, that there was no case where the testator makes use of these or the like words, " as
" touching the disposition of all my temporal estate, I give and
" dispose thereof as followeth," and immediately afterwards devises his several estates or his several lands to divers persons, that ever a fee was determined to pass. That by the words, *all my estate*, he must be understood to mean the *thing* (his lands) and not the *quantity* of estate, (the fee.)

This is a case in point, and rather stronger, since an argument in favor of a fee might there have been drawn from the reservation to the brother for life, and if this case is of conclusive authority, it will put an end to this part of the dispute.

But 1st, Does not this case lose its weight by proving too much? For it lays down the principle, that a devise of all the testator's estate, means the *thing* only, and not his *interest*; from which it would follow that by such a devise, a fee would not pass, contrary to the whole string of adjudications, from Lord Holt down to the present day.

2d, If the assertion of the chief justice " that there is no case where the word *estate*, in the preamble, had been adjudged to give a fee in lands afterwards devised without limitation," be true, then this single case might decide the present; but if it shall appear to be unfounded, it will evince the decision to have been made without due confideration, and the authority of the cafe muft be given up.

The cafes cited upon that occafion were *Hob.* 65, —1 *Salk.* 234, —1 *Vern.* 85, —*Prec. Chan.* 264, —2 *Vern.* 690, —3 *P. Wms.* 295,—Cole *vs.* Rowlinfon, 1 *Salk.* 234, was alfo cited—. In this cafe nothing is faid about the preamble, but the devife being of all the teftatrix's *eftate*, right, title and intereft, in whatever he held by leafe from fir John Freeman, and *alfo* the houfe called the Bell tavern, of which fhe had only the reverfion in fee after an eftate tail in the fon, to whom fhe devifed it; the whole was confidered as one fentence, tied together by the word *alfo*, and therefore the word *eftate* was carried to the devife of the Bell tavern fo as to pafs a fee.

1 *Salk.* 236 does not apply, for there the word *eftate* was in the devife and not in the preamble.

The cafe of Murray *vs.* Wife *Prec. in Chan.* 264, is fufceptible of the fame anfwer.

In Beachcroft *vs.* Beachcroft. 2 *Vern.* 690, the preamble is ftated and referred to by the lord Chancellor, when he fays, " *my worldly eftate* comprifes all he had in the world real and " perfonal." This however is not material, fince the word *eftate* is ufed in the devife itfelf. But this hint, probably gave rife to the idea of looking to the preamble for aid, in this pious work of fulfilling the will of the dead.

3d *P. Wms.* 294, Tanner *vs.* Wife, turned upon the queftion whether the real eftate was comprehended in a devife after perfonal bequefts, of " all the reft of his eftate, goods and chattels whatfoever, real and perfonal, to his wife."

Here the word eftate in the devife being explained by *goods* and *chattels* would naturally mean perfonal eftate; nor would the words *real* and *perfonal* help it, as there might be chattels real. Recourfe was therefore had to the preamble, in which he declared his intention to difpofe of all his *temporal eftate*, which the counfel for the heir infifted more properly applied to perfonal eftate, and leafes for years, which were in their nature temporary, and would wear out in time, than to permanent real eftate. Lord Chancellor referring to the preamble alfo, fays " *temporal eftate* means the fame as *worldly* eftate, or all a man has in the world real or perfonal, and adjudged that the real eftate pafled to the wife, and in fee.

In this cafe alfo, the Chancellor furnifhed an inftance of incorporating the words of the preamble with the devife. He fays, " reft and refidue are words of relation, and muft refer to fome eftate mentioned before." Now here was an eftate mentioned

tioned before his temporal eſtate, which brought it to ſignify the ſame as if he had ſaid " I deviſe the reſt and reſidue of all my temporal eſtate."

This caſe alone might have made the chief juſtice pauſe at leaſt, before he made the bold aſſertion now under conſideration. But there are others much ſtronger.—Ibbetſon *vs.* Beckwith *Cas. Temp. Talb.* 157, was this: the teſtator in the preamble declares " as touching my wordly eſtate, I diſpoſe of the ſame in " manner following: to my ſiſter Mary Beckwith, all my eſ- " tate *at* H. in hither dale, leaſing at Crew, and all my eſtate at " Cubeck, paying and diſcharging all legacies *before* charged " by my father's will. To my loving mother all my eſtate at " Northwith-cloſe, North-cloſes, and my farm at Roomer with " all my goods and chattles for her life; and to my nephew " Thomas Dodſon after her death, if he will change his name " to Beckwith; if not, I give him £20 to be paid him for life, " out of the cloſes, and farm, which I give her, upon that re- " fuſal, to her and *her heirs forever*."

The queſtion was, if Thomas took a fee in that which was deviſed to him, after the death of the mother, or only an eſtate for life?

The word *eſtate* is in the deviſe to the mother, but muſt be deſcriptive of the *thing*, and not of the *intereſt*, becauſe it is his eſtate *at* Northwith-cloſe, which means the ſame as my houſes or lands at thoſe places: and though the Chancellor cites ſome caſes, to prove that a fee will paſs by a deviſe of all his eſtates *at*, or *in* ſuch a place, the point is certainly very diſputable, and there are many expreſs caſes to the contrary. However, thoſe he mentions may ſerve to ſhew the growing influence of the teſ- tator's intention over rigid rules of conſtruction: another reaſon why it muſt be deſcriptive of the thing, and not of the intereſt, is, that it is given to the mother for life.

However, the caſe is mentioned for the ſake of Lord Talbot's reaſoning on the preamble, enforced in his uſually clear and perſpicuous manner. He ſays, " in order to come at the teſta- " tor's intent, the whole complexion of the will has been pro- " perly taken into conſideration on both ſides. The words, " *wordly eſtate,* in the preamble, prove him to have had his " whole eſtate in view. Indeed he might have made but a par- " tial diſpoſition afterwards; but if the will be general and tak- " en in one ſenſe, it will make a compleat diſpoſition of the " whole, and in another will create a chaſm, and leave a part " undiſpoſed of; that ſenſe ſhall prevail which is agreeable to " his intention to diſpoſe of the whole." To

To apply this to the present will, which has the same declaration in the preamble.—Has the testator made but a partial disposition of the lands to his sons? The feudal law says so, but *he* does not, since he gives it to them without restraint, or direction that their estate shall cease at any fixed period, or on any event. Is not this the very case *Ld.* Talbot puts, of a testator using general words, which he says shall be so construed, as to pass a fee; because that will best agree with his intention declared in the preamble, to dispose of the whole? So far the case may not apply strongly, as there is no residuary clause, and the word *estate* is in the devise.

In Grayson *vs.* Atkinson, 1 *Wils.* 333, the testator, after declaring in the preamble his intention to dispose of all his temporal estates, devises several legacies, amongst others to A. and having empowered him to sell all, or any part of his real or personal estate, for payment of his debts and legacies, adds, " as " to all the rest of my goods and chattles, real and personal, " moveable and immoveable, as houses, gardens, tenements, " my share in the copper works, &c. I give to the said A."

The question was, if A. took a fee, or a life estate only in the real estate? Here were no words of limitation, nor was the word, *estate*, used in the devise, which was of houses, gardens, and tenements, and the preamble must be referred to, for that important word. Lord Hardwicke doubted at first, and had he as hastily decided as chief justice De Grey did, he might also have pronounced that the word estate had never been so used or applied, and adjudged it only an estate for life. But he searched for, and examined the principles of the cases; and then said, he was clear in his opinion that a fee passed; and his first and third reasons inform us of the ground of his conviction, which was the cases of Beachcroft & Beachcroft, Tanner and Wife, and Ibbetson and Beckwith; particularly the last, for he repeats *Ld.* Talbot's reasoning, drawn from the word *estate* in the preamble. He mentions another reason which no doubt had some influence, namely, that the estate was charged with, and might be sold for the payment of debts and legacies. But this I consider as the weakest argument, and placed by him, (as such generally are) in the middle, between the two stronger ones. For his power to sell was in a distinct devise, which he might exercise at all events, so as to be no looser, whether he took an estate in fee, or for life only, in the residue.

The cases of Coghill and Noel in the old General Court, and Halstead *vs.* Halstead, may also be here mentioned.

If

If this were a new cafe, I fhould feel no hefitation in declaring it as my opinion, that the rule as applied to common law conveyances, did not extend to wills; fince the ftatute refpecting them, allows men to difpofe of their lands, not by any technical terms but at their will and pleafure. But fince we have precedents to follow, I have no difficulty in thinking myfelf warranted by the opinions of thofe great men *Ld. Cowper, Ld. Talbot, & Ld. Hardwicke*, to fay, that by connecting the word *eftate* in the preamble, with the devifes to the two fons, a fee fimple eftate paffed to them in the lands; which will fulfil the will of the dead, and fettle the peace of the family; and it is for this purpofe, that the point has been fo thoroughly inveftigated and difcuffed—yet as the cafes of Dean *vs.* Gafkins, refered to in Mitchel *vs.* Sidebottom *Dougl.* 759 as well as the principal cafe, and that of Wright *vs.* Wright are in oppofition, the point is left undetermined.—For as to the prefent queftion, let this point be determined the other way, it will not warrant a recovery againft the heir.

1ft, Becaufe he will take by defcent, and not under the will: and 2d, becaufe the reverfion in neither of the fons lands will pafs by the refiduary claufe.

1. The rule is, that where the teftator makes the fame difpofition to the heir which the law would have made, or where it is made in fuch general terms, that the intention is left doubtful, the heir fhall take by defcent, as his better title, and not under the will. 2 *Bac.* 79—*Mod. Ca. Law. & Eq.* 23. 1 *Ld. Ray.* 728.

Here is a devife of lands to the heir, unlimited as to eftate; unincumbered with any charge, and therefore it amounts to no more than pointing out the lands which his heir fhould take by defcent.

In Smith *vs* Triggs 1 *Str.* 487, it was determined, that a devife in fee, by a mother to her daughter, who was her heir, would not make the daughter a purchafer fo as to caft the defcent from her upon the heir on the part of the father. In Beachcroft *vs.* Beachcroft, a clofe in St. Peter's, Derby, is devifed to fir Robert (who was probably heir) without limitation; the reverfion is never mentioned as having paffed either to the wife, or to the brother Jofeph, under the refiduary devife.

I was very attentive during the argument, to difcover, if any cafes were cited of a devife of lands to an heir without limitation, where the reverfion was adjudged to pafs to another under a refiduary claufe in the fame will, however large and comprehen-

five

five the words might be; not recollecting any fuch, and inclining to believe from the feudal reafoning and principles, favoring the heir, that none fuch were to be found.

The gentleman of counfel for the appellee, (whofe laborious refearches on fuch occafions are pleafing to the court, as they generally imprefs an opinion, that what is not produced by him in favor of the fide he advocates, does not exift,) very candidly acknowledged he could find no fuch cafe, except one in Fearne's eflay on contingent remainders page 170; and I believe that gentleman on reviewing this cafe, will think it not a fufficient foundation for an exception to his admiffion. In a fubfequent page the author fays " it fometimes happens, that a remainder is " limited in words which feem to import a contingency; tho' " in fact they mean no more than would have been implied " without them, or do not amount to a condition precedent, but " denote the time when the remainder is to veft in poffeffion." This he illuftrates by feveral cafes to the page which was read by the counfel, and then, for the fame purpofe, he quotes the cafe of Fortefcue vs. Abbot from Pollexfen & fir Thomas Jones. A teftator devifes a houfe to each of his eldeft fons, and three other children, without words of limitation, but willed, that if either of his faid children fhould die, then the houfes fhould be divided between thofe that were living.

The eldeft fon died, and it was contended that the limitation over, to the children then living, was a contingent remainder to the furvivors; that the eldeft fon's eftate for life in the houfe was merged in the fee, which defcended upon him as heir, and deftroyed the contingent remainder. But it was adjudged not to be a contingent but a vefted remainder; each child took a particular eftate in the houfe devifed to him, with a vefted remainder to the others for their lives.

As this cafe applied to the author's pofition, there was the appearance of a contingency in the words "if either of my children die;" yet it being certain, that they muft die, there was really nothing contingent in the event, and therefore it was a vefted remainder on the death of a child.

To the prefent cafe it does not apply at all, fince there was an exprefs remainder devifed upon the death of the eldeft, as well as of the other fons, which does not prove, that where there is a devife of lands to the heir without words of limitation, the reverfion in fee will pafs to another, by a general refiduary claufe in the fame will.

In Peal *vs.* Powell. *Ambl. Rep.* 387, tho' there was an appearance of intention, that the eldest son should take the freehold lands, by his being directed to confirm the leasehold lands to Giles, yet there was no devise of any kind to the eldest son, to take those freehold lands out of the general devise of all the rest and residue of his estate real and personal.

In Urry &c. *vs.* Harvey 5 *Burr.* 2638—the lands were not particularly devised to any person, and adjudged to pass to the wife by a devise of all the rest and residue of his estate whatsoever, and wheresoever: and Ld. Mansfield says " the word " estate carries every thing, unless tied down by particular ex- " pressions."

In the case before us, there is an express devise of the lands in question to the heir, without limiting the duration of his estate, leaving it to the fee which the law cast upon him, which acts exclusively of this subject upon the words *rest and residue* of my estate, and ties them down to other estate, not disposed of in former parts of the will.

So much for what is particular in respect to the heir.—Let us now

2dly, Enquire in general, whether in any case of lands devised without limitation, where only an estate for life shall be supposed to pass, the reversion in fee will pass by a general devise, *of all the rest of the estate, real and personal.*

The word *rest* is a relative term, and refers to the whole of a subject before contemplated by the testator. That subject here, was all the testator's property, which the preamble shews, he placed in his view, in one collected mass of lands, slaves, stocks, &c. In his disposition he takes out for Robert two tracts of land, six slaves, and ten horses.

For Theoderick one tract of land, two slaves and the same number of horses.

The *rest* to his wife and daughter—rather two considerable, and therefore, he excepts a young negro girl for Theoderick.— Strange that he should do so, and yet leave in it, the more valuable reversions of the three tracts of land given to the two sons.

A plain man would understand this word *rest*, to mean, what remained of the mass of property undisposed of, and would never suppose it could reach what had been given to the sons, at any period, or on any event, since the testator had not appointed any time, or any event, on which their rights were to cease.

It is true, a testator might devise lands for years, or for life, and limit no particular remainder, and in that case, the reversion would pass in the residuary clause. Skinner 150. Allen 28. 2 *Ventr.* 285. 2 *Vern.* 461, 621. *Eq. Ca. Ab.* 211. 3 *Atk.* 486. In these cases, the testator, having given a limited estate, shews his intention, that on the termination of that estate, the land should return into the mass of his property, and making no further particular disposition of it, means it shall pass in the residue.

But in a general devise of lands without limitation, I will not say there is no case, but I have not met with one, which determines that the reversion will pass by a general residuary devise in the same will.

And the distinction is obvious—since by such a devise the testator means to give a fee, as the judges all agree, and therefore he could not intend to include it in the residue. If the devisee must lose the land upon the rule of law, it goes to the heir, for whose benefit the rule was made.

In Davis *vs.* Saunders 2 *Black. Rep.* 736 and *Cowp.* 420, a devise to the eldest son and his wife for life, remainder to their eldest son and his heirs; if no male issue, to daughters and their heirs, and if they die without issue, to the testator's *right heirs.* To his son in law Humphrey Davis, and his heirs he gives all his estates freehold and copy-hold, tenements and premises, not before devised, for payment of debts, and the surplus to be equally divided amongst his children; and then he devises all the residue and remainder of his estate real and personal to the said H. Davis. The eldest son and his wife died, and never had issue—The question was, if his reversion passed to H. Davis; and it was determined, that the devise, to *right heir*, tho' nugatory, excluded it from passing as part of the residuum, tho' latent reversions might pass.

Strong, Clark, *vs.* Mervyn 2 *Burr.* 912. Audly Mervyn seized in fee of lands in Tyrone, on the marriage of Henry his eldest son, settled those lands to the use of himself for life, remainder to Henry for life, remainder to the first and other sons of the marriage in the usual form, remainder to the right heirs of Audley the father.

The father seized of other lands by his will devised several parcels by specific descriptions in the counties of Tyrone and Meath, " and also all other the lands, tenements and heredita-
" ments in the said counties of Tyrone and Meath, or either of
" them, whereof I am seized in fee simple, or of which any
other

" other perfon is *feized in truft for me* to his wife Olivia," in truft for feveral purpofes. Henry afterwards dying without iffue, the queftion was, if the reverfion in fee of the lands fettled on him at his marriage, paffed by the general refiduary devife to the wife? It was determined in Ireland, that it did pafs: but upon a writ of error, the whole court of King's Bench in England decided that it did not. Among other reafons given by Ld. Mansfield, he fays, " if the queftion had been between " the iffue male of Henry by a fecond wife, and the refiduary " devifee, could it poffibly be imagined that the teftator intend-" ed in fuch a cafe, that Henry's fons by a fecond wife fhould " be difinherited? and yet they muft have been fo, if the rever-" fion of this fettled eftate paffed by this devife."

If it could not be imagined, that the teftator there intended to difinherit remote, and barely poffible, children, of his fon by a fecond wife, when he had a firft wife, living, whofe children were provided for, much lefs can it be imagined that the teftator in this cafe intended to difinherit all the children of his fons by any wives, by devifing thefe reverfions in this refiduary claufe; and what gives additional weight to the objection is, that we are all fatisfied that the teftator believed he had fully difpofed of the lands to his fons, and had no reverfion to pafs by the refiduary claufe.

If the *law* raifes that reverfion contrary to his intention, the law muft difpofe of it, fince *he* has not, and give it to the heir at law. It might have had fome weight (though but litttle) to prove thefe reverfions included, if there had not been other lands undifpofed of, to have fatisfied the words *real eftate*. See the reafoning of the court upon this point in the cafe of Knotsford *vs.* Gardiner 2 *Atk.* 450. And if in that cafe it were thought, that the teftator could not intend to mangle a tenement by feparating the freehold from the leafehold, to give part to his wife from his only child who was a daughter: it would feem equally, or more ftrange, that this teftator fhould mean to mangle the intereft in thefe lands, to give the inheritance from his fons, to his wife and daughter. See 1 *P.Wms.* 286, where it is decided, that under a devife " of all his freehold lands," if there be none, leafehold fhall pafs rather than defeat the will.

2 Bacon 92. 1 Rolls *Ab.* 613—a man feized in fee of 3 tenements, and poffeffed of a leafe for years, and alfo of goods, devifes two tenements to one of his fons, and the other to a daughter and adds, " I make my two fons executors of all my goods moveable

moveable and immoveable, and all my lands, debts, dues and demands,"—determined, that no estate passed in the three tenements, (I suppose in the reversion,) because the words, *all my lands*, might be satisfied with the leasehold lands.

The case, of a devise of lands to A in fee, and of all the residue of his real and personal estate to B and C.—is stated in Goodright *vs.* Opie *Cas.* in *L.* and *Eq.* 123 and in Wright *vs.* Horne (same Book p. 222.) A dies in the testator's lifetime and the question was, if his lands passed to the residuary devisees, or descended to the heir? in both, the reasoning is strong for the heir, but neither is determined—it is strange, that in so plain a case it should not. For if a nugatory limitation to the right heirs, (nugatory, because it does what the law would do without it,) shall prevent that reversion from passing in the residue, much more shall an actual devise effectual at the time, but defeated by a subsequent accident prevent that land from passing in the residue.

Upon the whole, we think the law is with the appellant and therefore reverse the judgment of the District Court.

CASES DETERMINED
IN THE
COURT OF APPEALS
IN
THE FALL TERM OF THE YEAR,
1792.

SCOTT'S Executors, *against* CALL.

THIS was an action of debt, brought by the appellee against the appellant, upon a protested bill of exchange, drawn by the testator of the appellant, for £187 : 15, sterling for value received: as also, for the damages at the rate of 10 per cent. together with the charges of protest &c. The declaration demands the £187 : 15, sterling *of the value of* £250 : 6 : 8, *current money;* and 4/6 sterling *of the value of* 6/. *current money* and interest at the rate of 10 per centum per annum, on the said £250 : 6 : 8, from the date of the bill : it states also the protest; " whereby and by virtue of the act of Assembly in that case made, " action accrued to the plaintiff, to have and demand of the " defendant the said £187 : 15 sterling, of the value aforesaid, and " the said 4/6 sterling of the value aforesaid, and interest as aforesaid:" the breach assigned is, in the non-payment of the said several sums of money and interest &c. to the plaintiff's damage of £500. Upon the plea of payment, the jury found that the defendant's testator had not paid the debt in the declaration mentioned, and assessed the plaintiff's damage to one penny. The court gave judgment that the plaintiff recover £509 : 3 : 6 sterling, the principal, interest and charges of protest, together with interest thereon, after the rate of five per centum per annum from that day; and they settled the exchange at 33¼ per cent.

Exceptions being taken to the opinion of the court, upon certain points moved by the defendant's counsel, an appeal was prayed to this court. The

The question made by the bill of exceptions was; whether the plaintiff, to entitle himself, under the act of Assembly, to 10 per cent. damages beyond 18 months, ought not to prove an *actual presentation of the bill protested to the drawer* within that time.

CARRINGTON, J. delivered the opinion of the court.

The point which was argued at the bar, and which grows out of the bill of exceptions, need not be decided, as the court think the judgment erroneous in this, that the demand in the declaration is for the *current money value* of a debt, due in *sterling money*, on a protested bill of exchange, which is recoverable in sterling money only.

The judgment therefore must be reversed with costs.

WHITE *against* JONES.

THIS was a suit, instituted originally in the County Court, on the Chancery side, by the appellant. The bill states: that the complainant in 1761 or 1762, purchased a tract of land from H. Hatcher for which he paid a valuable consideration. That this land was surveyed for the said H. Hatcher in 1740, and that a patent for the same was made out on the 17th August 1756; but, on account of a dispute then depending before the king in council, respecting a claim, set up by governor Dinwiddie, of a pistole for signing patents for lands; this patent was so long withheld from H. Hatcher, that the land became forfeited for non-payment of quitrents, and for want of seating. That the complainant, in order the better to secure his title to the land, petitioned for the same as lapsed, and with the consent of H. Hatcher, obtained a patent in his own name in 1764.

That the defendant in 1743, obtained an order of council for surveying 2000 acres of land, including the land in question, and pending the above dispute between Virginia and governor Dinwiddie, fraudulently paid the pistole fee demanded by the governor, and obtained a patent. The prayer of the bill is, that the defendant may be compelled to relinquish his title to, and possession of, the land in dispute, to the complainant.

The

The Anſwer of the defendant, the heir at law of the original patentee, relies principally upon the want of equity in the bill; and denies notice of Hatcher's ſurvey.

The cauſe coming on upon bill and anſwer, together with the certificate of ſurvey, the order of the governor in council, and the grants before mentioned, read as exhibits, the plaintiff obtained a decree for the land in the County Court, which was reverſed by the High Court of Chancery upon a petition of appeal: the decree of reverſal is in the following words, to wit: "This court is of opinion, that the appellee's title, if any he hath, to the land in controverſy, muſt be ſupported on this foundation: That the grant to Henry Hatcher operated retroactively, giving to his title like vigor as if the conſummation thereof, by the grant, had been cotemporaneous with the commencement, which preceded the commencement of the appellants right; or on this other foundation: that the grant to Wood Jones was obtained ſurreptitiouſly, when the officer, to whoſe function the tranſaction of that buſineſs belonged, did not know part of the land comprehended in the grant, to have been appropriated, or claimed by another, who, in not perfecting his title, had been in no default; or was obtained by colluſion between the officer and the grantee; and upon ſuppoſition that the grant to Henry Hatcher by relation, was prior in effect, although poſterior in date, to the other, or that the latter was fraudulent, this, ſo far as it tended to intercept his right, was void; and the appellees remedy in a court of common law was proper and adequate; and this court, diſcerning no ground for application, by the appellee to a court of equity,—eſpecially, when ſo great a length of time had elapſed, after the commencement of Hatcher's title, before any one appeareth to have attempted to aſſert it, and the manner in which it was derived to the appellee, are remembered,—is of opinion that the ſaid decree of the County Court, by which the appellee recovered the ſaid land againſt the appellant with coſts, is erroneous; and therefore doth reverſe the ſaid decree; and doth adjudge, order, and decree, that the bill of the appellee be diſmiſſed."

From this decree, there was an appeal.

The PRESIDENT delivered the opinion of the court.

It was objected to by the counſel for the appellant, that the decree of the County Court having been carried into execution by the return of an *habere facias poſſeſſionem*, executed, the petition of appeal was made too late, and ought not to have been granted, ſince the *ſuperſedeas* thereupon awarded, could have nothing to operate upon. A

A *superfedeas* in England, is merely an auxiliary procefs; and fo it is, in fome inftances, in this country. But in general, it is a mode by which the record of a judgment of an inferior court, is removed before a fuperior jurifdiction.

When merely auxiliary, it can have no effect after the decree, or judgment is carried into execution; fince is can only ftay the proceedings in the ftate in which they are; but yet the fuit goes on, in the fuperior court, by the other procefs; and if the judgment be reverfed, a writ of reftitution iffues, to reftore the party to that, of which he has been difpoffeffed by the execution.

Where the *superfedeas* is the only procefs, by the laws of this ftate, it may have one, or both of thefe operations, as the judgment happens to be executed or not.

At law, a party may appeal at the time the judgment is rendered; or he may afterwards obtain a writ of error, which, it is admitted, may iffue after the judgment is executed.

Upon the merits, though the court is of opinion, that the decree of the Chancellor ought to be affirmed, yet we do by no means coincide with him, in the reafons and arguments upon which he feems to have grounded his opinion.

The plaintiff has ftated a very fair and proper cafe for a Court of Equity.—He was a purchafer, againft whom the defendant unfairly and fraudulently obtained a preference; and in queftions like this, where fraud is fuggefted and proved, courts of equity have competent jurifdiction, and can afford the moft ample and adequate relief.—But in this cafe, the plaintiff not having fupported the allegations in his bill, which charge Wood Jones with fraud in obtaining his patent, this court is of opinion, that there is no error in the decree, and that it muft be

affirmed with cofts.

WINSLOW *againft* DAWSON.

THIS was a fuit brought by the appellee, in the High Court of Chancery, to be relieved againft a judgment for £50, which by an award of arbitrators (made under a rule of court) he had been adjudged to pay with intereft;—infifting that the £50 was only intended as a penalty to enforce the punctual payment of £100, or to compel the appellee, in lieu thereof, to take up the appellant's bond to one Garret, for that fum, and which he was prevented from doing by the appellant himfelf;

felf; and praying an injunction againſt a judgment rendered upon the award. The bill ſtates and the depoſitions prove, that the memorandum was torn from the bond at the time the caſe was before the arbitrators, that the arbitrators refuſed to hear the appellee's witneſſes, but permitted a ſtatement to be read by the appellant's counſel of facts which were controverted by the appellee. The anſwer ſtates: that the defendant agreed to ſell a tract of land to the plaintiff, and to receive payment in any one of the three following modes: 1ſt, £200 in hand, or 2d, £250 in twelve months, or 3d, £300 upon a longer credit. That the plaintiff acceded to the firſt propoſition, if credit for a few months were allowed; and if not punctually paid, then, that the ſecond propoſition ſhould prevail. This being agreed to by the defendant, two bonds were executed, one for the payment of £100 at the time laſt mentioned, and another for £150 in twelve months after:—but, to the latter bond, a memorandum was annexed, that it might be diſcharged by the payment of £100 by a certain time, ſooner than that mentioned in the condition.

The Chancellor decreed a perpetual injunction, and the coſts at law to the complainant. From which decree the defendant in equity appealed.

THE PRESIDENT delivered the opinion of the court.

Taking the caſe to have been as ſtated by Winſlow in his anſwer, the inſertion of the £50 muſt be confidered, either as a conſideration for forbearance—and of courſe within the act of uſury,—or as a penalty, for which a compenſation may be made, and therefore relievable againſt in a court of equity:—for he admits, that the firſt propoſition for £200 was acceded to, and adopted as the agreement between the parties.

The caſe of Groves and Graves, in this court, has decided this principle: viz, that ſuch a contract to pay a larger ſum at a future day, upon non-payment of the ſum agreed upon, at a prior day, is not uſurious; but that the increaſed ſum ſhall be confidered as a penalty, againſt which a court of equity ought to relieve, upon compenſation being made.

That compenſation—in caſe the condition be for payment of money—is legal intereſt; unleſs ſome ſpecific damage be ſhewn, which may induce the Chancellor to direct a jury to aſſeſs the quantum of it.

In this caſe, Winſlow ſpeaks of difficulties to which he was ſubjected, but of no particular injury ſuſtained, which could entitle

title him to a compensation beyond legal interest: so that upon his own statement of the case, Groves and Graves would be a direct authority in affirmance of the decree. But take the case either way, there is no difficulty in it. For since Dawson might have performed what was required of him in order to save the forfeiture, by taking up the bond to Garret by the 10th of February 1784, and was prevented by the interposition of Winslow himself from doing so, that ought in equity to be considered as done, and the penalty of course relieved against.

But, as the injunction is made perpetual for £3:12:8: more than ought to have been injoined, the decree must be reversed with costs, and the injunction dissolved as to so much, and stand for the residue of the sum, and the costs at law, which were properly decreed, since the appellee appears to have tendered to the appellant, before the institution of the suit at law, more money than was due at that time.

ROSS *against* POYTHRESS.

THIS was an action of debt brought by the appellant in the District Court of Petersburg, upon a prison bounds bond; the breach assigned in the declaration, is nearly in the words of the condition of the bond, with an averment, that the prisoner did depart and escape from the bounds, without being discharged by due course of law.

Pleas, 1st, Conditions performed. 2d, That the bond was given to the sheriff for and concerning a matter relating to his office, whilst the defendant was in custody of the said sheriff; contrary to the act entitled an act " prescribing the method of appointing " sheriffs, and for limiting the time of their continuance in office; " and directing their duty therein."—Issue was taken upon the first plea, and liberty reserved to the plaintiff to file his demurrer to the 2d plea, at the next court, if he please.

The jury found a verdict for the plaintiff: but if, in the opinion of the Court, a *subpœna of injunction* issued from the High Court of Chancery, and delivered to the sheriff having the prisoner in custody, and served on the plaintiff's attorney, whereby the judgment, on which an execution had issued, under which the defendant was confined, was injoined, was a sufficient authority to the sheriff to discharge him from custody under

that

that execution, then they found for the defendant. No notice was taken of the second plea.

Judgment for the defendant upon the special verdict in the District Court, and appeal to this.

Ronold for the appellant.

Until a final decree was rendered for the plaintiff in equity, the injunction granted by the Chancellor could not operate, so as to deprive the plaintiff at law, of a right already vested in him. The lands of a defendant, are actually bound from the time a judgment is rendered against him; as are also his chattels, from the time a writ of fieri facias is *delivered* to the sheriff.

It would be highly unreasonable to give to an injunction, an effect so extensive, as that which must be contended for. The principal, as well as his securities, might remove or become insolvent, pending the injunction. The estate seized by the sheriff on a writ of *fieri facias*, might during that time perish, and thus, might the plaintiff at law lose entirely the effect of his judgment. Injunctions are not authorised, or in any manner regulated, by the laws of this country, and therefore we must resort to the rules observed in the courts of England. There, the money is always brought into court by the party obtaining the injunction, unless, in special cases, it is dispensed with, a *Harr. Ch. Prac.* 224, 226. So if goods are taken on execution, or money levied, or paid in execution, and in the sheriff's hands, the process of injunction will *stay them there Ib.* 225. Upon the same principle it is, that a bill of review does not prevent the execution of the decree impeached; but obedience is actually to be paid to the decree, as far as it can, without prejudice to the right of the party preferring the bill, 1 *Harr. Ch. Prac.* 171. Neither does a *superfedeas* set aside the execution, or stop the sale of the property seized under it. *Dalt. Sheriff.* 225—534. A *capias*, not executed, is arrested by a *superfedeas*; but if executed, the body must be returned with the *superfedeas*. Neither will an action for false imprisonment lie, if the body be taken on a *ca. sa.* without notice of the writ of error. If then, we are to take as our guide, the rules and principles of the English law, (and we have none other to follow,) we find, that an execution once served, is not interrupted by an injunction, or other proceedings subsequent to the judgment, until the debt is levied, or received by the officer, and is then only stopped in his hands.

The old Chancery law, passed in the year 1777, *Ch.* 15, §. 31, seems to give to injunctions, merely the power of *staying* executions. It neither authorises the discharge of the person, or property already taken in execution, nor does such an effect follow, as a necessary or reasonable consequence, from the order.

If the whole effect of the execution be done away by the granting of the injunction, I am at a loss to know, what return the sheriff can make upon the execution, or in what manner, the plaintiff is to proceed upon the dissolution of the injunction.

MARSHALL for the appellee. The cases read by Mr. Ronold, only prove that there are certain rules observed by the Chancellor in England, which neither are, or ought to be guides for us; and this necessary departure from those rules, results from the very nature of our situation, compared with that country. In that, much of the wealth of the nation consists in money; it is easily procured by those who can secure the repayment of it; therefore no inconvenience can follow from requiring a deposit of the debt recovered at law, as the condition of granting an injunction. So too, nothing can stop the progress of an execution once served. Yet even there, we find that in some instances this rigid rule is dispensed with, as the cases referred to by Mr. Ronold prove. In this country, the wealth of the people consists principally in real property—there is so much of that, and so little money at market, that the latter cannot be procured on loan, with any security.

This difference, will furnish a strong argument, why the rule in England, even in cases of executions against the property, should not prevail here; and the argument is fortified considerably, if we view the case by analogy to forthcoming and replevy bonds, which are unknown in that country, yet induced by necessity to be authorized in this. In these cases, the lien is entirely gone, and a compensation for it, provided in the security given by the debtor.

So too in England, if goods be taken by way of distress, and replevied, the distrainor loses his lien on the goods, and is left to his remedy on the replevy bond, *Brow. Ch. Rep.* 427: so that the loss of the lien upon property once seized, is not unknown even in England, much less in this country.

But the case of an execution against the body, is much stronger than if it were against the property. For if the body might still be kept in confinement, the injunction would be an idle and vain thing; since the plaintiff, if entitled to equity, might receive the same benefit from an original bill, as he could by obtaining the

the injunction. The plaintiff at law cannot complain with reason, since his security is certainly bettered.

Mr. RONOLD in reply. The act of 1791 *Ch.* 3, § 3, tho' it was made subsequent to this transaction, shews, from the manner in which it is expressed, the sense of the legislature upon this subject, by directing that the sheriff, having received money under an execution, shall, upon an injunction being granted, *repay* the money to the plaintiff in equity. But this was unnecessary, if, before the law was made, an injunction produced the extensive effect now contended for.

THE PRESIDENT. We shall give no positive opinion, as to the effect of an injunction obtained upon an execution against the *goods and chattels*, after seisure; as that case is not before us: probably it would be considered as settled by the act of 1791, which directing a restitution of the money levied, would seem to include inferior cases, and to extend, by an equitable construction, to the restitution of goods seized in execution, and not sold.

The reason is much stronger in the case of an execution against the *body*, where the injunction would have no effect at all, if it did not operate to discharge the body from confinement.

Judgment affirmed.

JENKINS *against* TOM and others.

THIS was an action of trespass, assault and battery, and false imprisonment, brought by the appellees in the District Court of Northumberland to recover their freedom. Plea, that the plaintiffs are slaves. Replication, that they are free, and not slaves; upon which issue is taken.

At the trial, the defendant tendered a bill of exceptions, which was sealed by the court, stating: that the plaintiffs had offered in evidence sundry depositions of antient people to prove, that certain women named Mary and Bess, when they came first into this country, were called *Indians*; and had a tawny complexion, with long straight black hair: to strengthen this testimony, the plaintiffs produced a witness to prove, that he heard a certain other person now dead, say in the year 1701, that when he was a lad about 12 years old, these women were brought to this colony in a ship, and were called *Indians*; that they had the appearance of *Indians*, and that the former of them

was

was called the grandmother of the latter. To the admission of this testimony, the defendant objected, but was over-ruled by the court.

The jury found a verdict for the plaintiffs. In the record there is a certificate of the judges, stating: That the defendant's counsel, in his argument, insisted much upon a clause in an act of Assembly, entituled an act "for the better government of servants and slaves", passed in the year 1753, which enacts "that all persons who have been, or shall be "imported into this colony by sea or land, and were not "christians in their native country,—(except Turks and "Moors in amity with his majesty, and such who can prove "their having been free in England, or any other christian "country before they were shipped for transportation hither)—" shall be accounted, and be slaves, and as such, be here bought "and sold, notwithstanding a conversion to christianity after "their importation:" and argued from thence, that all Indians as well in America, as elsewhere, not particularly excepted in that clause, might be sold as slaves: that the court informed the counsel, that he misstated the law; that there was a time at some period in the last century, when a law was in existance, which declared Indians at war with the people of this country, slaves, when taken prisoners: that under that law, many Indians were made slaves, and their descendants continue slaves to this day:—but that this law was some time after repealed; from which period, no American Indian could be sold as a slave, and that all such as had been brought into this country since that time, and who had sued for their freedom, had uniformly recovered it. That the same counsel still insisted upon his former argument, and considering the court's address to the bar, as a misdirection to the jury, had prayed this certificate to be entered at the foot of the judgment.

From this judgment the defendant appealed.

*After argument the Court affirmed the judgment.

THOMPSON

* *The reporter was not in Court, when the opinion in this case was delivered.*

OF THE YEAR 1792.

THOMPSON Appellant,

against

D. & J. DAVENPORT Appellees.

THIS was an appeal from a decree of the High Court of Chancery. The bill was filed by the appellees, to be relieved against a judgment at law, on a bond payable the 2d of March 1784, executed by the appellees for £113: 16: 4, being the amount of a tract of land, mortgaged by a certain David Davenport to the appellant, to secure a debt of £40: 18: 7, with interest from the 19th of August 1756, and sold under a decree of the County Court of Hanover, and purchased by the appellee James the younger, for whom the other appellee was security.

The ground of equity is, that the mortgage had been paid off by David Davenport:—that under a deed of trust, or power of attorney, from the said David, to Lewis and Ross, the land, had been long before the decree of Hanover Court, sold at public auction, and purchased by the appellee, James Davenport, the elder, at £30, the appellant being then present, and silent as to his title. That James the elder, paid the purchase money to Lewis, has been ever since in possession, and in 1779 received a conveyance from David Davenport for the land; so that James the younger, has had no benefit from his purchase under Thompson's decree, and ought therefore to be relieved against the payment of the money.

Both grounds of equity are flatly denied by the answer. So far from the mortgage money having been paid off, the defendant states an account, commencing in December 1756, by which, after crediting the said David with every payment contended for, he makes him debtor £7 : 5: 4, over and above the mortgage money.—The defendant insists, that the intention of the mortgage, was to secure subsequent advances of money, or other things; and that the balance due, for posterior dealings, ought to be satisfied out of the mortgaged premises. He denies, that he concealed his incumbrance from the plaintiffs, but, that on the contrary, he disclosed it to them, on the day of Lewis and Ross's sale; that besides this, James the elder, is a brother to David; has been a near neighbour to the defendant, ever since the purchase was made, and finally, that the price which he gave for the land, was not more than the value of the equity of redemption.

The proofs in the cause, relate principally to Thompson's confessions, that the mortgage was paid off, and his silence at the sale. Amongst the exhibits, is a letter from David Davenport to the court of Hanover, desiring a decree to be entered up, in the suit of Thompson against him, for the principal sum mentioned in the mortgage, and interest from the date, which he says is justly due. The account stated, and reported by the master, after crediting Davenport with all his payments, and debiting him with the posterior account of Thompson, down to the last payment made by Davenport, makes a balance of £29 : 1 : 3, due upon the mortgage in June 1762, and £31 : 5 : 7½, due for subsequent dealings.

The court injoined the defendant, from proceeding to levy more of his judgment at law, than so much of £29 : 1 : 3, with interest from the 28th of June 1762, as shall remain, after deductions therefrom, of the costs expended by the plaintiffs, in their action at common law, and in the said High Court of Chancery.

The PRESIDENT delivered the opinion of the court.

The evidence of Mr. Thompson's confession, respecting the payment of the mortgage money, is loose and desultory; liable to the objections justly stated by the Chancellor, and to others also important; amongst which, one is, that none of the witnesses mention the time, or near it, when those confessions were made—the proof respecting his silence at the sale, is also very defective.

To sustain the decree so far as it goes, the counsel, made several observations upon the evidence, which need not be further noticed, since we agree with the Chancellor on that ground.

The counsel for the appellees, upon this point, supposing that the evidence should be adjudged insufficient, to prove the mortgage to have been paid off, insisted, that no day of payment being mentioned, it was a conditional purchase, and not a mortgage; that Davenport might repurchase at any time, upon payment of principal without interest; which not being mentioned, cannot properly be demanded.

In questions, whether a deed should be considered as a mortgage, or an absolute purchase, chancellors have said, they would govern themselves by the intention of the parties; and

if

if the former appeared to have been intended, they would not suffer it to be changed into a purchase by any form of words, which might elude the justice of the Court, in permitting a redemption.

In aspect, form, and essence, this is a mortgage without a trait, indicating a purchase. No price for a purchase was contemplated, or discussed, as in a sale. The vendor retains possession, which is uniformly the effect of a mortgage, and not of a sale. There is also a covenant for payment of the money; and tho' interest is not mentioned, yet the principal debt was due on demand, and bore interest from the date, as in the common case of a bond.

In the case of a purchase, the vendee, has possession of the property, in lieu of interest, and therefore, if there be a condition to purchase, it is done on payment of principal only, unless interest be expressly mentioned; because otherwise, the vendee would have double satisfaction, namely, interest, and the use of the land. But, in this case, Thompson has received no equivalent for interest, since Davenport retained the possession of the land. Upon the whole, it is clear, that this is a mortgage, and as such, is redeemable upon the common terms, of paying principle and interest.

But the decree, reducing the mortgage from £40 : 18 : 7 principal debt in 1756, to £29 : 1 : 3, principal in 1762, is complained of, by both of the parties. The appellant's counsel insisting, that since there was a running account between the parties, on the close of which, a balance was due to Thompson, there ought therefore, to be no deduction from the mortgage debt. On the other side it is insisted, that since payments were made subsequent to the mortgage, more than sufficient to discharge both principal and interest, they ought to be so applied, and the balance should be credited in the account.

The rule as it respects the application of payments is agreed; but the question is, how it operates on the present case?

It is insisted, that the credits, are not to be considered as payments, but as forming so many items in a running account. Whether this would be the case or not, if the credits were mere matters of account, we will not now determine, as we understand, that it will be made a question in some other cause which is to come on.

But in this case, the credit in June 1762 of £80, which reduces the mortgage, is not of goods, or produce, so as to be a matter of account only; but was a payment made in money, or what was equivalent thereto, by two orders on Jackson and Crenshaw.

After the account was paid off, to that time, there was no choice of application, there being no debt but the mortgage.

The decree therefore is right, so far as it respects the balance due, but is defective, in not decreeing a conveyance, and disposing of the surplus.

As to the costs in Hanover, and the District Courts; whether it proceeded from a difference in opinion between the Chancellor and this court, or that it was not attended to by him, we cannot say; we rather suppose the latter, since we cannot discover any ground for making the defendant pay those costs; since he was certainly entitled to a considerable balance, and was pursuing regular methods to recover it. The costs in the Court of Chancery, were properly awarded against him, since the plaintiff was relieved.

The decree as also the first decree dismissing the bill with costs must be reversed with costs.

HILL & BRAXTON
against
SOUTHERLAND'S Executors.

THE appellant Hill, with two others, were endorsers of a bill of Exchange, drawn by Braxton in favor of Southerland, which returned protested. The parties, having agreed upon the sum due by the said bill, in current money; the drawer and endorsers gave their note to Southerland on the 28th of February 1776, directed to the clerk of King William Court, where a suit on the bill was pending, agreeing, to confess judgment for the amount due, (being at that time £778 : 7 : 4, at the exchange of 15 per cent.) with interest at the rate of five per centum per annum, from the 1st of June following. Southerland, held up this note until 1784, when without notice to any of the parties, he procured a judgment to be entered up for 361 : 6 : 10, the balance which appeared by an account filed by the said Southerland, to be then due to him. An execution being sued out upon this judgment, Braxton, obtained a supersedeas,

and

and reversed it. Southerland, then instituted a new suit against Hill alone, and got judgment in 1787, for £ 1400 : 5 : 9.

The appellant Hill, filed his bill in the High Court of Chancery, praying an injunction to this judgment, and stating, as the ground of his equity, that the bill had been nearly, if not wholly paid off by Braxton, and that, in consequence of a mistake in his counsel, no defence had been made at law, but the judgment had passed by default in the office, and was afterwards confirmed against him in court.

Upon the answer of Southerland to the injunction bill, the court directed Braxton to be made a party complainant, who filed his bill, stating the same facts, as those set forth by Hill, and further, that he Braxton, had in the year 1783, paid to the said Southerland, two bonds of Thomas Butler, amounting to £ 935 : 15 : 1, which were to be applied to the credit of the protested bill. That Southerland was also indebted considerably to him in account, the balance of which, if necessary, ought also to have been applied to that debt.

The defendant, in his answer to this bill, admits the payment of the bonds, but denies that any application of them to the credit of the judgment, was directed by Braxton ; that the defendant had applied £ 661 : 12 : 8 ¼ of those bonds to the credit of this judgment, and part of the residue, (by Braxton's particular directions,) to the discharge of a bond dated in February 1776, due to him from Braxton, in which Claiborne was security ; and the balance to a private debt of Braxton's.

There is no positive evidence in the cause, that Braxton directed the application of this, or of any other payment, to the credit of the judgment.

It is proved, that immediately after the payment was made, Braxton sent a message to his endorsers, informing them he had discharged the judgment; but this was not delivered in the presence of Southerland, nor does it appear, that any thing passed between them at that time, upon the subject. It is proved by one witness, that sometime after the bonds were received, Southerland declared he should lose money by taking them ; but it does not appear, whether this happened before, or after the first judgment was entered up in 1784. That as late as the year 1786, Southerland, enclosed to Mr. Braxton his, and Claiborne's bond, with some accounts, which Braxton, received without objection, and that some time afterwards, Southerland mentioned, that he had been advised to deliver Mr. Braxton those papers, and to rest his demand upon the protested bill.

The commissioner, to whom the accounts between the parties were referred, in his first report, applied the full amount of the bonds, to the credit of the protested bill, leaving a balance of only £34 : 17 : 9¼ due upon it. A similar statement had been before made by auditors, to whom the accounts had been referred. In stating this account, the commissioner charges interest on the £778 : 7 : 4, at the rate *of five per cent.* from June 1776, to December 1784, when the last payment was made; and credits all the payments, with interest on each, from the time they were made, until the same period in 1784. The report, contains also the private account of Braxton with Southerland, which is composed, of the bond of the former to the latter, in which Claiborne was security, and of some other items on the debit side; and of goods sold to Southerland, by Braxton, in the years 1777, 1778, & 1780, on the credit side. The commissioner made two statements of this account, in one of which he scales the credits, and in the other, fixes them at their nominal amount, submitting that question to the court.

The cause coming on to be heard; the court of chancery made a decree, in conformity with the following opinion, viz. " That the goods and merchandize, sold and delivered by the " plaintiff Carter Braxton, to the said Fendall Southerland, be-
" tween the years 1776 and 1781, ought not to be discounted, " at the money prices then charged, against a debt contracted " before the commencement of that period; but ought to be " discounted at their true value, which, in this case, may be " nearly perhaps ascertained by reducing those prices according " to the scale for proportioning the depreciation of paper mo-
" ney; that the payments made to the said Fendall Southerland, " by the plaintiff Carter Braxton, not appearing to have been " directed by him, at the times of payment or before, to be en-
" tered to his credit in that account, wherein he is made a debi-
" tor for the bill of exchange, the said Fendall Southerland " might enter them to the credit of the plaintiff Carter Brax-
" ton in any other account, subsisting between those parties; " and that for the principal money, damages, and charges, due " by the protested bill of exchange, in consequence of the set-
" tlement thereof, made the 28th of February, in the year 1776, " the said Fendall Southerland was entitled to no more than " £778 : 7 : 4, of current money of Virginia, with interest " thereon, at the rate of five per centum per annum, from the " first day of June, then next following."

The injunction is made perpetual, except as to £225 : 18 : 5¼ appearing, by the accounts stated according to the principles of the above opinion, to have been due to the said Fendall Southerland

therland, the 7th of December 1784, with interest from that time; and except also as to the costs in the action at common law.

From this decree the plantiffs appealed.

THE PRESIDENT delivered the opinion of the court.

The first question which presents itself in this case, is, whether the agreement of 1776, shall stand as the basis of settlement between the parties, or, if that should be set aside, because Mr. Braxton superseded and reversed the judgment, for want of a declaration as it is said, but for what cause, does not appear?—

If the judgment had been entered up *immediately*, and Mr. Braxton had reversed it for want of form, there might have been reason in the objection. But since it was kept up until the year 1784, (I will not say fraudulently, because the evidence does not warrant it,) and considerable payments intervened, which, Mr. Southerland himself admits, reduced the balance of £778 : 7 : 4, principal in 1776, and interest, to £361 : 6 : 10, principal in 1784; surely, fair dealing required, that these payments should have been mutually adjusted, previous to the entry of the judgment; or at least, that Mr. Braxton should have had notice, that the judgment was then to have been entered. If the judgment thus entered, was for too much, according to the agreement of 1776, surely, Mr. Braxton might complain of it, without violating that agreement. The proper remedy, was certainly in equity; but perhaps he was advised to seek redress in a court of law, as being the most expeditious. Be this as it may; what is a Court of Equity now to do? to set aside an agreement, (of the fairness and justice of which, neither party complains,) because subsequent disputes have arisen, about payments made in execution of the agreement, and so, subject Mr. Braxton to 10 per cent, instead of 5, from 1776, and to 40 per cent exchange, instead of 15, on the final balance.— This would be, for that meliorating court, not to relieve against penalties and forfeitures, but to assist in enforcing them. For after all negociation of a bill is at an end, and forbearance, the only object, the additional 5 per cent must be considered as a penalty, being beyond the legislative compensation allowed for the use of money. On the contrary, that court, applying one of its fixed principles, namely, "that what ought to have been done, shall be taken as done," will consider the judgment as having been entered up, immediately after the agreement in 1776,

1776, for the £778: 7: 4, current money, and intereſt at 5 per centum per annum, and on that ground will adjuſt the ſubſequent diſputes.

In doing this, we ſhall have two points to conſider—the firſt, and moſt important is, the application of Butler's bonds, paid and received in 1783. Whether the whole, amounting to £955: 15: 1, ought to be applied to the credit of the bill, (and which will with other ſpecie payments reduce the balance to £44: 0: 11, in 1790?) or whether £ 205, part thereof, ought to be applied to the bond, in which Mr. Claiborne was ſecurity for Braxton, and to an account, the balance of which is in favor of Braxton, more than the £ 44: 0: 11, if his paper money account is to ſtand at the nominal, and not at the reduced value?

The rules, reſpecting the application of payments, are not diſputed; but the queſtion is, how they are to apply, under the circumſtances of the preſent caſe? How Mr. Braxton intended it, appears from his declaration to Mr. Butler, made recently after the payment. It was natural, that he ſhould apply them to the relief of his friends, who ſtood bound as his ſecurities; and in the choice between them, he might have motives, for prefering the endorſers of his bill; and accordingly, when theſe bonds were paid in 1783, Mr. Braxton, ſent a meſſage to the indorſers, that he had made this payment on account of the bill. This meſſage, was not delivered in the abſence of, nor was it communicated to Mr. Southerland, ſo as to fix his aſſent to that application. But the appellants ſuppoſe, that this aſſent is to be infered, 1ſt, from Southerland's declaration, (which is proved,) that he ſhould loſe by taking thoſe bonds—and 2dly, from Mr. Southerland's application to Mr. Claiborne in 1784, (which is alſo proved,) warning him of his danger, and preparing him for the expected payment: and tho', he afterwards ſaid, that he believed this bond might be paid, yet he refuſed to give it up, and never did do ſo, 'till 1786, when the judgment was reverſed; then by the advice of his counſel, he ſent it with other papers to Mr. Braxton.

On this view of the evidence, the auditors, and the maſter thought, that the whole ſhould be applied to the credit of the bill. The chancellor thought otherwiſe, and applied part of it to the bond and account. Whether he was right in doing ſo, this court is to decide; and upon this queſtion it depends, whether Mr. Hill be at all concerned with the other parts of the diſpute; or is liable beyond the £ 44: 0: 11, in caſe that was not paid off by Mr. Braxton?

Although,

Although, if the debtor neglect to make the application at the time of payment, the election is then cast upon the creditor, yet it is incumbent upon the latter, in such a case, to make a recent application, by entries in his books or papers, and not to keep parties and securities in suspence, changing their situation, from time, to time, as his interest, governed by events might dictate. The endorsers, were made easy by the message from Mr. Braxton, "that the payment was applied to their relief," and might in consequence of it, have declined asking for counter security. On the other hand, Claiborne was not deceived, because it does not appear, that he considered his debt as discharged by those bonds.

Besides, it is more probable, that so large a payment would be applied to the credit of a still larger liquidated debt, than that it should be split, and placed, part of it to the credit of a small bond and account, and the residue to this large bond.

Upon the whole, we are of opinion, that the payment should be applied to the bill; and consequently, that the balance due upon that account, is but £34 : 17 : 9½, with interest from the 7th of December 1784.—Respecting the mode of stating the interest, a doubt arose, which induced one judge to decline giving his opinion, and he would have retired from the discussion, considering himself affected in the question, in his character of administrator; but the other judges, not considering the point as important in its operation, in this case, chose to pass it over, on the ground of the master's report not having been excepted to, or the point argued in court, rather than by a decision, either way, to establish a precedent in a bare court, which in other cases might be important.

The next question, arises between Braxton and Southerand, respecting the articles of their account, and principally, on Braxton's account, for goods sold to Southerland. It is to be considered at what rate those goods shall be estimated.— The account begins in September 1777, in which year it amounted to - - - - £8:
In 1778 to - - - - 97 : 1 : 6.
and ends in 1780,——one article - 142 : 10 :

247 : 11 : 6.

The court is of opinion, that an account for goods, not delivered or accepted as a payment, nor liquidated between the parties, ought not to be taken as a payment in paper, so as to stand at the nominal value, according to the strict words of the act

act of Assembly, but should be viewed in the light of a set off, and to be adjusted, (especially in equity,) upon just principles. In this proceeding, we are of opinion, that the legal scale, so far as it operates in the years 1777 and 1778, is not a just rule in itself, not corresponding with the general opinion of the citizens at the time, as to depreciation, nor does the scale at any period, give a proper rule for fixing the price of *imported* goods, which was influenced by the expence and risque of importation, as well as by the depreciation of the paper money. The account therefore, for goods delivered by Braxton to the end of the year, 1778, ought, at the *nominal value*, to be set off against the principal and interest of Claiborne's bond, and Southerland's account; and so much of the residue of his account, as will pay off the interest of the balance remaining due to Southerland, ought also to be set off at the nominal sum; but the residue of the amount of this account, ought to be subject to the legal scale of depreciation, for May 1780, of 60 for one, and at that reduced rate, to be set off against the principal of Southerland's debt:—a precedent for this distinction, between the principal and interest, is supposed to have been furnished in this court.

Upon the whole; the decree is right in sustaining the suit for relief, but is erroneous in the relief afforded, not only in the adjustment of the quantum, but in the application of it, as between the appellants.—It is to be reversed with costs—and upon payment by the appellant Hill, of the first mentioned sum of £34: 17: 9½, with interest from the 7th of December 1784, 'till payment, and the costs of the judgment at law, (the said appellant, retaining thereout, his costs in chancery, and in this court,) the injunction is to stand and be perpetual. But on failure in such payment, the injunction is to be dissolved as to so much, and the appellee to be at liberty to sue out execution for so much as he is entitled to by this decree.

The court, then proceeded to correct the account of the master commissioner, (upon the principles before stated,) as to the residue of the dispute, between the appellee, and the appellant Braxton; and find a balance due from the latter to the former, of £70: 0: 4, on the 30th April 1783—and since Braxton by applying to a Court of Equity for an account, has subjected himself, though plaintiff, to a decree for the balance found due from him; we must decree him to pay to the appellee the sum of £70: 0: 4, with interest from the 30th of April 1783, retaining thereout his costs in chancery and in this court.

Decree reversed.

SMITH *against* WALKER, Ex'r. of Mickie.

THIS was an action upon the case, brought by the appellant in the County Court of Albemarle, in the year 1787. The declaration states, that the plaintiff in 1773, being disposed to engage in matrimony with a grand-daughter of the testator of the defendant, the testator promised the plaintiff, that if he should marry the lady, he would give him as much of his estate, (except land,) as he should give any one of his own children—avers that he did marry her, relying on the said promise, yet the said testator did not give the plaintiff as much of his estate, (land excepted) as he gave to some of his children, tho often required &c.

Pleas—1st, That the testator did not assume, &c. 2dly, that he did not assume within five years, concluding to the country.

The jury found, that the testator did assume upon himself, in manner and form as set forth in the declaration, but that he did not assume within five years, and assess the plaintiff's damages to £240 : 14, upon which the court gave judgment.

The defendant filed exceptions, stating, that on the trial, the defendants offered as conclusive evidence, a decree of dismission in a suit in chancery brought by the plaintiff, against the defendant, for a specific performance of the contract laid in the declaration—That the plaintiff's counsel, opposed the admission of this evidence as conclusive, to which opinion the defendant excepted. It is not stated that the court admitted the evidence.

The judgment of the County Court, upon an appeal to the District Court, was reversed, because the evidence offered by the defendant, was rejected.—From this judgment, an appeal was prayed to this court.

THE PRESIDENT. There appear to be many imperfections in this record, from the institution of the suit, to its final decision in the District Court. The declaration states a promise by the testator, to give the plaintiff as much, as he should give to any of his own children; and a breach of this promise is alledged, without avering, *how much he gave to either of his own children, or to what the plaintiff's claim amounted.*

The plea is non-assumpsit within five years, without saying *before the institution of the suit*; so that strictly, it must refer to the time of the plea, which was in October 1787: and it concludes to the country, instead of the court; by which, the plaintiff is precluded, from bringing himself within the benefit of some of the exceptions from the act of limitations, by a replication.

The jury find one issue for the plaintiff, and the other for the defendant, and yet give damages to the plaintiff, upon which judgment is rendered by the court.

The bill of exceptions, (which is not sealed by the court,) states very imperfectly, the record offered in evidence, and does not state, that the court gave any opinion upon the subject. The District Court merely reverse the judgment, without dismissing the suit, directing a new trial, or awarding a repleader. The latter, this court would have directed, if they had found in the record, any good pleading to begin at. But the declaration is too faulty to be sustained. The breach assigned, is not sufficient, as is does not aver the quantity, or quality of the gifts made by the testator to his own children, or at what time they were made, so as to reduce the demand to some kind of certainty.

This might have been aided by verdict, if that had been rendered upon the trial of a proper issue: but when we are seeking for a good foundation, upon which to erect future pleadings, and find all defective, including the declaration itself, the uncertainty cannot be cured. In giving the judgment therefore, which the District Court ought to have given, we must dismiss the suit with costs.

NELSON *against* NELSON.

THIS was a suit instituted in the High Court of Chancery, by the appellant, for the specific execution of a parol agreement made between himself and the defendants, his brothers, in the life-time of their father, that whether their father should die testate or intestate, they would make amongst themselves an equal distribution of his estate. The bill states, that the father made a will and gave to the plaintiff a very unequal portion of his estate, tho' his eldest son and heir.

The Chancellor dismissed the bill, and the plaintiff in that court appealed.

THE PRESIDENT delivered the opinion of the court.

The great objection made to the relief prayed for by the appellant is, that agreements of this sort, are opposed to the rules of society, carrying with them strong marks of disrespect

and

and irreverence to the parent, and ought therefore not to be countenanced in a Court of Equity.

It is true, that obedience to parents during infancy, and respect through life, is not only a natural duty, but one, on which depends the peace and happiness of families, and consequently of society; and therefore if the present agreement could by any means produce effects like those stated at the bar, however strong the evidence might be that such an agreement was made, it would meet with no favor with us, as being leavened with moral turpitude, and unfit for discussion even, in a Court of Equity. Yet we cannot say, that a case may not exist, where such an agreement might be acquitted of those objections——and the present is a strong instance of such a case.

The parent, had always declared a settled intention to make an equal distribution of his estate amongst his sons. As he approached to the weak and infirm state of old age, when the mind, having lost its wonted vigor might be easily susceptible of any impressions; it was to be apprehended, that he might be induced to make considerable changes in the disposition of his estate. His eldest son having left the family and settled himself elsewhere, leaving his brothers around the father, might justly, or unjustly entertain suspicions, that they might derive advantages from this circumstance. A jealousy of this sort tho' unfounded, might produce heart burnings, and domestic feuds amongst them. To prevent this, might have been the prevailing motive which governed the brothers, and an agreement founded upon such a motive could not be objected to, as tending to produce public, or private inconvenience. To effect this end, we should expect to see a written agreement, ascertaining clearly the intention of the parties, deposited with some common confidential friend, under injunctions of secrecy, which would certainly answer better the object of the parties, than by making it the subject of conversation to house-keepers and overseers, as in this case. Tho' a written agreement might have been more proper, as being thereby less liable to misconstruction, yet a parol agreement, made before the act against frauds and perjuries took effect, might be enforced in this court.

In this case, the proof of the agreement is too slight. A casual conversation amongst the parties is heard, not respecting the agreement, or the particular terms of it, but the division of the father's estate. The agreement was made in March 1787, a few months after the act of frauds took effect; but as this is not noticed by the parties, or the counsel, it may not be important

important, and all events it is not neceſſary to conſider it; for there is no ſerious, ſolemn agreement proved, upon which a decree can be founded.

The decree muſt be affirmed.

KEEL & ROBERTS
against
HERBERT'S Executors.

A SUPERSEDEAS in this cauſe, was obtained againſt Herbert, who afterwards, and before ſervice of the writ, died. This court, on motion, awarded a new ſuperſedeas againſt the executors, which was executed, but afterwards quaſhed it, and awarded a *ſci. fa.* to hear errors againſt the executors; being of opinion, that the ſecond ſuperſedeas, could not be conſidered as a continuing proceſs, but a new one, and therefore, that the executor could not ſue upon the bond firſt given for proſecuting the ſuperſedeas.

THORNTON Executor of CHAMP,
againſt
JETT.

THIS was an action brought by the appellants in the Diſtrict Court of Northumberland, laying an aſſumpſit to themſelves. At the trial, the court, thinking the action not ſuſtainable upon the evidence given, directed a nonſuit, to which the plaintiff ſubmitted, but filed a bill of exceptions to the opinion, and obtained a ſuperſedeas to bring up the record before this court.

THE PRESIDENT. Whether the action was ſuſtainable or not, it is unneceſſary for the court now to decide—the plaintiff having ſubmitted to the nonſuit, which he was not bound to do, he has deſerted his cauſe, and therefore, he cannot now avail himſelf of an objection to the opinion of the court, in awarding it—the writ of ſuperſedeas muſt be quaſhed.

As

As to the costs, the court (except the President) were of opinion, that the assumpsit being laid to the plaintiffs themselves, they ought to pay the costs.

THE PRESIDENT said, that the reason why executors pay no costs, is, that they are in pursuit of their duty; and therefore he could see no reason, why this case should be distinguished from others, where the action is brought upon an assumpsit to the testator.

CATHARINE & BENJAMIN TURNER,

against

CLEAR TURNER Executrix of SAMPSON TURNER, deceased.

THE appellee, brought an action of detinue against the appellants in the County Court, in 1783, for the recovery of two slaves. The declaration states a possession in the testator, and in the plaintiff as executrix. Upon the general issue, the plaintiff offered to give in evidence, a parol gift of the slaves in dispute to Sampson Turner, by his father, a few years previous to the institution of the suit; which being admitted by the court, an exception was taken to the opinion, and a verdict being rendered for the plaintiff below, at a court held in the year 1789, the defendant appealed to the District Court of Suffolk, where the judgment being affirmed, an appeal was prayed to this court.

The PRESIDENT. The court are of opinion, that the judgment of the County Court is erroneous, in admitting the appellee, to give evidence of a parol gift of the slaves in dispute, supposed to have been made by Joseph Turner, the father, to his son Sampson Turner, the testator of the appellee; since if such gift had been really made, it being subsequent to the year 1758, no estate in the slaves passed to the said Sampson thereby, for want of a deed, or will in writing, according to the act of Assembly, passed in the year 1758, intituled, "an act to prevent the fraudulent gifts of slaves." And although it should appear, that the gift in this case was such, as was meant to be declared valid, either by the act passed in the year 1785, intituled,

led, " an act to prevent frauds and perjuries," or the act passed in the year 1787, intituled, " an act to explain and amend the acts for preventing fraudulent gifts of slaves;" yet nevertheless, the proof in the present case, was inadmissible, and the gift void; both of those acts, being prospective in their operation, and not retrospective of cases happening before; especially as to this supposed gift, on which the suit was commenced in 1783.

The judgment of the District Court is therefore erroneous, and must be reversed. The judgment of the County Court must also be reversed, the verdict set aside, and a new trial awarded; upon which, no evidence is to be admitted, to prove a gift of the slaves in dispute, except a deed in writing, or last will as the said act of 1758 required.

WILCOX *against* ROOTES and others.

THIS cause, came on before the District Court of Prince Edward, upon a summons issued by the order of the court, on the motion of Mrs. Wilcox the widow, and of Susannah Wilcox, the heir at law of Edmund Wilcox against Philip Rootes and others; requiring them to produce the will of the said Edmund Wilcox; and on a cross motion of the said Rootes and others, against Mrs. Wilcox, and the heir at law, to admit the said will to record.

The will being produced, it bore date the 25th of April 1781, and contained bequests of his whole estate to the appellees. The probate was contested by the appellants, who produced evidence, to prove the marriage of the testator, with the appellant Susannah, the widow, after the making of this will, and the subsequent birth of the other appellant.

The whole of the evidence is spread upon the record, as well that, which proves the execution of the will, as that, relating to the subsequent marriage of the testator, and the birth of a child. The record further states, that the testator married in 1783, had a child, and died in May 1785. That there was strong reasons to believe, that one of the devisees in the will, was the natural son of the testator—That the testator, the night before his death, expressed a desire to make a provision for his said supposed son.

The court admitted the will to record, from which order, the widow and heir at law appealed.

The

The queſtion made was, whether the will ought to have been admitted to record, ſince it was revoked by the ſubſequent marriage of the teſtator, and his having a child. It was contended for the appellant, that no principle of law was better eſtabliſhed, than this; that marriage and the birth of a child is an abſolute revocation of a will, made prior to the happening of thoſe events. If ſo, it is, as if it had never been made, and of courſe, it is improper that it ſhould be proved as a will.

To this it was anſwered by the counſel for the appellees, that let the doctrine concerning implied revocations be, as it is ſtated on the other ſide, yet on a collateral motion like this, the court have nothing to do with inquiries of this ſort. If all the requiſites of the law, which give validity to the will, have been complied with, the court, on a motion to receive the probate of it, are bound to admit it to record; leaving the parties to conteſt the force and validity of it, upon collateral points, in ſome other form. The only queſtions before the court on ſuch a motion, are, whether the will was duly executed by the teſtator, is it his laſt will, and was he capable of making it at the time?

Beſides, tho' ſubſequent marriage and having a child, be a revocation of the *bequeſts* in a will, it does not render the party *inteſtate*; and if the will be not proved, the executor cannot qualify. The will may be good to ſome purpoſes, and void as to others: but becauſe the bequeſts are revoked, it does not follow that the appointment of an executor, ſhould alſo be revoked, which muſt be the caſe, if the will could not be proved, and admitted to record.

The PRESIDENT delivered the opinion of the court.

The ſubſequent marriage, and having of a child, was clearly an implied revocation of the will, and ought to operate as ſuch; ſince the teſtator did not after thoſe events took place, republiſh his will, or ſignify an intention, that it ſhould be eſtabliſhed, or have any force or effect after that period: that his mind upon this ſubject, was otherwiſe inclined, appears clearly from the evidence ſtated in the record. The judgment muſt therefore be reverſed, without prejudice to any written or nuncupative will, made after the marriage and birth of the child, which may be offered, and proved according to law.

CASES ARGUED AND DETERMINED IN THE SPECIAL COURT OF APPEALS IN THE FALL TERM OF THE YEAR, 1792.

THORNTON Executor of THOMPSON, & GEORGE GRAY and Wife,

against

ALEXANDER SPOTSWOOD.

THIS was a suit in equity, instituted originally by the appellants against the appellee, in the County Court of Spotsylvania. The material facts in the case are as follows *viz.*

A. Spotswood the grandfather of the appellee, on his marriage, settled an annuity of £500 on his wife payable quarterly, and charged his Mine tract of land therewith; with power of distress, and *nomine pœnæ*. By his will, he devised all his estate to his son John, the father of the appellee, in tail. After the death of the G. father, John entered upon the estate devised to him; and his mother, by deed, released to him one half of her annuity, and then intermarried with Mr. Thompson, the father of Mrs. Gray, and the testator of the other appellant. John Spotswood previous to his death, gave to Mr. Thompson two bonds, and drew two several bills of exchange in his favor, for the amount of the arrears of the annuity then due, and shortly after died. The bills were negociated by Thompson, and finally came by assignment into the hands of a Mr. Walker, who commenced suits thereon, against the executors of John Spotswood, and having obtained judgments, took out executions, which

which were returned "*nulla bona.*"—It does not appear, in whose possession those bills are. The plaintiffs have them not. Mr. Thompson, having by his will devised to the appellant Mrs. Gray, *all the debts due* to him from the *estate of John Spotswood*, also departed this life. The appellee, is the eldest son and issue in tail of John Spotswood.

The County Court, decreed to the appellants Gray and Wife, the full amount of the bills of exchange, with 10 per cent damages; also the amount of the two bonds, and nearly one years annuity, which became due after the bills and notes were given; (deducting therefrom, a sum due from Thompson, for land of the appellees, sold to him by John Spotswood the father,) with interest thereon: and the Mine tract was decreed to be sold, to satisfy this decree, unless discharged by the appellee, within a limited time.

John Spotswood the father, by his will, devised all his estate (not intailed) to his son John.

The decree of the County Court was upon appeal to the High Court of Chancery reversed, from which, the present appellants appealed to the Court of Appeals; and a majority of that court not chusing to sit in the cause, a Special Court was summoned.

WARDEN for the appellants. There are two questions to be considered.—1st, Whether the mine tract is liable to satisfy the appellant's demand.—And 2dly, Whether a Court of Chancery has jurisdiction of the case.

The first point is dependent upon another, to wit, whether the annuity be extinguished or not, by the bills and bonds? I am to contend that they are not. The annuity, being of as high dignity as a bond, and higher than a bill of exchange, cannot be extinguished by them at law, or in equity: they are only additional securities. If the annuity exist at law, surely a Court of Equity will not assist, to take away the security, so long as the debt continues unpaid.

Upon the second point; it is the peculiar province of a Court of Equity, to assist in cases, where there is not a compleat remedy at law. This is to be presumed in the present case, as the defendant in his answer, hath not set forth, that there was property on the premises subject to distress, sufficient to satisfy the annuity.

WASHINGTON for the appellee. A Court of Chancery has not jurisdiction in this case, whether the annuity be extinguished or not. If the latter, then the executor by the 32 *Hen.* 8

might have diftrained on the land, in the poffeffion of any perfon, claiming by, or from the G. father; or, he might have maintained an action of debt at common law, againft the executors of John Spotfwood, for the rent accruing in his life-time. *Co. Litt.* 162 *b.* 5 *Co. Rep.* 118, 4 *Co. Rep. Ognels* cafe. Fairfax *vs.* Lord Derby, 2 *Vern.* 612, which laft cafe, is in point as to jurifdiction. A Court of Chancery will never interfere in cafes of this fort, unlefs the remedy be loft at law, by fraud in the tenant, as by depafturing the land &c. 1 *Eq. Ca. Ab.* 32.

If the annuity be extinguifhed, then it is too clear to be argued, that the remedy was only at law againft the executors of John Spotswood. But if the appellants do come into a court of equity, then I contend, that though the annuity might not be extinguifhed at law, yet it will be confidered as being fo in that court, and of courfe, the remedy could only be againft the *executors*, and not againft the *iffue in tail.* After fo long an acquiefcence on the part of Thompfon; his abfolutely negociating the bills; and of courfe receiving the amount of them, long ago, this court, will prefume an agreement between the parties, that the bonds and bills, fhould be accepted as a difcharge of the annuity, and as an exchange of the fecurity. In any point of view then, the decree of the County Court againft the iffue in tail, was erroneous.

But this is not the only error. The decree, is for the amount of the bills of exchange, in favor of the legatee, although neither the legatee, nor the executors of Thompfon are in poffeffion of the bills, or entitled to the benefit of the judgments recovered upon them, by affignment from Walker, or otherwife; and although Thompfon, has once received the value of them, from the perfon, to whom he endorfed them, (as is to be prefumed,) and neither he, nor his executors have been called upon by Walker to pay them, and probably, never may be called upon.

The moft which the appellants could afk for, would be fecurity, to indemnify them in cafe the amount of thofe bills fhould be hereafter recovered of them, and even this, could not with propriety be required of the *heir.*

But if the appellee be liable, to pay the amount of thefe bills, Mrs. Gray has no right to it, fince this is *not a debt due to Thompfon from Spotfwoods eftate,* and therefore is not included in the devife to Mrs. Gray.

The court was unanimoufly of opinion, that the appellants remedy, if any he had, was at law. That whether the
annuity

annuity was extinguished or not, at law, it was so in equity, under all the circumstances of this case, and that of course the appellants had mistaken their right, as well as their remedy.

The decree of the High Court of Chancery

was affirmed.

The Executors of WILLIAM HUNTER, and

the Executors of HERNDON,

against

ALEXANDER SPOTSWOOD.

THIS was a suit brought by the appellee in the High Court of Chancery, against the appellants. The case as extracted from the bill, answer, depositions, and exhibits was shortly as follows, viz. John Spotswood the father, died sometime in the year 1758, seized of a considerable entailed estate, part of which, consisted of very valuable iron works, and leaving a widow, (who afterwards intermarried with John Campbell,) as also the appellee his eldest son and heir at law, and one other son. Campbell, after his intermarriage, agreed with the said Hunter, to sell him the proportion of the iron made at the works, to which he would be entitled, in right of his wife's dower in the same; and Bernard Moor, the guardian of the appellee, and executor of John Spotswood, agreed to deliver the same to Hunter, upon his undertaking to pay for Campbell, a debt due from his wife to the executor, for property belonging to the estate, and sold to her before her intermarriage; and also one third of the expences, which might be incurred in carrying on the iron works. In consequence of this agreement, the iron was delivered to Hunter, who paid to the executor, the debt due from Campbell on account of his wife, and part of the expences. Campbell having left this country, attachments were

were sued out against his effects by Hunter, who had a considerable claim against him; as also as by Bernard Moor, to recover the amount of the expences due from him on acount of the iron works, which then remained unpaid. B. Moor obtained a judgment in the County Court, which was reversed in the General Court, and the attachment quashed, "it appearing to that court, that Campbell had given public notice of his intention to leave the country, which was known to his creditors." But Herndon (the sheriff,) having levied the attachment upon property belonging to Campbell, the court directed, that he should sell the same, and pay the money to Hunter, he giving security, to be accountable for it, in such manner as the court should thereafter direct.

At the sale of the attached effects, Hunter purchased to the amount of £650, but failed to give security, according to the direction of the court. He declined receiving the balance of the money, amounting to about £750, which *with interest*, is now claimed from Herndon's executors.

The appellee also claims from Hunter's executors, the £650 with interest, and also about £300, the balance of Campbell's debt, due for the expences of the iron works.

Hunter's executors answered, and also put in three pleas; to wit: 1st, to the jurisdiction—2d, the act of limitations; and 3d, want of right in the plaintiff to sue.

Herndon's executors in their answer say, that the money died in the hands of their testator, and therefore it ought not now to be paid in specie.

The bill being taken for confessed, as to Campbell, for £1717 : 0 : 10¾, the court decreed the same to be paid by that defendant. That £697 : 3 : 11½ part thereof, in the hands of James Hunter, should be paid by his executors, and £722 : 13 : 7½ other part thereof, remaining in the hands of Herndon (both sums bearing interest from the 3d of May 1770,) should be paid by his executors to the plaintiff, after deducting the costs of those defendants: the plaintiff to give such bond and security as the law requires.

WASHINGTON, for the appellee began.

The plea to the jurisdiction cannot be sustained.—This suit, is brought for the purpose of enforcing a settlement, of a long and complicated account, subsisting between different persons, but the whole so interwoven, that compleat justice could not be done, unless all those persons were before the court. In cases where an *action of account* may be brought, a suit in equity may properly be sustained. 1 *Eq. Ca. ab.* 5.

Much

Much stronger is this case, when, by resorting to this tribunal, multiplicity of suits are prevented. Thus, if Spotswood had sued B. Moor and recovered, Moor would recover against Hunter. So, if he recover against Herndon's executors, they must recover against Hunter's executors. All the parties being before the court, a decree is made against Herndon's executors, for the money retained by that testator, and against Hunter's executors, for the money received by theirs.

The next objection to a recovery, is the act of limitations—as to the £650 received by Hunter, from Herndon, there can exist no doubt. Hunter was not only a trustee for that money, in the same manner as Herndon would have been, had he retained it, but he is guilty of a fraud, in obtaining the possession of Campbell's property, from *an officer of the court*, against the order of that court; and that too, under a promise to give bond and security, as the order required, which he afterwards refused to do. Cases of trust, or fraud, are without the operation of the act of limitations.

As to the remaining sum of £300, respecting which an account is directed, there is more difficulty; but I am inclined to think, that there are sufficient circumstances in the case, to take it out of the operation of the act.

Hunter, having received the profits of an infant's estate, he is a trustee for those profits, and therefore cannot protect himself by length of time. Again—the iron in the hands of Hunter, was a deposit, placed there by Campbell, chargeable with the payment of a certain debt to Spotswood, which places him in the situation of a trustee, bound to execute the trust for which the pledge was placed in his hands. But I principally rely, upon the particular circumstances of this case. The appellee after his arrival at age, appears to have been totally in the dark as to his affairs, which had been conducted by his guardian, until a few years before the late war commenced; and this suit was brought shortly after its conclusion. There are many cases, which do not come within any of the exceptions from the act of limitations, and yet are construed to come within the equity of them. as if the time has elapsed during a period when no executor has qualified, or where there is a contest respecting the right of administration.

As to the right of the appellee to sue, it is clear that if he cannot, no other person can. He is entitled to the subject of recovery, namely, the profits of the land, and whatever objection might have been made to him at law, in this court none can exist. Objections

Objections are made to the depositions of two of the witnesses, on the ground of interest. To one of them, because he is the executor of one of the securities of B. Moor, in his capacity of guardian; to the other, because he was security for B. Moor, on his suing out the attachment against Campbell. As to the first, the record does not shew that he is executor. But if it did, the interest is too remote to preclude him from giving testimony—4 *Burr.* 2255—1 *Str.* 575 are stronger than the present. Again—both witnesses were cross examined by the objecting party, which estops him now, to impeach them on the ground of incompetency—*Vern.* 254—2 *Bac. Ab.* 289—4 *Burr.* 2252 1 *Ld. Ray* 730.

As to the objection to the other witness, there is no colour for it; because, whether Spotswood succeeds, or fails in this cause, it will not bar Campbell of his action, on the attachment bond, if the attachment issued illegally.

As to Herndon's executors, the principal objection is, to the claim for interest on the money retained by him. I admit, that if he actually kept the money by him during the whole time, he ought not to pay interest. But the answer admits, that this was not the case; for if it were, the money could not die in his hands, but would at this day, be specifically the same, that it was when received. A tender, will not even in equity prevent interest from running, unless the money were kept, and no profit made of it; and this should be sworn to by the party. 2 *Ch. Cas.* 206—2 *P. Wms.* 378—2 *Vern.* 192.

For the appellants, it was argued by MARSHALL, WARDEN, and STARK.

They contended that this was a stale demand, putting the act of limitations out of the question, and ought not to be countenanced in a Court of Equity. The plaintiff came of age in 1768, and this suit was not commenced until 1784. It appears, that within a short period after his taking possession of his estate, he had a schedule of it delivered to him. Even if Hunter, is to be confidered as a trustee of the profits, received during the infancy of the plaintiff, still, the act of limitations will run, against a suit to recover those profits. 1 *Eq. Ca. Ab.* 304—if the iron is to be considered as a deposit in the the hands of Hunter, and so like to goods pledged, there cannot exist a case of a sale, where the same argument may not be urged. The truth is, that the iron was sold by Campbell, to Hunter, and he, assumed to pay so much to B. Moor for it. As to the fraud charged upon Hunter, there is not more, than exists in every case

case of a breach of promise to pay money, or to perform any act. But if it were a fraud, still the act of limitations will begin to run, from the time it is discovered.

The objection to the jurisdiction was not relied upon.

They observed that the order of the General Court, directing Herndon, to pay the proceeds of the attached property to Hunter, was very unusual and improper, upon attachments of this sort, and could be accounted for in no other way, than by supposing, that the money was intended to be paid to him as a creditor of Campbell: the General Court at that time, having an equitable jurisdiction in cases of attachments against absentees.

The cases cited to prove, that the cross examination of a witness, amounts to a waiver of all exceptions to his competency, must have been decided upon the principle, that the party knew of the objection at the time of the examination, otherwise the doctrine would be unreasonable and absurd.

As to Herndon's executors, it was contended to be a settled rule, that a sheriff, or a stake holder, pays no interest. Interest is a retribution for the use of money, and therefore, if the person having the principal money in possession, is not permitted to use it, (being liable at any moment to be called upon for it,) he ought not to pay interest.

The answer (it is said,) does not state that the money was unemployed by Herndon: if it had, it would not have been evidence, since the contrary not being charged in the bill, such an allegation would not have been responsive to it. Herndon was not bound to keep the identical money by him. He might have deposited it with a friend for safe-keeping, by which means it might have been lost. The money might well have died in his hands, as the answer states, without his having parted with it, when it is recollected, that this country, was at that time full of James river bank notes, which were totally lost to the holders, by the war.

The Court, were just about to deliver an opinion, when it was observed by Mr. Marshall, that it did not appear in the record, or by the decree, that publication against Campbell, had been made in the Gazette, which ought to have been done, he being an absent debtor, and not served with the process—that without a publication, Campbell was no party to the suit: and therefore a decree, against persons called upon to pay *his* money, would be as improper, as if he had been *personally* decreed to pay it. And tho' the Chancellor ordered, that publication should be
made,

made, yet the execution of that order is not to be presumed, unless there be evidence of it in the record.

A certificate, was then produced from the clerk of the High Court of Chancery, stating, that due publication had been made; but this was not considered as sufficient, by a majority of the court.

In answer to the objection, it was argued, that no person could take advantage of this omission, but Campbell, who had not appealed.

But the court, for this reason only, reversed the decree, and sent back the cause to the High Court of Chancery.*

CASES ARGUED AND DETERMINED

IN THE

COURT OF APPEALS

IN

THE SPRING TERM OF THE YEAR,

1793.

HOYLE *against* YOUNG.

THIS was an action of slander, brought by the appellee, in the District Court of Petersburg. The declaration states, that the plaintiff was a merchant of good fame, and free from the crime of embezzlement or keeping false and unjust accounts, and that the defendant not ignorant &c. but maliciously intending to deprive him of his reputation as a merchant, and to subject him to infamy &c. falsely &c. spoke of the plaintiff then being a merchant, certain false &c. words to the following purport, viz. "Mr. Young I must tell you, that you have received

---

* The Chancellor having corrected the error, by stating in his decree, that evidence of publication was proved to him, the cause went back to the Special Court of Appeals, where the decree was affirmed in *toto*.

"ceived more tobacco than you have accounted for to the house, (meaning the mercantile house of which the plaintiff and defendant were partner's.") No *colloquium* is laid. Plea not guilty. At the trial, the defendant offered a demurrer to the evidence, stating the testimony given at the trial on the part of the plaintiff, which was objected to by the plaintiff, because the defendant had given evidence on his part, tho' he admitted, that that testimony was only offered in mitigation of damages: what that evidence was, does not appear. The Court refused to receive the demurrer after the defendant had introduced testimony on his side, to which opinion the defendant excepted.

Verdict and judgment for the plaintiff from which the defendant appealed.

CAMPBELL and WICKHAM for the appellants. As to the point relied upon in the exceptions, it must be given up.

The question will then be, whether the words laid in the declaration, be actionable, or not? Some words, are actionable in themselves, if spoken of *any person*—as to charge him with the commission of such a crime, as might endanger his life &c. others, are actionable only, when spoken of a person, whose *office* or *profession* distinguishes him from others; with respect to such persons, some words are actionable, without any averment, or explanation whatever: as to call a merchant a bankrupt. Others, are not of themselves actionable, unless spoken of the person, *in his official* or *professional character*, any more than they would have been if spoken of a person not bearing that character. In cases of this sort, therefore, the words ought to be made to apply to the person in *that particular character*, by laying a *colloquium*. 2 *Esp.* 235. The words as laid in this declaration, do not necessarily impute any crime, or improper conduct to the defendant: besides, they are too general, 2 *Espinasse*, 252.

The PRESIDENT.—Although the appellant's counsel in their argument of this cause, abandoned the exception taken to the opinion of the Court, refusing to receive the demurrer to evidence, yet we have considered it, thinking it important to the practice, and necessary to be settled. We have been able to derive but little aid upon this subject, from the English books, and have therefore taken it up, on principle. To permit a party to go fully into the trial, and after demurring to the evidence, take his chance with the jury, and failing there, to try the court, would be highly improper, and repugnant to the spirit of the law, which prevents a plaintiff from suffering a nonsuit after the jury have retired. On the other hand, it would be equally improper to preclude him from a demurrer, because he had examined ed witnesses. We think the proper rule is, to allow a demurrer to evidence at any time before the jury retire, altho' the party demurring may have examined witnesses on his part. the whole evidence on both sides being stated; (which in all cases ought to be done) unless the court think the case clear against the party. In which case, the books agree, that the court may refuse to receive the demurrer. In this case, the opinion of the court as to this point was right, 1st, because the whole evidence was not stated, and 2dly, because we think the case was clearly against the defendant.

To consider the main question relied upon in this court, upon principle. The law has liberally provided remedies for every person injured in his person, property, or reputation. The plaintiff in this case, complains of a wrong done to his character. The jury think his complaint well founded, and that he has sustained damage thereby to a certain amount. Yet the court is applied to, to set aside the verdict, by declaring that the words charged in the declaration are not actionable. If a man be injured in his property to the value of five shillings, he may recover reparation therefor; and yet, if the injury tho' an hundred times more grievous, be offered to his reputation, it is said he is without redress by the principles of law, tho' the fact be established by a jury. If the books be consulted, it will be found, that in ancient times, the judges to discourage actions of slander, were very rigid indeed in their decisions, from whence arose the doctrine (long since exploded) that words should be taken in *mitiori sensu*. Discovering afterwards, that slanders were by this mean encouraged, a more rational and just principle was introduced, viz. " That words should be understood in the sense they were understood by the byestanders." In the case of How *vs.* Prinne, 2 *Lord Ray* 812. it was decided, that to charge a man with evil principles was actionable. In the present case, the words laid in the declaration, clearly import a charge against the defendant in his mercantile character. The declaration states him to be a merchant, and the whole of it taken together shews, that the words were spoken of him *as such*. It was contended, that the words, do not in themselves import a charge against his reputation. We admit that they might have been innocent. One man may properly say to another in private, by way of asking for information, or in the necessary discussion of a disputed point, that that other had not accounted for property placed in his hands. The case is quite different here— the charge is made publicly—it is laid to have been *maliciously* spoken

spoken, with intent to injure the plaintiff, and so the jury have found it. After this it would be highly improper in the court to set aside the verdict.

The judgment must be affirmed.

WILLIAMS & ROY, Executor of CORRIE,

against

CAMPBELL.

THIS was an appeal from the District Court of King and Queen. The appellants, on the 12th of October 1787, sued out of the General Court, a writ, in case, against the appellee, without any indorsement of the nature of the action. The sheriff executed the writ, and took appearance bail, and so returned the writ. At the rules in July 1788, a declaration in trover and conversion was filed, and a common order entered against the defendant, and sheriff, which was confirmed in July.—There were then continuances for five or six terms, in the General and District Courts, at two of which, the plaintiff and defendant, obtained commissions for examining their witnesses.

At the April term 1791, on the motion of the defendant, the District Court upon inspection of the writ, dismissed the suit with costs, it appearing, that the cause of action was not endorsed on the writ; to which order, the plaintiffs excepted, and filing a bill for this purpose, appealed to this court.

THE PRESIDENT delivered the opinion of the court.

By the law, as it formerly stood, the sheriff was often perplexed to decide, in what cases, he ought to require appearance bail. To remedy this, the act of 1777 describes the actions, in which it should, or should not be required; and as a direction to the sheriff, the plaintiff, on pain of having his suit dismissed with costs, is to endorse on the writ, the true species of action. Trover is one of those actions, in which appearance bail is not required.

It is contended, 1st, That the court could not dismiss the suit, (if in other respects it were proper,) upon inspection of the writ, without a plea in abatement.

This objection cannot be sustained.—If the motion had been made in proper time, the court, might have directed a dismission, upon inspection of the writ. 2dly,

2dly, That the motion was made, at an improper stage of the cause.—

As to the defendant himself, the motion was certainly made too late. He might have made it, during the term next after the judgment was confirmed in the office, but not after; and even if he had not been precluded by this omission, he would have been so, by his appearance afterwards in the District Court, without then making the objection.

As to the sheriff, he was not bound to take bail, and therefore, there was no pretence for entering judgment against him, either for want of a bail bond returned, or for insufficient bail. Of this judgment, it does not appear he had any notice; he might conclude the contrary, by hearing of the defendant's appearance, and that the contest was going on between the parties.

This being disclosed, before executing the writ of enquiry, the court, ought to have set aside the judgment against the sheriff—they might also have set it aside as to the defendant if moved for, without bail, on his pleading to issue.

The judgment must be reversed with costs, and the suit remanded; with directions to the District Court, to set aside the judgment as to the sheriff, and to proceed to execute the writ of enquiry against the defendant, unless he shall move to set aside the office judgment which he is to be allowed to do upon pleading to issue, and proceeding to trial immediately, without delay to the plaintiffs on that account.

DANIEL *against* ROBINSON'S Executors.

THE appellee, being dead, Warden moved, to enter his appearance for the executors, without waiting for a *sci. fa.* which he said was only necessary to force an appearance. The court granted the motion, and tried the cause, at the instance of the counsel for the appellee, altho' it was objected by Mercer, J. that a trial at this term would be a surprize upon the appellant, who might consider the appeal as abated until regularly revived. But it was said by the court, that the appellant ought to follow the cause.*

EDWARD.

---

* In the case of Wood *vs.* Webb, determined afterwards in October 1795, the court, upon a similar motion, refused to revive the appeal upon an appearance being entered, and directed a writ of *sci. fa.* to issue, saying, that the above case had not been duly considered, at the time the motion was granted.

EDWARD STEVENS,

against

John Taliaferro, Adm. of John Thornton, dec.

THIS was an appeal, from a judgment of the District Court of Fredericksburg, reversing a judgment of an inferior court, and awarding a repleader from the plea.

It was an action of debt, brought by the appellant, against the appellee, upon a bond given by the testator, and a certain John Pattie. The defendant, without taking oyer, plead in bar, " that the said John Thornton, was jointly bound with a cer- " tain John Pattie, in the said identical writing obligatory in " the declaration mentioned, and that the said John Pattie, " survived the said John Thornton, and this he is ready to ve- " rify wherefore, &c." To this plea, the plaintiff replied, " that he ought not to be precluded &c. because he says, in the " said writing obligatory, it is not expressed, that the said John " Thornton was jointly bound with the said John Pattie, as is " alledged in the plea, and if they were jointly bound, that by " an act of Assembly passed in the year 1786, " intituled, an act " concerning partitions, and joint rights and obligations; it is " therein declared, that the representative of one, jointly bound " with another, may be sued, as well as the surviving obligor him- " self; and he insists therefore, that the said action does not survive " against the said Pattie, but is maintainable against the said " John, &c. and this he is ready to verify—wherefore, &c." the record then proceeds thus, " and thereupon an issue was join- " ed by the parties."

Verdict and judgment was rendered for the plaintiff, in the County Court, and an appeal prayed to the District Court, where that judgment was reversed as above stated.

MARSHALL for the appellant.

The plea in this case, is faulty in two respects, and therefore, could oppose no legal bar to the plaintiff's recovery. 1st, It does not state, that the obligors *were not severally bound*, which they might have been, altho' they were also *jointly* bound. 2dly, It does not set forth, at what time John Thornton died; for if that event happened, after the law mentioned in the replication took effect, which was in 1787; then I conceive, that this case would come within the operation of that law, altho' the bond was executed long before. The same inconvenience, which

which is generally, and properly chargeable upon retrospective constructions of laws, would not exist in this case; for the two obligors, if they were both alive when that law took effect, stood upon equal ground, as to the chance of survivorship. If there had been a demurrer in this case, (let it have come from which ever side it might,) there could have been little doubt, but that judgment must have been given for the plaintiff; because the first fault in pleading being committed by the defendant, the demurrer would have reached it, however defective the replication might be.

Tho' there may be an objection to the informality in joining the issue, yet it is cured by the statute of Jeofails, and the verdict will not on that account be set aside.

The court informed Washington, who was about to argue the cause for the appellee, that there was no necessity to say any thing, as there was no difficulty in the case.

THE PRESIDENT. The plea is certainly sufficient, and if the act of 1786, were material in the case, the plaintiff might have set forth the time of Thornton's death in his replication, by way of avoiding the bar, relied upon by the defendant. What would have been the opinion of the court, upon the operation of that act, if the time of the death had been stated in the replication, need not be mentioned. The replication is certainly faulty, and containing the first slip, the District Court did right in reversing the judgment, and in setting aside the pleadings subsequent to the plea.

We are also of opinion that the judgment of the County Court is erroneous, there being no issue joined in the cause.

Judgment of the District Court affirmed.

PLESANTS SHORE & Co. & ANDERSON

against

ROSS.

THIS court, upon an appeal formerly taken in this cause from a decree of the High Court of Chancery, having ordered an issue to be directed by the Court of Chancery, to try, " what was the current and average price, in sterling mo-" ney, on the 18th day of April 1781, of tobacco passed at the inspections

"inspections of Page's, Richmond, Manchester and Petersburg;" the issue was made up accordingly, and directed to be tried in the District Court of Richmond.* The parties waving the trial by jury, consented, to submit the decision of the issue to five persons appointed by them for that purpose, or to any three of them, and that their report should be certified, and returned into the High Court of Chancery, in lieu of, and to have the same effect as the verdict of a jury, directed to be taken.

The referees made their report, and determined, that the current and average price in sterling money, on the 18th of April 1781, of tobacco passed at the inspections of Page's, Richmond, Manchester and Petersburg, was 17/6 one third per cwt.

This report being certified into the Court of Chancery, the appellants filed a bill, praying to set it aside, and stating, as the ground of their objection to it, that the referees had gone upon a palpable mistake in the rule adopted by them, in ascertaining the current and average price in sterling money, of the tobacco (mentioned in the issue,) on the 18th of April 1781. That instead of taking the current and average sterling price of the tobacco, as it was bought and sold, *just previous and subsequent* to the 18th of April 1781, (for on that very day there was no proof of any purchases having been made) the referees, had first fixed a paper money price to the tobacco, and then applied the scale of depreciation to that sum, in order to obtain the specie value, which they again converted into sterling money, according to the rates of exchange in a Northern state, where it varied very considerably, from what it was in Virginia. That by this circuitous and uncertain mode of calculation, a result was produced, in no manner corresponding with the real sterling value of tobacco about that time.

This bill was accompanied with affidavits, proving, that the sterling price of tobacco just before, and after the time mentioned in the issue varied from 6/, to 12/ sterling.

No answer was put in to this bill, and the court being satisfied with the report, entered a decree pursuant to what the Court of Appeals had prescribed, making the current and average price of the tobacco, as reported by the referees, the rule, by which the money was turned into that commodity.

From

---

* See the Chancellor's Rep. p. 147, where this case, from its commencement in the Court of Chancery, to its termination there, is very fully stated.

From this decree, Pleasants Shore & Co and Anderson appealed.

THE PRESIDENT delivered the opinion of the court.

The issue directed in this cause, was intended to satisfy the conscience of the Chancellor. It appears that his conscience was satisfied, and there is no doubt, but that his decree was formed in strict conformity with the conviction thereby produced. But as this court has the power of examining and correcting his decrees, we must be guided by the same conscientious principles; and if we are not satisfied with the award, we must pronounce, that he ought not to have been satisfied. For myself, I am so far from being satisfied that the price is rightly fixed, that I feel the fullest conviction on my mind of the contrary.

But the difficulty is, how we are to discover the principles upon which the decision of the referees was really made; and how the subject is to come before the court? If we consider the persons chosen by the parties in the light of arbitrators, and that the objection is made on the ground of mistake, as to facts, or principles, the answer is, that this mistake must appear upon the face of the award; and in this case, there is no such ground of objection. Affidavits may be introduced, but they must tend to prove partiality, or misbehavior in the arbitrators, and not mistake in law, or fact. When an issue is to be tried, it is under the superintendance of the court, who will prevent the introduction of improper testimony; and if the verdict be against evidence, they will certify this together with the verdict, and the Chancellor will not be satisfied. If no such certificate be made, still the Chancellor will in some instances direct a new trial, on affidavits proving misbehavior in the jury, afterwards discovered: but this he will not do, upon affidavits tending to prove that the verdict is contrary to evidence. The parties, have in this instance substituted referees for the court and jury; and the question is, whether the party objecting to the report, is bound by it, as if it had been a verdict certified without exception, and must abide the consequence of his own act, in taking the case out of its legal course? or whether, he may bring the mistaken principles on which the referees proceeded, before the court, as a ground for a new trial of the issue?

If the referees had certified the principles upon which they proceeded, there would seem to be no difficulty: it would come within the reason of those cases, where the mistake is apparent upon the face of the award. If the paper annexed to the

the bill, were really evidence of thofe principles, it would produce the queftion, whether the miftake was thereby rendered *apparent*; and in that cafe, I fhould feel no difficulty. But, there is no proof of the ground upon which they proceeded. They once agreed to give a certificate, but afterwards refufed. Whether they were right or wrong in doing fo, is immaterial. The plaintiff having alledged that this paper contains the ground of the report, the only difficulty is, whether the Chancellor ought not to have fufpended the confirmation of the report, until that fact was afcertained. On a thorough confideration of the fubject, and of its cofequences as a precedent, we think he was right, and

affirm the decree.

WHITE *againft* JOHNSON.

THIS was a fuperfedeas to a judgment of the General Court. The cafe was—Johnfon brought an action on the cafe in the General Court, againft one Watfon, and the writ, which was directed to the fheriff of —————— county, was returned executed, by White, thus, " executed, W. White D. S." without mentioning the name of his principal, or of the county in which he acted as deputy fheriff. No appearance being entered for Johnfon, a common order was entered againft him, and againft William White, deputy fheriff of ————— county, which was afterwards confirmed againft the defendant and fheriff, and a writ of enquiry was thereupon executed. The jury found damages for the plaintiff, and the judgment was entered up, againft the defendant Watfon, and *W. White, deputy fheriff of Louifa county.* To this judgment, a writ of fuperfedeas was awarded by this court.

RONOLD for the plaintiff in error. The judgment is not warranted by any of the proceedings, which appear in the record. The writ is not directed to the fheriff of any county; it is not executed by the deputy fheriff of any county; nor is the interlocutory judgment, rendered againft the deputy fheriff of any county; and yet, final judgment is entered againft W. White deputy fheriff of *Louifa* county. How did it judicially appear, that *White* who executed the writ, was deputy fheriff of *Louifa* county? There might be two perfons of that name, each of them deputy fheriffs of different counties.

But

But if this objection could be removed, there is another, which muſt be fatal: the judgment is rendered againſt the deputy inſtead of the *high* ſheriff.

By the General Court law, paſſed in October 1777, C. 14, § 14, if bail be not returned with a copy of the bail bond, the remedy is againſt the ſheriff; and that the *principal* is intended, when the legiſlature ſpeak of the reſponſibility of the ſheriff generally, will appear evident, by referring to other laws upon this ſubject. Thus, by the act of the 27th George II. C. 1, § 36, a remedy is given againſt *the ſheriff*, for not paying money received by him on an execution: and by the 3d *Geo.* III, C. 5, a ſpecific remedy is provided in ſuch a caſe, for the creditor, as well as for the *high ſheriff*, againſt the *deputy*. And this is exactly conſonant with the principles of the common law, by which, the high ſheriff alone, is liable for any breach of duty in the office of ſheriff, and no action will lie againſt the duputy. *Cowp. Rep.* 43.

DUVALL, for the defendant in error.

The act of 3d *Geo.* III, C. 3, § 3, requires, that where the deputy executes any writ, he ſhall endorſe thereon, the day and month when the ſame was executed, and ſubſcribe, as well the name of his principal, as his own. If the deputy in the preſent caſe, had purſued this direction, it might have been known, againſt whom to enter the judgment; and he ough· not, by having omitted to perform this part of his duty, to be permitted to take advantage of his own miſconduct. The declaration ſtates the county in the caption;—and therefore, it ought to be preſumed, that White was the deputy ſheriff of that county. As to the blank in the writ, that is cured by the act of feofails 5, *Geo.* I. The deputy ſheriffs in this county, are very different from thoſe officers in England, who act under a ſpecial authority from their principles. They qualify in open court, with the ſame formalities which are obſerved in reſpect to high ſheriffs, and in many caſes, they are recognized by our laws.

RONOLD in reply.—Though the deputy be puniſhable for a falſe return, in omitting to endorſe on the writ, the name of his principal, yet this omiſſion cannot warrant the entering up a *judgment* againſt him.

The PRESIDENT delivered the opinion of the court.

The caſes all prove, that in England, the remedy is againſt the high ſheriff only, (in whoſe name every thing is done,) for the official acts of his deputy; unleſs in inſtances, where by

particular

particular statutes, a remedy is given against the deputy. The same principle of law prevailed in this country, and was general, until the year 1763; when a law was made, giving to the creditor, a remedy by motion against the deputy sheriff, for money received by him on an execution. By the same law, the deputy was directed under a penalty, to put the name of his principal, as well as his own, to all *mesne* process executed by him. But if he failed to do so, neither this, nor any other law, authorized the entering of judgment against him, for not taking appearance bail upon such *mesne* process. The General Court law passed in 1777, warrants a judgment against the *sheriff*, which certainly means the *principal*, and not the *deputy*. The practice in the General Court, both before, and since the revolution, was to enter up judgment in such cases, against the deputy sheriff. But we are of opinion, that such practise was wrong, and unwarranted by any law.

The judgment therefore must be reversed, and the proceedings subsequent to the declaration set aside. The cause is to be remanded to the General Court, to be proceeded in *de novo*, from the return on the writ.

IRVIN, GALT, and Company,

against

ELDRIDGE & BRACKENRIDGE.

THIS was an appeal, from a judgment of the District Court of Prince Edward. The appellant, moved that court for judgment upon a forthcoming bond, executed by the appellees, the condition of which, (after reciting the execution, seizure, and re-delivery of the property by the sheriff in the usual form,) is, " that if the said Eldridge and Brackenridge do " deliver to the said sheriff, the said property, taken in execu- " tion and restored, at Buckingham courthouse, on the 26th day " of this month, or pay the said sum of £ 75 : 8, then the obli- " gation to be void, &c." The court over-ruled the motion, considering the bond to be informal and defective, in not stating, that the 26th day in the condition mentioned, was the day appointed *for the sale of the property.*

THE PRESIDENT. The act of 1769, C. 3 § 2, declares, "that if the owner of goods taken in execution, shall tender "sufficient security, to have the same forthcoming at the day "of sale, the sheriff shall take a bond from such debtor and se- "curities, payable to the creditor, reciting the service of such "execution, and the amount of the money, or tobacco due "thereon, and with condition, to have the goods forthcoming "at the day of sale appointed by such sheriff, and shall thereupon "suffer the goods to remain with the debtor at his risk, 'till "that time." But this court, in the case of Wood and Davis, determined, that it was not necessary for the bond to state, that the time when the property is to be produced, *is that appoint- ed for the sale of it*: that it is more proper, and more benefi- cial to the parties, that the bond should ascertain the *time*, and *place* of delivery, than that it should pursue the literal words of the law, which, do not require either to be inserted in the condition, but merely, that the property should be forthcom- ing, *at the day of sale appointed by the sheriff*. It is remarkable, that the next clause of the law, which gives the remedy, drops the expression of *the day of sale*, and says, "if the property be not delivered, *according to the condition of the bond*," a motion may be made. The court are therefore of opinion, that the bond in question, is neither defective nor informal.

The judgment must be reversed, and we should now proceed to enter it up for the appellant, as the District Court ought to have done, if it appeared to us, that the appellee had no other objection, or defence to make against it, than that, upon which we have decided. But as it is possible, that the defendants may have made payments, or may have other objections, which were not brought forward, in consequence of the opinion of the court be- ing in their favour, it will be most proper, to remand the cause to the District Court, that they may proceed to render judgment upon the bond, open however, to the defendants, to make any other objection thereto, than such, as respect the legality, or formality of the bond.

KENNEDY *against* BAYLOR.

THIS was a suit originally brought in the County Court of Berkeley, by Baylor, to foreclose the equity of redemp- tion, which Kennedy had in a tract of land. Kennedy in his answer,

answer, claimed certain credits, and the court directed an account to be settled by commissioners, which being done, and returned, the record states, "that it appearing to the court, "that the mortgagee had had possession of the land for some time, during which, it had sustained damage," other commissioners are appointed, to value the same—a second report, pursuant to the last order being made, the court, after deducting the amount of the damages so ascertained, from the sum found to be due by the first report, decreed the balance to the plaintiff—no replication was made to the answer, nor were any exceptions taken to either of the reports.

This decree was affirmed in the High Court of Chancery, from which an appeal was prayed to this court.

MARSHALL for the appellant, insisted upon the following errors in the decree.

1st, The cause coming on, upon bill and answer, the latter must be considered as being true in every part of it; and therefore, the payments alledged by the defendant to have been made, ought to have been allowed by the commissioners, two of which were not.

2d, The commissioners do not state when, or where they met to settle the accounts, or whether, the defendant had notice of their meeting.

3d, The decree is for more than the commissioners report to be due.

4thly, and principally.—The rents of the land, and the *injury it sustained*, during the plaintiff's possession, are referred to *commissioners*, instead of a *jury* to ascertain.

The PRESIDENT. As to the first objection, there is no doubt, but that the answer in this case, must be considered as being perfectly true. But the counsel mistakes, when he supposes, that the payments insisted upon in the answer, have not been allowed. All of them are, except a credit of wheat, the price of which the defendant could not ascertain, and perhaps did not, for that, or for some other reason bring before the commissioners.

The third objection is, that the decree is for more than the balance stated to be due by the report, and that too, with accumulated interest. But it does not appear, that the interest upon interest, amounts to a greater sum, than that, for which a deduction is made by consent of parties, on account of *miscalcu-*

lation

lation of interest. As to the principal sum, it does by no means appear, that the decree is for more than the report makes it. The decree therefore must be affirmed.*

REYNOLDS

against

WALLER'S heir at law, and administrator.

THE appellees instituted this suit in the High Court of Chancery, in order to recover back certain warrants, and the interest received upon them, also warrants for about 5000 acres of land, which their testator had obtained for his services during the war, and which had been unfairly purchased from him by the appellants, for the trifling consideration of £20, at a time when, the testator was intoxicated with liquor, and incapable of contracting. The purchase was made by Valentine, on account of himself and Reynolds, the latter of whom, afterwards became the sole proprietor, by purchase from the former of the whole interest. The fraud, was clearly proven to the satisfaction of the Chancellor, who decreed; that Reynolds should restore to the plaintiff, the military certificate received by him from the auditor, for the pay, and depreciation of pay due to Waller, with interest thereon from the 1st of January 1782; or if that certificate could not be restored, to deliver to the plaintiff other certificates, of the same kind, and of equal value, with like interest. And (part of the land warrants having been assigned by Reynolds, to Waller, in his life-time,) the court directed an issue, to ascertain what damages the plaintiff had sustained, by his intestate's not receiving the military land warrant, for the remainder of the land, to which he was entitled.

From this decree an appeal was prayed.

The PRESIDENT delivered the opinion of the court.

A more palpable imposition, was never practised, or better established, than in this case. Reynolds, though not a party in the fraud, was nevertheless, a partner with the person who committed it, and is therefore answerable. The

---

* The court took no notice of the other objections.

The decree, so far as it annuls the contract, is therefore right: it is also right in the relief afforded, as to the land.

As to the certificates, the relief granted is not exceptionable, so far as it compels restitution of them in specie, or others of equal value, in case, the identical certificates cannot be returned. But, if he can do neither of these things, to compel him to purchase at market, or to pay in specie, the nominal amount of the certificates, is in our opinion improper. The true period, at which to estimate their value, (in case the certificates cannot be restored,) is that, at which the cause is tried—this, is not like the case of Groves and Graves, which was a contract to deliver a certificate *at a future day*; after the day had passed, the party who was to have received the certificate, not being compellable to accept it, was entitled to its value on that day. But in this case, there was no contract. The bill is, for a specific restitution of the certificates fraudulently obtained, and therefore, if the appellant had at any time offered to restore them, or will now do so, the other party must receive them, or its value; of course, the present value ought to be the rule of compensation, if the certificates themselves cannot be restored.

The opinion and decree, was entered in the following words, viz.
" there is no error in so much of the decree, as sets aside the
" contract, pretended to have been made by Edward Valen-
" tine, with Edward Waller, decd. for the purchase of the lat-
" ter's claim on the public, for pay and depreciation, and a
" bounty in lands, nor in the relief afforded, so far as it relates to
" the land. But, that the said decree is partly improper, and
" in some instances defective, so far as it respects the certi-
" ficates, for the pay and depreciation. It is therefore decreed
" and ordered, that so much of the said decree, as sets aside the
" contract for the purchase, and directs the mode of relief as to
" the land, and costs, be affirmed, and that the residue of the
" said decree be reversed. And this court, proceeding to make
" such decree as to that part so reversed, as the said High Court
" of Chancery should have pronounced, it is further ordered
" and decreed, that the appellant restore to the appellee, the mi-
" litary certificate or certificates received by him from the au-
" ditor for public accounts, the 4th day of April 1785, for the
" pay, and depreciation of pay, due to the said Edward Waller,
" amounting to £ 283 : 16 : 7: or if those certificates can-
" not be restored, that he deliver to the appellee other certifi-

" cates,

"cates, of the same kind, and of equal value, if such he hath, to
"be ascertained, by an examination before the master commis-
"sioner of the said court, on the oath of the appellant upon in-
"terrogatories; but if not, then, that he pay to the appellee,
"the present specie value of such certificates, to be ascertained
"by the said commissioner, or by a jury, if either party shall
"require it. That the appellant also account before the said
"commissioner, for the specie value of all interest arising on
"the said certificate, as the warrants for such interest were
"worth, at the time he, or his assignee received, or might
"have received the same; and pay the amount thereof in specie
"to the appellee, discounting therefrom, the sum of £20, paid
"for the purchase, on the 23d of December 1784, with interest
"thereon from that day, until the money shall appear to have
"been repaid, by the receipt of interest as aforesaid.

WHITE, WHITTLE, & Company,

against

BANNISTER'S Executors.

THE appellees, as executors of Bannister, under a power in his will, leased certain mills called Battersea, belonging to the estate of their testator, to the appellants, who having received an assignment of a judgment obtained against the executors, insisted upon retaining so much of the rent, as was equal to the amount of the said judgment, they having fully paid up, what was due on account of rent, except as to this sum.——

The executors, refusing to admit the offset, distrained for the balance of the rent due, and the appellants filed their bill, praying an injunction, a discovery of assets, and that they might be permitted to retain, and be acquitted of so much of the rent. The ground of equity is, that the Battersea mills are subjected to the payment of debts by the following clause in the will, viz, " my will is, that my estate be kept together, and worked for the payment of all my just debts, which I wish to have done, in fair, and equal proportions,"—that the assets are thereby rendered abundantly sufficient to pay all the debts, as the executors had acknowledged.

The

The executors by their answer, insist, that under another clause in the will, the profits of the Batteriea mills are specifically devised, for the maintainance, and education of the three younger children of the testator, and contend, that they are not made liable to the payment of debts.

They say that all the estate has been sold, and applied to the payment of debts, superior in dignity to that, assigned to the plaintiffs. That there are claims yet unpaid, for several thousand pounds, more than they expected; and that, if the residue of the profits of the Batterlea mills, beyond the dower, be subject to the debts, present and ensuing rents, will not be more than sufficient to discharge debts, which have a preference to the plaintiff's; that they cannot ascertain the amount, or dignity of the debts yet unpaid, but are confident, they will exceed, what is yet due from the sales of the estate, and from sperate debts owing to the testator.

The cause coming on to be heard, on the bill, answer, exhibits and examination of witnesses, the court dismissed the bill, from which the plaintiffs appealed.

THE PRESIDENT delivered the opinion of the court.

A bill, to retain, and to set off a debt against rents due, has an unfavourable appearance. If creditors, purchasing from the executors, or, as in this case, renting an estate from them, shall be permitted to bring forth their claims against the testator, in discount, they might thereby gain an improper advantage over other creditors. The executors, might be involved in the trouble of accounting for the assets on every purchase, and in case of mistakes, might subject themselves to a devastavit.

The objection, has additional weight in this case, where the plaintiffs were not original creditors, but purchased up the debt for the purpose of a discount; or if in fact, they are not the real owners of the debt, (a point not clear,) they are endeavouring to gain a preference for another, by taking an assignment in trust, whilst they complain that the executors are preferring favorite creditors.

The appellants, aware of these objections, charge, that the executors were assured, and had acknowledged that the estate would be sufficient to pay all the debts, in which case, no objection could be made to the reasonableness of the discount. But this being denied by the answer, that foundation fails, and the injunction should be dissolved.

But another question occurs, and that is, whether the bill cannot be sustained as an original one, for a discovery of assets?

1st, A creditor may at law, either sue out execution upon a judgment obtained against the executors, and levy it on the visible property of the testator, if any,—or, if none to be found, 2dly he may proceed against the executors, as for a devastavit, on account of a misapplication of assets, or for that, which amounts to an admission of assets. Or 3dly, a creditor may not know the state of the assets, the amount, nor the claims against the estate. He may therefore file his bill in equity, to have a discovery of those matters, and on that discovery being made, may either proceed at law, or that court may retain the cause, and determine disputes between the parties.

Now, although at law, the judgment in question would be considered as amounting to an admission of assets, so, as to charge the executors, and a Court of Equity, would not interfere, to relieve against the consequence of that judgment, yet it would not by an original decree, charge an executor on that ground.

The bill in this case appears to be for a discovery. After charging, that the profits of the Battersea estate are assets, which would make the estate fully solvent, it calls upon the executors, to set forth the amount of the assets, and of the debts due from the estate; prays to be allowed to retain for this judgment, against the rent, and for general relief. The executors, answer very properly as to the Battersea estate, insisting, that the profits are not assets, but are made (by the will,) a fund for the education and maintainance of the three younger sons, who are entitled to the proceeds of the estate when sold.

But as to the discovery sought for, the answer is not so proper. The executors speak of sales, but do not specify the amount; they say, they have paid all that has come to their hands, in discharge of debts of superior dignity to the plaintiffs, without stating the amount, or even the names of the creditors, and the nature of the debts: thus, taking upon themselves, to judge of the dignity, and preference to which they were entitled, and thereby precluding, not only the court, from deciding upon those points, but the plaintiffs, from contesting that preference, by making those creditors parties. They say further, that there are claims against the estate, for several thousand pounds more than the testator thought he owed, the accounts respecting which, are not liquidated. They cannot ascertain the amount, or dignity of the debts due from the testator, but are confident, they will exceed the sums yet due for sales, as well as the sperate debts; but of these, they give no account. "They add, that if the residue beyond assets, be subject to debts, as much is due by specialties, and judgments entitled to a preference, as the present and ensuing years rents will discharge." The answer was filed in October 1791, so that it speaks of the two first years rents only, and there are consequently, three years, which may be clear of those superior demands. It does not appear (as the appellant's counsel contended,) that debts of inferior dignity had been paid.

Upon this view of the case, three questions arise. 1st, Whether the plaintiffs had a right to retain, or to set off. 2dly, Whether the answer is so satisfactory, as to entitle the executors to a dismission of the bill? and 3dly, whether the profits, are in part, or in the whole, assets, under the will.

The first question, is clear against the appellants, and therefore the injunction ought not to have continued.

The second question, has been shewn to be against the executors, and therefore, the bill should not have been dismissed, but a decree for a settlement of the executors accounts, should have been made.

The third question is a difficult one, yet we should have decided it, if there had been a full court. Upon a settlement of the accounts, the decision may be unnecessary.

The decree must be reversed with costs, and the injunction dissolved. An account is to be taken of the out-standing debts due to the testator at the time of his death, what have been collected since, and the balances yet due, distinguishing in the latter, such as are sperate, from such as are supposed to be desperate. An account is also to be taken of the sales of all the estate, real and personal, stating when sold, and the profits made from each tract of land, and of the slaves, until the sale thereof, and what hath been received, or is yet due of the amount of such sales. Also an account of any estate real or personal remaining unsold, and the profits thereof, (the Battersea estate excepted) also an account of administration as far as the executors have gone, shewing the application of what money hath come to their hands; also a state of liquidated debts yet due from the testator, with their dignity, and of the nature of such claims as are unliquidated; and also an account of the profits of the Battersea estate, distinguishing those of the mills, and tradesmen from each other and from those of the plantation. When these accounts are returned to the High Court of Chancery, it is to be decided, if necessary, whether the profits of the Battersea estate, beyond the widow's dower be subject in the whole, or in part to satisfy the demands of the appellants.

BAIRD

BAIRD & BRIGGS,

against

BLAIGROVE Executor of BLAIGROVE.

THIS was an action on the case, brought by the appellants in the District Court of New London. The declaration states, that the plaintiffs having obtained a judgment against a certain Jeremiah Glenn, and being willing to give to the said Glenn, an opportunity of disposing of his property to the best advantage, to enable him to satisfy the judgment, an agreement was entered into between the plaintiffs, the said Glenn, and the testator of the defendant, (which is set forth verbatim) whereby, the testator of the defendant bound himself to see the balance of the aforesaid debt, interest, and costs, (which should remain unsatisfied, by the property which the said Glenn might sell, for that purpose,) paid by October 1775: That the intention of the said agreement was, to favor the said Glenn, by enabling him to sell his property at the highest price. That in consideration thereof, the said testator, afterwards, &c. assumed upon himself, to pay such balance when required. The declaration then avers, " that the sale by G. was made, and a balance still remain-
" ed unsatisfied, of which the testator had notice; whereby an
" action accrued to the plaintiffs, to have of the said testator,
" the said balance, nevertheless," &c.

The agreement stated in the declaration, has three *scrolls*, opposite to each signature; but no part of the agreement, either in the beginning, conclusion, or attestation, says any thing, about its being sealed. The conclusion is thus " as witness our hands" &c, The attestation thus " teste."

Upon the general issue, the plaintiffs had a verdict, and upon motion, the judgment was arrested. From this judgment, the plaintiffs appealed.

RONOLD for the appellant. The error stated as the ground for arresting the judgment is, that this action is not sustainable; being founded upon an instrument under seal. This might have been a serious objection, if the fact had been true: but it is not; or at least it does not appear to be so, upon the face of the record; for in the first place, the court cannot say, that the agreement was sealed, and if they could, then 2dly, the action is not brought upon the agreement.

It

It is true, there are scrolls to the agreement, which might, or might not have been intended for seals; but it cannot be considered as a deed, unless it be mentioned to be sealed.

But if it were sealed, the agreement is not the foundation of the action. It is true, the declaration states the agreement, but yet, it avers, that the testator assumed in consideration of the *indulgence given to G.* not in consideration of the *agreement*.—This consideration is sufficient to maintain the action, since it might produce loss to the plaintiffs.

MARSHALL for the appellee—Whether this instrument be sealed or not, *the court* must determine upon an inspection of it, and if so, there can exist no doubt, that there are three seals to each signature. The calling it a sealed instrument, cannot make it one, unless it be actually sealed, which is the substantial part.

It is not easy to read this declaration, and not consider the agreement, to be the very foundation of the suit. It is set out in *hæc verba*, and the cause of its being made, is mere tautology, that being expressed in the deed, and would have resulted without the averment—the consideration is plainly referable to the agreement and to nothing else.—If it be to any thing else, it is to the *intention* of making it, which would certainly be an insufficient consideration—an assumpsit, in consideration of an intention in the other party to do a thing, would be clearly a *nudum pactum*.—The assumpsit is not stated to have been made, in consideration of an indulgence *actually* granted. Of course, it must refer to the *intention*, or to the *agreement*—if to either, the plaintiff cannot recover—if to the first, there was no right for want of a valid consideration, if to the second, the remedy was misconceived.

THE PRESIDENT. The court are not satisfied, that this is to be considered as a sealed instrument. It is in no part of it expressed to be sealed—the attestation is the same, as in common simple contracts, not under seal, nor does the declaration speak of it, as being of that dignity—it is true, there are scrolls annexed, but it may nevertheless remain a matter of doubt, whether they are to be considered as the seals of the parties?

However, it is unnecessary to determine this point, as we are of opinion, that if it were a sealed instrument, this action is sustainable. The agreement is only stated as inducement to that, which forms the real ground of the consideration afterwards alledged. The foundation of the action, is the subsequent assumpsit which is stated in the declaration, and there is no doubt, but that a parol agreement made subsequent to one under seal, may be declared upon, tho' it should alter the terms of the written agreement.

Judgment of the District Court reversed, and entered for the plaintiff upon the verdict.

KERR & Co. *against* 'LOVE.

THIS was an appeal from a decree of the High Court of Chancery, in a suit brought by the appellee for an account.

The PRESIDENT delivered the opinion of the court.

The debt claimed by the appellee, originated before the year 1776. The only evidence produced by him, respecting a quantity of molasses delivered by him, to the distillery at Norfolk, on account of the appellant, is, his own books, and oath.

The appellant in his answer, having denied, that this article was delivered by his direction, the oath, and books of the appellee, (in no case admissible, to charge a person with goods delivered by order to a third person, unless such order be otherwise proved,) ought not to have been admitted as evidence, to prove that article. And as there is no other testimony, to charge the appellant therewith, except his own admission, and a consent to be charged *upon certain conditions*, it ought to be made upon the terms of that concession, and should operate only so far against him.

Another charge exhibited by the appellee, is of sugar and wine, delivered on board a vessel of the appellant's, to the master thereof, for safe keeping; and this, is proved by an entry on the books of the appellee, made by his clerk, who is not now to be found; together with the oath of the appellee, to ascertain the quantity. This sort of evidence, tho' admissible in the case of a sale and delivery of goods, is not proper in this case, to charge the appellant with those articles, delivered for safe keeping, to the master of the appellant's vessel; since there is no evidence, that any part of them, came to his hands, except, what the answer admits—and therefore, this admission ought to be the rule by which the charge should be regulated.

As to the question of interest, this court, without controverting the general principles stated in the decree, are of opinion, that as the accounts in question were unliqidated, and disputed nated between the parties; they might have been adjusted, (notwithstanding the absence of the appellant,) with George Kerr his partner, or agent; or if such a connection were doubtful, an attachment bill might have been filed, at any time, for that purpose.

Under these circumstances, interest ought not to commence, but from the institution of this suit.

Decree reversed.

BANNISTER'S Executors
against
SHORE.

THIS was a bill filed in the High Court of Chancery, by the appellee, as administrator of his wife, against the appellants, to recover £1000, which (the bill states) Bannister had agreed to give as a marriage portion with his daughter the appellee's late wife. The evidence of this promise, was the deposition of the widow of Mr. Bannister, who proved, that her husband in different conversations with her previous to the marriage, had declared his intention once to have been, to give his daughter £1000. But upon a particular occasion, and previous also to the marriage, he told her, his embarrassments would oblige him to substitute 500 acres of land on Hatchers Run, in lieu of money. Also a letter from Bannister, addressed to his daughter, after marriage, in substance as follows, viz. " I mean to give my daughter in lieu of £1000 her
" intended portion, and I do hereby give to my said daughter,
" and her heirs, 500 acres of my Hatchers run tract, and 5
" slaves, as her dowry in marriage, subject to her husband's le-
" gal claim, whose unconditional right thereto is plain. And
" if I should be prevented from executing a conveyance to this
" effect, this shall stand as one—as witness my hand and seal:"
to this paper a seal was annexed. This letter was sent to Shore, and in his bill, he acknowledges that he received, and retained it, without any act proving his dissent; but says, that he did not mean to assent to it, supposing that there would be time enough afterwards, to shew his disapprobation. One of the defendants in his answer states, that previous to the marriage, he informed

the

the appellee, at the requeſt of Banniſter, that he intended to give his daughter land, inſtead of money, with which the appellee ſeemed well ſatisfied—another witneſs proved, that he had ſeen Banniſter and the appellee, upon the land mentioned in the above letter, ſearching out a fit place, whereon to erect buildings. Shore had a child by his wife, after which, the wife, and then the child died. After this, Banniſter conveyed the land before mentioned to his ſon John, but upon what conſideration does not appear.

The Chancellor decreed the £1000 to the plaintiff, from which the executors appealed.

WICKHAM for the appellants.

If Shore be entitled to the £1000, his remedy is entirely a legal one, and he might have recovered in an action upon the caſe. If ſo, a ſolid objection will lie to the juriſdiction of the court of Chancery.

Upon the ſubſtantial merits of the caſe, there ſeems to be but little difficulty.—Becauſe a father from the particular ſituation of his eſtate, may at one time intend to give a certain portion to a child, will it be contended, that he is afterwards bound to purſue that intention, whatever changes may take place in his fortune, and however inconvenient it may prove to him? Surely it cannot—beſides, this *intention*, if it can be called a *promiſe* in the preſent caſe, is merely an intended teſtamentary diſpoſition, which is at any time revocable. The anſwer ſtates, that Mr. Shore was informed of this alteration of Mr. Banniſter's intention, before his marriage, and was ſatiſfied.

This fact, is compleatly eſtabliſhed by the retention of the letter or deed, without diſſenting from the terms contained in it.

He ought not after circumſtances are altered, to be permitted to ſay, that he did not *aſſent* to thoſe terms, or to complain, of being deceived by them.

If then, Shore has no title to the money, the next queſtion is, whether he can have any to the land?

The letter from Banniſter, tho' it may not have all the forms, moſt certainly contains the ſubſtantial parts of a deed. It is ſigned, ſealed and delivered.—Of courſe, the daughter was entitled to an immediate ſeiſin in fee, in the land, and the huſband to the enjoyment of it during her life, and of his own alſo, as tenant by the curteſy, in conſequence of the after birth of a child. But Shore, not having obtained a ſeiſin in *fact*, during the life of his wife, is not entitled to his curteſy.

But

But if he be entitled to his curtesy, still the objection first made occurs; which is, that he has an adequate remedy at law, to recover the possession, and damages. Upon every principle therefore, it would seem, that the decree for £1000 is erroneous—since, if Shore has any title whatever, it can only be to the land, or its value, for his life, to ascertain which, an issue ought to have been directed.

RONOLD and MARSHALL for the appellee.

The objection made to the jurisdiction of the court, is now too late, after answer filed, and no plea in abatement, or demurrer put in; see the act of 1787, C. 9. Besides, this court has concurrent jurisdiction with the law courts, in cases of marriage agreements, 1 *Vern.* 110.

As to the merits;—after the father hath declared an intention, to give his child a certain marriage portion, in consequence of which a third person is induced to make his addresses, and thus engage his affections, it would be monstrous if the father could change, or diminish that portion, by any subsequent secret declaration— 2. *Vern.* 499, 764. The declaration therefore of Mr. Bannister to his daughter, is an underhanded agreement, and void.

The proof of Mr. Bannister's promise to give £1000, could not have been more compleat, unless Mr. Shore had demanded it in writing; an indelicacy, which the law did not require him to commit. As to a supposed waver of the money portion, in consequence of his assent first given, and his subsequent acquiesence, the first, is not proved, and the second, is the result of a false deduction from the fact. The answer of one of the defendants, which states the assent of Shore, is not evidence of the fact, because not responsive to any allegation in the bill. And if it were, yet Mr. Shore may have conceived, that he was to enjoy the same interest in the land, which he would have had to the money; else, it is not probable, that he would have given up £1000 for a *life* estate in land, which was worth no more *in fee.* His conduct in retaining the deed, can furnish no presumption of acquiesence, since there was no necessity for expressing his dissent from the terms of it, until the promised conveyance was *tendered* to him. Besides, the contract contained in that letter, was made with the daughter, at that time a married woman, and was therefore void: it could not operate, to deprive the husband of an antecedent vested right—a right which cannot be considered as surrendered, but for a real, valuable consideration. But admit that Bannister had an election to substitute land, in the place of money; yet having deprived

himself

himself of the power to do the one, he shall be compelled to perform the other.

WICKHAM in reply.

It is true, that in England, Courts of Equity exercise a jurisdiction in cases of marriage promises, because they can, and always do compel the husband, to make a suitable settlement thereout upon his wife. But this is never done in this country. The act of 1787, which has been relied upon, can only apply to cases, not strictly within the jurisdiction of the Court of Chancery, as to the *person* or *property*. But surely, this court may dismiss a bill for the want of that equity, which can alone entitle it to jurisdiction, altho' no plea in abatement is put in. If the construction contended for be right, then it will follow, that the courts of law, may by the combination of the parties, be entirely ousted of their jurisdiction, and every subject of controversy, may be transferred to, and decided in Chancery.

I do not contend, that the express promise of a father, to give a certain portion to the person who shall marry his daughter, is not obligatory upon him. But I insist, that it would be mischievous in the extreme, if general declarations of his intention, and more especially those, made (as in the present case,) in the bosom of his family, should bind him, whatever inconveniences might result from it.

THE PRESIDENT, (after stating the case, and observing that the clerk had certified, that the infant child of John Bannister the son had been made a defendant, tho' no process was prayed against him,) delivered the opinion of the court.

There is no evidence in the cause, that the appellee was ever entitled to any thing, except the paper referred to in the bill, addressed by Mr. Bannister to his daughter. This was received by the appellee, and retained by him, without any evidence of his dissent from the terms of it. Independant of this tacit acquiescence, it is in proof, that Mr. Bannister and the appellee, went to view the land, spoken of in that letter, and that the former, in the presence of the latter, informed the witness, that they had been to examine it, for the purpose of fixing upon a proper situation for a house.

The executor in his answer, states, that he was sent by Bannister, to inform the appellee of his intention to give his daughter land, with which the appellee appeared well satisfied.

But independant of this—there is no proof at all, whereon the claim of the appellee can be founded. Mr. Bannister's public declarations are relied upon. These are denied by the executors

executors—But whether this denial be evidence or not, is of little consequence, because that which is relied upon, to sustain the claim, falls very short of its object. What is it?—a private, confidential, domestic conversation, between a husband and his wife, wherein the former, speaks of an *intention once formed*, and then for influential reasons altered. And because it was once formed, it is supposed to be irrevocable.

The claim if at all founded, is merely a legal one; and if a suit at law should be brought for the land, it may then be discussed with propriety, whether any act of the appellee, amounted to such a seisin, as to secure his right to be tenant by the curtesy.

It was objected, that the conveyance of the land to John Bannister the son, put it out of the power of the father, to perform his engagement respecting it. But the fact is, that by the death of Mrs. Shore, and of her child, in 1784, the land descended to John Bannister, the brother, as her heir at law, to whom it was afterwards conveyed by the father.—But this deed does not appear in the record.

The decree therefore must be reversed, and the bill dismissed.

John Clayborn Executor of A. Clayborn,

against

HILL.

THIS was an appeal from a decree of the High Court of Chancery, in a suit commenced there by the appellee, to set aside a conveyance from Herbert Clayborn, to Augustine Clayborn, his father and the testator of the appellant, as being fraudulent. The prayer of the bill is, that the appellee may be let in to have the effect of an execution, issued against the estate of the said H. Clayborn.

The bill states, that the plaintiff sued out an execution against the estate of Herbert Clayborn, which in November 1784, was served upon certain slaves, some corn, stocks of cattle and tobacco, then being on a plantation in King William county, in the possession of the said Herbert Clayborn, who exercised over the whole property, every act of ownership. That the property was claimed by Augustine Clayborn, under certain deeds of conveyance to him, from the said Herbert. These conveyances are charged to be fraudulent.

The answer states, that long previous to the 11th of June 1780, A. Clayborn, and Carter Braxton, having engaged in a commercial

commercial connection, the former being entitled in right of his wife, to an estate in England, did with her consent, sell it to Braxton for £6000, which formed his part of the stock in trade. That A. Clayborn, some time afterwards, withdrew himself from the business, which had been profitable, and on the 11th of June 1780, relinquished his share of the profits, to his son Herbert, for the consideration of £3000, which Herbert, by articles in writing of that date, (reciting, that those profits had been made from a capital, furnished by the wife of A. Clayborn,) agreed to pay to the said A. Clayborn and his wife. That H. Clayborn becoming afterwards indebted to C. Harrison, in a considerable sum of money he, on the 1st of February 1783, by indenture, conveyed to his father, and to the said Harrison, jointly, and to their heirs, 60 slaves by names, some horses, described by names, colour, and the use made of them—sundry articles of household and kitchen furniture, *together with sundry other articles of household furniture*; also 36 head of cattle, 40 of sheep, and 100 of hogs; to have, and to hold, all the above property, *as per list delivered in*, and a charriot and harness, unto the said A. Clayborn, and C. Harrison, &c. in trust, that after default in the said H. Clayborn, in paying the £3000 to the said A. Clayborn, and the debt due to the said Harrison, they, or either of them, or the survivor, or their heirs, to take and sell the property thereby granted, or a sufficiency thereof to pay the same, and the surplus, to be paid to said Herbert. This deed was recorded in the court of New Kent county, on the 14th of August 1783.

In April 1783, H. Clayborn, by deed of trust, conveyed to said A. Clayborn, C. Harrison, and another, three tracts of land lying in King William and New Kent counties, to be by them sold, and the proceeds thereof, applied to the discharge of debts, due from him to the trustees, and of engagements entered into by certain other persons on his account, the surplus to be paid to the said Herbert. This deed was proved in New Kent County Court, on the 14th of August following, and was recorded.

On the 20th of November 1783, Augustine Clayborn, assigned the two deeds above mentioned, so far as he had an interest in the lands, slaves, and other property conveyed by them, to John Nash, in trust, as a provision for the wife of the said Augustine; this was done, in consideration of her interest in the English estate, which her said husband had sold. This deed of assignment, was recorded in Sussex County Court.

On

On the 12th of August 1783, Herbert Clayborn (to satisfy an execution, the benefit of which belonged to C. Braxton,) sold and conveyed to Braxton, 30 slaves, part of those before conveyed to Clayborn and Harrison, but with the assent of Griffin, a prior mortgagee. The debt due by Herbert Clayborn, to Braxton, being on the same day, paid by A. Clayborn, Braxton assigned, over to him and his wife, this bill of sale for the 30 negroes; and this assignment, was proved in New-Kent County Court two days afterwards.

The answer states, other claims of Augustine Clayborn against Herbert Clayborn;—and admits the possession of Herbert, (of all the property conveyed to his father,) on the day, when the plaintiff's execution was levied.

On the 5th of May 1784, an account was stated, between Herbert, and Augustine Clayborn, commencing in October 1783; wherein Augustine is charged, as of that day, for slaves
(by name,) that day sold   £445: 0
  sundries as by account settled 20th November,   540: 18:
  negroes [by name] then sold   500:
  May 5th 1784, personal estate then sold   303:
                1788: 18:

And on this day a bill of sale was executed by H. Clayborn, to A. Clayborn, for the above property; the amount to be credited him on his agreement with the said Augustine and his wife, dated the 11th of June 1780. This bill of sale is proved, and admitted to record in New Kent County Court, on the 14th of April 1785, The property conveyed by this bill of sale, is the same, which had before been mortgaged to the said Augustine Clayborn.

The court decreed the deed of the 1st of February 1783, to be fraudulent, and void as to the creditors of Herbert Clayborn; and that the defendant, out of the assets of his testator should pay to the plaintiff, the amount of his judgment and costs. From this decree, the defendant in chancery appealed.

DUVAL, for the appellant. The first decision we meet with, upon the subject of fraudulent conveyances of personal estate, is Twine's case 3 *Co. Rep.* 80. But it is to be recollected, that the English cases are for many reasons too high toned, to apply in this Country. The bankrupt laws, which forbid one creditor from being prefered to another, have excited a desire in the courts of that country, to make the same principle as general as possible; and consequently a jealousy is entertained against all conveyances, which give such a preference:
                       and

SPRING TERM

and thus it is, that small circumstances are caught at, to set them aside—again, in that country, deeds respecting personal estate are not registered, and of course, possession is the highest evidence of property. But by our law, mortgages of personal property, and of slaves, are required to be recorded; see the act of 1748, C. 1. So that there is not the same danger of fraud, as to subsequent purchasers and creditors, in this, as in that country. That the consideration in this case, was *bona fide*, is compleatly established; and if so, all the arguments of inconvenience, which can be urged, may be repelled by the maxim, *caveat emptor*, which strictly applies to this case—he cited 2 Durnf. and East 375—3 Atk. 44.

MARSHALL for the appellee. Whether the reason assigned, why the English cases, do not apply in this country be a substantial one, or not, will depend upon the just construction of the act of 1748, which is certainly very obscurely expressed. The first clause of that law declares, that no lands, tenements or hereditaments, shall alter, pass, or change, whereby any estate of freehold shall be made to take effect, unless the same be recorded in the General Court, or court of that county, where the land shall lie, within a certain time.—Now, this clause cannot possibly apply to *slaves*, because the deed is to be recorded in the *county where the land lies*. The fourth clause declares, that *all* deeds of trust, or mortgage, must be recorded *according to the directions of this act*. But the directory part of that act, as to the *place* of registration, is applicable to *land* only, for the reason before given.—But, if *slaves* are meant by the law, then by analogy to land, this deed, ought to have been recorded in King William County Court, because, the slaves were *in that county*, at the time the deed was made, and the execution served upon them. So that, either a mortgage of slaves is not comprehended within the law, or if it be, then, this deed has been registered in an improper county.

Lyons, J. requested Mr. Marshall, to read the tenth section of the law, which requires, that a memorial of all mortgages, containing the number, and names of the slaves, and the description of the personal estate, if any be mortgaged, shall be registered in the General Court.

Mr. MARSHALL. I contend that if the law apply to a mortgage of slaves, the deed in question, was not recorded in the proper County.

It is also an important question, whether the mortgagor of personal property, can retain the possession of it. The English cases lay it down, that a security upon personal property, is not properly a mortgage, but a pledge, or deposit, and remains in the pawnee's possession. What influence, the custom of this country (which is otherwise,) may have upon this point, I will not pretend to determine. But, if all these points be against me, I rely with confidence, upon the many badges of fraud which attend this case.

In the first place, consider the *connection* between the parties; a mortgage by a son, to the father.—*The time*;—just previous to the affairs of Herbert Clayborn becoming desperate, and whilst his creditors were pressing him. A conveyance too, of *every thing* he possessed, down to a knife case, with a sweeping clause, that nothing might be omitted. It is remarkable too, that only that species of property is conveyed, which might be resorted to by his creditors: for his real estate (not encumbered) was considerable, and is not conveyed.—If the transaction were *bona fide*, would he deprive himself of all the comforts of life, and the means of deriving profit from his lands? or would he not rather have retained a part of his personal, and in its room, substituted some of his real estate. All the cases agree, that a total disposition of a man's estate, or the remaining in possession, are certain badges of fraud—there is also something remarkable in the consideration stated—to wit, that the father, and Braxton, in 1777, had formed a commercial connection—the father's capital was £6000.—In 1782, it is decided to have been a loosing business; and yet, in 1780, the father sells the profits of this trade, to the son, for £3000 sterling, which is the consideration of the mortgage. But again: in 1784, the son makes an absolute conveyance to the father, for £1788: 18; after which, it must be agreed, that the son's retaining the possession is so strong an evidence of a secret trust, as not to be fairly accounted for. The property continues in his possession, when the execution is served, he receives the crops, disposes of them, converts the cattle, hogs, &c. to his own use, and in short, exercises the most compleat ownership over the whole.

WARDEN on the same side. No case can come more compleatly up to Twine's case, than this. The conveyance is general, and possession is retained by the mortgagor. In Powell on mortgages it is laid down, that the possession of personal property, which is mortgaged, should remain with the mortgagee; or if it do not, the reason should appear, from the *nature and import of the mortgage*, from p. 1 to 66. So,

So, where a supercargo on a voyage, mortgaged by way of Bottomry and Hypothecation, the vessel and cargo, and proceeded on the voyage, and sold the cargo, and bought other goods with the proceeds, and so bartered it two or three times; this was determined not to be fraudulent, because from the very nature of the transaction, it was understood, that the supercargo was to make the most of the property. But where in a mortgage of personal property, it was stipulated, that the mortgagor should retain the possession, and receive the profits, it was adjudged fraudulent against creditors—so that, even an express agreement to retain possession, will not save such deeds from being fraudulent, unless the *transaction itself*, necessarily accounts for, and justifies it.

MARSHALL. There is but one possible way of construing the act of assembly, so as to make all its parts consist together, and at the same time, effect the purpose, for which deeds ought to be registered. The first section of the law directs, that deeds of land shall be recorded in the General Court, or Court of the County, in which the land lies.—The 4th section directs, that all mortgages, shall be recorded according to the directions of that act.—The 9th and 10th sections declare, that for the purpose of giving notice to purchasers of lands, slaves, &c. of prior incumbrances, memorials of all deeds of lands, slaves, &c. shall be registered, by the clerk of the General Court; and the clerks of the different County Courts, are also directed to furnish the clerk of the General Court, with memorials of all deeds, recorded in their respective courts, which are also to be registered in the General Court. If then, the deed be of *lands and slaves*, it ought to be recorded in the General Court, or court of the county *where the land lies*—if of *slaves* only, then in the General Court: In this way only, will there be compleat notoriety of all deeds—if it may be recorded in the county where the mortgagee lives, a purchaser must first know, who is the mortgagee, before he can know to what County Court to apply. If it may be recorded in any county, then, if the clerk should fail to send forward the memorial to the General Court, the registration will afford no notice whatever.

The PRESIDENT requested Mr. Marshall, to read the act of 1758, respecting the fraudulent gifts of slaves, observing, that this question might perhaps be determined by analogy to that.

Mr. MARSHALL.—That act relates to *positive* gifts, the act of 1748, to *mortgages*—that, to conveyances *without* consideration.—This, to conveyances with consideration.—The deeds
spoken

spoken of in that law, may be proved by two witnesses. Those mentioned in this law must be proved by three.—That is passed ten years after, and has no reference to this: there can therefore be no analogy between them.

CAMPBELL for the appellant in reply.

This case, depends entirely upon principle, and its own peculiar circumstances—no aid can be derived from English cases, because the reason, which has produced them in that country, do not exist in this.

I contend 1st, that the deed in question, is valid under the act of 1748, and 2dly, that the circumstances attending the transaction, cannot invalidate it upon the principle of fraud.

First, the law of 1748, is not creative of the right to mortgage personal property, because it existed at common law, but it directs the manner of giving notoriety to such deeds. The notice intended, is to be obtained, by referring to the registration of the memorials of them, in the General Court. It is therefore unimportant, in what county they are recorded, since the General Court is the place, where information is to be obtained, respecting the county in which the deeds were recorded. And if the officer, whose duty it is to forward these memorials fails to do it, the parties are not thereby to suffer.

Secondly, Before the English cases are considered, let us recollect how this subject stood, at the time when Twine's case was decided; and it will be found, that the facility, with which secret conveyances might be made, rendered it proper for the judges, to exercise a strictness (in order to defeat every attempt to commit a fraud,) which would have been unnecessary, if a mean had been adopted, whereby creditors and purchasers might have guarded themselves against it. This inconvenience, produced the statutes of Elizabeth, respecting fraudulent conveyances. The preamble, recites the mischief which resulted from the possession remaining in one person, whilst the property was transferred to another, whereby creditors, and purchasers were defrauded; and the judges stretched as far as they well could, to carry this statute into full effect. The cases referred to in Powell, furnish a satisfactory reason for the distinction, between real, and personal property, continuing in possession of the mortgagor. In the first, purchasers may obtain notice, by recurring to the vicinage in cases of feoffments, or to the records, in cases of bargains and sales. But in the latter, possession is the highest evidence of property. Attend to the difference between the statute of Elizabeth, and our law. The former, only punishes the fraud, which it did not attempt to prevent. The

latter,

latter, prevents its commiffion, by directing the deeds to be recorded. The principle of *caveat emptor* therefore, cannot with propriety apply in England, becaufe there is no poffible mode, by which a purchafer can guard himfelf againft prior, fecret conveyances; it is otherwife in this country.

Under all the inconveniencies above pointed out, Twine's cafe came forward. The conveyance was abfolute and was of all his property. No inventory of the particular articles; and want of notoriety, is there ftated as the foundation of the decifion. This, is the cafe of a mortgage, which from its nature imports, that the poffeffion is to remain with the mortgagor. There is a fpecification of the property conveyed, and an appraifinent annexed. As to the inconveniences arifing from the want of notoriety, fee 2 *Blac. Com.* 338---342---*Pow. on Mortg.* 2 *Ed.* p. 286---290.

If then, poffeffion remaining with the mortgagor, be not in this country, an evidence of fraud, what are the other circumftances relied upon? *relationfhip*---if the tranfaction be otherwife fair, the preference given by a fon to a father, can be no evidence of fraud. *The time*,---Since there are no bankrupt laws, or principles growing out of them in this country, which prohibits a debtor from preferring one creditor, to another, the circumftance of time is unimportant, if it be antecedent to the *execution delivered*. But the ftrongeft proof that this tranfaction was real, and not colorable, is, that in April 1784, H. Clayborn, mortgaged his land (which his creditors could not have touched,) to his father, Harrifon, and William P. Clayborn, whofe claims were found to exceed the value of the property firft mortgaged. If he found himfelf fafe in the power of a father, would he alfo have thrown himfelf upon the mercy of ftrangers, if the tranfaction had not been real?

THE PRESIDENT pronounced the following opinion and decree, viz. "The deed of mortgage, dated the 1ft of February 1783, from Herbert Clayborn to Auguftine Clayborn, "in the decree mentioned, if made for a valuable and *bona fide* "confideration, was not void by reafon of Herbert Clayborn "the mortgagor, retaining poffeffion of the flaves and other ef- "tate thereby mortgaged to the faid Auguftine, as the faid deed "was duly recorded, and that therefore the confideration fhould "have been enquired into, and accounts taken and fettled be- "tween the parties, before the deed was declared void on that "principle, which could not be properly done in this fuit, as
Charles

" Charles Harrison one of the mortgagees is not a party. But
" this court is of opinion, that as the said Augustine suffered the
" said Herbert to retain the possession of the slaves, and other
" estate, on which the appellees execution was levied, after the
" sales in October and November, for which bills of sale were
" made, (as referred to in the answer of the appellant, and filed
" among the exhibits in this cause,) releasing the equity of
" redemption, and conveying the absolute property in the estate,
" thereby conveyed and confirmed, to the said Augustine, which
" bills of sale were not recorded until the 14th of April 1785;
" that they were fraudulent and void as to the appellee, and
" neither the said sales, nor the prior mortgage which had ceased
" to operate, did protect the estate, (then sufficient to satisfy his
" demand) from his execution, and that there is no error in
" the decree for the payment of the appellee's debt and costs.

Decree affirmed.

TARPLEY'S Administrator
against
DOBYNS.

THIS was a suit in Equity, instituted in the County Court of Richmond, by the present appellant. The bill charges, that there were various specie dealings, between the intestate of the plaintiff, and the defendant; and that upon a settlement made in 1779, there being a balance found due from the defendant, he executed a bond for £54 current money, the amount thereof. That this was understood by the parties, to be a specie debt, and as a proof, that such was the meaning of the parties, the defendant, afterwards paid £6: 10, in specie, and still acknowledged himself further indebted to the plaintiff's intestate ; which could not have been the case, if the debt had been subject to the legal scale of depreciation, which in 1779, was 10 for 1. That the plaintiff, instituted a suit at law, against the defendant, and not suspecting that the defendant would attempt to contend; that the debt should be scaled, he was unprepared to prove the defendant's declarations, tending to shew, that he considered it as a specie debt.—In consequence whereof, the jury reduced the debt, to a smaller sum, than the defendant had actually paid, and found a verdict against the plaintiff. The bill prays, that the defendant may be decreed to pay the £54, in specie with interest, after deducting the above payments.

To this bill, the defendant demurred for want of equity. The demurrer being sustained in the County Court, as also in the High Court of Chancery where it was carried by appeal, the plaintiff below appealed to this court.

The cause, being argued here by Mr. Campbell for the appellant;

The PRESIDENT delivered the opinion of the court.

We feel no difficulty in declaring, that both decrees are right. Although the appellant might have resorted to a Court of Equity in the first instance, if his case would bear it, it is now too late, after having made his election, to take a trial at law. As to the surprise, which is made the pretext for this application to a Court of Equity, it ought not to benefit the appellant in the present case; since, when he discovered a disposition in the appellee, to avail himself of his legal advantage at the trial, he might have suffered a nonsuit.

Decree affirmed.

ANDERSON *against* BERNARD.

THIS was an action of trespass, brought in the District Court of Prince Edward, by the appellant, against the appellee, for taking a saddle from his possession. Plea, not guilty. The defendant at the trial offered in evidence to the jury, a record of his qualification as a deputy sheriff, and also a witness to prove, that the defendant, as deputy sheriff, had seized the saddle in the declaration mentioned, to satisfy certain fees due in 1781, to the clerk of the General Court. The account of the fees due, and stated in the record to have been produced in evidence, is headed thus, " Dr. Thomas Anderson, to Adam Craig, *deputy* clerk, General Court." To this evidence the plaintiff filed a bill of exceptions. Verdict and judgment for the defendant, from which the plaintiff appealed.

RONOLD for the appellant, contended, that the *deputy* clerk, was not entitled by law to demand fees from suitors, and therefore, the account offered in evidence, could not justify the sheriff in levying the distress. That these summary modes of enforcing the payment of debts, ought to be strictly pursued, to prevent oppression upon individuals.

The sheriff saw his authority, and ought to have known, that no fees could be distrained for, but such, as were due to the *principle* officers of the courts. The evidence therefore, was improperly admitted by the court.

MARSHALL for the appellee. By the act of 19th *Geo*. II. C. 1, §. 12, the sheriff, if sued for levying a distress for officers fees, is permitted to plead the general issue, and to give in evidence the special matter of his justification.

As to the mode of stating the account, by which the *deputy* clerk is made the creditor, no advantage can now be taken of it; because the account, though it appears in the record, is properly no part of it, nor is it excepted to, as inadmissible testimony.

The court being divided in opinion, the judgment was affirmed.

JOHNSON *against* BOURN.

THIS was an action of assault and battery, brought by the defendant in error in the District Court of Charlottsville. There were two pleas put in, 1st not guilty: and 2dly, a justification. The defendant, at the trial, offered the testimony of a witness, against whom a seperate action was then depending at the suit of the plaintiff for an assault committed at the *same time*. The court, refused to suffer the witness to be examined, considering him to be incompetent, on account of his being sued as a joint trespasser.

The defendant below filed a bill of exceptions to the opinion of the court, and a verdict and judgment being given against him, he obtained a supersedeas from this court.

RONOLD for the plaintiff. There seems to be no good reason, for rejecting this witness upon the ground of incompetency. A person named in the *simul cum*, may give testimony for the defendant, in an action of trespass, *Bull. Ni pri.* 285. Watson *v*. Shelly, 1 Term *Rep.* 301 is expressly in point. *Hardw. Cas.* 360 and 3 term *Rep* 27.—in the last case, this principle is laid down—that if the witness, is neither to gain, nor lose, by the event of the cause in which he deposes, or if the verdict cannot be given in evidence for, or against him, he cannot be objected to on the score of incompetency.

MARSHALL

MARSHALL for the defendant. My own opinion is, that the law is correctly stated by Mr. Ronold, but the point has been otherwise determined in the General Court, upon an indictment for an affault.

The PRESIDENT. The plaintiff, by bringing feperate actions, has removed all objection to the teftimony of the witnefs, fince the verdict in one fuit, cannot be given in evidence in the other. The objection therefore can only go to the *credibility*, not to the *competency* of the witnefs.

Judgment reverfed—verdict fet afide, and new trial awarded, with directions to admit the examination of the witnefs.

WILLIAM EUSTACE

againft

GASKINS Executor of EUSTACE.

THIS was a fuit in equity, inftituted by the appellant in the County Court of Lancafter. The object of the bill is, to recover a compenfation, for certain lands devifed to the plaintiff, by his father, William Euftace, and afterwards recovered from him at law, by fome perfon having a better title.

This claim, is founded upon a claufe in the will of the faid William Euftace the father, by which he defires, that in cafe the land given to his fon William, fhould be recovered from him, his fon John (the teftator of the defendants, to whom he devifed the principal part of his eftate,) fhould purchafe it for his faid fon William. In 1742, the recovery was obtained, and the teftator of the defendants, died in 1785.

This fuit was inftituted in 1788, and the bill, accounts for the delay in bringing the fuit, by charging, that the teftator of the defendant amufed the plaintiff, until his death, with promifes of providing for him by his will. Some proof of fuch a promife, as well as an acknowledgment by John Euftace, of the plaintiff's forbearance, appears in the record. The defendant, in his anfwer, principally relies upon the length of time. Exceptions were taken, and filed by the defendant, on account of the court's refufing to receive the anfwer of Mrs. Euftace, who is ftated in the exceptions to have qualified as executrix of John Euftace fince the inftitution of this fuit.

The

"The County Court, directed the value of the land in 1742, and the back rents, to be afcertained by commiffioners, and decreed the amount thereof, to the plaintiff, the prefent appellant.

This decree, was reverfed in the High Court of Chancery, and an appeal was taken from thence, to this court.

WASHINGTON for the appellee. The firft objection which occurs to the decree of the County Court is, that there is not fuch teftimony in the caufe, as could warrant a recovery upon any principal. The will of William Euftace the elder, is not made an exhibit, nor admitted by the defendants in their anfwer; neither is there any other evidence of the recovery ftated in the bill, but a judgment in ejectment againft John Euftace, an infant, of *fome* land; but whether of *that,* devifed by the will of William the father, does not appear.

But I rely principally upon the length of time, which has elapfed, fince the recovery ftated in the bill. Subftantial juftice and wife policy demand, that in all cafes, whether legal, or equitable, there fhould be a period, beyond which no claims fhould be litigated: fuch a length of time, as creates a prefumption of payment, or of fatisfaction made, is confidered as much an equitable bar in this court, as if it came within any pofitive act of limitation. In the cafe of Standifh, *vs* Radley, 2 *Atk.* 177, where portions, which became due in 1673, were fued for in 1717, lord Hardwicke determined, that fuch a lapfe of time, creates a ftrong prefumption, that they had been paid, and amounts almoft to the proving of a negative to induce the court to believe them ftill unpaid.

So, in the cafe of Smallman *vs* Hamilton 2 *Atk.* 71, an annuity devifed by will, was confidered, as being barred by length of time, on the prefumption, tho' forborne to be fued for 10 years only—fee alfo 3 *Atk.* 105—226, 1 *Harr. Cha. Prac.* 375.

MARSHALL for the appellant. I admit that length of time, which induces a prefumption, that the claim has been fatisfied, will create an equitable bar. But this prefumption, may be repelled by teftimony accounting for the delay, and in this cafe, there is a fufficient reafon affigned, and proved, for the appellant's not afferting his right, at an earlier day. It appears, that the teftator of the appellee had been long married, without having children—that he acknowledged his brother's lenity, in not coercing fatisfaction of his claim, and promifed, to make him an ample provifion at his death.

There is no room then, to let in a prefumption of payment, upon which alone, this equitable bar can be fet up.

The

The PRESIDENT delivered the opinion of the court.

The judge, who pronounced the decree of reversal in this case, seems to have considered no other question, but the presumption against the demand, on account of it's antiquity. It is undoubtedly true in general, that a right, for a length of time unasserted, is subject to a presumption of its having been satisfied, sufficiently strong, to defeat it. But it is equally true, that this presumption may be opposed by circumstances, accounting for the forbearance. In this case, we think a sufficient reason for the delay is assigned, and satisfactorily proved. The decree of the Chancellor is therefore erroneous, and must be reversed. As to that of the County Court, we have felt some difficulty in deciding, what ought to be done with it; it cannot be sustained upon any principle. The will not having been made an exhibit in the cause, and the only evidence of a recovery, of the land in question, being a judgment of the General Court, against John Eustace, for *some* land, (but *what* land does not appear,) the decree was certainly made, without sufficient testimony to warrant it. In the next place, Mrs. Eustace ought to have been made a party, so soon as it was known, that she had qualified as executrix to her husband John Eustace. Her answer might have disclosed something important, of her own knowledge. The court ought to have directed an *issue*, to try, whether any, and what part of the plaintiff's land, had been recovered, as well as the value and profits thereof, which being in the nature of damages, ought to be ascertained by a jury, and not by commissioners.

The decree of that court therefore, must also be reversed, as well as the proceedings subsequent to the answer. The plaintiff to have leave to amend his bill, so as to make Mrs. Eustace a party defendant, and the cause to be sent back to the County Court, to be there proceeded in.

TOMLIN, MITCHEL and HOW,
against
KELLY.

THIS was an action upon the case, for goods sold and delivered, brought by the plaintiffs in the General Court, from

from whence it was sent to the District Court of Northumberland. The jury found a special verdict, in the following words to wit, " we find for the plaintiff, £100: 9: 6½ dama"ges, if the court shall be of opinion, that an action can be "maintained, for goods, wares and merchandizes, imported "for sale by the plaintiffs, *who kept no retail store*, but who "sold the same at *public auction*, on a wharf, and delivered "them to the defendant *twelve months before this suit was brought*, "otherwise we find for the defendant."—

Judgment upon this special verdict was given for the defendant in the District Court, and a writ of supersedeas was granted by this court.

CAMPBELL for the plaintiffs in error.—The question is, whether this case shall be construed to come within the operation of the act of October 1779 Ch. 3, " for discouraging exten"sive credits, and repealing the act prescribing the method of proving book debts." I am to contend it does not.

The act passed in 1748, which is intended to be repealed, will serve to throw light upon the true intention of the legislature, in passing the law more immediately in question. The preamble to that law, as well as the enacting clause, is literally confined to the sale of goods by retail, and was intended to provide a species of evidence unknown to the common law; by which, retail merchants were permitted to prove their store accounts by their own oath. This law, not only opened a door to perjuries, and to infinite frauds, but tended to encourage extensive credits, from the facility of establishing such demands. To repeal this law, and to do away its effects as to extensive credits, was obviously the design of the act of 1779. The preamble recites, that the method of proving book debts, and the extensive credits formerly given by merchants and traders, had been found injurious to this commonwealth: the law then proceeds to repeal the law of 1748, and to enact, " that all actions, founded upon account for goods sold and delivered, or for any articles charged in any store account, shall be commenced within six monts, after the cause of action accrued, and not after". The mischief stated in the preamble, existed only in the retail business, which, almost entirely formed the internal commerce of this country, before the war, and of course, must have been alluded to, by the legislature.

The law requires each item in the account, to be truly dated, which is an additional proof, that the retail trade was alone contemplated.

WARDEN

WARDEN for the defendant. When a law is expressed, as this is, in general terms, reasons for forming constructive exceptions from it, ought to be so strong, as to leave nothing to conjecture—whenever we quit the plain expressions of a law, to wander at large in the wide field of construction, we should be sure, that the guides we take will not mislead us.

The legislature had two motives for passing the law of 1779—the one, to repeal the act of 1748, because it warranted an unsafe species of evidence—the other, to prevent extensive credits, as an evil independent of, and not growing out of the act of 1748—for if it had necessarily resulted from that law, it must have expired with the law, and need not have been stated as a primary mischief, intended to be cured. If it had been considered merely as a consequence, it was highly absurd to entitle the law, "an act to prevent extensive credits, *and* repealing the law prescribing the method of proving book debts." The second clause of the act, creates a bar against all actions founded upon account for goods sold and delivered, *or* for any articles charged in any store account.

Now, is this an action for goods sold and delivered, or not? If the law only meant store accounts, why is the former part of this clause inserted? the latter would have answered the purpose.

If it were politic, to prevent extensive credits in the confined sales of a retail store, the reason applies a *fortiori* to extensive wholesale negociations; if it were wise to prevent it, when transacted in a house by *private bargain*, was it not equally so, if sold upon a wharf at *public auction*.

THE PRESIDENT delivered the opinion of the court.

In discussing the case of Beale and Edmundson, it was agreed by the unanimous opinion of a full court, that the act of 1779, applied only to the store accounts of retail dealers; and we should feel ourselves bound by that opinion, unless it were over-ruled by as full a court, even if our sentiments at this time, respecting the principle then established were different from what they then were. But the present court retain the same opinion upon the subject; and must therefore pronounce the law to be in favour of the plaintiffs, upon the special conclusion of the verdict.

Judgment reversed, and to be entered for the plaintiff.

CASES ARGUED AND DETERMINED

IN THE

COURT OF APPEALS

IN

THE FALL TERM OF THE YEAR,

1793.

JAMES M'ALISTER
against
JOHN M'ALISTER.

THE defendant in error brought an action upon the case against the plaintiff, in the County Court of Berkeley—Plea *non assumpsit*. By a rule of court entered in November 1789, the parties, submitted all matters in difference between them in this suit, to the final determination of two arbitrators, mutually chosen, and in case of their disagreement, they to chuse an umpire, whose award, or the award of such umpire thereupon, to be made the judgment of the court.

The two arbitrators not agreeing, named an umpire, who, "after examining the papers filed in the suit, and after consi-
"dering the claim of the plaintiff, and the various charges ex-
"hibited in an account rendered by the defendant, in bar to the
"claim of the said plaintiff, declared his opinion; that the
"plaintiff should not recover his said claim, but on the contrary, his
"suit be dismissed at his own costs." This award being returned, was objected to by John M'Alister, the plaintiff below, whereupon a rule was made, to shew cause, why the award should not be set aside?

Upon this rule, a motion was made to set aside the award, and the plaintiff, in support of his motion, offered to prove by the arbitrators and umpire, that the umpire had admitted the depositions of James M'Alister, the defendant, and of his wife, to be read as evidence before him. But the court, refusing to examine these witnesses, determined that the award should be made the judgment of the court. To this opinion, the plaintiff filed a bill of exceptions, which was sealed.

From this judgment, John M'Alister appealed to the District Court of Winchester, where it was reversed, the award set aside, and a new trial directed; the court being of opinion, that the oath of the party, was improperly admitted as evidence by the umpire.

The plaintiff in this court, obtained a supersedeas, to the judgment of the District Court, asigning for error, that that court reversed the judgment of the County Court, because the umpire admitted improper evidence, whereas, if the County Court erred in refusing to examine the witnesses, all that the District Court should have done, would have been to reverse that judgment, and to direct the evidence to be admitted to prove the admission of the improper testimony, if any there was.

The following is the opinion and judgment of this court.

" That the testimony of the defendant James M'Alister and
" Sarah his wife, was not proper in this suit, and ought not to
" have been admitted without the consent of the plaintiff; and
" that if the umpire on the proceedings mentioned, did receive
" and admit their depositions as evidence, in the matters in
" difference between the parties in this suit, submitted to him,
" his umpirage and award should have been set aside, and a tri-
" al by jury awarded *by the County Court*. The judgment of
" the District Court is therefore erroneous. The judgment of
" the County Court is also erroneous, in not allowing the plain-
" tiff to prove, that the depositions of the said James and Sarah
" M'Alister were admitted as evidence by the said umpire, as
" (it is stated in the bill of exceptions filed in this cause,) the
" plaintiff offered to do."

Both judgments reversed with costs. The cause sent back to the County Court, to receive such proof, and for further proceedings.

WILSON & M'RAE *against* KEELING.

THIS was an appeal from the High Court of Chancery—Keeling, the plaintiff in that Court, borrowed from M'Rae in April 1778, a sum of paper money amounting to £422: 18, not to be repaid in less than twelve months thereafter, which money, (the answer states,) belonged to the ward of M'Rae, being so much received by him in discharge of a specie debt due to the ward. Keeling conveyed to Wilson as a trustee for M'Rae, certain property by way of mortgage, to secure this loan—after the money became due, but not on the very day, Keeling tendered the debt in paper money, to Wilson the trustee, who refused to receive it. An ejectment being brought, to recover possession of the mortgaged premises, a judgment was thereupon obtained. Keeling filed his bill in the High Court of Chancery praying an injunction, and liberty to redeem, upon paying according to the scale of depreciation, at the time when the money was lent. The answer states, that the money was borrowed by Keeling, for the purpose of discharging a specie debt, and that it was actually so applied.

The Chancellor being of opinion, that the debt in question for money borrowed and secured by mortgage, might be discharged in the same manner, as a debt created and secured by a pact in any other form; and that by refusal of the money tendered, the right to interest, between the time when the tender was made and the time when the debt was demanded by M'Rae, was extinguished, decreed a reconveyance to the plaintiff upon his paying to the defendants, £84 : 11 : 8, with interest thereupon, from the time of the loan, until that of the tender, and from the 1st day of September 1784, (when a demand was made,) until payment of the principal debt, with the costs of the suit at law, and his costs in defending this suit; but upon his failing to do this, the court decreed a foreclosure and sale, in the usual manner.

CAMPBELL for the appellants. The appellant M'Rae, having gained the legal title to the mortgaged property, has thereby obtained an advantage, of which a Court of Chancery will never deprive him, without forcing the party, who seeks its aid, to retribute the other party by doing compleat equity. This is an over-ruling maxim in that court. If the appellee shall be found to sustain no injury, or to be deprived of no equitable right by paying the nominal amount of the debt in specie, what is it, that shall warrant the interposition of a court of equity, to deprive the mortgagee of the full benefit of his judgment at law? Keeling cannot lose any thing, by paying the full amount of the loan in specie, because he made a specie use of the money. On the other hand, M'Rae is injured, by applying the scale of depreciation to the debt; because the money

ney lent, tho' it confifted of paper bills, was the reprefentative of fo much fpecie, as it was received by him in difcharge of a fpecie debt.

M'Rae is to be confidered in this court, as ftanding in the fhoes of the perfon, to whom Keeling paid the fum he had borrowed, in the fame manner, as if that debt had actually been affigned to him. That the parties confidered this as a fpecie contract, is evident, from the value of the property mortgaged.

But the decree is furely erroneous, fo far as it ftops the intereft from the tender of the money, to the time of the fubfequent demand, fince the prefent cafe cannot be likened to that, of a tender made in fpecie. In the latter cafe, the money always continuing of the fame value, no injury can arife, if it be not tendered on the day of payment. But in the cafe of paper money, its value was continually leffening, and therefore it ought to have been tendered on the *very day*, as the lender, (relying on the punctual payment of the money,) might have made contracts, providing for the immediate application of it, and might lofe the benefit of fuch contracts by difappointment.

MARSHALL for the appellee, was ftopped by the court.

LYONS J. delivered the opinion of the court. The cafe is too clear to be argued. This is a downright attempt to evade the law, directing the mode of fettling debts contracted in paper money, without a fingle circumftance to countenance it.

In the cafe of Wily and Panky, in the General Court, it was determined, that the creditor who concealed himfelf in his houfe, to evade a tender, fhould fuftain the lofs by the depreciation of the money.

Decree affirmed.

WILLIAM PAYNE, Executor of John Payne,

againſt

WILLIAM DUDLEY, Executor of Fleet.

THIS was an appeal from a decree of the High Court of Chancery. The appellant filed his bill in that Court, ftating, that his teftator was indebted to the teftator of the appellee by bond, upon which a judgment had been obtained in the year 1766, during the lives of the parties. That the bond, being

being afterwards found by the defendant amongſt the papers of his teſtator, the defendant had inſtituted an action upon the ſame bond, againſt the plaintiff, in a different court from that in which the original judgment had been obtained: that the plaintiff, not knowing of this judgment, was prevented from pleading it in bar, in conſequence of which, a ſecond judgment was rendered in the year 1789, againſt the plaintiff. The ground of equity is, that the teſtator of the plaintiff had, in the year 1766, conveyed the greateſt part of his property to John Semple, in truſt for the payment of the debt in queſtion, (amongſt many others,) provided, the enumerated creditors would within a reaſonable time accede to, and accept of that ſecurity. That Fleet was one of the acceding creditors, and had been fully ſatisfied for the above mentioned debt out of the truſt eſtate. An injunction was prayed for and granted.

The defendant in his anſwer, denied any knowledge of the judgment in 1766, or that the debt had been ſatisfied either by Payne himſelf, or by Semple out of the truſt eſtate; and inſiſts, that the debt (for which the judgment ſought to be injoined was rendered) being yet due and unpaid, it ought now to be ſatisfied by the plaintiff, whether Fleet was, or was not an acceding creditor.

The judgment in 1766 was entered upon confeſſion; no declaration or bond was filed, and conſequently, it was entered generally, without aſcertaining any preciſe ſum.

The Chancellor upon a hearing of the cauſe, diſmiſſed the bill, being of opinion, that the equity ſtated, was neither admitted by the anſwer, nor ſupported by the evidence.

CAMPBELL for the appellant. I am aware of an objection, which may be urged againſt the relief ſought for by this bill; which is, that the defendant at law, having loſt the opportunity of availing himſelf of a legal advantage, cannot expect the favor of a Court of Equity, unleſs he ſhew, that the judgment is an unconſcientious one. But it ſhould be obſerved, that this legal advantage being gained, (and that too by the ignorance of the appellant) he has loſt the opportunity of availing himſelf of the preſumption, that the firſt judgment (obtained ſo long ago as the year 1766) had been paid; a defence which he might fairly have uſed if inſtead of improperly inſtituting a ſecond ſuit upon the ſame bond, a ſci. fa. had been proſecuted to revive that judgment. The preſumption ariſing from length of time, is much ſtronger againſt a judgment, than againſt a bond; for in the firſt caſe, a ſci. fa. cannot be ſued out after 7 years, but by permiſſion of the court. There are ſtrong circumſtances in this cauſe to ſtrengthen the preſumption. On the day when the firſt judgment was to be confeſſed, Payne executed a deed of truſt, conveying his property to Semple, to ſecure ſuch of his creditors as ſhould accede thereto. That Fleet was one of the acceding creditors, appears from the circumſtance of one of his ſons being found in poſſeſſion of a part of the truſt eſtate; after which it does not appear, that any demand of payment was made.

MARSHALL for the appellee. The principle ſtated and admitted by Mr. Campbell, furniſhes a compleat anſwer to all the objections relied upon; for it is clear, that where a man has neglected to avail himſelf of an advantage merely legal, equity will not aſſiſt him, ſo as to defeat the juſtice of the caſe. Fleet by receiving part of the truſt eſtate, is not thereby barred from recovering the balance of his debt, if other property can be found. It is like the caſe of a mortgagee, who if not fully ſatisfied by the ſale of the property mortgaged, may proceed to recover the balance from the mortgagor.

LYONS J. in caſe of a *foreclofure*, how would it be, if there were no covenant for payment of the debt,

MARSHALL. In that caſe, the mortgagee muſt be ſatisfied with the ſecurity he has taken; but he may elect to have the property ſold, in which caſe, he may proceed againſt the mortgagor for the balance left unſatisfied by the mortgaged property.

As to the preſumption of payment, it was a fit ſubject to have been relied upon at law. But ſurely it cannot be ſeriouſly contended, that the acceding creditors are precluded from claiming ſuch part of their debts, as remained unſatisfied under the truſt.

The PRESIDENT. The preſumption of payment ariſing from length of time, beſides being defeated by the acknowledgments of the debtor in 1775 and 1779, is ſufficiently repelled, by conſidering the delay neceſſarily incurred, whilſt the creditor was waiting to ſee what the truſt eſtate would produce. The creditors are not barred, by the terms on which they acceded to the deed of truſt, from demanding any balance not ſatisfied under the truſt—nor does it even appear, that the debtor had a letter of licence, which on ſuch occaſions is generally given.

It never was ſuppoſed, that the property of an inſolvent debtor, acquired after his diſcharge, was exempted from the claims of his creditors, until the debts before contracted were fully ſatisfied. It is his perſon only, which is protected.

We

We come now to confider, the nature and extent of the relief fought for. Courts of Equity never interfere, to deprive the plaintiff at law, of any legal advantage which he may have gained, unlefs the party, feeking relief, will do compleat juftice by paying what is really due. Indeed, they have (upon the fame principle,) gone fo far as to refufe their affiftance, in relieving againft a judgment, obtained by fraud. The truft deed furnifhes no equitable bar to the creditor, fince he has waited, to know the refult of that fund, as long as could have been expected. If Payne's executor had fuppofed, that a balance of the truft property were ftill remaining unapplied, he might have made the reprefentatives of the truftees parties, and called for an account.

Decree affirmed.

WILLIAM M'WILLIAMS
againft
LEWIS WILLIS.

THIS was an action upon the cafe, brought by the appellee againft the appellant in the Diftrict Court of Frederickfburg. The declaration contains two counts. The firft ftates; that a certain difcourfe was had between the plaintiff and the defendant, concerning the renting of a piece of ground of the defendant's, for the ufe of the *Jockey Club*, whereupon, the plaintiff, (*called in the faid agreement Colonel Willis*) agreed to rent the faid ground to the defendant, for the ufe of the Jockey Club, for the term of feven years, and the defendant agreed to pay for the fame, the fum of £30, a year, the field to be enclofed by the plaintiff, with a good fence, and the defendant, in behalf of the Jockey Club, agreed to have the field reftored to the plaintiff at the end of the term, with the fence in as good order, as when it was received, and the defendant, in confideration of the plaintiff's promife to do every thing &c. on his part agreed to be done promifed to do every thing on his part to be performed: avers performance on the part of the plaintiff, and lays the breach, in the non-payment of 2 years rent, and in not reftoring the field enclofed as he received it. The 2d count, is an *indebitatus affumpfit* for the ufe and occupation of a race field,

field, and an affumpfit *of the defendant* to pay &c.—upon the general iffue, the jury found a verdict for the plaintiff—at the trial, the plaintiff produced in evidence, an agreement in writing, correfponding with that ftated in the declaration, except, that the defendant is ftiled in the agreement, *Treafurer of the Jockey Club*, which defcription is omitted in the declaration. The court, having over-ruled the motion of the defendant that this agreement fhould not go in evidence to the jury,—an exception was taken to the opinion, and an appeal prayed.

WARDEN for the appellant.—The plaintiff having declared upon a *parol* agreement, the court ought not to have permitted him to give in evidence, an agreement in *writing*. The defendant, might probably have made a different defence from what he did, if the cafe had been truly ftated in the declaration. He might have fhewn that he was no longer treafurer of the Jockey Club; or that the plaintiff, was himfelf a member of that fociety.

But if this objection can be obviated, there is a material variance, between the written agreement offered in evidence, and that declared upon. The declaration does not charge the defendant as *treafurer*, although by the agreement, he had charged himfelf in that character. As treafurer, it is to be prefumed he had funds in his hands, to indemnify himfelf; and he would therefore have been authorifed, (if the judgment had been rendered againft him *in that capacity*,) to apply thofe funds to the difcharge of it. But as the cafe now ftands, he can neither make fuch an appropriation of the funds, if he *have them*, nor can he have recourfe againft the members of the Club, if he have them not.

Upon the fubftantial merits of the cafe, the defendant is not chargeable at all. He acted as agent for a fociety, to whom alone, the credit can be prefumed to have been given. It is like the cafe of a factor, who, when acting for a known principal, is never confidered as being individually chargeable. 3 *P. Wms*, 290, 2 *Str.* 1168. The cafe of Macbeath *vs* Haldimand, 1 Term *Rep.* 172, is much like the prefent. Suppofe the appellant had ceafed to be treafurer, before the expiration of the feven years; it will not be contended, that he could have been liable under this contract, for rents accruing after that time, even if he were fo, for rents antecedently due. But the declaration not charging him upon the *written agreement*, and in his true character, it was impoffible for him to avail himfelf of fuch a circumftance, if the facts would have warranted it.

If

If thefe obfervations be correct, the plaintiff could not, recover upon the firft count; and if fo, he could not go into proof, to enable him to fucceed upon the fecond—*Str.* 648.

WASHINGTON for the appellee. The firft point made by the appellant's counfel is, that the declaration being upon a parol affumpfit, the written agreement was improperly admitted as evidence.

No rule of law to warrant this objection is recollected. Where a *deed* is the foundation of the action, it ought to be declared upon; becaufe the defendant may plead *non eft factum*, and the court upon infpection, may determine, whether the inftrument poffefs the neceffary qualities of a deed. No fuch reafon, and therefore no fuch neceffity exifts in the cafe of an agreement, *not under feal*. It may be produced as evidence of the agreement ftated in the declaration; but the plaintiff muft prove the hand writing of the defendant, and muft produce fuch an agreement, as fubftantially fupports the charge, as laid. Doing this, the defendant is expofed to no fort of inconvenience, becaufe the declaration gives him complete notice of the allegation, to which he muft anfwer, and if it do not, the plaintiff muft be nonfuited. The defendant is at liberty to give in evidence, upon non affumpfit, any thing material for his defence. In an action upon the cafe for money lent, the plaintiff may give in evidence a promiffory note, 2 *Str.* 719. This is a very ftrong cafe, and not diftinguifhable, upon principle, from the prefent.

The fecond objection, is founded upon a fuppofed variance, between the declaration and the agreement.—It is true, that in a fpecial action upon the cafe, the allegations and the proofs muft agree; and fo they fubftantially do, in the prefent inftance. The naming of the appellant, *treafurer of the club*, in the agreement, is a mere *decriptio perfonæ*, not affecting his refponfibility. It is as unimportant, as if he had been ftiled, *Efquire*, or *yeoman* in the agreement, and no notice had been taken of the title in the declaration.

The third point is more connected with the merits of the cafe. It is contended, that the appellant was not *perfonally* liable—This is by no means a novel cafe—It is no more, than the agreement of one man, to pay a fum of money for a third perfon. The agreement in queftion, is not made with the *Jockey Club*, nor with the *treafurer* of that Club, but with *William M'Williams*, for the benefit of the Jockey Club, and therefore, he makes himfelf perfonally refponfible for them.

The

The cafe of Cullen *vs* the Duke of Queenfberry, *Brow. Cha. Rep.* 101, is by no means fo ftrong a cafe againft the appellant, as the prefent; and yet, it was there determined, that the individuals who contracted for the benefit of a company, were perfonally liable.

But at all events, we are entitled to recover upon the fecond count, notwithftanding the cafe of Weaver *vs* Boroughs, 1 *Str.* 648, which is not law at this day.

LYONS J. delivered the opinion of the court.

A parol agreement reduced to writing, does not in any manner change the nature of the contract; the writing is merely evidence of the parol agreement, and being the beft evidence, ought to be produced, though not fpecially declared upon. We can difcern no difference between this cafe, and that cited from 2 *Str.* 719, where in an action for money lent, a promiffory note was allowed to be given in evidence, to prove the charge laid in the declaration.

The variance between the declaration and the agreement, in the former, omitting the addition of *treafurer*, is not material; and if it were, the defendant might have taken advantage of it, as well in the prefent mode of declaring, as if the written agreement had been fpecially fet forth. It was as unimportant to name the appellant, *treafurer*, in the declaration, as it would have been, to give the appellee the title of *colonel*, becaufe he was ftiled fo in the agreement. We cannot prefume, that any circumftance exifted, to do away the refponfibility of the appellant, becaufe none are proved, nor even pretended. The perfon with whom he contracts, cannot be prefumed to give a credit to the members of a club, perhaps numerous, and difperfed through different parts of the country. The agreement is made with the appellant, and he binds *himfelf perfonally* to perform it. He is liable therefore, whether he receives the money fubfcribed by the individual members of the Club, (as in the cafe of Cullen *vs* the Duke of Queenfberry, cited at the bar) or not. This is not like the cafe of merchants and partners, becaufe, in contracts made by them, they are all jointly and feverally bound for the whole.

In this, each fubfcriber is liable only for his proportion, and therefore an individual, contracting with the treafurer, knows nothing of the ftate or value of the fund, which the treafurer does; confequently, he cannot be fuppofed to go upon its credit.

Judgment affirmed.
KEEL.

KEEL & ROBERTS *against* HERBERT.

THE appellee brought an action of *indebitatus assumpsit*, for the moiety of a vessel, sold to the appellants. Plea *non assumpsit*—and *non assumpsit* within 5 years. Replication that the defendants did assume. Verdict for the plaintiff, that the defendants did assume, as declared against. The defendants filed a bill of exceptions, stating specially, what each witness, examined in the cause had deposed, and that not one of them, established an assumpsit *within five years*. This appears from the bill of exceptions to have been the case; but it does not state, that the testimony therein set forth was the *whole evidence* given in the cause. The court, upon the motion of the plaintiff's counsel, instructed the jury, that the evidence produced by the plaintiff, was good and effectual in law to maintain the issue on his part. From this judgment, the defendants below, appealed to this court.

WICKHAM for the appellants. The jury having found a general verdict, without taking notice of the second plea, have left the question arising upon that plea entirely undetermined, and the verdict is consequently inconclusive.

But I rely principally upon this—that the court exceeded the due exercise of their powers, when they undertook to decide upon the *weight* of the testimony given to the jury. It was certainly their duty, to see that the evidence was proper. But in estimating its weight, the jury were exclusively the judges.

If the defendant had demurred to the evidence, as stated in the bill of exceptions, there is no doubt but that he must have succeeded. Yet this is merely formal, and since the bill of exceptions states all the evidence, the court may with propriety decide, that the plaintiff, not supporting the issue on the second plea, ought not to have had judgment.

By the Court.

The District Court most certainly did wrong, in directing the jury, that the evidence *was sufficient* to maintain the issue.

This was a question, which belonged exclusively to the jury, and ought to have been left with them, without any such declaration, or direction, unless the court, (by a demurrer to the evidence having been filed,) had been compelled to decide upon it.

But the court mistook even upon the point which they improperly undertook to determine, for there appears no proof whatever, of the purchase of the sloop, by the appellants. The bill of exceptions, states an offer of £1100 by the appellant—a demand by the appellee of £1200—but no agreement as to the price. There is no proof of any contract, but such as is derived from the appellee himself.

The judgment must be reversed, and a new trial awarded.

JOHN HAWKINS's Executors,
against
NELSON BERKLEY.

THIS was an action of debt, brought by the appellee in the County Court, upon a bond, given by the testator of the appellant, with condition, that the said John Hawkins, would faithfully collect on commission, certain debts due to the appellee by bonds, (as by list annexed,) and would pay the amount so collected, and return an account of his collection, and also surrender up all bonds not fully paid, when required; (except such as might be lodged with clerks, or with lawyers, to bring suit on,) the obligor agreeing, to perform the duty of a collector, and in all things relative to the business, to act for the benefit of the obligee, to the best of his skill. The defendant pleaded, that he had performed the conditions of the said bond. To this the plaintiff replied, protesting that the defendant had not performed the conditions of the said bond, and assigned as a breach, that the said Hawkins, did not well and truly collect the several sums of money, due on the bonds contained in the list, to the said writing obligatory annexed, nor use his best endeavors to collect the same without delay; but that he omitted, to make timely application for those debts, *and neglected to bring suits for their recovery*, tho' often requested so to do, as also to render an account of his collection; but that on the contrary, he refused to account, or to pay the whole of the monies collected at any one period, and at all times, retained a considerable part thereof, as well as of the bonds, &c. to this the defendant rejoined generally. The jury found a verdict in favor of the plaintiff, for £5, which was set aside by the court, and a new trial awarded. The second verdict was in favor of the defendant, which being also set aside, the jury upon the third trial, found for the plaintiff

plaintiff, £914 in damages. The defendant then moved for a new trial, which was over-ruled. The judgment was affirmed upon an appeal to the District Court of Richmond, where judgment was entered for the damages and costs of that court, to be levied of the goods &c. of the testator, in the hands of the executrix, if so much she had, if not, *then of her own proper goods.* From this Judgment the executrix appealed.

MARSHALL for the appellant.—The objection relied upon in the District Court went principally to the number of new trials awarded by the County Court, but I do not consider that as a point which can be insisted upon.

I shall confine myself to the variance, between the breaches assigned, and the condition of the bond upon which the suit is founded; and if it should be considered as material by the court, it will of course be fatal to the judgment. The rule of law is well established, that if any one of the breaches assigned, be for the non-performance of a duty, which the obligor hath not undertaken to execute, and general damages are assessed, the verdict is bad. One of the breaches in this replication is, that the testator *did not bring suits upon the bonds put into his hands*, and there is no part of the condition of his obligation, which imposes this as a duty upon him. If I am right in this objection, the judgment of the County Court must be reversed.

The next error, which I think the record exhibits, is in the judgment of the *District Court.* The executrix is condemned, to pay the *damages* out of her *own estate*, in case of a deficiency of assets. I do not recollect any precedent of this court upon the point, and therefore, if I am not precluded by any such from making the objection, I shall contend upon principle, as well as upon the act of assembly, that the damages ought not in any event, to be paid by the executrix. Nothing could be more unjust, and unreasonable, than to punish an executor, for his endeavours to preserve his testator's estate, from the effects of a judgment, which he may suppose to be erroneous.

It would seem, to be a duty imposed upon him, from the very nature of his office. He would, (I conceive,) be highly reprehensible, were he to submit to a decision, (perhaps ruinous to creditors and legatees,) in his opinion erroneous.

The damages upon reversal, are given in lieu of all damages, or interest, which makes them a part of the *debt* due from the estate, and should therefore be chargeable upon the same fund, as the principal.

RONOLD

RONOLD for the appellee.—I admit the law upon the firſt point, to be as Mr. Marſhall ſtates it; but I deny the application of it to the preſent caſe. By the condition of this bond, Hawkins undertakes *to uſe his beſt endeavours to collect the debts*, and if coercive meaſures were neceſſary for that end, he was bound to make uſe of them. It was an eſſential part of his duty, which he was as much bound to perform, as he was to demand payment of the debts. So that the breach, tho' not aſſigned in the very words of the condition, is in ſtrict conformity with the meaning and ſpirit of it.

As to the ſecond objection, if it were to prevail upon the ground of hardſhip, it might go a great deal farther than Mr. Marſhall expects; for it certainly is not more unjuſt, that the executor, ſhould out of his own pocket, ſatisfy the damage occaſioned by his own act, where his teſtator's eſtate is inſufficient, than in caſes, where he is charged for a falſe, or perhaps unſkilfully drawn plea.

MARSHALL in reply. The right of a collector, to inſtitute ſuits indiſcriminately, and thereby, to ſubject his principal to the poſſible payment of coſts, muſt depend upon the ſpecial authority given him. A collector, may certainly be cloathed with ſuch powers—or a man may collect, and yet not poſſeſs them. If they are meant to be delegated, it is eaſy to expreſs ſuch intention, and words of excluſion cannot be neceſſary. The agreement of the obligor, to return all bonds not in ſuit, proves nothing againſt me, becauſe Berkley might chuſe to direct the inſtitution of ſuits himſelf.

LYONS, J. delivered the opinion of the court.

The variance between the condition of the bond and the breach aſſigned is not *material*. Agreements are always to be conſtrued, according to the evident intent of the parties, appearing from the deed itſelf, without a rigid adherence to the letter. This rule is laid down in the caſe of Freſhwater *vs.* Eaton. *Str.* 49, and is certainly a correct one. It is plain, that the intention in this caſe, was to veſt in the collector a power to bring ſuits, and that the exerciſe of ſuch a power, was neceſſarily involved in the undertaking on his part.

The caſe of Bache and others againſt Proctor Dougl. 382, is ſtronger than the preſent. The condition of the bond was, to render a fair, juſt, and perfect account in writing, of all ſums received. It was determined, that the obligor was guilty of a breach of the condition, by neglecting to *pay over* ſuch ſums. Beſides, the objection in this caſe comes after a verdict. The defendant, if he had considered the variance as material, might have demurred.

Judgment affirmed.

HOOE & HARRISON & others
against
GEORGE MASON.

THIS was an action upon the case, upon an *indebitatus assumpsit, and quantum meruit* brought in the District Court of Dumfries, by the appellants, owners and masters of the ship General Washington for freight and primage. Upon the plea of *non assumpsit*, the jury found a special verdict, in substance as follows: That on the 31st of August 1780, the defendant shipped at Amsterdam, on board of the General Washington, a letter of marque, bound for Alexandria, in Virginia, and owned by the plaintiffs, two parcels of goods, and paid the freight and primage on the small parcel, before the ship sailed.

That the captain signed two bills of lading, binding himself to deliver the goods to the defendant, or to his assigns, at Alexandria, the danger of the seas only excepted; the defendant, paying, $12\frac{1}{2}$ per cent freight, upon the nett proceeds, upon their delivery at Alexandria, and the captain's primage, at the rate of five per cent.

That the ship was a merchantman employed in transporting goods for hire, provided with a letter of marque and that by the ships articles, the captain was not to cruise or sail out of his way after the enemy, for the purpose of making prizes or in pursuit of an enemy.

That the captain, on his voyage, did change his course two or three points, and gave chase to a ship and brigantine belonging to the enemy, for three or four hours. That the ship was supposed to mount, 12, or 14, nine pound caronade guns, and the brig, 8 or ten four pounders; that the General Washington, mounted two nine pounders, and 16 double fortified six pounders.

That the Gen. Washington, out sailed the ship and brig; the two latter, after the action began, acting upon the defensive & offensive. That the attack was begun by the captain of the General Washington,

ington, who after a long engagement had nearly made prizes of the enemy, and would probably have done so, if he had not been too much disabled to pursue.

That the captain, was then obliged to stop six or eight days to refit, and altered his course to Dartmouth, in New-England, a good harbor, for ships of the burthen of the General Washington. That the disabled situation of the ship, was produced by the action, and rendered it prudent in the captain to put into this port.

That the goods were all landed, and stored at Dartmouth, and that it was necessary to unload, in order to refit,—which being accomplished, the ship was fitted for a privateer, and sailed in about four months after her first arrival, and was taken.

That the defendant wrote to colonel Henly of Boston, a letter dated the 22d of November, 1780, informing him, that he had goods on board this ship, which were intended for his own use, and not for sale, and requesting him, in case the ship should not be directed to Virginia, or the managers should not bring part of the goods hither, to have all his goods stored, and forwarded by the first good vessel, to Potomack, or if none offered, then to send them to Philadelphia, or Baltimore: if the managers sent any part of the cargo to Virginia, then his goods were to come by that conveyance.

That in consequence of this letter, the agent for the owners, delivered the defendant's goods to col. Henly; that they were imported for the defendant's own use, and not for sale—That from Dartmouth, there was no opportunity to ship them to Virginia.—That they were removed from thence to Boston, from whence they were sent to Rappahanock river in Virginia, and from thence, by a circuitous land and water carriage, to the defendant.

That as soon as the arrival of the ship at Dartmouth was known, the plaintiffs sent on an agent, to fit her out as a privateer, and to sell their own goods, which being made known to the defendant, produced the above letter.

That it was frequently practised by merchants, during the late war, to receive and sell their goods, and to pay freight for them, tho' landed at other ports, than the port of delivery.

If upon the whole, the plaintiffs be entitled to full freight, they find for them £96: 3: 4 $\frac{1}{2}$—if to freight *pro rata*, then they find £20—if the law be for the defendant, then they find for him.

Upon

Upon this verdict, the District Court gave judgment for the defendant, from which the plaintiff appealed.

LEE for the appellants. I shall put out of the case, the articles of agreement, entered into between the appellants and the captain, which, tho' operating in our favor, are improperly brought into view, inasmuch as the defendant being no party to that agreement, they ought not in any manner to be affected by it.

Freight, is a compensation for the carriage of goods, and is deserved, in proportion to the trouble. The appellee, therefore, ought unquestionably to pay for the carriage to Dartmouth; and if the non-delivery of the goods at the port of destination should be found to have been caused by himself, he will be answerable for full freight. I admit, that from the terms of such engagements as the present, if the goods be not delivered at the port of destination, in consequence of a voluntary and faulty departure of the captain, he is not entitled to claim any part of the freight. This will lead to an enquiry, into the conduct of the captain of the General Washington. It is found, that he went out of his course, a few points, for the purpose of attacking, and this, I contend, he was justifiable in doing. A letter of marque, is not obliged to act upon the defensive. She may *chace*, may attack, may even go a few points out of her course to do this; but she cannot cruise. Park on *Insu.* 341—*Dougl. Rep.* 510. Thus far then the captain acted properly.

His next step, was to put into Dartmouth, and this is found by the jury, to have been dictated by prudence. Being there, the owners were entirely at liberty, either to refit, and compleat the voyage, or to transport the goods to Alexandria in some other vessel. It is a right, of which the freighters cannot deprive the owners. Although the General Washington was not intended to bring the goods to Alexandria, yet, the owners might have sent them in some other ship, and in fact they did so with respect to a part of the cargo, belonging to other persons. The defendant's might have been also sent, if his agent had not taken them.

He ought not therefore, to avail himself of this act of his own, to deprive the owners of full freight.

MARSHALL for the appellee. I admit, that freight is a compensation for the carriage of goods, from one place to another. It is bottomed upon some contract, either written, or parol, and by the mercantile law it is considered, as being neither due nor demandable, until the service is performed. The performance of the service, then, must be first established, before the reward can be claimed, and in strictness, it cannot be demanded, if from any cause whatever, the goods are not carried to the port of delivery agreed upon. I must admit that in some instances, the compleat fulfillment of the contract may be dispensed with; and yet, freight *pro rata* allowed. But as this is merely a matter of excuse, it must be proved by the owners, and must appear to be such an one, as fixes the blame upon them, or upon the captain. In this case, the conduct of the captain is attempted to be justified, and authorities for that purpose are relied upon. But it is easy to discern, that the cases cited by Mr. Lee, do not apply. They relate merely to disputes between the *assurer*, and *assured*, and not to the subject of *freight*, which involves quite different considerations.

One party agrees to insure, provided the other conforms to certain rules, well established and known by both, and which are therefore calculated upon, in estimating the rate of hazard.

If the captain be not permitted to cruize, or to act offensively, the risk is the less, and of course, the premium diminished. A deviation therefore, avoids the policy, and the cases cited, define what is such a deviation, as to produce this effect. But the freighter, knowing that the ship is by contract, (as in this case,) prohibited from chasing, and that his property is on that account, more safe in her than in another vessel, is induced to give her a preference.—A violation of this contract, is a plain fraud upon him, and consequently, deprives the owners of an excuse, for not strictly complying with their engagement. Were it otherwise, the captain would be thereby induced, to chace every vessel, of which there was a chance of making a prize, and thus, not only prolong the voyage, but endanger the cargo. Though the defendant was no party to that agreement, yet as it is natural that his enquiries would go to every circumstance relating to the risk, it is to be presumed, that it was known to him.

As to the letter written by the appellee, to col. Henly, it appears to be very much misunderstood by the counsel who rely upon it. It is in the alternative; if the Washington should not bring the goods, or if the owners should not chuse to send them in some other vessel, then, and not otherwise, his agent is directed to take possession of them. As it is not presumable, that the owners would have delivered the goods to Henly, without an order from the appellee, it is plain, that this letter was shewn to their agent. The goods being delivered, amounts to a declaration, on the part of the owner, that the Washington was not

intended

intended to come to Alexandria, and that they did not mean to send the goods, in some other veſſel. A different determination, afterwards formed, and executed, could not juſtify their prior conduct. Upon the whole, I think it clear, that the conduct of the captain in the firſt inſtance, and of the owners in the ſecond, was ſuch, as to deſtroy all claim to freight, either upon principles of juſtice, or of law.

LEE in reply—I willingly conſent, that the agreement, between the owners and the captain, ſhould be conſidered as part of the caſe. The ſecond article of it, directs the mode of arming, and ſtipulates for a reward, to the *mariner firſt diſcovering an enemy*, which proves, that it was intended to chace, and to act offenſively. Nor is it difficult, to reconcile this with the firſt clauſe, which was evidently meant to prohibit the captain from committing a *deviation*, which we find, from the caſes cited, to mean *cruizing* and not going a few points out of the courſe *to chace*. In fact, it was intended to expreſs, what would otherwiſe have been underſtood.

THE PRESIDENT delivered the opinon of the court.

The deviation, and putting into Dartmouth, being found by the jury, to have been prudent and unavoidable, in conſequence of the action, no objection againſt the payment of freight, can on that account be made, if the conduct of the captain, in attacking the enemy, were juſtifiable. The general principle of law, that a merchantman, having letters of marque, may *chace* an enemy in ſight, but cannot *cruize* out of her courſe to look for one, is well eſtabliſhed, and ſeems not to have been controverted at the bar. This is ſurely a very reaſonable diſtinction; for ſince commerce is the principal object of ſuch a veſſel, it would be improper, that ſhe ſhould loſe ſight of this, and go in ſearch of prizes.—On the other hand, as letters of marque are obtained at ſome expence, a veſſel would have them to little purpoſe, if ſhe could never act but on the defenſive, and could not, whilſt purſuing her great and primary object, embrace a probable chance of making prizes, ſo as to procure a reimburſement. But to this, two objections are made by the counſel for the appellee.—1ſt, That the doctrine, tho' applicable to caſes of inſurances, is not ſo, to thoſe, where the queſtion is about freight. The court cannot diſcern any diſtinction between them; for if the inſurer be ſuppoſed to know the principles and rules of inſurance, and to calculate the rates of hazard accordingly, why is not the freighter to be preſumed equally well informed? The

The second objection is, that the captain was restrained by the articles, from giving chace. But upon a view of those articles, it is evident, that the parties well understood the distinction between cruizing, and chasing an enemy in, or near the course, the former of which is alone intended to be prohibited. We are therefore of opinion, that the conduct of the captain, has not deprived the owners of their claim to freight. We are equally clear, that the claim cannot go beyond a freight *pro rata*. The letter of the appellee, did not prevent, or in the most distant manner, intend to prevent the owners, from sending the goods to the port of delivery; on the contrary, he appears to have preferred their doing so, and only requested the interference of his friend, in case they should not take that step. The delivery of the goods to col. Henley, was evidence enough, that the owners had no intention of sending them, and that they had abandoned their claim to full freight.

Judgment reversed and entered for £20.

HOOE & HARRISON,
against
THOMAS PIERCE, Admr. of Thos. Pierce.

THIS was an action of detinue for a negro, called Jack Robinson, alias Taliver, instituted by the appellants, and determined in the District Court of Suffolk. The jury found a verdict for the plaintiff, if the law, upon the facts *agreed to be stated*, be for him, if not, then for the defendant. Before these facts were agreed, Thomas Pierce the defendant died, and a *sci. fa.* issued against the appellee, his administrator, to shew cause, why the said facts should not be agreed, and the matter of law thereupon argued. The appellee appeared, and the parties agreed the following case.

That on the   day of July 1779, the Bishop, an enemie's vessel, was taken on the high seas by the General Washington, an American vessel, belonging to citizens of the United States. That the slave in the declaration mentioned, was on board the Bishop at the time of her capture, and was then known on board by the name of *Jack Robinson*. That the vessel and cargo, together with the slave, was brought into Virginia, and condemned as lawful prize, and purchased under the sentence of the court, by the plaintiffs. That the slave in question, was once the property of the testator of the defendant, known by the name of *Taliver*, and so continued, until the year 1777, when he ran off from his master, and got on board a British vessel. That the slave, *Jack Robinson*, was taken from the possession of the plaintiff in September 1783, by the defendant, in pursuance of a warrant, granted according to an act of the General Assembly passed in 1782, * entitled, "An act for the recovery of slaves, horses and other property, lost during the war," and that he still detains him.

If the court shall be of opinion, that by the sale of the slave under the sentence aforesaid; the defendant lost his property therein, then judgment to be entered for the plaintiff, otherwise for the defendant.

The District Court gave judgment for the defendant, from which the plaintiff appealed.

LEE for the appellants. The only difficulty on the part of the appellants, is created by the special conclusion of the jury, which would seem to confine our title, to the purchase made *under the sentence of a court, in a suit, to which Pierce was no party*. And yet, hard as it may at first appear, that the rights of third persons should be affected by judgments, as to them, *ex parte*; yet, it is better, that a private injury like this should be sustained, than a public inconvenience produced, by discouraging persons from purchasing under the judgments of courts having competent jurisdiction: a consequence to be certainly expected, if the title of the purchaser could afterwards be questioned.

The appellants claim a right to the slave in question, under the acts of congress, passed in 1775, and 1776, making slaves, the subjects of lawful prize.

WICKHAM for the appellee. It appears from the facts agreed in the cause, that the enemy did not acquire the slave in dispute, by *plunder*, in which case only, the property, by the law of nations, is changed. On the contrary, it is agreed, that the testator's right was not divested by any act of his own.

But, if the slave had actually been seized by the enemy, in action, the recapture would revest the property in the original owner, by the right of postliminium, which extends to all kinds of property taken in war, except moveables; and these,

on

---

* Rev. Laws, Page 157. Ch. 8.

on account of the uncertainty in *identifying* them, are never restored. It is true, that slaves are not mentioned in any modern cases, because they are a property, unknown in the greatest part of Europe. But Vattel states, that amongst the ancients the rights of postliminium extended to them. However, a discussion of this point is rendered unnecessary, by the special conclusion of the verdict—I shall proceed then to consider the title of the appellants, as derived under the sentence and sale.

There is no principle more clear than this, that in Courts of Common Law and Equity, those only can be affected by their judgments or decrees, who are parties to the suit, or those who claim under them. I acknowledge, that the sentence of a court of admiralty is binding upon all persons, who are in possession of the property, or who claim under those who are; because, the parties interested are not known, and consequently not named. But in this case, Pierce was neither in possession himself, nor did he claim under any person who was: his title was adverse to that, claimed by the enemy and the captors.

If there be a decree for the sale of mortgaged property, it was never contended, that the rights of third persons, not parties to the suit, could be thereby affected.

I shall not acknowledge the authority of the resolutions of Congress, which have been read, because, that body were cloathed with no powers to legislate for the respective states; but if they were, these resolutions, being no more than private regulations, and not being found, cannot be noticed by the court.

I will beg leave to submit to the consideration of the court, another point, which tho' not connected with the merits of the cause, is certainly very important. The suit was abated by the death of Pierce, and ought to have been so entered. Detinue will not lie against an executor, for a conversion, or in consequence of a detainer by the testator, nor unless the property afterwards come into the possession of the executor. The judgment is for the slave, if to be had, if not, the value. Now the executor cannot perform one of the alternatives, if he never had possession of the property. *Bro. Ab.* 227—*Cowp. Rep.* 371, in which it was determined, that the action would not lie against the executor, for a finding and conversion by the testator.

The jury therefore, should either have found, or the parties have agreed a detainer by the appellee. It may perhaps be contended, that the act of 22 Geo. II, C. 5, § 5, which declares, that the death of either party between verdict and judgment, shall not abate the suit, furnishes an answer to this point. But that

that law muſt mean, a *perfect* verdict, and not ſuch an one, as might be ſet aſide, and a venire *de novo* awarded, or which either party, by refuſing to agree the facts, muſt render ineffectual. Neither can I admit, that the appearance of the executor, and his actually agreeing the facts, will alter the caſe; becauſe, he only did, what the writ of *ſci. fa.* commanded him—beſides, this agreement can extend no farther, than to the facts themſelves, and cannot cure the errors before committed.

LEE in reply. The act of Aſſembly which Mr. Wickham has read, ſeems to apply ſtrictly to this caſe, becauſe, it ſpeaks of verdicts *generally*, without diſtinguiſhing between perfect and imperfect verdicts. But if this were an imperfect verdict, the court, upon the trial of the *ſci. fa.* would direct a new trial, and not an abatement. The intention of the law was, to prevent the operation of the act of limitations.

THE PRESIDENT delivered the opinion of the court.

The firſt queſtion to be conſidered is, whether the ſuit ought to have abated, by the death of the original defendant.

The act of Aſſembly declares, that the death of either party between verdict and judgment, ſhall not abate the ſuit, but that judgment ſhall be entered, as if both parties were living.

It is contended, that this is no verdict, and therefore, not provided for by the law. It is true, that verdicts muſt be certain in themſelves, or ſuch as may be made ſo, by reference to that which is certain.

It is common for them to refer to records or to other papers equally certain. On a demurrer to evidence, a conditional verdict, dependent upon the opinion of the court as to the demurrer, is common and proper. So a verdict, to depend upon the opinion of the court, on a caſe ſtated on the record, is an uſual and legal proceeding. Caſes agreed, are ſometimes ſubſtituted in the room of ſpecial verdicts. But it is very novel, to find both in the ſome record, and connected together. Even this might have been unexceptionable, if the verdict had referred to a ſtate of facts *before agreed to*. But to ſupply the uncertainty of a verdict, by referring to that, which, ſo far from being certain, did not exiſt for five years afterwards, cannot poſſibly be right. Suppoſe the parties had refuſed to agree a caſe; or had in reality diſagreed about the facts: this might well have happened, and what could have been done. The court could not coerce them to agree upon a caſe, nor could any thing be ſubſtituted in its room.

We can find no caſes determined in England, upon the ſtatute of the 8 and 9 *W ill.* 3, C. 11, (from which our law was copied,) like to the preſent. Upon

Upon principle, we have no doubt, but that the administrator was not bound to cure the uncertainty in the verdict, by agreeing to a state of facts, of which he might be totally ignorant, because his inteſtate having more knowledge of them had conſented to do ſo.—That he might therefore have abated the ſuit, if he had choſen it, is clear. But he certainly might wave this advantage, and prefer a trial upon the merits. This he has done, by agreeing to a ſtate of facts. But then, the cauſe muſt reſt upon the agreed caſe, independent of the verdict.

Upon the merits, there is not much difficulty. The condemnation in the court of admiralty, could not bind the inteſtate, who was no party to the ſuit. If the ſentence of a foreign court of admiralty had condemned this ſlave, as a prize to the Britiſh, we ſhould have regarded it, though Pierce had been no party; becauſe it would not have been in his power to have become a party. So, if in this caſe, Pierce had put in his claim, and it had been decided againſt him, that deciſion, whilſt unreverſed, would have bound this, and all other courts. But the ſlave in queſtion, was libelled, and condemned, by the name of *Jack Robinſon*, inſtead of that, by which he was always called; and therefore Pierce could not be *preſumed* to have had notice, that his intereſt was involved in the ſuit, ſo as to enable him to aſſert his right.

The firſt reſolution of Congreſs, which paſſed on the 25th of November 1775, authoriſes veſſels commiſſioned by that body, to capture and make prizes of all armed veſſels, belonging to the enemy, employed in the war, and of all tranſports carrying troops, warlike, or naval ſtores, or proviſions, and directs the diſtribution of the prizes.

The next reſolution which paſſed on the 23d of March 1776, extends the right of capture to all veſſels, and to all goods, wares and merchandize, *belonging to any inhabitant of Great Britain:* but ſlaves are not mentioned. Whether they ſhould be conſidered as goods &c. within the meaning of this reſolution, or whether they are to be claſſed with lands, or ſhips and cargoes, ſo as by the rules of poſtliminium, to require the ſentence of a Court of Admiralty to change the property, or whether they are to be conſidered in the light of moveables, and the property in them changed by capture, without condemnation, are queſtions, which the court think unneceſſary to conſider, ſince it is not ſtated, that the ſlave belonged to an *inhabitant of Great Britain,* ſo as to bring the caſe within the reſolution of Congreſs: neither is it ſtated, that he was taken *in war by the enemy,* and recaptured,

recaptured, so as to bring it within the exception in the act of Assembly passed in 1782. It appears, that he was the property of Pierce, and being such, ran off, and was found on board an enemies vessel, where no person claimed a right to him.

The sale therefore, in the present instance, could not divest the right of the original proprietor, however inconvenient this doctrine might prove to purchasers—for though equitable rights may, in favor of fair *bona fide* purchasers, for valuable consideration, and without notice, be lost by a sale, legal rights never can, unless there be fraud, as in the case of a prior mortgagee standing by, whilst another is throwing away his money by purchasing the mortgaged premisses, without giving notice of his prior incumbrance—in cases of legal rights, the principle of *caveat emptor* properly applies.

Judgment affirmed.

THWEAT & HINTON,

against

ADAM FINCH.

FINCH brought an action upon the case, in the District Court of Petersburg, against Thweat and Hinton as inspectors at *Robert Bolling's* warehouse. The declaration states, that the defendants, having inspected and passed three hogsheads of tobacco, the property of the plaintiff, they refused to deliver him the usual notes, or receipts for them, as by law, and the duty of their office, they were bound to do; but had delivered the notes, and the tobacco to other persons, having no authority from the plaintiff, to receive the same, contrary to law, and the duties of their office. Plea, not guilty. Verdict and judgment for the plaintiff, from which the defendants appealed.

The defendants filed a bill of exceptions, at the trial, stating, that the plaintiff gave in evidence that John Finch, by direction of the plaintiff, applied to the defendants in the year 1784 for the tobacco in question. That the defendants shewed him the warehouse books, by which it appeared, that the defendants had received, and inspected the three hogsheads of tobacco in the declaration mentioned, as the property of the plaintiff, and that the same had been shipped; the defendants alledging, that they had issued notes for it, in obedience to a written order to do so in the name of the plaintiff, which they shewed to John Finch, who is certain, it was not the hand writing of the plaintiff, of which he informed the defendants.

That the plaintiff, afterwards gave a written order, directing the inspectors to deliver the notes for the tobacco, to the said John Finch, who presented the same, and demanded the notes, but the defendants refused to deliver the notes, or tobacco, for the reasons before given; but that no proof was made of a personal demand, by the plaintiff himself. The defendants alledging, that the evidence was not sufficient to maintain the issue on the part of the plaintiff, moved for a nonsuit, which was over-ruled.

CALL, for the appellants. The first objection which is to be made to this judgment, respects the imperfections of the declaration. Though it states that the defendants were inspectors at Bolling's warehouse, it does not charge them to be *public* inspectors of a *warehouse established by law*, and unless this were the case, this action could not be sustained. Robert Bolling, might have owned a private warehouse, and the appellants might have been inspectors at it, for any thing that this court can judicially know. The contrary is not to be presumed.—The appellants, could not with propriety, traverse this material fact, as it was not charged in the declaration.

The declaration is also liable to objection, on account of its being double, and thereby forbidding an issue upon a single point, or at least tending to produce confusion in the trial, and to conceal from the defendants view the point intended to be controverted. It charges, 1st, A refusal to deliver the notes to the plaintiff; and 2dly, a delivery of them to a third person, unauthorized to receive them. If the plaintiff may bring two distinct charges into discussion, in one court, he may multiply them without end.

As to the bill of exceptions, I think it shews that the appellee ought not to have recovered upon the evidence produced by him. It appears, that no demand was made by the *appellee himself*, and the act of Assembly does not authorise inspectors to deliver the notes to *the order* of the owner, but to the owner himself. If the appellants were chargeable in this case, it would place inspectors in this dangerous dilemma: if they deliver the tobacco to the forged order of a person, whose hand writing they

they never saw, they subject themselves to an action, and to a penalty also: if they do not deliver it, and the order should be genuine, they will still be liable to an action. The law, authorises the delivery of the notes, to the person who brings the tobacco, and from any thing appearing in this record, the notes, might have been delivered to the overseer of the appellee.

MARSHALL for the appellee. What weight there might be in the objections to the declaration, if they had been made at a proper time, it is unnecessary now to decide, because, after a general verdict, the court will presume, that those things were proved to the jury, without which, they ought not to have found as they have done. The court, after verdict, will not, for the purpose of destroying it, hunt after objections, or enquire, whether there might not be a possible case, in which this action would not lie. It is notorious, that there are no private warehouses for the inspection of tobacco, in this country. The declaration, pursues the words of the law. The act of Assembly, which establishes tobacco warehouses, is a public one, and the court will therefore take notice, that *Bolling's warehouse* is one, created by this law. But there may be enough collected from the declaration, to defeat this objection; for it charges, that the defendants refused to deliver the *usual notes*, contrary to his *office of inspector*. Another objection to the declaration is, that it is double. But if there be two acts, either of which will sustain an action, it cannot be error to state them both, by way of aggravating the damages.

The point made in the bill of exceptions, having been before decided in this court, it will be unnecessary to take notice of it. It is settled, that the court cannot direct a nonsuit in any case, and that if they do, the plaintiff may refuse to submit to it.

CALL in reply. As to the power of the court, to direct a nonsuit, I admit, that the point has been settled as Mr. Marshall has stated. But certainly, if a bill of exceptions exhibits the *whole evidence*, and shews, that the plaintiff had no cause of action, judgment may be rendered against him, as well in such a case, as if it had appeared, in the form of a demurrer to evidence.

The PRESIDENT delivered the opinion of the court.

Upon a motion for a nonsuit, the court may give their opinion, that the plaintiff has no cause of action, and may direct him to be called. But he may nevertheless appear, and refuse to be nonsuited, nor can the court compel him against his will.

So on the other hand, the court may declare, that the action is maintainable—or may refuse to give any opinion to the jury, and so leave the whole question with them: if they do instruct, still the jury may find against the opinion of the court, who have no remedy left, but to grant a new trial.

So, if the party file a demurrer to the evidence, the court may, if the evidence be clear, refuse to compel the other party to join in demurrer, leaving the jury at liberty to determine.

But if in either of these cases, if the Superior Court should be satisfied, that the plaintiff had no cause of action, they will reverse the judgment.

This bill of exceptions, exhibits a very different case—the whole question was, whether the order, on which the notes and tobacco were delivered, was genuine, or counterfeit. This was a mere matter of fact, proper only for the enquiry, and determination of the jury. As to the hardship, which it was contended inspectors would be subjected to, it is no greater than that to which they might be exposed, by delivering tobacco on counterfeit notes, in which case, they would clearly be liable, to the holder of the real notes. It is a common and known risk of office, contemplated when undertaken.

We are next to confider the objections to the declaration.

The first is, that the warehouse is not stated to be a *public* one. If it were possible to suppose a *private* warehouse, at Robert Bollings—*Inspectors* there, to *view*, and *pass tobacco*—compelled by *law*, and the *duty of their office*, to give notes obligatory upon them, to deliver the tobacco on demand—that the inspectors had refused such notes, by which the plaintiff had lost his tobacco: if, I say, we could suppose all this, and consider this as a *mere private contract*, it would even then be difficult, to support the objections to the action, upon principles of common law.

But such a case is altogether visionary. The record, and the public laws upon the subject, warrant the court in saying, that the warehouse, and the inspectors, are such as the law has established.

The second objection is, that the declaration is *multifarious*.

The act of Assembly requires, 1st, that the notes should be delivered to the owner of the tobacco, but inflicts no penalty for refusing to do it. 2dly, It imposes a penalty upon the inspectors, for delivering the notes to any, but to the proprietor of the tobacco, without a written order from him.

This

This action is brought, not for delivering the notes to a third person, unauthorized to receive them, but for not delivering them, when demanded, to the owner.—The former offence, tho' charged, is merely by way of special damage, and intended to shew the remedy complete for the whole value of the tobacco, since the defendants had put it out of their power, ever to deliver it.

Judgment affirmed.

BROWN'S Administratrix,

against

GARLAND & others.

THE appellant instituted an action of debt in the District Court of Richmond against the appellees, (stiling herself, administratrix of W. B. Brown) upon a bond taken to herself as administratrix. The declaration is in the *debet et detinet*—Plea, payment. The defendant Garland having given six months previous notice of offsets, offered as such at the trial, two bonds due from the intestate, and which had come to his hands by assignment since the institution of this suit—also two receipts signed by the plaintiff, the one for money, and the other for a bond due by the intestate, and assigned to the same defendant; all which offsets had been acquired since the institution of this suit. They also produced in evidence an advertisement of the plaintiff's, offering for sale the property of the intestate at public auction, and agreeing to allow a discount of five per cent to such of the creditors of the estate, as chose to purchase at the sale. They also offered at the trial to prove a sufficiency of assets to pay the debts, and tendered the costs of suit. All these facts appeared in a bill of exceptions taken by the plaintiff to the opinion of the court, admitting the testimony—verdict for the defendant and appeal.

WASHINGTON for the appellant. The defendant at common law could shew nothing in discharge of a bond but something of an equal dignity with itself, such as a release, &c. offsets are permitted in England by a statute, which is not in force here. In like manner, the defendant is permitted by a
statute

statute in that country as well as by the law of this, to plead payment. But there is no law of this state which authorises offsets. If this were a question in Westminster Hall, it would be decided against the appellees under the English law; for the debt to be offset must be in the same right as the debt demanded. Thus in an action by the assignee of a bankrupt, a debt due from the bankrupt cannot be set off. *Wils. Rep.* 155. So where after the testators death the defendant received rents which became due before, he was not permitted to set off against the claim of the executor for those rents, a debt due to him from the testator.—Shipman *vs* Thomas, *Espinass* 274. The reason is, that where there are mutual debts, there must be mutual remedies; and unless there are, the doctrine of offsets cannot apply.

So a man cannot set off a debt due in right of his wife, against one due from himself. *Bull.* 179, 180—3 *Atk.* 691.

Though the bond in question were actually given for property of the testator's sold to him (which does not appear) yet it became a debt due to the executrix—she must sue in the *debet et detinet*, and is accountable for *the amount of the property so sold*, to the persons entitled to demand it. The remedies therefore are not mutual—The debts are not mutual—and consequently the offsets inadmissible. If they were, it might subject the appellant to a *devastavit* in cases of debts of superior dignity and an insufficiency of assets.

WARDEN for the appellees. The act of assembly 22. *Geo.* II, *C.* 27. §. 6, which permits the defendant to make *all the discounts he can*, is more comprehensive than the statute relating to offsets, and sufficiently so to embrace the present case. But I rely principally upon the advertisement, as imposing upon the appellant an obligation to receive the bonds in question in discharge of the debt for which the suit was instituted. He cited, 3 *Wils.* 396, 2 *Bur.* 821—1229.

MARSHALL on the same side.—The first question in this cause is, whether the discount offered is proper, under the act of Assembly—2dly, if not, what operation the advertisement will have upon the case.

1st, The words of the act are very extensive; much more so than the statute of offsets. The adjudications in England therefore are not applicable, because the statute speaks of *mutual debts* which our law does not. In the present case, the bond being given for property of the testator sold, the money when received is to be administered as other assets, and may therefore be properly subjected to the discount insisted upon at the trial.

MERCER,

MERCER, J.—Ought not the defendant to have pleaded this offset? The plaintiff might then have replied, no assets.—That it was not given for property of the testator, or the like; in which case the issue would have been upon the proper point.

MARSHALL. The act of Assembly does not require it to be pleaded, but declares that the discount if proved, shall be allowed.

But 2dly, the advertisement strengthens the case very much, because it creates an obligation on the appellant to admit the discount, is a tacit admission of assets, and of course does away the danger of producing a devastavit.

DUVAL on the same side, perhaps the appellee might have been induced to take the assignment of these bonds in consequence of the advertisement, and therefore the rejection of them as a discount would be a fraud upon him.

WASHINGTON in reply. If the defendant upon the plea of payment, can give in evidence offsets of this sort, it is impossible for the plaintiff to know how to meet the plea at the trial.—The bonds may be void, or paid off.

In the construction of the act of Assembly, the question, what are the proper discounts is still left open for the court to decide upon, and no better, or more just rule can be adopted than that, which prevails in cases of offsets in England. By confining is to mutual debts, it prevents confusion at the trial, or the possibility of eventual injustice to any of the parties.

The advertisement does not better the situation of the appellee, because neither of them were *purchasing creditors*; and to such only, are the benefits offered or intended. If the offset were in this case permitted, the appellant might be subjected to this inconvenience. A purchaser at the sale gives his bond, not claiming to be a creditor, for if he were, he would be entitled to a discount of five per cent, and ought not to have given a bond at all. The debt belonging to the administratrix and she being accountable for the amount to those intitled to distribution, she may have paid them, and afterwards upon bringing suit upon the bond, the defendants obtain assignments of debts due from the intestate to destroy the demand.

As to the defendant's offer to prove assets, it does not better the case, because it not being a point in issue, the plaintiff could not be prepared to meet such evidence.

CARRINGTON, J.—delivered the opinion of the court.

The court considers the motive of the advertisement, which was only to enhance the sales by offering the inducement of five per cent discount to the *purchasing creditors*.

But

But Garland not being of that defcription, can claim no benefit under it. The advertifement therefore is out of the queftion; and without it, there is no doubt, but that the admiffion of the bonds as offsets was improper. Neither the advertifement, nor the bonds ought to have been given in evidence to prove a payment, upon the plea and iffue joined in the caufe.

Judgment reverfed and a new trial awarded.

Sir JONATHAN BECKWITH,

againft

BECKWITH BUTLER & others.

THE appellees filed their bill in the High Court of Chancery, praying for a diftribution of the perfonal eftate of Sir Marmaduke Beckwith, and to fet afide a deed made by Sir Marmaduke to the appellant for 14 flaves, upon a fuggeftion of fraud in the obtaining of it, and for a divifion of them amongft the reprefentatives.

The defendant in his anfwer denies the fraud in obtaining the deed, and contends that it was but a reafonable provifion for him, the heir of the family and title, otherwife unadvanced. He ftates that there were little other eftate except a debt due by bond from Col. Tayloe which his father gave him in his lifetime as a compenfation for his having confented to the fale of a large Englifh eftate which would have defcended to him.

The allegation in the anfwer refpecting the gift of Tayloe's bond is not fupported by teftimony.

The Chancellor having directed an account of advancements made by Sir Marmaduke Beckwith to his children and grandchildren with the value of fuch advancements, alfo an account of the value of fuch of the flaves, named in the deed from the faid Sir Marmaduke to the defendant Jonathan Beckwith and their increafe, as were living, a report was made, to which fundry exceptions were taken by the defendant. Thefe exceptions being over-ruled by the court, the defendant was decreed to pay (out of the eftate of his inteftate in his hands to be adminiftered) to Beckwith Butler £610: 12: 4 ¼ and to Lawrence Butler £813: 2: 3 ½ with intereft from the 1ft of September 1781 appearing by the faid report to be due to them. From this decree Beckwith appealed.

The

The PRESIDENT delivered the opinion of the Court.

The anſwer of a defendant in chancery is not evidence where it aſſerts a right affirmatively in oppoſition to the plaintiffs demand. In ſuch a caſe, he is as much bound to eſtabliſh it by indifferent teſtimony, as the plaintiff is to ſuſtain his bill. The appellant, who is the heir at law and executor of his father, ſwears in his anſwer, that the father in his life-time gave him Tayloe's bond, the amount of which forms the great bulk of the perſonal eſtate ſought to be diſtributed. It would be monſtrous indeed, if an executor when called upon to account, were permitted to ſwear himſelf into a title to part of his teſtator's eſtate.

As to the fraud charged in the bill, in the obtaining of a deed for the 14 negroes, it is not ſufficiently proved. Some of the witneſſes prove an incapacity in the donor to contract at certain times: but the ſubſcribing witneſſes ſwear to his capacity at the time of executing the deed, and as the ſettlement is by no means an unreaſonable one, the court think it moſt proper and ſafe to eſtabliſh it. It reſembles the caſe of a will which was conteſted in this court, where the proof as to the ſtate of the teſtators mind, when the will was ſigned, overcame all the teſtimony reſpecting his capacity both before and after. But then the negroes conveyed by this deed muſt be conſidered as an advancement, as to which a queſtion was made at the bar, whether the encreaſe of the ſlaves, and intereſt on money advancements ought to be brought into hotchpot? The court are of opinion, that where a child is advanced with money, or negroes, he need not bring into hotchpot the encreaſe of the one, or account for the intereſt upon the other. For as he muſt ſuſtain the loſs, by accounting for the property at it's value *when given*, and by ſupporting and raiſing the negroes, ſo he is entitled to the encreaſe of them. There does ſeem to be a hardſhip, where one ſon has been advanced for many years, that he ſhould account with an unadvanced child only for the principal; yet no better rule than the above can be adopted.

Some objections were made at the bar to the mode purſued by the maſter, in aſcertaining the value of the negroes advanced; but we are of opinion, that though the value ſeems to have been gueſſed at, it does not appear to be unreaſonable either way, and as no exception is taken to the report, the objections now made ought not to be regarded.

The report is in favor of all the plaintiffs and is confirmed by the Chancellor. Yet a decree is given in favor of the Butlers only, without noticing Marmaduke Beckwith, another of the plaintiffs. This we suppose to have been a mistake of the clerk.

The decree therefore must be affirmed so far as it goes, and the cause remitted to the High Court of Chancery, for a hearing as to Marmaduke Beckwith.

WARDEN and WASHINGTON for the appellant.
CAMPBELL for the appellees.

SALLEE, *against* YATES & Wife.

THIS was an appeal from a decree of the High Court of Chancery—The bill was brought by the appellees to recover a legacy of £300, devised to the female plaintiff, by the will of Benjamin Harris her father, made in the year 1776, of which, £100 was to be paid in a year after the legatee should attain the age of 18 years, and the residue, so soon as the executors could raise it. The first payment was made to Sallee, the guardian of the legatee, on the 12th of September 1778, some time after she arrived to the above age, as was also the residue, on the 3d July 1779.

The guardian lent out the £200 on the day he received it, which was repaid to him in the year 1780—the £100 remained in his hands, not lent out, nor used, until the paper money was called in, when he funded the whole sum of £300 together with his own money, at the rate of one, for a thousand. The legatee refused, (before the money was funded) to receive it from the guardian, and instituted this suit, against him, as also against the executors and residuary legatees of the testator, praying that the £300 may be reduced according to the scale when it was paid, and that the balance may be made good out of the residuary estate. The Court, decreed the executors to pay the £300 to the plaintiffs, after deducting therefrom, the payments, made according to the true value at the time of such payments with interest from the time the plaintiff was entitled to recover her legacy. From this decree, the defendants appealed.

The PRESIDENT delivered the opinion of the court.

This is certainly a very hard case, but we think there is no ground for relief. The legislature in the year 1781, contemplating, no doubt, all those cases of hardship, and at the same time, the infinite mischief and confusion which would be introduced,

troduced, by a re-settlement of paper money claims, passed a law, declaring " that all actual payments made by any person " or persons, of any sum, or sums of the paper currency, there " mentioned, at any time, or times, either to the full amount, " or in part payment of any debt, contract, or obligation, " whatsoever, the party paying the same, shall have full credit, " for the nominal amount of such payments, which are not to " be reduced." It is remarkable, that to the words *debt* and *contracts*, are added, *or obligations whatsoever*, which comprehend legacies. Courts of Equity, are as much bound by this legislative declaration, as courts of law. The executor therefore, by the payments made to the guardian, was by this law totally discharged, and since the guardian was guilty of no fault, either in receiving, or in the application of the money, he ought not to be subject to the loss, by further depreciation, subsequent to the payment by the executors. The bill must be dismissed as to the executors and residuary legatees, and the cause remanded to the High Court of Chancery, as to the guardian, for an account to be taken of the money received by him, according to the principles of this decree.

JACOB WESTFALL,
against
JOHN SINGLETON.

THIS was an appeal from a decree of the High Court of Chancery. Sometime in the year 1749, Lord Fairfax, by a public advertisement, invited settlers, to that part of the Northern Neck where the land in question lies, promising to make rights to such, as would settle there. A man of the name of Vanderpool, having previously made a settlement upon the tract in dispute, he, about this time, sold the same to Abel Westfall, who took possession, and continued to hold it, until the year 1755, when he died, intestate, leaving two sons, Cornelius his eldest, and John. Lord Fairfax, having granted a very large tract of country, (including within it, the land in question,) to Bryant Martin, received a reconveyance of it, and laid off the whole into a manor.

In the year 1770, upon the application of the settlers, he, by a writing under his hand, agreed to convey to them their respective settlements, for three lives, renewable for ever, reserving an annual rent; which agreement was proved and recorded. Cornelius Westfall, who at the time of his fathers death, and long after, lived in the state of New Jersey, removed to this commonwealth, and took possession of the land in question, about the year 1773, and continued to hold it until his death, in 1780, having by his will devised it to his sons Isaac, and Zachariah, who afterwards conveyed the same, to Jacob Westfall, the plaintiff. Cornelius, paid rent for this land for some years, tho' lord Fairfax had refused to convey it to him.

The defendant (who claims under a purchase from John Westfall, the younger, son of Abel Westfall, by the defendant's father, and a deed in consequence thereof from lord Fairfax in the year 1773, to the defendant) states in his answer, that it was customary in that part of the country, for persons, having mere settlement rights, to transfer the same, by death-bed donations, which were always considered as valid. That Abel Westfall made such a disposition of the land in question, to his son John, who had shared with him in the toil and danger of making this settlement, and of securing it from the Indians; that the defendant and his father held possession until 1774, when Cornelius Westfall took possession.

There is some evidence, proving a custom, similar to that mentioned in the answer. The defendant having recovered the land in ejectment, this bill was filed praying an injunction and a conveyance.

The Chancellor dismissed the bill, being of opinion, that the equity therein stated, was neither admitted by the answer, nor established by the evidence.

The PRESIDENT delivered the opinion and decree of the court
" as follows: If lord Fairfax had not originally invited settlers on his
" lands on the South Branch, by a promise of making them titles,
" he was nevertheless bound, by his advertisement of the 5th of
" August 1749, to grant such titles to all persons then settled
" thereon. That Abel Westfall, being at that time settled on
" the land in dispute as a purchaser from Vanderpool, the origi-
" nal settler, was entitled to a grant thereof, from lord Fairfax,
" on the usual terms of granting his lands; and Abel, dying so
" entitled, in possession of the land, in the year 1755, without
" making a will, or other disposition of it, his equitable interest
" therein, descended to Cornelius Westfall, his eldest son and
" heir at law; who not appearing to have done any act, to for-
" feit, or to shew that he abandoned his title, but on the con-
" trary,

" trary, having entered on the land, within 20 years, (the time
" allowed by law for his entry if it had been a legal title, and
" he in the state,) he was entitled to the like grant from lord
" Fairfax, which his father might have claimed: But as it ap-
" pears, that the settlers within the manor, generally agreed,
" to accept leases on the terms of lord Fairfax's advertisement
" in 1770, and Cornelius himself, applied for such lease, and
" paid the annual rents accordingly, which amounted to his
" consent, to wave the claim to an absolute title, that he ought
" to hold the land, under the heirs, or assigns of lord Fairfax,
" on the terms, and subject to the covenants contained in the lease.

" That John Westfall, the younger, son of Abel, having no
" title in law or equity, to the land, no right could be derived
" to Thomas Singleton from him; and therefore, it is imma-
" terial, whether their contract was for an absolute purchase,
" or for a term only.*

" That lord Fairfax being bound in equity, to lease the land
" to Cornelius, at the time he executed the lease to John Sin-
" gleton the appellee, the latter, ought to be considered in
" equity as a trustee for Cornelius, and those claiming under
" him, as to so much of the said land, as was within Abel
" Westfall's settlement.

" The decree therefore must be reversed with costs, and it is
" decreed and ordered, that the appellee do, at the costs of the
" appellant, execute to him a proper deed, for assigning to him,
" his heirs and assigns, the said lease, made to him by lord Fair-
" fax, and bearing date the 3d day of August 1773, with all the
" benefits, and subject to the covenants and conditions therein
" contained, on the part of the said Singleton. That the in-
" junction granted by the said Court of Chancery, to stay the
" proceedings on the judgment at law, obtained by the appellee,
" against the appellant in the county court of Hampshire, stand
" and be perpetual. That the appellant be quieted in his pos-
" session of the said land, and that the parties bear their own
" costs in the said Court of Chancery: Liberty however, be-
" ing reserved to the appellee, to state, and shew to the said
" Court of Chancery, that part of the land contained in the
" lease, was not included in Abel Westfall's settlement, and to
" the said Court of Chancery, on that being made to appear, to
" vary the decree, so as to confine the assignment of the lease,
" the injunction, and quieting of possession in the plaintiffs, to
" the lands, to which Abel Westfall was entitled." JONES

---

* There is some contradictory testimony in the cause upon this subject.

JONES,

against

WILLIAMS & TOMLINSON.

THE appellees filed their bill in the High Court of Chancery against John J. Jacobs and wife, praying for a conveyance of a tract of land to which they were entitled in right of a settlement, made before the year 1775, and which had been granted to the said Jacobs and wife, by patent dated in 1784, in virtue of a survey made upon a military warrant by David Rodgers under whom Jacobs and wife claimed. This warrant was located in 1775, and the survey was returned in 1776; long subsequent to the settlement of the plaintiff's as asserted in their bill. Tomlinson's right of settlement having been affirmed by the commissioners in the year 1780, Williams alone entered a caveat against the emanation of a grant to Rodgers, but by an accident attending the transmission of subpoenas for his witnesses, the caveat was dismissed.

Jacobs and wife by their answer insist, that Rodgers had a right of settlement prior to that of the plaintiff's, and amongst other things disclosed, that they had sold to the appellant Jones.

Depositions were taken, which prove the prior settlement of the plaintiffs. After this, a new bill was filed by the plaintiffs, making Jones a party defendant, who appeared and put in an answer, in which amongst other things, he asserts a right in Rodgers by settlement, prior to that of the plaintiffs. No replication was put in to this answer, but the cause coming on to be heard upon the bill, answers, exhibits and *examinations of witnesses*, the court decreed in favor of the plaintiffs, from which decree the defendant Jones appealed.

MARSHALL for the appellant. This cause, as to the appellant, is to be considered as having come on, upon bill and answer: for the depositions having been all taken, before he was a party to the suit, and an entirely new claim being made, and new matter brought before the court, the evidence could not with any propriety be used against him. It would be most unreasonable, if claims not put in issue by the former bill, could be supported by the evidence taken on that bill. In 1 *Harr. Ch. Prac.* 108. It is laid down, that at any time before hearing, upon cause shewn, the plaintiff may obtain an order to add parties to his bill, but in this case, the cause is to be heard as to such new defendant, upon bill and answer. In the same book p. 150, it is also said, that when a supplemental bill is filed, after publication, the court never gives leave to examine that, which was in issue in the former cause, and it is irregular to examine witnesses, to a matter, that was in issue, and not proved in the original cause, and such proof, is not to be read. So, if there be no proof of the new matter in the supplimental bill, it must be dismissed, unless such matter be admitted by the defendants answer.

If then, the cause is to be heard on the bill and answer, the state of the case will be simply this. The answer, positively denies the plaintiff's title; states a completely equitable right in the defendant, under a prior settlement by Rodgers, and that, converted into a legal title, by being carried into grant.

THE PRESIDENT delivered the opinion of the court.

The depositions are clearly inadmissible. The first answer is filed in 1789, disclosing the sale to Jones, but at what time, does not appear. If it had been, *pendente lite*, the depositions might perhaps have been read. The bill against Jones, is neither supplemental nor amended, for it contains new matter entirely, without noticing the former bill. The cause must therefore be heard upon the bill, answer and exhibits.

It appears, that under the act of Assembly passed in 1779, Rodgers was entituled to a grant on a military survey, returned in 1776. This however was subject to a caveat, upon the trial of which, the merits might have been heard, and decided.

A caveat was entered by Williams, and in consequence of an accident was dismissed; we shall therefore consider the case, as the General Court would have done, on a hearing of the caveat.

As to a right by settlement, Rodgers appears to have had the best; but no right whatever, could be acquired in this way, in lands formerly belonging to the crown, until the act passed in May 1779—before that time, those lands might have been entered, and patented by any person, notwithstanding prior settlements by others: and even this act, which considers settlers as entitled to some compensation for the risk they had run, allows them only a preference to such settlements in lands, as at that time were *waste & unappropriated*. As to priority of settlement, it might still remain a question between persons, both of whom claim under the same sort of title; but the law of 1779, does not set up rights of this sort, so as to defeat those legally acquired under warrants; it applies to controversies between mere settlers.

The

The land in question therefore, was not *waste and unappropriated* in 1779, nor subject to the claim of a settler, however just it might be, because Rodgers was then entitled to a patent for it.

Decree reversed with costs and bill dismissed, each party paying his own costs in the High Court of Chancery.

BYRD *against* COCKE.

THIS was an action of debt brought by the appellee against the appellant as high sheriff, for levying an execution on the property of the plaintiff's tenant, without paying him an years rent, due at the time. The declaration "demands "£80, which the defendant owes and detains, for that the "defendant refused to pay the plaintiff the said sum of £80, "though he the defendant, as sheriff, levied an execution on "the property of J. Stith, which property was on the plaintiff's "premises, rented to the said Stith, for the said £80 a year, "and notwithstanding, the said Stith was in arrear to the "plaintiff, for the last years rent, to wit, for 1780 and although "the defendant was applied to for the said £80, contrary to "the form and effect of the act of Assembly &c. and the defen- "dant still refuses to pay the said £80 tho' often required &c. "to the plaintiffs damage £150" &c.—Plea *non assumpsit*—verdict and judgment for the plaintiff for £83 : 13 : 4 damage.— This judgment, being affirmed in the District Court, an appeal was prayed to this court.

The attorney general for the appellant.

This record though small, is as full of error as it can well be.—The writ is in case—the declaration in debt—the issue is *non assumpsit*, and verdict and judgment is entered for the plaintiff, though the jury have not found that the defendant *did assume*.

The declaration being in debt, makes an incurable error in the proceedings, at the very threshold. Debt will not lie in a case of this sort, where no contract exists, unless it were given by statute. It is brought too, against the sheriff for an act of *commission*, for which, even an action on the case would not lie. But if the action were proper, still the issue is immaterial, for tho' the defendant did not assume, yet he might be liable to the recovery of the plaintiff.

WICKHAM

WICKHAM for the appellee. That an action will lie against the sheriff, for levying an execution upon the property of a tenant on the demised premises, without paying a years rent to the landlord, if the same be due, is settled by the cases of Palgrave *vs* Windham, 1 *Str.* 212, and Gore *vs* Gofton, 1 *Str.* 643, both of which, being adjudications upon the statute of *Ann*, from which our act is copied, will be considered as authority.

The objection to the declaration, is more to the form, than the substance of it, tho' it begins like a declaration in debt, by stating the defendants *to owe and detain* &c. yet upon a view of the whole of it, we shall find it to be in fact a declaration in case; and if so, the *debet et detinet* may properly be rejected as surplussage. It states the act of Assembly—the rent due, and execution levied, notwithstanding notice to the sheriff, and demand of the years rent.

As to the issue, it is only informal, and therefore cured by the act of Jeofails—*nil debet*, may be pleaded to an action upon the case—not guilty to an action of debt; and tho' neither are formal, yet they are cured by verdict.

The PRESIDENT delivered the opinion of the court.

If the declaration could be supported, the court might get over the errors which precede and follow it, either by considering them, as cured by the verdict, or by awarding a repleader, from the first fault. But the declaration is certainly in debt, and tho' after a verdict, objections to the form of a declaration will be disregarded, yet we can find no authority, to justify a rejection of that part of it, as surplussage, which designates it a declaration in debt. As an action of debt, it is not sustainable under the act of Assembly, which does not impose a *penalty* upon the officer; and therefore, an action upon the case, for consequential damages, was most clearly the proper remedy.

Both judgments must be reversed with costs.

COLEMAN, *against* DICK & PAT.

THIS was an action of assault and battery, and false imprisonment, brought by the appellees, in the District Court of Petersburg. Plea, that the plaintiffs are slaves—Replication, that they are free and not slaves, and issue thereupon.

The jury found a special verdict in the following words viz. "We find, that the plaintiffs are lineally descended by the maternal line from Judith; that Judith was an Indian, *or the descendant* of an Indian. That she was brought into this state by a certain Francis Coleman, sometime after the year 1705, and was held as a slave, to the day of her death. If the law be for the plaintiffs, we find &c."

The District Court, gave judgment upon the special verdict for the plaintiffs. From which the defendant appealed.

WICKHAM for the appellant. I shall in the argument of this cause, rely upon three points. 1st, Admitting Judith to be an Indian, that she was nevertheless a slave. 2dly, That it does not sufficiently appear, that she was an Indian, entitled to freedom. 3dly, That the plaintiffs cannot recover in *this action,* tho' both these points be against me.

1st, The first act respecting Indians, passed in the year 1662, C. 136, *Purv. Ed.* of the laws p. 96, which does not relate to the subject of slaves. The next was in 1670, C. 12, p. 172, which enacts, that all servants, not christians, imported into this country by shipping, shall be slaves for life, but that those, who come by land, shall serve for a limitted time.

The next law passed in 1672, C. 8, p. 184, which speaks of Indian slaves, or servants for life, and proves, that the act of 1670, did not prevent Indians from being made slaves. The act of 1679. C. 1. p. 235 declares, that Indian prisoners taken in war, should be free purchase to the captor. Then comes the act of 1682, C. 1, p. 282, which repeals that part of the law of 1670, relating to slaves, and enacts, "that all servants, (except Turks and Moors, whilst in amity with his majesty,) which shall be brought, or imported into this country by sea or land, whether negroes, Moors, Mulattoes, or Indians, who, and whose parents and native country were not christian, at the time of the first purchase of such servants by some christian, though afterwards, and before such their importation and bringing into this country, they shall be converted to the christian faith, and all Indians which shall be hereafter sold by our neighboring Indians, or any other trafficking with us, and for as slaves, are deemed to be slaves, to all intents and purposes."—The act of 1705, C. 49, which is re-enacted by the acts 1748, and 1756 declares, "that all servants, imported and brought into this country by sea or land, who were not christians in their native country, (except Turks and Moors in amity with his majesty and others that can make
"due

"due proof of their being free in England, or in any other christian country before they were shipped in order for transportation hither,) shall be accounted and be slaves, and as such, be bought and sold, notwithstanding a conversion to christianity."

It is true, that in this law, there is a repealing clause of all other laws within the purview of it; yet, as this law differs not materially from that of 1682, it cannot be considered as intended to repeal that, but is merely a revision and collection of all the laws upon the subject. The act of 1682, makes slaves of Indians within our territory, which this act does not, and therefore, that part of the former law may be repealed by this. I am aware, that a notion has prevailed, that Indians could not be made slaves; this can only be accounted for, by considering the opinion, as applying to Indians *within the limits of this country.*

2dly, The verdict is so insufficiently found, that no judgment can be entered upon it. It finds, that Judith was an Indian, or *the descendent of one*; but it does not find *expressly*, that she was an Indian. Admitting the plaintiffs to be descendents from Judith, in the maternal line, it does not follow that they are Indians *intitled to freedom.* Suppose Judith had only been stated to be the *descendent of an Indian*, that might as well have been in the paternal as maternal line. The jury in tracing the plaintiff's descent, derive it from Judith in the *maternal line*, but when speaking of Judith's ancestry, they state her to be a descendent from an Indian *generally*, which shews that they understood the principle, that the issue, as to the question of slave or no slave, follows the condition of the mother. We may therefore, fairly conclude, that the jury could not ascertain, in which line Judith was descended.

Thirdly; There is no principle of law better settled, than this: that in personal torts, two or more cannot join as plaintiffs in the action, because the injury done to one is not an injury to the other. I submit it therefore, whether upon this point, the present action can be maintained.

CAMPBELL for the appellees. In favor of freedom, we are bound to construe all laws tending to its destruction, with the greatest strictness. From a view of all the acts which have been cited, it is evident, that the legislature never intended, that Indians *generally* should be made slaves, tho' some particular Indians, in special cases might. When therefore we speak of an *Indian*, unqualified by circumstances of any sort, we as certainly ly speak of a freeman, as if an *Englishman* had been mentioned. To associate the idea of slavery with the condition of this class of men, it is necessary to speak of them, as Indians of a *particular description*, who, by some law might loose their freedom. The preamble to the act of 1705, C. 52, shews, that the design of it was, to regulate the trade and intercourse with *all Indians* whatsoever, proving thereby, the sentiments of the legislature as to the free state of the Indians.

If then, Judith were *an Indian*, she was free—if a descendent from one, the court will presume her equally free, unless, they should presume the descent to be from such an Indian, as might by law be made a slave. For as Indians, generally speaking are free, the presumption, (unless opposed by circumstances proving her to be of that description, which might be made slaves,) will be, that the descent was from a free Indian.

The third objection is not a solid one. Actions of this sort are merely fictitious, and intended for the purpose of trying the single question, whether free or not? They are under the controul of the court, as much as actions of ejectment, and will be so moulded, as to bring into view the only point to be tried, and to favor the most complete attainment of that object. Besides, it is a benefit to the master that they should all join.

MARSHALL on the same side. The act of 1670 does not speak of Indians *generally*, but of such only, as are captured in war by each other, and sold to the whites. The act of 1679 does not make slaves of any, but only declares, to whom the property, *such as it is*, belongs. The Indians, mentioned in the recital to the act of 1682, (on whom alone that law operates,) are such only, as were captured by other Indians in war and sold, as mentioned in the act of 1670. This law speaks only of Indian *servants*, (not of Indians in general,) and authorizes such, as were held in servitude in their native country, to be made slaves, tho' Indians in general could not. But whatever may be the construction of these laws, I take the act of 1705 to be conclusive upon the subject. It not only repeals, in *express* terms, all former laws upon the subject, but establishes an intercourse with the Indian nations, as with *freemen*—it authorizes a free commerce with them. Is it usual for freemen to treat, or to trade with nations as free, the individuals of which, if caught, become slaves? The act of 1705 therefore, shews, that Indians in general could not be made slaves, but such of them only, as were *servants* in their own country.

The

The second objection goes to the insufficiency of the finding. But if I am right upon the first point, then it follows, that if Judith were an Indian she was free, unless she were also found to come under that description of Indians, who, by law might be made slaves. As to the alternative finding, the court must presume, that Judith was a descendent from an Indian in the maternal line, because where marriages are unknown, the father can never be certainly ascertained, the mother always may, and consequently the presumption in all such cases is, that the descent, when generally spoken of, is in the maternal line. In the case of illegitimate issue, the law acknowledges no father.

The third point, I consider as being completely settled, by the affirmance of the judgment, obtained by Tom *and others vs* Jenkins, (all of whom joined in one suit) in the Northumberland District Court. *

Wickham in reply. The act of 1705, (which I call the treaty law,) could only relate to Indians *within our territory*. 1st, because the preamble so states it, and 2dly, because Virginia had no right to make regulations, respecting Indians without her limits. This law is intended to regulate trade with Indians, considered in a *national* point of view, which is by no means incompatible, with the right, or the policy of purchasing the individuals of those nations for slaves. Suppose this had been a statute of the Parliament of England respecting a trade with Guinea, tho' that nation is acknowledged to be free, and is so treated, yet it would not follow, that a traffic carried on for the purchase of the individuals of that nation, as slaves, would be incompatible with that acknowledgment. I admit, that no Indians, but such as were brought in, in a state of servitude, could be made slaves; but I contend, that Judith's situation was such, is fairly to be inferred from the verdict, which finds that *she was brought in by Coleman, and held by him as a slave;* that is, brought in as a slave, and held as a slave, which is the plain construction of the finding. The mother being stated to have been retained in slavery, is at least *prima facie* evidence that her posterity are so, and ought to require some opposing testimony to defeat it. If this be not the case, what, let me ask, will be the situation of our negro property? If the master in every instance, is bound to prove his negro to be of that particular description, which subjects him to slavery, there is not one in ten thousand instances, where he could do so.

But

---

* See Ante 123.

But upon the second point, I still rely with confidence. If the finding Judith to be an Indian, is finding that she might be either free or a slave, it leaves the question as to that fact in a state of too much uncertainty, for a decision either way. This court can presume nothing for, or against the plaintiffs. As *individuals*, they may form their own conjectures as to the fact. As *judges*, the fact must be found for them, and that with certainty. But if presumption is to be let in, I must still controvert the rule mentioned by Mr. Marshall. A bastard, is said not only to have no father but no mother. He is *nullius filius*.

MARSHALL. The question seems to be narrowed to a single point; and that is, whether Judith, being found to be an Indian, unqualified by any circumstance, or description whatever, is insufficient, or can amount to a finding against the plaintiffs? Now I hold the rule to be, that where an affirmative is proven, and can only be defeated by a negative, the party who would claim a benefit under the negative, must prove it. Thus, a verdict which finds, that the plaintiff's ancestor died seized, and that the plaintiff is his heir, need not find also that the ancestor died *intestate*, in order to perfect the plaintiff's title, but the defendant must prove that he did not die intestate, if being true, he would avail himself of that fact. So here, Judith is stated to be an Indian—an Indian generally speaking is free.— But some Indians are not free—yet Judith is not found to be such an Indian, as could not be free: the affirmative therefore being found, clear of the exceptions, the latter is not to be intended, so as to destroy the former. It is useless to cite cases to establish such plain principles of law.

WICKHAM.—The cases cited, are not in point. The court intended matter *collateral* to the issue, in order to sustain the verdict, but they did not, and could not intend the *very point* in issue, for that would be in fact, a finding of the court, not of the jury. I will examine one of the cases. The dying intestate, was a point merely collateral to the issue. But suppose the issue had expressly been, whether the person died intestate, or not; would the finding in that case have been sufficient? So here—the point in issue is slavery or not: but whether in the affirmative, or negative, is not deducible from the verdict: for tho' Judith was an Indian, yet she might be either a slave, or free. Can this court then intend she was free? Surely not.

THE PRESIDENT delivered the opinion of the court.

We considered the last point first, because if this were against the plaintiffs, it would have been unnecessary to decide the others.

others. The objection, when applied to common cases of personal torts, is well founded: but actions like the present, are merely fictitious, and were very properly in this respect, likened to actions of ejectment. For if many persons may unite as plaintiffs, to try a joint right to land, (which no doubt they may,) no good reason can be given why they may not unite, to try a joint right to freedom as in the present case. Although suits for freedom may be instituted without the leave of the court, yet it is usual to petition for such leave. The court, generally require the opinion of the counsel upon the plaintiff's right; and if it appear, that the plaintiff has probable cause for suing, the court will make special orders for the purpose of protecting the plaintiff from the master's resentment, or ill treatment on that account, and for allowing him reasonable time to prepare for his trial.

As to the first point made at the bar, the court are of opinion that the act of 1705, is a compleat repeal of all former laws on the subject, and that since that period, no *American Indian*, can be reduced into a state of slavery. *Foreign Indians* coming within the description of that act, might be made slaves. When therefore, we speak of *Indians generally*, it is to be understood, that some might, but others might not be made slaves in this country.

This principle being ascertained, we were led to a consideration of the second point, which respects the insufficiency of the finding. Upon this, the court are divided.

Two judges think, that finding Judith to be an Indian, *brought in* by Coleman, without saying from whence, whether by sea, or land, is insufficient to warrant the judgment. That whatever lengths the jury might have gone in presuming the fact, the court cannot supply those circumstances, necessary to establish it. On the other hand, two judges, presuming in favor of liberty, think that the verdict is sufficient.

The judgment therefore must be affirmed.

KEENE *against* LEE.

EJECTMENT in the District Court of Northumberland, brought by the appellee. The parties agreed a case, in substance as follows, viz.

That William Keene the 1st, being seized &c. by his will, made in 1681, devised 240 acres of land, (part of the tract in question)

question) to his son William and his heirs for ever, and if he died without issue, remainder over.

That William Keene the 2d, being seized of the said 240 acres of land, as well as of 260 acres bequeathed to him by Mrs. Banks, (the residue of the land in the declaration mentioned) devised the whole to his son Newton and his heirs for ever.

That Newton, being seized &c. by his will made in 1770, devised to his executors his lands in Fairfax and Loudoun, and all other the lands and slaves to which he was entitled, as heir by the mother's side to John Woodbridge, to sell for payment of debts; and if there remained more slaves than were necessary for this purpose, he devised them equally amongst his children. He then devised as follows, viz: "I give to my wife my dwel-
"ling plantation, and tract of land, (being the land in questi-
"on) during her widowhood, and after her death, or widow-
"hood, I give the same to my eldest son William, to him and
"his heirs, on this condition, that my said son shall, as soon as
"he arrives to the age of 21 years, join in, and make sufficient
"deeds for conveying to the purchaser or purchasers of my said
"land in the county of Fairfax, an absolute estate in fee sim-
"ple, and shall also join in the sale of the aforesaid negroes, as
"my said executors may sell for the payment of my debts, and
"suffer the remainder of the said slaves to be enjoyed, and go
"for ever as I have before bequeathed them; but in case my
"said son does not comply with the aforesaid condition, then,"
he gives the dwelling plantation and tract of land under the same condition, first to his son Thomas, and then to his son John.

The testator then proceeds to devise as follows: "Item, it
"is my will, that if my son William, die without heir of his
"body, before he comes to the age of 21 years, that the land
"above devised to him, shall go to my son Thomas and his
"heirs, yet it is my meaning, that if he attain that age, he
"shall enjoy a fee simple in the said land, with the condition
"aforesaid annexed."

That William the 3d, in the year 1775, and after the death of his father executed a paper under his hand and seal, which was duly recorded, by which, after reciting that he had just attained full age, and had considered his father's will, he declared that he would abide by, and perform the directions of the same, and the conditions therein contained.

That the executors sold the land in Fairfax, pursuant to to the power given them by the will of Newton Keene, and
that

that his son William, joined them in a conveyance of it to the purchaser.

That the negroes, to which the said Newton Keene was entitled, as heir by the mother's side to John Woodbridge, mentioned in the will of Newton Keene, were at the time of his death, and have been ever since, in the adverse possession of George Yerby; and that a suit has been commenced by the executors, and is still pending for the recovery of them.

That in the year 1789, William Keene the 3d, executed a deed, conveying to trustees all the slaves mentioned in his father's will, (to which he was entitled as heir on the mother's side to John Woodbridge,) for the use of the wife and children of the said William; with a power to the trustees, to sue for and recover the said slaves, for the uses mentioned in the deed.

That the said William Keene the 3d, did in the year 1779 sell and convey all the land, to which he was entitled under the will of his father, and which is the land in the declaration mentioned, to the lessor of the plaintiff, in fee simple.

That after the execution of this deed, the lessor of the plaintiff used the land in the declaration mentioned, for some years, for the purpose of a cart way, to and from his other land; and that the defendant, who is the second son of the said Newton Keene, entered upon the same, about the year 1788, and still keeps possession.

That Robert Keene, the son of William the third, is heir at law of the said William, and is yet living.

That the widow of Newton Keene, after his death, viz. in 1771, appeared in court, and renounced all benefit under the will of her said husband; after which, William Keene the 3d, entered upon the lands in the declaration mentioned, and allotted to the widow her dower in the same, according to a survey and plat, which are annexed and agreed.

They agree the lease, entry and ouster, and if upon the whole matter, the law be for the plaintiff, they agree that judgment shall be entered for him, for his term yet to come, in the land in the declaration mentioned; if the law be for the defendant, then judgment to be entered for him.

Judgment upon this special verdict was given for the plaintiff, in the District Court.

CAMPBELL for the appellant. I am to contend, that the estate in question, devised to William Keene, by the will of his father Newton Keene, was to take effect upon the performance of a *precedent* condition. The eftate is not to veft, until his arrival at the age of 21 years; immediately after which, he is to join in a conveyance of the flaves. It is neceffary therefore, that William Keene, or thofe claiming under him fhould fhew, that he had ftrictly performed the condition; fince no obftacles however great, could excufe him from the performance. The declaration made in 1775, *agreeing* to perform the conditions in the will, cannot be faid to amount to a performance, becaufe this is a thing merely executory, whereas the thing to be done, fhould have been executed.

The caufe of forfeiture which I have juft confidered, is in the *omiffion* of the devifee, to convey the flaves. But the conveyance of thofe flaves to truftees, for the ufe of the family of the devifee, is a more *active* and deliberate breach of the condition, and has for ever put it out of his power to perform it, although all other obftacles fhould be removed.

WARDEN and WASHINGTON argued the caufe for the appellee.

There is certainly a material difference, between a condition precedent, and fubfequent, both in their nature, and effects; if the former, the condition muft be ftrictly performed, before the eftate can veft; but if the latter, the eftate is immediately vefted, and the continuance of it, depends upon the performance. As to the former, it is admitted that nothing, not even the act of God, or of the law, can difpenfe with a ftrict performance. In the latter, if the performance be prevented from any fuch caufe, the eftate becomes abfolute in the poffeffor; for conditions which go to *defeat* eftates, are odious, and to be taken ftrictly. *Sheb*. *Touch*. 129—130.

The condition in queftion is moft certainly *fubfequent*. Immediately after the death of Newton Keene, the remainder vefted in his fon William in *intereft*, and upon the death of the widow of the teftator, it vefted in *poffeffion*. But the condition was not to be performed, until William came of age, which muft have been fubfequent to the vefting of the eftate; and therefore, if the performance was prevented by the act of law, the eftate is abfolute in him.

Let it be here premifed, that as to the negroes, the condition is nugatory in itfelf; becaufe they being devifed to the executors, with a power to fell, it was entirely unneceffary to require, that William fhould join in the conveyance, and therefore if he had really refufed to do fo, tho' it might have prevented an eftate *from vefting*, it would not have *divefted* an eftate.

But

But suppose the act required to be done, were material; it is denied, that a forfeiture has taken place, either by *omission*, or by any act of *commission*.

As to the first, the charge is, that William has not joined in a conveyance of the slaves mentioned in his father's will. But before this is relied upon, it should appear, 1st, that the executors had found a purchaser for the slaves, and 2dly, that they had produced a conveyance of them, requesting him to join. For William Keene, is not authorized to *sell*, but is required, to *join in conveying to the persons*, to whom the *executors* had previously sold. But again: neither William Keene, nor the executors could convey the negroes until they were reduced into possession. Such a conveyance would have been *ipso facto* void, besides exposing the parties to a severe penalty. A condition to do a thing, which amounts to maintenance is void. *Shep. Touch.* 129, 1 *Hawk. pl. Cr.* 255, *Rolls Ab.* 417. If then this be a condition subsequent, the performance of it is forbidden by the law, and therefore, no forfeiture can have incurred.

2dly, What act has William Keene done, to disable himself from performing the condition? Let it not be forgotten, that so soon as he arrived to full age, he bound himself by a declaration, sufficient to restrain him from any active breach of the condition. But if not so, the deed of 1789 was not a breach. It is found, that at that time, the negroes were in the adverse possession of another; the deed therefore was void, both at common law, and by the act of Assembly against the selling of pretensed titles. If so, it could produce no disability whatever in William Keene, if the negroes should ever afterwards be recovered, and reduced to possession. If a feoffee, upon condition to reenfeoff, be disseized, and then he take wife, and enter into a statute, &c. yet before his entry, this is no breach of the condition, for 'till then, the charge doth not bind the land. *Shep. Touch.* 143, *Co. Litt.* 222, 2 *Co. Rep.* 59, *b*. Suppose then, that the negroes in question should hereafter be recovered, and admit that the trustees in the deed of 1789 could recover damages, under an idea, that this deed, though not valid as a conveyance, amounted to a covenant to convey, when the negroes should be recovered, still such a recovery would produce no disability, and most certainly, a Court of Equity, would never decree, in the very teeth of the statute, a specific execution of such an agreement.

William Keene then, cannot properly be charged with a breach of the condition, until, having it in his power, legally, to perform it, and being requested to do so, he refuses. Besides, the deed of 1789, is not only voluntary, but fraudulent as to the appellee, who had purchased and paid a valuable consideration for the land, ten years before this deed of trust was made.

But if all these points are against the appellee, he is most clearly entitled to the 240 acres, which were entailed upon William the 2d, by the will of his father, and therefore descended upon William the 3d, unclogged with the condition in Newton Keene's will.

The PRESIDENT delivered the opinion of the Court.

There can be no dispute about the 240 acres, which being entailed by William Keene the first, descended upon William the 3d; free from the conditions in the father's will, and being converted into a fee simple estate in 1776, he was enabled to convey to the lessor of the plaintiff, a compleat and absolute estate in this parcel of land, by the deed of 1779.

But as judgment is given for all the lands mentioned in the declaration, without distinguishing this part, from the other, it must be reversed, unless the plaintiff's title to the whole can be sustained.

The condition annexed to this devise in the will of Newton Keene, is active, so far as it requires the son, when of age, to join with the executors in a conveyance of the slaves to those, who might purchase from them; or passive, as it injoins him, to suffer this property to be enjoyed by the devisees, in case they were not sold. The condition was certainly nugatory, since the devise to the executors to sell, or to the legatees, was perfect, and would have included the heir, without any act on his part. It was added, probably, from abundant caution, to remove any doubts of the title from the minds of purchasers. But though it was unnecessarily required, the devisee was not therefore excused from the obligation of performance, since he took the estate subject to that condition. This then brings us to the question, whether it has been sufficiently performed, or not?

In January 1775, the devisee executed a writing under seal, reciting, that in the preceding month he had attained full age, stating the condition on which the land was devised to him, which he had considered, and declaring, that he would abide by the directions, devises, and conditions of the will, and join in any sale of the lands and slaves, according to the will.

It is objected, that this is not a conveyance, but merely an executory declaration. As to the lands, this is true; the title to them cannot pass at law, but by a regular conveyance; yet a Court of Equity would have compelled him, to release to the person, who might purchase from the executors. But it is unnecessary, to consider the extent of the obligation, which this declaration imposed upon William Keene, as to the land, since it is found, that he joined the executors in a conveyance of it.

As to the slaves, the declaration under consideration, is important. This species of property may pass, from one to another, without a deed or *written* contract, if a valuable consideration be given. And if William Keene had instituted a suit for the recovery of these slaves, the writing in question, would have been such an evidence of a contract, as to have created a bar to his recovery; not by way of estoppel, but as passing his title.

But it was contended, that he ought, as soon as he came of age, to have conveyed his right in the slaves to the executors, This would have been doing more than the testator required. He is only enjoined, (in case of a sale made by the executors,) to *unite with them in a conveyance to the purchaser*, and this he was not bound to do, unless *required* by the executors. If no sale were made by them, he was then bound, to suffer this property to be enjoyed by the devisees.

It is objected, that the deed of trust made in 1789, has disabled William Keene from conveying to a purchaser when required, and has also deprived him of the power, of permitting the enjoyment of the property by the devisees, within the meaning of the testator. To this, there are two sufficient answers.

1st, That the settlement is merely voluntary, and therefore fraudulent as to creditors and purchasers, and indeed as to all the world, except the grantor himself. It is therefore void, as to the appellee, who claims under a prior title from William Keene. Besides, the declaration made in 1775, and recorded, had passed away his interest in the slaves, to the uses mentioned in his father's will, and therefore the deed of 1789, could not operate to defeat it.

2d, If it could be admitted, that this deed produced a forfeiture, still the remainder man could not lawfully enter in 1788, before this deed was made.

Upon the whole, we are of opinion, that the conditions in the will of Newton Keene have been performed, and that the judgment must be affirmed.

GRANBERRY'S

FALL TERM

GRANBERRY's Executor,
against
JOSIAH & JAMES GRANBERRY.

THE appellees filed their bill in the High Court of Chancery against the appellant, the executor of their father; and their guardian, for an account.

To the report of Auditors made in the cause, the appellant took the four following exceptions. 1ft, That his receipts of money in depreciated paper, are reduced by the scale of depreciation, on the day they were received, without any proof that he received it unnecessarily, or delayed paying it away to those who were entitled to it.

2dly, Interest is allowed on monies in his hands, as if he were a debtor, or had retained the same improperly, and that too at a time, when borrowers of good credit were not to be met with, and when the executor neither did nor could make a profit thereby.

3dly, No commissions are allowed him.

4thly, That £500 due from him to the testator and to be paid in June 1779, and which was paid on the day, is charged to him as specie.

The report being confirmed by the High Court of Chancery, the defendant appealed.

RONOLD for the appellant. As to the first exception.—An executor, is in the nature of a trustee ; he receives no benefit from the execution of his office, and should therefore be subject to no injury, unless he hath produced it by his own misconduct. An executor is not only compelled to receive the debts of his testator, but is bound to solicit and to enforce the payment of them. For if they should be lost by his neglect, in not using the proper means of obtaining payment, he must sustain that loss. In this situation therefore, it would be unjust, to burthen him with the loss; by depreciation of money, thus forced into his hands, and at a time, when perhaps no opportunity offered of applying it. Some reasonable time then, should be allowed him, to dispose of the money, before the scale can with justice be applied.

Second exception.—Where the risk must be run by the executor, he is not bound to pay interest. This is laid down in the case of Ratcliff *vs* Graves, 1 *Vern.* 179; and tho' in that case, interest was decreed, yet it was upon a principle, which does not apply in this country : it was, that the money might be be infured. So, an executor who changes the nature of a debt, due to the teftator, becomes liable himfelf to pay it, out of his own pocket—1 *Vern.* 473. An executor is not liable to pay intereft, even in England, unlefs he make a profit by the principal. *Brow. Ch. Rep.* 359, Newton *vs* Bennet. The Chancellor was therefore miftaken, (as I humbly conceive,) when he prefumed the appellant had made a profit, becaufe the contrary was not fhewn. The executor could not in this cafe, diftribute the money amongft the legatees, who were under age, and who of courfe, could not give him a difcharge; he was therefore compelled to retain it, and unlefs it appeared, that he made ufe of it, nothing can be more unrighteous, than to force him to pay intereft.

It is true, that the appellant ftands in the double character of guardian and executor, but as the debts due from his teftator, were not all difcharged, he will be confidered as holding the money, in his capacity of executor. The intereft, I confider as a reafonable compenfation for his trouble, upon the fame principle, that he is entitled to the undifpofed furplus, unlefs barred, by an exprefs compenfation allowed by the teftator. There is no cafe to be found, which fubjects a guardian to the payment of intereft, from whence I conclude that he is not liable to pay it; and a guardian and executor appear to ftand, much in the fame fituation; for if the former, take a bond for rent due to his ward, he is liable to pay it out of his own pocket, and the bond is his own. 2 *Ch. Rep.* 97.

The law of this ftate, requires, that a guardian fhould annually return an account of the profits and of the income of the ward's, *eftate,* to court; but this can only mean the real eftate, to which, the words *profit and income,* are more properly applicable; unlefs indeed the guardian fhould lend out the money, in which cafe, the intereft would be income, and to be accounted for.

Third exception—The legacy given to the executor, is to be confidered as a gratuity, independent of his trouble in executing the truft, and not in lieu of his commiffions. If he had refufed, he would ftill have been entitled to the legacy, and having undertaken the trouble, he ought to receive a compenfation for it.

Fourth exception—The appellant, being an executor, was not thereby rendered incapable, of difcharging a debt he owed to the eftate of his teftator, at the time it became due, more efpecially, as it appears in this cafe, that the payment was applied to the difcharge of a debt, due from the teftator. If fo, he is entitled equally with others, to the benefit of the law, respecting payments in paper money.

CAMPBELL for the appellees. 1st Point—Nothing can be more just, or reasonable, than that an executor, claiming to be charged on a day posterior to that, on which he received money, or in other words, with less than he received, should shew some good reason for such a pretension. It is a subject, susceptible of proof and of explanation.

If the rule laid down by the Chancellor be rejected, to what other can we resort. The liability of an executor, if he do not recover his testator's debts in proper time, can only exist, where there was probable ground to apprehend insolvency, or the like; and in such cases only, can he be charged with such negligence as to render him personally liable. But at a time, when a depreciated paper money was in circulation, I should not hesitate, to consider an executor guilty of malfeasance in his office, who should press for the payment of his testator's debts, unless under an evident necessity.

2d point—The Chancellor, in the case of Newton and Bennet, which has been cited, says, that where it does not appear, that the executor applied the money to the purposes of the will, or unless he brings it into court, he shall be presumed to use it in the way of his trade, and be liable to pay interest for it. This case, is strongly in my favor. If there be debts due from the estate, and carrying interest, and the executor permits that interest to accumulate, when it might be avoided, it is right, that he should answer it out of his own pocket.

3d point—By the laws of this state, a guardian receiving the *estate* of a ward, must annually render an account; and he is confined to the *profits or other income*, for the support of the ward, without being permitted to go farther. The word *estate* includes *money*, as well as *land*.

THE PRESIDENT delivered the opinion of the court.

'The first objection made to the report is, that the paper money is reduced by the scale of depreciation, on the day it was received by the executor. Upon general principles, such a rule, would certainly be improper and unjust; and especially too, when the money was received in a state of rapid depreciation. The executor may not be able to find a creditor, or legatee, to whom he could pay the money, on the day it was received, or the payment might be suspended in some cases, by disputes amongst creditors for the preference.

But

But in this cafe, the appellant has neither objected to the mode *originally*, nor pointed out any other, the propriety of which might be confidered by the court: on the contrary, his accounts were stated by himfelf in the fame manner, the debits and credits being reduced by the fcale, on the day they were received and paid. He ought therefore to be bound by this mode, and the Chancellor did right, in over-ruling this exception.

The fecond objection, is to the charge of intereft, as if the executor were a *debtor*, or had received, or retained the money improperly. It is contended, that fuch a charge, at the time it is made, is peculiarly unjuft, as there were then no borrowers of good credit to be met with; and that the executor neither did nor could derive a profit from it.

There are no facts difclofed in the record, which can throw light upon this fubject. The bill is filent as to intereft, and fo is the anfwer, except that part of it where (fpeaking of the paper money which he had fcaled,) he ftates the injury arifing from confiderable fums having been on hand, from time to time, leffening every day in their value, without benefit to him, and without an opportunity of paying it away. Thus the queftion ftands upon the face of the accounts. It is true, that there is no general rule, which obliges an executor to pay intereft. We find from the cafes upon this fubject, that it has been determined both ways; and upon principle, it will appear, that no general rule can be formed.

Each cafe muft depend upon its own particular circumftances; in fome cafes the executor ought, and in others, he ought not to anfwer intereft. In this we think he ought to be accountable for intereft, on the money refting in his hands, from time to time. But for the reafons before ftated, in confidering the firft point, it would be too rigid, and injurious, to charge him with intereft from the day of each receipt of money. The accounts ought to be clofed at the end of *each year*, and intereft allowed upon the different balances, up to the year 1782, when the whole tranfaction clofed. But fuch intereft, ought not to be carried to the account of the fucceeding years, in order to deduct the fame, from the payments made in fuch fucceeding years. This though done in the common cafes of debtors is too ftrict as to truftees.

As to the rifk ftated at the bar, or the difficulty of procuring borrowers, it is an objection which does not come from th executor, nor is it ftated by him in his anfwer, but is mentioned in argument as a possible case. But if it were true, he might have applied to the Chancellor for his direction, as to lending it to individuals, or to the public, which would have made him safe; or he might have carried the money into that court. In this case there were children, whose fortunes were almost entirely pecuniary. It would therefore be unjust that the money should lie in the executors hands unproductive, so as to deprive the legatees of maintainance, or oblige them to resort to the principal of their legacies.

If the executor does not settle his accounts every year, he ought at least to strike the balance at the end of every year, that he may see the state of his accounts and of the funds in his hands. It is upon this principle, that we establish the rule before mentioned.

In stating this interest, the appellant ought to have credit for the £500, in 1773, which by the will was directed to be lent him without interest, and to be re-charged with it in 1778, when the loan was to cease.

The third objection is made on the score of commissions.

An executor, is certainly entitled to some compensation for his trouble, and that, by custom, is generally fixed at five per cent upon actual receipts. But it is objected, that the legacy left to him, is a bar of all further compensation. The rule, that a legacy given to an executor, defeats his claim to the undisposed residuum, is assimilated to the point under consideration. But that principle, seems to be much mistaken, in the application made of it. It is unnecessary for us to give an opinion upon that point, as in this case, there is no surplus; yet it may be observed, that if there were such a residuum, the legacy would be no bar, as there were several executors, to all of whom unequal legacies are given, and so this court decided, in the case of Shelton and Shelton. The present question therefore, like all others of this nature, depends, (as to the amount to be allowed,) upon the custom, and the intention of the testator. He clearly meant, to allow an adequate compensation. To one executor, he gives £250, and left that should be an insufficient recompence for his trouble, he authorises the other executors to encrease it, if necessary. In the codicil, he gives the appellant (who is not named an executor in the will itself,) a legacy, *as being his nephew,* and to this, he would have been entitled, tho' he had refused the office. It would seem, as if the testator did not at first mean to make him an executor, by his directing *his executors,* to lend him £500 with interest. So that it is

evident,

evident, he never intended the legacy as a compenfation for his fervices, but merely as a bounty. The appellant therefore, ought to have credit, for five per cent commiffion on his receipts of each year, before the accounts are clofed, in order to adjuft the intereft as before mentioned.

As to the 4th point, the court entertain fome doubt, whether the £500, ought to be charged to the defendant at all, or not?

In the exceptions, it is ftated as a debt due from the appellant, to the teftator, and paid in 1778,—in his account, he gives credit in October 1777, for this fum, as due in 1778, and reduces it by the fcale of October 1777. He is charged with it by the commiffioners, in 1778, as cafh, had five years, without intereft, and then due; in which cafe, he ought not to be charged with it, unlefs he received it in other money, that what came to his hands by collection, with the whole of which, he feems to be charged in the account. This fact therefore, muft be afcertained in the Court of Chancery.

If it appear, that he is fo charged, the credit in his account (as executor,) in October 1777, ought to be confidered as a payment on that day, in paper, and reduced by the fcale accordingly; for a debtor, by undertaking the office of an executor, cannot be prevented from exercifing, in common with others, the right of paying in paper money a debt due to the teftator. And as no better proof can be expected, the entry in his account, will be evidence of the *time* of payment, and from that time, he bound his fecurities, to be anfwerable for the proper application of the money.

The decree therefore muft be reverfed with cofts, and the caufe remanded to the High Court of Chancery for the enquiry to be made, and for an account to be taken, according to the principles of this decree.

CASES ARGUED AND DETERMINED

IN THE

COURT OF APPEALS

IN

THE SPRING TERM OF THE YEAR, 1794.

TAYLOR'S Administratrix,
against
PEYTON'S Administratrix.

THIS was an action of debt upon a bond, instituted in the District Court of Northumberland. The declaration was in common form, with a *profert* &c. Upon oyer, the bond is set forth at large, and the defendant pleads payment. The jury found the following verdict, viz: "We find for the plain-
"tiff the debt in the declaration mentioned, if the court shall be
"of opinion, that the copy of the original bond with the en-
"dorsements thereon, filed in this cause, and proven to be sto-
"len and burnt, all of which is well attested, is legal evidence
"to go to the jury and support the plaintiff's declaration,
"otherwise they find for the defendant."

Upon the copy of the bond is endorsed a memorandum signed by three persons, certifying that they had compared the copy with the original and found them perfectly to agree. Judgment for the plaintiff and appeal prayed.

WASHINGTON for the appellant. The copy of a deed, of which oyer cannot be demanded, may be given in evidence if the original be lost, or be in the possession of the adverse party. But if oyer be demanded, and must be given, the obligee has no remedy left but to resort to a Court of Equity, to establish the bond. Even if this court should consider itself bound by the case

case of Read *vs* Brookman in 3 *Durnf.* and *Eaſt* 151, ſtill that deciſion will have no influence upon this caſe, ſince the loſs of the bond is not ſtated in the declaration, or put in iſſue by the pleadings.

MARSHALL for the appellee. The caſe of Puered *vs* Duncombe, 2d *Ld. Ray,* 852, is an expreſs authority to prove that it is not neceſſary to produce the original bond. Why the party ſhould be forced into a Court of Equity, if he can at law prove the exiſtence, and ſubſequent loſs or deſtruction of the bond, I am at a loſs to imagine. The ſame evidence is required in both courts—The danger of ſetting up a forged bond, for the copy of the real one, is not greater in the one court than in the other. If a ſuit ſhould be brought in the Court of Chancery, and doubts be entertained concerning the execution, or loſs of the bond, that court would at laſt direct an iſſue to be tried at law. In the note to the caſe of Read *vs* Brookman, it was decided that the copy of a bond, or of a releaſe might be given upon oyer. But admit it to be true, that the bond muſt be produced, if oyer of it be demanded, yet if the defendant wave the neceſſity of ſeeing the original, and without denying the validity of the bond, avoid it by the plea of payment, it is ſurely too late after this to object.

WASHINGTON in reply. The caſe of Puered *vs* Duncombe was decided before the ſtatute of the 4th of Ann, C. 16, making the ſum mentioned in the condition, inſtead of the penalty, the real debt, and is therefore not to be relied upon.

The caſe of Matiſon *vs* Atkinſon, 3 *Durnf.* and *Eaſt* 753, in the note, is againſt the appellee, becauſe it proves, that where oyer of the original is diſpenſed with, the plaintiff muſt file a ſpecial declaration, ſtating the loſs of the bond, or obtain a rule upon the defendant, to ſhew cauſe, why profert of a copy ſhould not be accepted. This mode of proceeding, tho' new, ſeems liable to no ſolid objections, becauſe the loſs being put in iſſue, the defendant is apprized of the point he is to conteſt.

LYONS J. We will not now determine how the caſe would have been if the defendant had inſiſted upon oyer of the original bond: becauſe it is clear, that ſhe has waved the neceſſity of its being produced, by accepting oyer of a copy, and pleading to the action.

The caſe is completely within the reaſon of the modern practice, ſtated in the caſe of Read *vs* Brookman, in 3 Term *Rep.* and the notes ſubjoined.

Judgment affirmed.
BURWELL.

BURWELL, against COURT.

THIS was an appeal, from a judgment of the District Court of Williamsburg, rendered upon a bond for the forthcoming of property taken in execution.

Mr. Ronold for the appellant objected to the form of the bond, the condition of which is, "that the property shall be produced at the day of sale," but appoints no *place*.

By the court—The act of Assembly requires that the defendant should give bond and security to have the property forthcoming at the day of sale, but is silent as to the *place*.—The omission therefore cannot vitiate the bond.

Judgment affirmed.

SMITH & MORETON, against WALLACE.

THIS was an appeal from a decree of the High Court of Chancery. The case was as follows: The appellants instituted a suit in the General Court against Benjamin and William Piper, the latter of whom being arrested by the appellee (the sheriff) was discharged upon the parol agreement of Jett to become bail for his appearance.

The clerk being of opinion that this undertaking was not sufficient, and a bail piece being offered, and rejected by him, because it did not mention the name of the defendant on whom the writ had *not* been served, a common order was entered at rules against the defendant and sheriff. On the 8th day of the succeeding term (at which time the office judgments were to be set aside) the bail peice being again objected to by the clerk, for the reason before mentioned, it was shewn to the plaintiff's counsel, who thinking it sufficient, said that he should make no objection to it. It was then delivered to the clerk, who was directed by the counsel to file the same; but he, not knowing what had passed at the bar, entered the plea of payment *for the sheriff*, against whom judgment was afterwards obtained in the District Court. From this the sheriff appealed, pending which, the real defendant offered

fered to deliver himfelf up to the plaintiff's attorney, in exoneration of the fheriff, but was refufed. The gentleman who appeared as counfel for the plaintiffs in the General Court, being examined as a witnefs in this caufe, depofed, that when he declared he fhould not object to the bail piece, he only meant that in cafe a motion were made by the defendant's counfel to receive the bail piece, and to be permitted to fet afide the office judgment, he fhould not oppofe it; but that he ftill expected the fanction of the court was to be obtained, as was the practice where an objection was made to the bail piece.

To be relieved againft this judgment, the fheriff filed his bill in the High Court of Chancery, and a perpetual injunction was decreed, from which decree an appeal was prayed.

RONOLD for the appellants. I muft admit that the cafe of the fheriff is a hard one, and cannot fail to excite compaffion. It is to be regretted that he can be relieved only by fhifting the burthen from himfelf, to another, who on no principle whatever ought to bear it.

Let it be fuppofed, that the appellants and the appellee are equally innocent; equally clear of any charge of negligence, or improper conduct. Yet their relative fituations in this court are widely different. The former, has the law in his favor, and cannot lofe the advantage it gives him, unlefs it be oppofed by fuperior equity on the part of the latter. It cannot be pretended that this is the cafe. But the truth is, that the appellee has not equal equity with the appellants, becaufe he has been guilty of an unwarrantable negligence, which has operated to the prejudice of the party againft whom he now feeks relief.

By omitting in the firft inftance to take *a bail bond*, he deprived the plaintiff at law of the opportunity of excepting to the fpecial bail. For unlefs appearance bail be given, fpecial bail cannot be demanded. But admit that the bail piece was fufficient, and fo confidered by the plaintiff's counfel, it was the duty of the fheriff, againft whom the judgment was entered at the rules, to fee that the bail piece was filed, and a proper plea entered. He could relieve himfelf by no other means. He was legally, as well as equitably, bound to fubftitute fome other fecurity for the debt, before he could be difcharged.

Tho' he fhould be permitted to fhelter himfelf under the plea of ignorance or furprize, on the day the miftake (as it is pretended) happened, yet the orders of the court being extended, and read the fucceeding day, gave him abundant opportunity to correct it. His failing to do fo fubjects him as leaft to the charge of negligence, againſt which equity can never relieve, and for which a third perſon ought not to ſuffer. This negligence was calculated to impreſs the plaintiff's counſel with a belief, that the bail piece was withdrawn, and conſequently prevented him from objecting to the *ſufficiency of the bail*, which he was not precluded from doing by his agreeing not to object to the form of the bail piece.

Between perſons ſtanding in this ſituation, equity ought not to interfere.

MARSHALL & CAMPBELL for the appellee. If accident or ſurpriſe can ever furniſh a ground for the relief of a Court of Equity, the pretenſions of the appellee in this caſe muſt be well founded. But if Mr. Ronold be correct, it is impoſſible that accident, unmingled with fraud, can ever be relieved againſt; for in all ſuch caſes, both parties are, or may be equally innocent. If a bond be loſt, or deſtroyed, both parties are equally innocent, and yet a Court of Equity will relieve. No blame is imputed to the appellant, and none can with propriety be charged upon the appellee. Yet an accident has happened, which ſubjects the latter to unmerited injury at law.

The appellee did every thing which he was bound to do. When the bail piece was objected to by the clerk, his attorney had either to appeal to the court, or to adjuſt the difference with the adverſe attorney—he attempted the latter, and ſucceeded—the former became of courſe unneceſſary. The clerk was then directed to file the bail piece. Ignorant of the agreement of the counſel, he by miſtake enters a plea for the ſheriff. The blunder was in the officer of the court, not in the party, and therefore it ſhould not injure him. But it is contended that a real injury to the plaintiffs might have reſulted from this miſtake: ſuppoſe it might, yet none ſuch is proved: a *real* injury ſuſtained by one party, is not to be ſanctioned, becauſe *it is poſſible* that the other might alſo have been injured. But there is in truth no ground, even for the conjecture of the counſel. The ſheriff is not bound to take appearance bail. He may himſelf become ſpecial bail, or the defendant may give other ſpecial bail. Suppoſe the bail piece had been filed, would the appellant have been in a better ſituation than he now is? He could not have charged the bail, until after a *non eſt inventus* had been returned upon a *ca. ſa.* againſt the principal; and it appears that the principal offered to ſurrender himſelf.

LYONS

LYONS J.—The court are of opinion that the bail piece was sufficient, and must have been so considered if it had been objected to, at the time it was offered. The clerk therefore mistook the law when he rejected it, and entered a plea for the sheriff. That court might, and most certainly would, have corrected this mistake at any time, if it had been moved to do so. But the party was ill advised when instead of doing this, he applied for a supersedeas to the judgment, since the record furnished a Superior Court with no ground for an interference.

However, we are fully satisfied upon the equity of this case. A more complete surprize can hardly be conceived. It would be strange if an accident so mischievous as this in its effects, were beyond the reach of that court, whose peculiar province it is to grant relief in such cases. The negligence with which the appellee is charged, is fully excused by the agreement of the counsel, and the mistake which followed; and therefore cannot be urged as a ground for denying the relief which has been extended to him.

The decree must be affirmed.

WALTER PETER,

against

SAMUEL COCKE Executor of Henry Cocke.

THIS was an action of debt, brought in the District Court of Williamsburg by the appellant, upon a bond given to him *for and on account of Messrs. Glen and Peter*, merchants in Glasgow. The declaration states the debt as due to the plaintiff without mentioning for whose use.

The defendant without craving oyer, put in the following pleas.

1st Payment—2dly, That the debt was originally due to a British subject, and was acknowledged by the testator to the plaintiff, on account of Glen & Peter, merchants in Glasgow, who were British subjects; and was contracted before the 1st of May 1782, and was not transferred to a citizen of this state, nor to any person capable of maintaining an action in this commonwealth, at any time before the first of May 1775, for a valuable consideration. There are many other pleas, all unimportant

important in the decision. At the trial, an objection was made by the defendant to the admission of the bond in evidence; because the bond stated in the declaration was given to Walter Peter, and the one offered in evidence, is to Walter Peter *of the County of Surrey on account of Messrs Glen & Peter meerhants in Glasgow*. This objection being sustained by the court, the plaintiff filed an exception to the opinion; and a verdict and judgment being given for the defendant, the plaintiff appealed.

WICKHAM for the appellant. It was necessary that this suit should be brought in the name of Walter Peter, the trustee, as he alone had a right to recover at law. The use to which the money was to be applied when recovered, was unimportant to the debtor; it was stated in the bond merely as a memorandum for the obligee, and would have been very unnecessarily set forth in the declaration. It is not usual to set out the bond at large in the declaration, provided the material parts of it are stated, so as to apprize the defendant of the true ground of the action. It might as well be contended, that the title, or place of residence of the parties if mentioned in the bond, should be carefully recited also in the declaration.

LYONS J. There appears to be a defect in the declaration which has not been noticed. It charges that the said Henry Cocke and a certain Richard Cocke deceased, whom the said Henry Cocke survived, gave the bond in question. And the breach laid is, that "neither the said Henry nor the defendant hath paid", without averring non-payment by Richard the other obligor.

COPELAND for the appellant. It is a rule, that the plaintiff need not aver a matter, which it would be unnecessary for him to prove, if averred; and, if in the present case, the declaration had charged non-payment by the other obligor, the plaintiff could not have been required to prove it. The defendant pleads payment, and there can be no question, but that under the act of Assembly permitting him to prove all the discounts in his power, he might have availed himself of any payments made by the other obligor. The case of Busher *vs* Philips, *Bull. nisi prius* 163, seems to be in point. That was an action of debt, on a bail bond, against C. and the declaration stated, that the defendant and two others became jointly and severally bound; the breach was that the defendant had not paid.— The plaintiff had judgment, although the defendant demurred specially, and stated as a cause, that the declaration did not aver non-payment by the other obligors.*

LYONS J. delivered the opinion of the court. The first objection cannot be sustained upon any principle. It was unnecessary to state in the declaration, the use or consideration for which the bond was given; and if it had been stated, it would have been mere surplusage.

But we do not feel satisfied upon the objection to the declaration stated from the bench.

The cause must be sent back for a new trial, with directions to admit the bond as evidence but reserving to the appellee by the consent of the appellant the liberty of availing himself of any other legal exception to the proceedings already had, as if this judgment had not been rendered, or any appeal granted.

Judgment reversed.

HUBBARD *against* TAYLOR.

THIS was an appeal from a judgment of the District Court of Charlottesville, affirming the judgment of the County Court of Charlotte, upon a bond given for the forthcoming of property taken under execution.

The condition of the bond is, "that if the said Hubbard and "Tomkies, shall deliver to Samuel White, sheriff &c. on Fri- "day the 15th day of June next, at Charlotte court house, be- "ing the day of sale appointed by the said sheriff, three negroes "[by name] which were taken under execution by a writ of "fi. fa. issued from the office of the County Court of Charlotte, "to satisfy the said John Taylor the sum of £151: 6: 11¼, then" &c.

The objection to the judgment, insisted upon by Mr. Wickham, was, that the condition does not mention the person *against whom* the execution issued, or upon *whose property* it was levied.

By the Court. The law requires that the execution should be described in the condition of the bond which not being sufficiently

---

* See the case of Arscott and Heale, *Cro. Car.* 6. debt against 3 obligors, one pleads *solvit ad diem*. Replication that neither of the three nor any one of them had paid: on issue joined, verdict, that one had not paid, held good.

ciently done in this case, in the instances mentioned at the bar the judgment is erroneous.

Judgment must be reversed, and the motion of the appellee on the said bond over-ruled—The bond and execution quashed.

CARR *against* GOOCH.

THIS was an appeal from a judgment of the District Court of Charlottesville in an action upon the case, brought by the appellee. The declaration stated: that John Carr deceased, by his will, directed his executors (of whom the defendant was one) to sell a tract of land the property of the testator: that the plaintiff was employed by the executors, to cry this tract of land at public auction, when the same was purchased by a certain John Moore who was the highest bidder. That Nathaniel Anderson, one of the executors, complained of the sale as being unfairly made, and contrary to the directions of the executors, and insisted that the land should be again set up for sale. That the defendant objected to this, and promised that if the plaintiff would not cry it again but would confirm the sale so made, that he would indemnify and save him harmless from all actions or demands, which might be brought against him on account of the sale made to Moore: that the plaintiff in consideration of this promise did forbear to cry the land again, and did confirm the sale. The breach is, that the defendant not regarding his said promise did cause and permit an action to be brought against him, in his name, and that of the other executors, for and on account of the sale so made to the said Moore, and did cause and permit a judgment to be obtained against him, for £ 140.

Upon the plea of non assumpsit the plaintiff got a verdict. The defendant moved in arrest of judgement but was over-ruled.

WASHINGTON for the appellant. There is either no consideration at all laid in the declaration, or if there be, it is an illegal one. 1st, There is none laid. After the appellee had struck off the land to Moore, his power over the subject ceased. He had no longer an authority to vacate the purchase, and again expose the land to sale, or to confirm what had been done. If the transaction was fair and legal, nothing

remained

remained to confummate it, but for the executors to convey. If it was unfair or illegal, they alone could confirm or fell again. A promife then, made in confideration of the auctioneer's *not* doing what he could not legally have done, was entirely vain, and had no neceffary caufe to induce it. As little fo, as a promife to pay money to B. in confideration that he will not fell the land of C. which would undoubtedly be a *nudum pactum*.

But if there be a confideration, then 2dly, it was illegal and confequently infufficient to maintain an affumpfit. The defendant undertakes, that if the plaintiff will confirm an unfair and *illegal fale*, he will fave him harmlefs for fo doing. When the foundation of an agreement is fraud, immorality, or any thing againft law, a court of juftice will not be made the inftrument of enforcing the performance of it. The plaintiff himfelf ftates the confideration of the defendant's affumpfit to be bottomed upon a fraud.

MARSHALL for the appellee. Wherever a confideration, which is the foundation of a promife, produces benefit to the one party or injury to the other, it is fufficient to fupport an affumpfit. The defendant requefts the plaintiff not to do a certain act, and promifes to fave him harmlefs from the confequences of his compliance. The plaintiff is induced by this promife to gratify the wifhes of the defendant, which afterwards fubjects him to the payment of damages. Can it be ferioufly urged that in fuch a cafe, there is no confideration for the promife? If the cafe require further aid, let it be obferved, that the perfon bound to indemnify, is the very perfon who affifts in producing the injury.

The fecond point appears to be ftill more deftitute of foundation. The principle laid down, that a confideration illegal or immoral will not fuftain an affumpfit, is unqueftionably true. But I cannot difcern the application of it to this cafe. It does not appear that the plaintiff had done an unfair or illegal act. One of the executors fuppofes fo, and infifts upon a re-fale. The other executor thinks otherwife, and wifhes to confirm it. It is a mere conteft between them, each wifhing to prevail, and the one promifes to indemnify a third perfon employed by them to do a certain act, if he will obey his directions.

LYONS J. delivered the opinion of the court.

The principle, laid down at the bar by the appellant's counfel, as to the validity of a confideration, is certainly correct. A promife to pay money in confideration of another's doing an immoral or illegal act, would clearly be infufficient to fupport an action. But the prefent cafe is not chargeable with any fuch
objection

objection. The appellee was employed by all the executors to perform the duties of a cryer, in the selling of a tract of land. In that capacity, he struck it off to the highest bidder as he was bound to do. The sale, for any thing that we can know from this record, was fair and legal. But one of the executors thinking otherwise, desired a re-sale, which was successfully opposed by the appellant, in consequence of his promise to indemnify the cryer against all actions or demands on that account. Yet this very executor causes or permits an action to be commenced against the person he was bound to protect, and recovers damages. If there be fraud any where, it is properly chargeable to the appellant. Suppose a man is arrested at the suit of two executors, one of whom directs the officer to discharge the defendant, which is opposed by the other. The orders of the former are obeyed in consequence of a promise to indemnify and save the sheriff harmless. Yet this very executor unites with the other in an action against the sheriff, and damages are recovered against him. Can there be a doubt, but that the sheriff might well maintain an action upon this promise? It is difficult to conceive upon what principle the executors could recover damages from the cryer in the present case. As to the purchaser, he being the highest bidder, was most clearly entitled to the land, if he were not privy to a fraud, or apprised of a deviation in the cryer from the orders of those who employed him. In such a case, the cryer might certainly be subjected to damages.

But whether the judgment against the appellee was a righteous one or not, cannot be a question in the present action: he has sustained an injury in consequence of an act performed at the request of the appellant, against which the appellant promised to indemnify him.

We think there is no difficulty in the case and affirm the judgment.

COLE *against* CLAYBORN.

THE appellee brought an action of detinue to recover a number of slaves. Upon the pleas of *non detinet*, and the act of limitations, the jury found a special verdict as follows.

That William Cole the elder, by his will dated in 1729, made the following devises, viz. " I give to my wife, for ever, " two negroes named Will and Sarah, above and besides her " dower

"dower in my lands and negroes; as alfo one ninth of my per-
"fonal eftate." After which he devifed as follows, viz. "All
"the reft and refidue of my negroes and perfonal eftate, of
"what nature or kind foever, to my children for ever,
"equally to be divided amongft them, the furvivors or furvivor,
"fhare and fhare alike: My will alfo is, that my executors
"fhall work all my negroes, (except thofe particularly be-
"queathed) on my lands, until my fon William fhall come of
"age, and the profits of the faid lands and flaves, to be equally
"divided amongft my children; and in cafe my fon William,
"fhould moleft, fue, or demand account of my executors for
"ufing the entailed lands, then the faid refidue of negroes and
"perfonal eftate to my other children."

That the flaves, in the declaration mentioned, are the de-
fcendents of a female flave allotted to Mary Cole, the widow,
as part of her dower.

That William Cole the younger, father of the defendant,
was fon and heir at law of the faid William the elder, and died
in the year 17   having by his will devifed all his perfonal eftate, of what nature or kind foever, to his fon William and
his heirs for ever, fubject to certain charges and conditions.

That after the death of Mary the widow of William Cole the
elder, which happened before the year 1752, Bridget, one of
the flaves in the declaration mentioned, and the mother of the
others, was, on a divifion of the eftate of William Cole the
elder, allotted to Martha, one of his daughters, the wife of one
Leigh, as her fhare of the dower flaves of the faid Mary.

That the prefent defendant is the fon and heir at law of the
faid William Cole the younger, was born in June 1744, and
in the year 1769, commenced fuit againft the faid Leigh for
the flave Bridget, in the declaration mentioned, who at that
time had no children: That this fuit abated in 1779, by the
death of Leigh, who had retained the poffeffion of the flaves
ever fince the death of the widow, and the prefent defendant
became poffeffed in February 1783.

That the faid Leigh, by his will, devifed the negroes in
queftion to his daughter Mary, and her hufband William Clayborn the plaintiff, during their lives, and the life of the furvivor,
remainder over to their children; that immediately after the
death of Leigh, the plaintiff got poffeffion of the flaves in the
declaration mentioned, and continued to hold them until February 1783, when they came to the poffeffion of the defendant.
That Mary the wife of the plaintiff died in April 1783. And
if, &c. &c.   Upon

Upon this verdict the District Court gave judgment for the plaintiff, from which the defendant appealed.

Marshall for the appellant. The principal question in this case is, whether the slave in the declaration mentioned, from whom all the others have descended, passed under the residuary clause in the will of William Cole the elder? If they did, then the appellant has no title; if they did not, he has a complete title as heir at law.

I admit, that the residuary clause is sufficiently comprehensive to include the reversionary interest in the dower slaves; but if the whole of this clause be connected together, the intention of the testator may require a different construction. When he speaks of *all his slaves*, it is improbable that he meant to include the *dower slaves*, because he directs that *all his slaves* be worked on his lands by his executors. Now it would be improper to extend the generality of this clause to the dower slaves, which the testator knew he had no power over during the life of the widow. And if he could not mean to include those slaves in this part of the clause, it is not probable that he had them in view in the preceding part of the clause, which respects the disposition of them.—The clause is an entire one connected together by an evident continuation of the same idea, without any interruption, and must be supposed to embrace the *same subject*, throughout.

It would therefore seem to be a very strained and unnatural construction to break the clause, and make the testator mean, only a part of his negroes, when he speaks of the whole of them in one instance, and the whole of them, when he mentions them in another place, but in the very same sentence.

Duval for the appellee.—The devise of the residue of the negroes, though coupled in the same clause with the direction to the executors concerning the temporary employment of them, is nevertheless a distinct part of the sentence from that, and may with propriety receive a different exposition. It is not unusual, in the construction of wills, and even of deeds, to enlarge or limit the meaning of particular words, so as to fit them to the subject on which they are meant to operate, and to avoid contradiction or absurdity. Thus, though the word *all* would if unrestrained comprehend the dower slaves, yet, as the testator could exercise no dominion over them during the life of his widow, it is not probable that he meant to include them in that part of the sentence, which directs his negroes to be employed on the plantation. But if he did intend it, he mistook the extent

of

of his power; but he meant to pass all his slaves in the former part of the sentence is evident: 1st, Because the plain and natural import of the words include them; and 2dly, because it is a residuary devise, which from the very nature of it is intended to leave nothing undisposed of. The court always inclines against such a construction, as tends to produce a partial intestacy. But what strengthens this exposition in the present case is, that the heir at law is provided for by an estate entailed upon him, which is noticed by the testator, and operates strongly to repel a presumption that the testator intended to leave any part of his estate to descend upon the heir.

As to the possession, it is found to have been in Leigh from the year 1752 till 1769, before any suit was brought.

LYONS J. delivered the opinion of the court.

There is no difficulty in this case. A testator may carve out as many particular estates, from the fee simple interest in the property disposed of, as he pleases; and, whatever part is not specially given away, remains with him: If he disposes of the rest and residue of his estate, such remnant will pass, unless restrained by other parts of the will. There are no words in this will which limit the general operation of the sweeping clause.—*All the rest of his estate*, means every thing over which he had a power; and his intention, so far from appearing to controul these general expressions, seems to favor the operation of them in their greatest latitude. The testator had no doubt an equal affection for all his children. They are all equally provided for by the will, and can hardly be presumed that he would leave a part undisposed of in order that it might descend to the heir at law, who was otherwise provided for.

This case is not like that of Kennon & M'Roberts in this court. In that, the intention was very clear.

Judgment affirmed.

CASES ARGUED AND DETERMINED

IN THE

COURT OF APPEALS

IN

THE FALL TERM OF THE YEAR, 1794.

SHERMER *against* SHERMER'S Executors.

THIS was an appeal from a decree of the High Court of Chancery. The case was this; John Shermer, by his will, devised to his wife the use and profits of his whole estate, both real and personal, during her natural life, and after that was ended, then the whole of his estate, exclusive of that already given to his wife, to be equally divided between whoever his wife should think proper to make her heir, or heirs, and his brother Richard Shermer. He further directed, that his executors, as soon as the crops were finished after his wife's death, should sell and dispose of his whole estate, real and personal, as they might think most conducive to the receiver's benefit.

The wife died in 1775, a few days after the testator, without making any disposition, or appointment of her part of the estate. The executors sold the estate, agreeably to the will, and distributed one moiety thereof, amongst the relations of Mrs. Shermer; for the recovery of which, this suit was brought against the executors and distributees, by the present appellant, the son, heir and executor of Richard Shermer, the brother named in the will. It is proved that the testator frequently said, he would leave his wife one half of his estate, to dispose of as she should please, and that most of his estate was acquired by his intermarriage with her. Upon a hearing of the cause the bill was dismissed, from which this appeal was prayed.

RONOLD for the appellant. The principle upon which the appellant's claim is founded, is so fully explained, and so conclu-

lively

lively settled in the case of Tomlinson and Dyghton, 1 P. Wms. 149. that it is unnecessary to add any thing to it.

MARSHALL for the appellee. The devise to Mrs. Shermer, was intended to pass to her; the whole interest and absolute ownership in the moiety, given to her appointed heir. In last wills, it is not necessary that the testator should use technical words, in order to pass a fee; for however inartificially he may express himself, yet if his intention can be discovered to mean a disposition of his whole interest in the thing devised, the court will supply such words, as may be necessary to effectuate that intention. Thus, if the devise had been to the wife, to *dispose of as she pleased*, she would most unquestionably have been entitled to the fee simple; because such a power is the eminent quality of such an estate. But the case of Tomlinson and Dyghton is relied upon, to establish this principle, viz: that where an *express* estate for life is given, it cannot be enlarged by words of implication, tho' if the estate had been given *generally*, it might be otherwise. I shall contend 1st, that the principle is not true, and 2dly, if it were, still the case itself is not like the present.

1st, The principle is fully contradicted by the case of King and Melling, 1 *Ventr.* 214, and the great variety of cases there cited. Langly and Baldwin 1 *Eq. Cas. Ab.* 185.—Blackbourn and Edgley 1 *P. Wms.* 605.—The Attorney General *vs* Sutton, 1 *P. Wms.* 754. These cases clearly prove, that an express estate for life, may be enlarged by words of implication, if the testator's intention require it. The case Tomlinson and Dyghton is consequently founded upon a mistaken principle, and ought not to be regarded.

But 2dly; If that case be law, it is unlike the present. In that, the power of disposing is limited to particular children; in this, it is to the heirs general. The distinguishing feature of a fee simple estate, is consequently discernible in this case, and not in that. Again—in that case, as well as in that cited from 3 *Leon.* 71, the wife having made an appointment, the intention of the testator could not be frustrated, and consequently, the question, turning merely upon the validity of the appointment, the nature, or extent of the wife's estate, was a point only incidentally decided, and therefore, the opinion as to that point, ought not to be considered as a binding authority. Again; it will not be denied but that if an express estate for life had not been given to the wife, the latter words, would have enlarged the estate into a fee simple. In this case, the court, to effectuate

ate the intention of the testator, will consider the life estate given to the wife, as applying, not to her moiety, but to the moiety, which after her death is devised to the brother, and this will materially distinguish the present case, from that of Tomlinson and Dyghton, & will bring it precisely within that part of the rule laid down by the court, which makes the estate to the wife a fee simple.

WASHINGTON in reply. The case of Tomlinson and Dyghton, and the cases there cited, from 3 *Leon.* 71 & 1 *Mod.* 189, are so conclusive upon the point now under consideration, that it can only be necessary for me, to shew that the objections made to them are not well founded. Those cases are built upon this well established principle of the common law, viz: that an heir shall never be disinherited by implication, nor by words of uncertain and doubtful meaning. In last wills, an estate of inheritance is permitted to pass, by other words than those artificially appropriated to that purpose; but it is intention only, which governs in such a case; and where that intention can be clearly discovered, the court will give such a construction to the words, however inapt they may be, as will fulfill that intention. Thus in the case of Langly and Baldwin, the testator declared an intention, in one part of his will, to give an estate for life only; but it was equally clear, that he meant all the sons of the tenant for life to take estates tail in succession, before the limitations over were to take effect. But the 7th and other sons would not by the rules of law, come into the succession, if the ancestor took only an estate for life; because, where the ancestor takes an estate for life, the heirs, or issue, by such names, cannot take as purchasers. So is Shelleys case—here then, are two contending intentions, both of them equally clear, tho' depending upon different claims for fulfillment. A provision for all the children, was more likely to be the favorite intention of the testator, than the nature, or quantity of the estate to be enjoyed by the ancestor. How then, ask the court, is this prevailing intention to be effectuated? The answer is, by uniting the estate for life with that arising by implication, and thus enlarging that estate into an inheritance; by which means only, the whole issue could be provided for. By such refinements, do the judges govern themselves in cases of that sort, and thus ingenious are they in inventing some subtle mode or other for carrying into effect the *will* of dead men. They metamorphose an estate for life, into an estate of inheritance, to promote this primary object, but not otherwise. It is necessity only, which could justify it, since if this necessity did not require it, such

refinements

refinements would amount to the *making*, not to the *conſtruing* of wills. So too, in the caſe of the Attorney General *vs* Sutton, founded upon the ſame principle with that juſt ſpoken of; except that in this, if all the iſſue had been provided for, yet the court muſt have decided as they did; becauſe, from two clauſes in the will, (mentioned in a note in the laſt edition of *P. Wms.*) the teſtator expreſſes his intention to give an eſtate tail, in words too plain to be miſunderſtood. But the court never will convert an *expreſs* eſtate for life, into an eſtate of inheritance, by words of *implication*, unleſs compelled to do ſo by abſolute neceſſity; that is, where the intention is in the firſt place clear, and not merely a doubtful, or poſſible intention; and ſecondly where that intention *cannot otherwiſe be effectuated.* This is the principle, upon which I rely; it is laid down in all the caſes, and controverted in none. Thoſe cited upon the other ſide prove it, and it is the very principle, upon which they are decided. Tomlinſon and Dyghton does not oppoſe, but on the contrary ſupports it, and yet it ſeems to have been ſuppoſed by Mr. Marſhall, that the judge declared, " that an expreſs eſtate for life could not be enlarged by implication." Taking it as a thing granted, that this poſition was there aſſerted, he proceeds to prove its fallacy, by citing Langly and Baldwin, and the other caſes relied upon for this purpoſe. But theſe caſes, tho' they contradict the *ſuppoſed caſe* of Tomlinſon and Dyghton, are entirely conſiſtent with that caſe, as it *really* is. The Chancellor there ſays, " that where an expreſs eſtate for life is given, with a *power to diſpoſe*, the latter words, ſhall not by implication enlarge the former, into an eſtate of inheritance, but they ſhall be conſidered as a diſtinct gift, and as coming in by way of addition." Now the difference between that, which the judge is *ſuppoſed* to ſay, and that which he actually ſays, is obvious. An expreſs eſtate for life may be enlarged by words of implication, *if by no other means* the teſtator's intention can be complied with, and therefore, in Langly and Baldwin, it was done, becauſe there was no other way to effectuate the intention; becauſe, if the 7th and other ſons could not take by deſcent, it was ſuppoſed they could not take at all: but they were clearly *intended to take*; therefore *from neceſſity*, the anceſtor took an eſtate of inheritance. But in the caſe of Tomlinſon and Dyghton, the children of the teſtator might take by purchaſe, without doing this violence to the plain words of the will. Therefore no neceſſity exiſted, for enlarging the eſtate for life, by words of implication, for in that caſe, the wife

might

might, by exercising the power of appointment given to her, make the children take as purchasers. So upon this principle, the case before the court, and all others, where a power of appointment is annexed to the express estate for life, will be found to differ, from cases, where the issue are let in under words of implication, enlarging the estate for life into an estate of inheritance.

The next question is, does the case of Tomlinson and Dyghton differ from the present? The restriction of the power to dispose in that case, is noticed in the argument, and differs from this thus far only, that if that passed a greater estate than for life, it was a *conditional* fee, this an *absolute* one: if that only gave a power to dispose, it was a limited one, this is unlimited. But as to intention, there is no difference. The testator might as well intend the one, as the other, and both are equally distinguished by the marks of ownership, if there exist any in either. But it is contended, that in that case, the wife had made an appointment, and therefore, as to the other point, it was merely an obiter decision. But it is evident, that this was a material point in the cause, for if the wife took an estate in fee, it was unnecessary to decide the validity of the appointment; and therefore, this was a previous and important subject of consideration.

The last argument relied upon is, that the court to effectuate the testator's intention, will construe the express estate for life in this case, as applying only to the moiety, which after the wife's death, is given to the brother, and not to the other moiety devised to her appointed heir; and upon this difference, it is supposed, that the case of Thomlinson and Dyghton, does not apply. This argument tho' specious, has no solidity when examined for, I ask, where is that intention, which, without resorting to the construction contended for, will be defeated? What is the intention? To give an estate *for life*, for so are the express words of the will; in the next place, to limit the inheritance to the person, whom the wife should appoint. No person can doubt, but that this was the intention, because the words are too plain to be misunderstood. There is no room left for construction, where there is no ambiguity in the expression. But, can this intention, so expressed, be no otherwise effectuated, than by converting the life estate into a fee? If it cannot, then admit it must be done, and greater concessions ought not to be required, since all the cases, cited against us, shew, that the bold attack upon the plain words of the testator, can only be warranted, where otherwise, the intention would be entirely defeated.

defeated. To the question, I answer, let the wife take an estate for life; let her exercise the power of appointing her heir or heirs; let such heir or heirs take the inheritance, and then the testator's intention is fulfilled. Is not this what we contend for? and cannot all this be done, consistently with the rules of law? where then, is the *necessity* of giving the wife a fee? The heirs could have taken if she had *chosen* to name them, and if she did not chuse, but preferred leaving the estate to descend, where the law would cast it, it cannot alter the case, or make the intention of the testator mean, what was not meant when that intention was expressed. That intention, was either to give a *power*, or a *beneficial interest* to the wife in the inheritance, and this court, will decide at this day, as they would have done, had the question come on the moment after the testator's death. One would suppose, from the argument on the other side, that the heirs of the wife could not possibly take, unless the wife was construed to take a fee, and that the court were struggling to invent some mode, or other, to prevent this violence from being done to the testator's intention. Whereas, there is nothing more in the case, than that the wife has either neglected, or not chosen to exercise the power she had, and therefore, this attempt is made, in order to repair the consequences of this omission, by sacrificing to that end, the established principles of law.

There are some expressions in this will, not unworthy of notice, as tending to furnish additional proof of the intention.— He gives to the wife, the *use* and *profits* of his estate for life, and says, " *and after this is ended*" &c. Now these words strike me to be as strong as the words *and no longer*, in Target and Gant, 10 *Mod.* 402. Again, the devise is not of the *estate itself*, but of the *use* and *profits* for life, which is another strong evidence of intention.

The PRESIDENT delivered the opinion of the court.

It is contended by the appellant's counsel, that Mrs. Shermer was by the will, only tenant for life of a moiety, with a power to dispose of the fee; and that not having executed that power, the estate descends to the heir of the testator.

In support of this position, several cases have been cited; but they seem to verify the saying of a judge, " that in disputes upon wills, cases seldom illucidate the subject, which depending on the intention of the testator, to be collected from the will, and from the relative situation of the parties, ought to be decided upon the state and circumstances of each case."—To which

I will add, that I have generally obferved, that adjudged cafes have more frequently been produced to difappoint, than to illuftrate the intention; and I am free to own, that where a teftator's intention is apparent to me, cafes muft be ftrong, uniform, and apply pointedly, before they will prevail to fruftrate that intention.

The cafes produced tend to prove, that an exprefs eftate for life to the wife, with a power to difpofe of the fee, fhall not turn her eftate for life into a fee.

In the cafe of Target and Gant, the fubject in difpute was a chattel, and the objection to the remainder was, that it was void, being limited on too remote a contingency, being after an eftate tail, which, it was faid, the wife took, tho' devifed to her for life, being limited over on her dying without iffue. The lord Chancellor faid, that the eftate tail in fuch a cafe, as to lands, was raifed by implication, to favor the teftator's intention, and he would not make the implication, in the cafe of chattels, to deftroy that intention. So that if this cafe apply at all, it proves, that the teftator's intention fhall make fuch words either an eftate for life, or an inheritance, as fhall beft promote that intention.

In both the cafes from 1 *P. Wms.* and 3 *Leon.* where it was adjudged the wife took an eftate for life, with power to difpofe of the fee, the decifion of the point was unimportant, fince in both, the wife had executed her power, properly and effectually.

In thofe and all the cafes, the queftion turns upon a fee eftate in lands, here there is no doubt about the fee. It is in the purchafer from the executor, and the only queftion is how the money fhall go according to the will? whether this will make a difference, need not be decided, fince upon a view of the will, the intention is apparent, that the wife fhould have the whole eftate for life, and that at her death, one half (except his fpecific bounty to her) fhould go to *her family*, and the other to *his own*. Their relative fituation, and his prior declarations, only fhew fuch intention to be liberal and juft.

His words have been critically fcanned; he does not give her a power to *difpofe*, but to name the *perfon or perfons* fhe might chufe to fucceed to her part, to whom the teftator gives the money; and it is doing fmall violence to the words, even in their critical meaning, to fay that by *fuffering* her legal reprefentatives to fucceed her, fhe has *actually made them her heir or heirs*, as much fo as if fhe had pointed them out by an exprefs devife.

The decree affirmed.

BENTLY Executor of RONALD,

against

HARMANSON'S Executors.

THIS was an appeal from a judgment of the District Court of Accomack, reversing a judgment of the County Court. The appellant brought an action of debt against the appellee upon a bond executed by the testator of the appellee. The defendant pleaded payment, without craving oyer of the bond, and leave was given to offer special matter in evidence.

The bond produced in evidence at the trial, and which is set out in the record, has the signature and seal of a co-obligor, and is joint. The jury found that the defendant owed the debt, and judgment was thereupon entered for the plaintiff. Upon an appeal to the District Court, this judgment was reversed, *because there appeared to be a joint obligor who survived the defendant's testator against whom the charge survived.*

The PRESIDENT. The reason for reversing the judgment of the County Court, would have been a sound one, if the fact upon which it is founded had appeared in the record; but it does not. The declaration is upon Harmanson's bond alone, without taking notice of another obligor. A bond appears in the record, with the name and seal of another obligor, but 1st, it is doubtful whether it can be noticed, since oyer is not taken. 2dly, It does not prove this material fact, that the other obligor was the survivor. It might, if true, have properly been taken advantage of by plea. The defendant was permitted to give special matter in evidence, but what that special matter was, is not spread upon the record; if it respected the fact of survivorship, it was decided by the jury against the defendant.

> The judgment of the District Court is to be reversed, and that of the County Court affirmed, with damages and costs.

PLEASANTS & Co. *against* LEWIS.

THIS was an appeal from a judgment of the District Court of Charlottesville, over-ruling a motion made by the appellants, upon a bond given by the appellee, upon the service of an execution, conditioned for the delivery of 1000 bushels of wheat, at the day, and at the time of sale appointed by the sheriff. The facts stated in a bill of exceptions are, that on the day of sale, the obligor delivered a parcel of wheat to the sheriff, the quantity at that time unknown, but which the defendant at the trial acknowledged to be about 500 bushels, which the sheriff received, *without excepting to the quantity*, and proceeded to sell the same, but could not for the want of buyers. The court over-ruled the motion, from which this appeal was prayed.

The PRESIDENT. The condition of the bond was not performed by the partial delivery stated in the record, and of course the penalty became forfeited.

The judgment must therefore be reversed, and the cause remitted to the District Court, to proceed to judgment on the the bond, allowing credit for any money, which may be proved to have been paid to the appellants, or to have been raised by the sale of any part of the wheat delivered.

Judgment reversed.

WARD *against* WEBBER & Wife.

THIS was an appeal from a decree of the High Court of Chancery, upon the following case. A suit was instituted by Webber and wife, in the former General Court, on the Chancery side, against the father of the appellant, and of Mrs. Webber, stating, that the father, had by a deed executed in 1754, conveyed to his said daughter, whilst single, several tracts of land, together with 16 slaves, and all the furniture and stocks on those plantations. That previous to this deed, and before her marriage, the father had frequently declared his intention to give his daughter the greatest part of his estate, if she should marry to please him. That in consequence of these promises, the complainant courted the daughter, and married her. That the father, after executing the deed, got possession of it surreptitiously, and cancelled it. The object of the bill was, to set up the deed. The answer of the father denied the material allegations in the bill; admitted the existence of the deed, but that it was made on a condition, that the daughter married to please him, which she did not.

Upon

Upon the death of the father, the suit was revived against the appellant, the son, and against the executors, and a decree was made in that court, in favor of the complainant, as to the land, and part of the slaves, which were in the possession of the defendants. The same plaintiffs, afterwards, instituted a suit in the High Court of Chancery, for the balance of the negroes. The appellants filed a bill to review the former decree; and that being opened, the whole question came on again to be heard and considered. The ground now relied upon by the appellants to set aside the former decree, as well as to defend the last suit, is, that the father at the time of making the deed, labored under a prosecution which threatened his life, and that the deed was executed, in order to screen his estate from forfeiture, in case he was convicted, and under a trust, to re-convey the estate to the father, if he should get clear of the prosecution. Sundry depositions were taken, upon the weight of which, the present cause very much depended.

The Chancellor dismissed the bill of review, and decreed for the appellees upon their bill, from which decree this appeal was prayed.

MARSHALL for the appellants. It might perhaps be made a question in this cause, whether the deed of 1754, being made without consideration, can deserve the aid of a Court of equity to set it up? But as this is a point upon which I do not rely, I shall pass it over, and insist, that there are circumstances in this case, which would render it iniquitous in a Court of Equity to aid the plaintiffs, and that it will therefore leave him in the situation in which the law has placed him. That there was a secret trust and confidence between the father and daughter, is so strongly to be presumed from circumstances, that aided by the positive evidence of one of the witnesses, the fact can scarcely be doubted.

1st, the *time* when the deed was made,—the father then labouring under a perilous prosecution, which he appears to have been very apprehensive would affect his life.

2dly, The *person* to whom the deed was made—a child—in whom this secret confidence might with safety be reposed if with any person.

3dly, The various expressions of the father about that time, indicating his apprehensions, and the mode by which he expected to save his estate, (all of which are abundantly proved) at a time too when it is not to be supposed, he was preparing for future litigation. 4thly,

4thly, The father continuing in poffeffion of the property. Thefe circumftances ftrong as they are by themfelves, are very much ftrengthened by a fact proved and admitted, viz: that the daughter, declared, that the deed for one parcel of land (about which there is no difpute) was to be recorded, but that the other (which is the deed in queftion) was not to be recorded. The fact is, that one deed was recorded, and the other was not, which proves, that as to the deed which was not intended to be recorded, a mere truft was underftood. If then the court be fatisfied that a truft was intended, its aid will not be afforded in an attempt to violate that truft.

WARDEN for the appellee. Before the deed was made, or a profecution apprehended, it is in full proof, that the father had frequently made parol declarations of his intention to give the greateft part of his eftate to his daughter when fhe married. If the deed in queftion had not been made, this court would have decreed a fpecific performance of thofe promifes; being made, it muft be confidered as done in execution of them. The title of the daughter therefore is paramount to, not dependent upon that deed.

CAMPBELL upon the fame fide. I lay down this as a principle of equity not to be controverted, viz: that where a father makes a deed to a child, it will be confidered as an advancement and not a truft. 2 *Vern.* 19—28—436. *Eq. Cas. Ab.* 382. 1 *Vern.* 467, 2 *Ch. Cas.* 26, 231. The principal circumftances relied upon in this cafe to eftablifh a truft, is the proof of a fraud intended by the father, for the purpofe of defeating the crown of its eventual dues. It would be ftrange, if a perfon who hath committed a fraud, could be permitted to defend himfelf by averring it. It is not pretended that this truft was declared in the deed itfelf, and parol evidence is relied upon, not to explain a doubtful conftruction, but to eftablifh one, totally different in its operation, from that which the real deed upon the face of it imported; and this, no court has ever yet gone fo far as to fuffer. Even in the cafe of laft wills, evidence is received with great caution, and even then only, to rebut an equity. 2 *Vern.* 98, 337—648, 736.

The firft point having been given up, it will be unneceffary to take up time in proving, that a Court of Equity will aid a volunteer, againft a volunteer. But if it fhould be doubted, I will refer the court to the following cafes, 1 *Vern.* 219, 365—464 2 *Vern.* 473. 1 *P. Wms.* 60.

MARSHALL

MARSHALL in reply. A Court of Equity, will never lend its aid to set up a deed, (tho' destroyed by fraud) if it would do iniquity. I may go farther, and say, that it will not even assist in setting up a hard and oppressive deed. It is contended, that independent of the deed, this court would enforce a specific performance of the parol promises of the father. But there is abundant proof, that those promises were conditional, and that the father, was always strongly opposed to the marriage of his daughter with Webber. Besides, the bill does not claim the property upon that ground; those promises are not put in issue, and of course the evidence as to them is irrelevant to the real merits of the cause.

The principle contended for by Mr. Campbell, that every thing is to be presumed against him who commits a fraud, applies not to this case, because there is no dispute between us, as to the contents of the deed. If there were, then I admit, that every thing should be presumed against the person who destroyed the deed. But I contend, that the deed, tho' absolute on the face of it, was intended to pass a beneficial interest, only in case the grantor should be convicted, and that a resulting trust was meant, in the event of his escaping the prosecution. Whether the fact be so or not depends upon the evidence. I admit therefore, that if this case were unconnected with those circumstances relied upon to prove a trust, that the deed would be considered as an advancement to the daughter, in which case the authorities cited would apply. But since a child, may as well as any other person be a trustee for a father, evidence to establish the trust may as properly be admitted in such a case, as if the conveyance were made to a stranger.

I do not contend, that if *Ward* had applied to the court to *set aside* the deed, that he would have been entitled to its aid: But on the other hand, that court will not assist the *daughter to set up* the deed. For if *he* were guilty of a fraud by intending to defeat the crown of its rights, *she* was *particeps criminis*, and can be in no better situation than he is. We ask no favors, nor do we require the aid of the court; we only desire that none may be granted to the other side, but that the parties may be left where the law has placed them.

As to the propriety of admitting parol evidence in this case, I do not contend, that it ought to be received to *explain*, or to *contradict the words* of a written contract; but it is every days practice to admit such evidence, to prove a *secret trust*. As for instance, to convert a deed absolute upon its face into a mortgage, which is a case parallel with this. So too the establishment of resulting trusts, depends almost always upon parol evidence varying the nature of the written deed. Upon the whole, I rely upon this principle, that tho' equity may aid a volunteer in setting up a deed against another volunteer, yet the plaintiff in such a case, must have compleat equity, and must come to ask relief with clean hands.

CAMPBELL.—The case stated of an absolute deed being considered as a mortgage is not apposite to this, because in that, it is a fraud in the grantee not to insert the defeasance. Besides, the mortgagee is active, and is a real purchaser; whereas in this case the daughter is merely passive, and cannot be guilty of a fraud in accepting the deed.

MARSHALL.—If he who conveys, commits a fraud, the receiver, knowing of it, is equally guilty, because to all deeds there must be at least two parties, and if there were no fraudulent grantees, there could be no fraudulent grantors. A mere volunteer may as well be guilty of a fraud, as he who pays a valuable consideration, and all trustees are volunteers.

THE PRESIDENT delivered the opinion of the court.

The first point mentioned, tho' not relied upon was, that equity will not aid one volunteer against another, but will leave them to the law, their equity being equal. It is generally true, that this court will not aid a volunteer in *supplying legal defects* in a prior deed, against a subsequent volunteer. But there are exceptions to this general rule, one of which is, the cases of advancements for younger children otherwise unprovided for, in favor of whom the court will supply such legal defects; the counsel probably considering this as such a case, did not press the objection; but he insisted, that applicants to this court must come with clean hands and a fair case, as this court will not enforce iniquitous or even hard bargains.

As to the first, the whole proceeded from the father, and if there were any evil in his intentions, it is not to be imputed to the daughter, who was wholly passive, and used no means either fair or otherwise to procure the deed. Nor can it be thought immoral in her to accept the voluntary bounty of her father, securing to her a provision for life. Natural affection imposes upon parents a moral obligation to provide for their children, and it hath been esteemed both in law and in equity a good consideration for supporting such provisions.

As

As to the second branch of the objection; it is true that the court will never decree iniquity, and there are instances, where they have refused to decree hard bargains though fair, but these are rare, and are generally cases of glaring hardships. For in general, the court will not undertake to estimate the speculations of parties, in a contract, but will deem them the best judges of their own views, and will compel a performance, though they may be eventually disappointed in their expectations.—As to *iniquity* the court discovers none in this case, at least on the part of the daughter, and upon the ground of hardship how does it appear? It is suggested, that the father left himself nothing to subsist upon; but the fact is not proved. On the contrary, it being charged in the original bill, that he had a considerable estate, he who best knew the truth or falsity of the assertion, does not deny it, nor does he complain of hardship, but rests his defence on quite another ground, viz that the promise was conditional, and was broken by the daughter. So that the principles of the objection do not apply to the present case.—If they did, it might be worthy of consideration, whether the present application *to restore a deed to its legal force, which it had lost by fraud or accident*, is not distinguishable from an application to *supply original defects* in a deed. The difference seems to be a strong one, and the court recollect the case of applications to supply defects in bonds against *securities*, which is constantly refused; yet if a bond in which they are *legally* bound be lost, the court will not on account of the securities, withhold the usual relief in giving it the same validity as if it were produced. The argument seems a *fortiori*, that a deed, deprived of its legal force by fraud in the donor, will be restored tho' in a hard case, the court considering that as undone, which should not have been done; but as I said before, it is unnecessary to decide this point, since the facts do not support the objection.

Two other objections remain to be considered. 1st, That the promise was conditional and broken. As to this, there is no proof.

2ly, That there was an implied trust for the father, in case he survived the impending prosecution for felony. Upon this head, the proof is generally derived from the vaunting declarations of the father, that he had secured his estate to his children. That he would face his enemies, and was a proper person to go to law. Mrs. Cotterel is a positive witness, that when he delivered the deed to his daughter, he said, it was not to have effect, if his life were saved, and the circumstances stated by the counsel might have weight to induce a presumption of the truth, if there were nothing to encounter them—but there is abundant proof to over-rule both.

1st, The deed was absolute—without trust or condition—if the former could not safely be inserted, the latter might and ought to have been, in order to prevent imposition upon her future husband.

2dly, There were three subscribing witnesses to the deed and a fourth present, who did not subscribe it, all of whom swear, that no mention was made at the time of either trust or condition.

3dly, Mrs. Woodson's deposition is material—she says that when Ward was speaking of the condition and trust, he was asked if there were any agreement at the time either verbal or in writing to that purpose, and he answered there was not.

4thly, As to the trust. Ward himself who certainly knew more of the matter than Mrs. Cotterel, does not mention it in his answer—whereas he ought to have relied upon it, if it were true, and ought to have brought a cross bill to discover and establish the trust—He did neither, and upon what ground can it now be set up?

The decree must be affirmed.

FIELD'S Executors,

against

SPOTSWOOD.

THIS was an action on the case brought by the appellants against the appellee in the County Court. The declaration contained two counts: the 1st, a special one, stating, that the plaintiff's testator was authorised by the defendant's father to lease out certain lands of which he was seized in tail. That he made a lease to one Dillon of a parcel of the said land for three lives; that Dillon assigned the same to Sisson, and that Field and Dillon gave their bonds to Sisson with condition to procure for him a lease from the defendant, (on whom the estate tail had by that time descended,) on the usual terms of his former leases, and that the defendant promised the said Sisson to make him a leafe. That the defendant for many years received rents from Siſſon, and then turned him out of poſſeſſion; that Siſſon ſued Dillon upon the bond and recovered damages, and that Dillon afterwards upon motion recovered over againſt Field: that whilſt the ſuit was depending, the defendant in conſideration of the premiſes, promiſed Field to ſave the ſaid Dillon and the ſaid Field harmleſs on account of the ſaid bond and ſuit aforeſaid, and of their engagements to Siſſon. The breach aſſigned is, that the defendant has failed to indemnify &c. The 2d count was for money laid out and advanced for the defendant's uſe. Verdict for the plaintiff. An exception was taken to the evidence of Dillon, who proved, that he carried a letter from Field to the defendant upon the ſubject of his indemnifying the ſaid Field, and that immediately after reading the letter, the defendant promiſed that Field ſhould not ſuffer on account of his contract for the ſaid leaſe &c. The judgment of the County Court was reverſed in the Diſtrict Court of Frederickſburg, from which this appeal was prayed.

WILLIAMS for the appellant. It is unneceſſary to enquire whether the 1ſt count be ſuſtainable or not, although I have no doubt myſelf but it is. The 2d count is certainly a good one, upon which the plaintiff below might well recover. The only queſtion then will be, whether the inferior court did right in admitting the evidence ſtated in the bill of exceptions? The witneſs was certainly diſintereſted, and his teſtimony was properly left to the jury, who were the only judges of the weight to be given to it. They were ſatisfied that it ſupported the claim of the plaintiff, and found for him.

WASHINGTON for the appellee. The firſt count certainly cannot be ſuſtained, becauſe the conſideration ſtated being altogether paſt, it was not ſufficient to ſupport a valid promiſe. The undertaking of Field, either as it reſpected the leaſe, or his bond to Siſſon, was not induced by the requeſt, knowledge, or permiſſion of the defendant. Both had been given, before Spotſwood was conſulted upon the ſubject. The reſponſibility which Field drew upon himſelf, was the reſult of his own conduct, unauthoriſed by the defendant, and no new motive appearing to induce the undertaking of the defendant, it is clearly a *nudum pactum*. The acceptance of rent by the defendant might poſſibly have amounted to a confirmation of the leaſe, and might have ſubjected the defendant to the action of Siſſon for ouſting him from the poſſeſſion. But the preſent, is a different action brought by a different perſon, and for a different cauſe of action—If the firſt count be without conſideration, the ſecond cannot be ſupported, becauſe the money paid by Field could not be for the defendant's uſe, and the whole caſe appears in the record.

As to the exception, my objection is, that the promiſe being made to Dillon and not to Field, the latter could not bring this ſuit and avail himſelf of that promiſe. 1 *Eſp.* 105.

The PRESIDENT delivered the opinion of the court.

The bill of exceptions furniſhes no ground for reverſing the judgment of the County Court. Dillon was a diſintereſted witneſs, he having been indemnified by his recovery againſt Field, and the promiſe, tho' made to him, was intended for Field, it being given in anſwer to the letter of Field upon the ſubject of ſaving him harmleſs.

As to the want of conſideration in the firſt count, which has been relied upon at the bar, the court is of opinion that there is nothing in the objection. A tenant in tail might at that time have made leaſes for three lives, under certain reſtrictions preſcribed by the act of Aſſembly; but if he could not, yet ſurely he might promiſe to make a leaſe, and might be compelled to pay damages for breach of ſuch a promiſe. In this caſe, it is evident that he did make ſuch a promiſe, and received rent in conſequence of it, which was a ſufficient conſideration to uphold the undertaking.

The judgment of the Diſtrict Court muſt be reverſed, and that of the County Court

affirmed.

DOE, Leſſee of TOBIAS P. MURRA,

againſt

NORTHERN.

THIS was an ejectment brought in the Diſtrict Court of Northumberland by the appellant, in which the jury found a ſpecial verdict, to the effect following, viz: That in 1666 the governor of Virginia, with the advice and conſent of the council of ſtate, granted the land in queſtion to Thomas Freſhwater, who afterwards aſſigned the patent to Robert Siſſon,

son, who in 1698 devised the land to his grandson George Sisson in fee tail.

That George Sisson in the year 1725, by deeds of lease and release, conveyed the land in question to Edmund Northern, the father of the defendant, under whom the defendant claims, as heir or devisee, and that the said Edmund Northern was thereof seised and possessed.

That in the year 1736 George Sisson sued forth a writ of *ad quod damnum*, and proceeded regularly to dock the intail of this land, after which he by deed of bargain and sale dated in 1737, and recorded as the law directs, conveyed the land in question to Tobias Purcell the ancestor of the plaintiff, who, by virtue of the said conveyance, entered, and was *seised and possessed* thereof at the time of his death, which was after the year 1747, when he, by his will, dated in 1761, devised the same to the lessor of the plaintiff.

That the defendant's ancestor E. Northern was seised and possessed of the land in question after the year 1737, and that after his death, his son peaceably delivered up the possession to the ancestor of the plaintiff. That the guardian of the plaintiff was in possession of the land for many years, and continued so, till he was turned out by the defendants.

The District Court gave judgment for the defendant, from which this appeal was prayed.

WASHINGTON for the appellant. The single question in this case is, whether George Sisson in 1736 could legally dock the intail, and convey to the ancestor of the plaintiff under the law of 1748, which permits a person *seised* of an estate in fee tail, to dock the same by a writ of *ad quod damnum*. It will be objected, that Sisson legally divested himself of the estate during his life by the deed of 1725, and consequently that he was not *seised of an estate tail in* 1736, so as to bar the same under the words, or under the meaning of the above mentioned law. In answer to this objection, I submit it, whether after so great a length of time, and under all the circumstances of this case, the court will not presume a surrender by Sisson of his life estate, for the purpose of giving validity to the inquest and deed of 1736. In England, it is necessary for the tenant in tail, if he would suffer a common recovery, either to have a sufficient estate and power, to enable him to do it, by being tenant in tail in possession, or he must have the concurrence of the tenant of the freehold. The rule there is, that where a person has a right

right to suffer a recovery *omnia præsumuntur rite et solemniter acta*, till the contrary appears; and a surrender of the life estate will be presumed, unless opposed by circumstances which contradict the presumption. 2 *Str.* 1267, 1129. So in the case of Bridges *vs* the duke of Chandos, 2 *Burr.* 1065, this principle is laid down, and fully explained. In the case from 2 *Str.* 1129, the presumption was rebutted by the production of an *imperfect* surrender. In the case from 2 *Burr.* the presumption was sufficiently contradicted: 1st, on account of the tenant in tail having other lands which he might bar, and upon which the recovery might operate, without resorting to presumption, in order to bar the estate tail, whereof he was not in possession. 2dly, because it was not fortified by proof of possession under the recovery. But the principle is fully established and admitted in both the cases. Now in the case under consideration, if the writ of *ad quod damnum* and inquisition did not operate upon the land in question, it could not operate at all, but was a nullity: No imperfect surrender appears; and seisin and possession is found in Sisson, by the inquisition taken at the time, and upon the premises. Possession is also found in Purcell, under the deed of bargain and sale founded upon the inquisition. *Acquiescence* on the part of the issue in tail appears: acquiescence on the part of Northern is found, by his son quietly delivering up the possession, and finally these circumstances are fortified by length of time. A stronger case for presumption cannot be imagined.

WARDEN for the appellee. If the plaintiff's title be in any part of it defective, it is sufficient for the tenant in possession, however destitute he may be himself of right. The objections to the plaintiff's title are, 1st, that the patent found by the jury is not a compleat one, not containing any of the formal parts of a deed, but is a mere skeleton. 2d, From the patentee it is transferred by *assignment*, which is not sufficient to convey a title to lands; the law of 1748 declaring, that no estate of inheritance in lands shall pass, alter, or change, from one to another, but by deed indented, &c.

3dly, The inquisition is taken the 10th day of March in the year 1736, and the writ of *ad quod damnum* is dated the 3d day of March in the 10th year of the reign of Geo. the II, which is subsequent to the inquisition, and therefore it was taken without a writ to warrant it.

4thly, The findings in the verdict are contradictory to each other. It is found that after 1725 and after 1737 Northern was seised, and yet it is found, that Purcell, after the deed to him was

was seised and possessed during his life. Again—by the will of Purcell, the land is devised to his wife for life, who, the jury find, died in 1766; and yet that the guardian of the lessor of the plaintiff was turned out of possession in 1764.

5thly, As to the point which has been anticipated, I think it too strong to be got over. By the deeds of lease and re-lease to Northern in 1725, which contains a warranty, the tenant in tail deprived himself of all interest in the premises, and, by discontinuing the estate tail, he no longer had any power under the law, to dock the intail, or to make the deed of 1737. The court will presume a great deal to support a recovery, which is a matter of record, and of course will be considered as having been rightly done, which they will not do, as to matters transacted in pais. This I consider as a full answer to the cases which have been cited.

WASHINGTON in reply. As to the 1st and 2d objections, the case of Birch *vs* Alexander, (see ante 34.) where these points were much contested, is a complete authority.

3d objection. I have not time to examine whether Mr. Warden be accurate or not, in his calculation of dates; I am almost satisfied that he is not. But suppose it otherwise, I contend that any inaccuracy in this respect is supplied by the verdict, which finds, that a writ issued, in *hæc verba*, that in obedience thereto an inquisition was taken, and the deed recites both. Now the writ must *in fact* have issued before the inquisition was taken, and both must have existed before the deed.

4th objection. If the verdict be so contradictory that no judgment could be rendered upon it, then the judgment of the District Court must be reversed, and a *venire facias de novo* awarded; a decision which I did not expect to hear pressed for by the counsel for the successful party below. But though it might be my interest to consent to this, yet candor compels me to say, that I think the verdict may very well be reconciled, by the court's presuming, what I have contended they ought, in order to support the deed of 1737, viz: that Purcell consented, that, if Northern would surrender his life estate, for the purpose of giving effect to the deed of 1737, he should enjoy the land during his life—that Northern did so: in consequence of this, Sisson became seised again, (as the jury find he was,) and the intail being docked, Purcell became seised under the conveyance to him: afterwards Northern re-entered by curtesy, and held the possession during his life—and that his heir knowing all this, quietly delivered up the possession to Purcell the rightful owner.

These

These are the circumstances, which I rely upon, to aid the presumption arising from length of time.

The principal part of the fifth objection has been before answered. The form of the deed to Northern is relied upon. It is of little consequence, what sort of conveyance was made, as to the point we are discussing. But if it were material, I would contend, that the deed of lease and release set forth in the record, is a statutary conveyance, as much so, as a deed of bargain and sale, and that therefore neither could work a discontinuance, nor pass a greater estate than the grantor might lawfully part with. There might perhaps be a common law deed of lease and release at this day, but then the lease must not (as in this case,) be by bargain and sale, and recite that it is made for the purpose of enabling the lessee, under the statute of uses, to receive a release. As to the warranty, the jury have not found assets descended upon the issue in tail.

I do not ask the court to presume any thing, so as to supply *defects* in the writ, or *inquisition*, but merely a *fact* done in pais as well in this case, as in that of a common recovery, viz. a surrender: so that the difference contended for, does not weaken the authorities cited.

The PRESIDENT delivered the opinion of the Court.

The question on the merits is, whether George Sisson's deed of lease and release to Northern in 1725, prevented the operation of the writ of *ad quod damnum* in 1736, and his deed to Purcell in 1737. This may very much depend upon the actual seisin and possession of the parties; as to which, the findings are uncertain, and directly contradictory to each other.

1st, They find that George Sisson entered by virtue of his grandfather's will in 1698, and was seised and possessed, and being so seised and possessed, did in 1736 sue out the writ, and in 1737 conveyed the land to Purcell. Afterwards they find, that in 1725 (an intervening period between 1698 and 1736) the same Sisson conveyed the same land to Northern, and that he was thereof seised and possessed, in contradiction to the former finding.

Again; they find that by virtue of the deed of 1737, Purcell entered, and was seised and possessed, and was so seised and possessed at his death in 1761. Afterwards it is stated that Northern was seised and possessed after 1737 and that his son after 1747 delivered up the possession to Purcell.

These might be reconciled by a strained construction, so as to avoid a contradiction, but the court do not think it right to proceed

proceed to judgment upon so uncertain a verdict as to this fact.

The judgment of the District Court must be reversed for these reasons, and the cause remanded for a new trial.

ELIZABETH APPLEBURY & others,

against

ANTHONY'S Executors.

THIS was an appeal from a decree of the High Court of Chancery, reversing a decree of the County Court in favor of the appellants, the children of Thomas Applebury, in the suit, who were plaintiffs. The bill states a marriage agreement between Thomas Applebury, father of the plaintiffs, and James Anthony, their grandfather, by which the grandfather promised to give to the said Applebury, a slave named Lucy, in marriage with his daughter, the mother of the plaintiffs. That the marriage took effect, and the grandfather refusing to deliver the slave, the father brought a suit to recover her. That the suit was refered to arbitration, when the grandfather finding it would be decided against him, he proposed to convey the slave to all the children of his daughter, begotten, or to be begotten, with which proposition Applebury closed, and dismissed his suit.—That in May 1769 the grandfather executed a deed for the slave according to the terms of the compromise, which deed is lost or mislaid. That the grandfather died in 1784, and that the defendants are his executors, and refuse to deliver Lucy and her children; and to compel them to do so, is the prayer of the bill.

The answer admits the marriage contract; the suit and reference thereupon; that Lucy was determined to be the property of Applebury, and she was soon afterwards delivered into his possession. That upon an application made by the grandfather to Applebury, the latter agreed to exchange Lucy and her children, for a slave called Dinah, and two notes of hand for £60 which were delivered, and Lucy was retained by the grandfather; that a receipt, expressing this exchange, was signed by Applebury, in May 1769. They admit a deed from the grandfather to Applebury, for Lucy, which was put into the hands of a third person, and which was after the exchange delivered to the defendants by an order from Applebury.

The deed of the grandfather dated in May 1769 to the *children* of Applebury is proved by the deposition, and that it was delivered to a third person to be recorded. The answer is fully supported by the testimony.

The decree of the County Court which was in favor of the plaintiffs, was reversed in the Court of Chancery.

COPLAND for the appellants. The *children* of Applebury taking a legal estate under the deed, as purchasers, not under their father, but under James Anthony the grandfather, the father had no right to sell, exchange, or in any manner to defeat that right. They stand upon the same ground as all other persons who apply to a Court of Equity to set up deeds lost or destroyed by accident or fraud; and the deed in question having been destroyed by the testator of the defendants, this court will establish it without regarding the unauthorised interference of the father.

MARSHALL for the appellees.—The *equitable* right to these slaves was originally in the father himself; and the subsequent conveyance to the *children* being without consideration, they are merely volunteers against the representatives of James Anthony, whose testator was a purchaser, for valuable consideration, of the father's original equitable title.—So that this is not the case of a contest between volunteers, but that of a volunteer asking the aid of this court against a purchaser for valuable consideration; in which case, I conceive, a Court of Equity will not interfere. The only deposition in the cause is that of the father, who says, that he considered himself entitled to dispose of the negro mentioned in the deed, which leaves a strong presumption, that the deed was delivered as an escrow.

COPLAND in reply. I do not rely upon the deposition, because the answer admits the conveyance. As to the main point, there can be no good reason, why this court should not set up a deed destroyed by the party who gave it, because he had purchased the property from a person, who he knew had no right to dispose of it. Such a bargain could not bind the present plaintiffs.

THE PRESIDENT delivered the opinion of the court.

This being an application to a Court of Equity, to restore a lost deed to its legal validity, it becomes important to consider whether the deed, if restored, has any legal force. It is the
the

the deed of the grandfather, for slaves, to which he had, at the time, no title. For upon the state of the case, the title appears to have been in Applebury the father.

But it is said, that this deed was made with the consent and privity of Applebury, and therefore ought to bind him; to this there are two answers. 1st, It is admitted, that if a man has an equitable title only, and stands by, and suffers another to purchase without disclosing his title, he is guilty of a fraud, which shall defeat him of his equitable claim. But it is supposed, that a legal claim could not be so lost, even in favor of a purchaser; and it is doubted, if even an equitable claim would be destroyed by that circumstance, in the case of a mere voluntary conveyance.

But 2dly, Suppose the children had this equity against their father, it is but an equity, which may be opposed by circumstances of superior equity on the other side, especially on behalf of the grandfather, who was a fair purchaser, and had his deed delivered to him without the same having been recorded.

The whole transaction was fair. The grandfather who was bound to give Lucy to Applebury, conveyed her to his children with his consent and approbation. The next day an agreement was made between the same parties to substitute a valuable consideration for Lucy, and this, not with any fraudulent view, but upon the laudable motive of gratifying the wishes of the slave. The consideration was paid; Lucy redelivered; and the deed restored to the grandfather. And now, the grandchildren are endeavoring to set up this voluntary deed, made upon a contract between their father and grandfather, who agreed without any fraudulent intention to change the contract, and to cancel the deed, whilst it was in their power to do so, (it not being recorded,) notwithstanding their father's estate was thereby augmented, in consequence of the consideration paid for Lucy. So that they have a chance at least, of receiving an equivalent, if they should get Dinah and the two other slaves purchased with the £60 which the father may give them in lieu of Lucy. The grandfather has already paid Applebury his wife's fortune, and if the plaintiffs were to succeed in this suit, they would compel the grandfather to pay it over again.

Upon the whole, the plaintiffs have neither law nor equity in their favor. The defendant Anthony has both, and the decree of the Chancellor is right. But it may be necessary to distinguish this case from that of Ward *vs* Webber and wife, (see ante p. 274) where a voluntary conveyance by a father to a child, being cancelled by the father, was restored to its legal validity:

1st, In that case the father was proprietor of the estate, and had a power to convey. In this the grandfather had no title and this original defect was to be supplied in equity by the consent of the father, and so liable to be opposed by superior equity.

2dly, In that case the deed was delivered into the daughter's keeping, who was of full age, and was privately cancelled by the father, without her consent: in this, the children, if they were in being, had no hand in the transaction, nor had they even the deed. The father who consented to accept it, relinquished it the next day, and gave it up to the donor.

3dly, The defendant in that case, was a mere volunteer, here, he is a fair purchaser, for a valuable consideration, so that the cases are wholy dissimilar, and the decree perfectly reconcileable.

Decree affirmed.

SMALLWOOD,
against
MERCER & HANSBOROUGH.

THIS was an appeal from the High Court of Chancery, dismissing the bill of the appellant. The case was as follows.—Mercer being in possession of a tract of land, to a part of which Hansborough was entitled as heir to his mother, (and which had been sold to the father of Mercer, by the father of Hansborough, without the privy examination of the mother) proposed selling it to Smallwood, who hearing of the title of Hansborough, objected thereto. Mercer, to remove this obstacle, applied to Hansborough, and a bond dated March 26th 1783, was entered into, with a condition, the material parts of which are as follows, viz: " whereas certain matters of controversy
" now depend, and subsist between the above named Mercer,
" and the above bound Hansborough, that is to say, a claim
" which the said Hansborough pretends to have to $133\frac{1}{3}$ acres of
" land, now in the possession of the said Mercer, and which the
" said Hansborough claims as heir at law to his mother Lettice,
" whom the said Mercer admits to be one of the daughters and
" co-heiresses

"co-heiresses of Joseph Sumner deceased; and also admits the
"said land to be the same, which the late John Mercer, father
"of the said Mercer, purchased of the father of the said Hans-
"borough, as, and for, the reversion of one third of 400 acres,
"called the dower of the widow of the said Joseph Sumner;
"also a claim the said Mercer has, or may have against the said
"Hansborough, as executor of his father, for the value of the
"said land, in case the same shall be adjudged to the said Hans-
"borough,—he the said Hansborough, hereby acknowledging
"assets in his hands sufficient to make satisfaction for the said
"$133\frac{1}{3}$ acres, and also acknowledging the said Mercer to have
"all the right of his father, under the deed from the said Hans-
"borough, which several disputes the said Mercer and the said
"Hansborough have agreed to submit to the arbitration &c. of
"Joseph Jones, Alexander Rose and Andrew Buchanan, or a-
"ny two of them, to be adjudged &c. and in manner following,
"viz: if they shall adjudge the said Hansborough to be entitled
"to said land, they shall award the said Mercer to pay the said
"Hansborough, the value thereof in money, upon receiving
"a conveyance of the said land from said Hansborough; and
"as to the dispute between the said Mercer and the said Hans-
"borough, as executor of his father, it is agreed, the same
"shall be adjusted as follows, viz; if the said arbitrators shall ad-
"judge the estate of the said Hansborough liable to make good
"the value of the said land, they shall adjudge what value shall
"be paid, and may allow the said Hansborough to retain such
"value in his hands, in full, towards the consideration they
"shall adjudge to be paid for the said lands. The condition is,
"if the said Hansborough shall in all things do and perform the
"award &c. which the said arbitrators shall make touching the
"premises, (provided the same be made in writing ready to be de-
"livered *on or before the 30th of June next*) then &c, &c. To
"which was annexed the following memorandum, viz: "It
"is agreed, if the legatees of the said J. Hansborough, (the fa-
"ther) shall dissent from the claim of the said Mercer, against
"the said Hansborough, on the covenants in the deed of the said
"J. Hansborough being arbitrated, then the arbitrators shall be
"discharged from that part of the business before submitted to
"them. And it is agreed, the said Hansborough shall
"enter an appearance at the suit of the said Mercer, in an acti-
"on of covenant in the General Court, and allow the same to
"go on with all legal dispatch to a judgment, 'till when, said
"Hansborough agrees to wait with said Mercer, for whatever
"the

"the said arbitrators shall adjudge the said Mercer to pay for the said 133½ acres, and then to discount therefrom what may be recovered in the action of covenant; and further, the said Hansborough agrees that he will make the said Mercer deeds for the said lands, immediately upon payment of the value to be awarded, or upon receipt of a bond for the same, with such security as the said Hansborough shall agree."

This bond being shewed by Mercer to Smallwood, the latter after consulting counsel was induced to make the purchase, and paid the consideration money agreed upon. The award was never made, on account of the refusal of one of the arbitrators to act, because he had previously given his opinion to Hansborough with respect to his title. Mercer offered to concede the title to be in Hansborough, and to give him bond and security to pay as much per acre for the 133½ acres, as he was to receive from Smallwood for the whole tract, which offer was refused. Hansborough brought an ejectment against Smallwood, upon which Smallwood exhibited this bill praying for an injunction and conveyance. Upon the institution of this suit, Mercer brought an action of covenant against Hansborough as executor to his father.

MARSHALL for the appellant. This bond contains a positive agreement on the part of Hansborough to sell the land in question, and the agreement as to the sale, could not be dependent upon the award, the object of which was, merely to decide upon *the title of Hansborough*, to fix the price of the land, and the damages to be paid by Hansborough out of the assets of his father, for the breach of his contract, in not warranting the title of the land. The circumstances which attended the giving of that bond, prove incontestibly, that this was the intention and design of the bond. Hansborough knew of Smallwood's intention to purchase, and his objection on account of Hansborough's claim to the land. To remove this objection, he gave the bond, which was shewn to Smallwood, and it had the expected effect. A third person paying his money in consequence of this agreement, ought not to be affected by the fault either of Hansborough, or of Mercer, in failing to adjust those other matters of dispute, which only concerned themselves. The proviso, that the award should be made, and delivered within a stated time, does not alter the case, because it could only relate to the matters submitted, which were the *price and damages*, not the *sale*, which is positively stipulated for, whatever might be the event of those subjects of dispute. But further; Hansborough, by appointing a referee, who he knew could not act, committed a fraud, and he will therefore be bound to submit to some other equitable mode of adjusting the price.

CAMPBELL for the appellee. If this court be called upon to decree a specific execution of an agreement, it must be done in the way agreed upon by the parties, and in no other. For otherwise, it would be to *make*, not to *execute an agreement*; and if, from any circumstance, it cannot be executed in that way, this court must leave the parties to their legal remedy. It is to be observed, that Smallwood, knowing of Hansborough's title, can stand in no better situation than Mercer would, if he were plaintiff. This obligation is to be binding in the whole, or not at all. Now what does Hansborough bind himself to perform? The award of the arbitrators. That is, if they say, he hath a title, they are to decide upon the price which Hansborough shall take for the land. But upon what condition is Hansborough bound to sell for that price? That the decision be made *within a limited time*. If this condition be not performed, he is not bound at law, and upon what principle can he be bound in equity? He might, for the purpose of putting an end to litigation, and with a view of receiving the value of the land within a short period, be disposed to sell his right, which otherwise he would not have been induced to do, if kept in suspence beyond that time. But after that time is passed,—litigation still hanging over him,—the purchase money at this day unpaid, and he forced at length to assert his right in a court of law:—after so great a lapse of time, and after he has been compelled to incur all the trouble and expence, which he so anxiously wished to avoid;—can it be just or equitable, that he should be still bound to sell, tho' he agreed to do so upon a condition only, which has not been performed? It is impossible. But what can this court do? They cannot appoint referees; for they may not be agreeable to the parties. And if the court could appoint them, still the award cannot now be made within the time fixed upon by the parties, and consequently, the prayer of the bill which is for a specific execution of that agreement, cannot be decreed. The result of the whole is, that this court must remain neuter between the parties, and leave them to the law.

MARSHALL in reply. I yet insist, that the agreement to sell is absolute. The business of the arbitrators is stated in the preamble to the condition, namely, to decide the right of Hansborough to the land, the price to be paid by Mercer, and Mercer's claim

claim to damages. But the arbitrators are not to decide, whether Hanſborough is to ſell, or not. If they were, then I admit the full operation of the proviſo. But that is not ſubmitted: the bond itſelf is compleat evidence of a prior agreement to ſell; for in all bargains, it is uſual for the vendor to agree to ſell, before the price is ſpoken of. This previous point being ſettled, the conſideration and terms follow next, and is either fixed by the ſtipulation of the parties, or left to depend upon other modes of aſcertainment. I admit, that the court cannot appoint referees; but if it be clear, that a ſale was agreed upon and that the award which was to fix the price, has been prevented by accident or fraud, this court may compel a ſpecific performance as to the ſale, and direct a jury to ſettle the price. In the caſe of Roſs and Anderſon in this court, a ſimilar decree was made transfering this power from arbitrators to a jury. With greater reaſon ought it to be done in this caſe, where the party himſelf prevented the award by appointing an arbitrator, who he knew could not, or ought not toact, and knowing too, that Mercer's view in obtaining the bond was to enable him to ſell to another.

The PRESIDENT delivered the opinon of the court.

The queſtion is, whether a Court of Equity, upon the agreement, and the facts ſtated, will compell Hanſborough to convey his land, upon receiving the value thereof, to be aſcertained either by the price which Smallwood gave Mercer; by appointing new valuers, or by a jury.—It is to be premiſed, that Smallwood, is in no better, or worſe ſituation than Mercer, ſince he purchaſed with notice of the written agreement, without any further information, or promiſe from Hanſborough, who is not bound by any miſtaken opinion formed of that agreement, either by Smallwood, or by his counſel. He ſeems to have conſidered as fixed, ſundry events, then contingent; namely, that the arbitrators would decide the title, and, if in favor of Hanſborough, that they would aſcertain the price to be paid for the land, and that Mercer would, in caſe that price was not diſcounted by his claim, pay the value, or give bond with ſatisfactory ſecurity for the ſame. If all theſe things had been done Hanſborough would indeed have been compellible in equity to convey. But Smallwood never could conceive, that Hanſborough was to convey his land at all events, without even knowing the price he was to receive for it, or without having any ſatisfactory aſſurance, that he ſhould ever get any thing. Such a

conveyance

conveyance I believe no Court of Equity ever compelled a defendant to make.

It was contended by Mr. Marshall, that the *sale* was not refered to arbitration, but was made by the parties themselves, and that the arbitrators were only to settle the value. It would seem a strange sale, in which such necessary ingredients, as price, and the vendor's right to sell, were in suspence. It would be more properly described, by calling it an inchoate contract for a sale, provided the arbitrators determined in favor of the vendor's title, fixed the price, and that the other requisites were complied with, none of which were done, and consequently the contract never was compleated.

In cases of bonds to perform awards, there are two remedies, 1st, at law upon the bond, in which, a plea that the arbitrators made no award, would, if true, defeat the plaintiff's action. 2dly, If any act be awarded to be done, for which a compleat remedy cannot be had at law, such as to make a conveyance, a bill in equity for a specific performance of the award is common and proper. But how the Court can decree the specific performance of the condition of a bond to perform an award, when in fact no award has been or can be made, is not discernible. But the bond is relied upon, as containing an agreement to sell, which agreement is sought to be specifically executed. That agreement it has been shewn was only a treaty, never brought to perfection, for want of the award. And that this was the effect of the arbitrators refusing to act, seems to have been well understood, both by Mercer and Hansborough. The former makes new propositions which the other declines, and brings his ejectment, and Mercer brings his action of covenant, each pursuing his original remedy, as if no agreement had ever subsisted. It is true, if the agreement had been perfect, (since Smallwood purchased under it, and both the defendants knew it,) and they had consented to dissolve it, it would have been a fraud upon the plaintiff, against which, a Court of Equity would have relieved. But no such ingredient appears, and every thing depends upon the original agreement. That agreement never having been perfected, there is no foundation for the interposition of the Court of Equity, and therefore we

affirm the decree.

BUCKNER

PUCKNER & others, trustees of BEVERLEY,

against

Smith, Stubblefield, Graham, and Dixon's executors.

THIS was an appeal from the High Court of Chancery dismissing the bill of the complainants who are now appellants.—The case was as follows: Beverley during his infancy lost a considerable quantity of tobacco at unlawful gaming with the defendant Smith; who for valuable consideration gave to Stubblefield an order upon Beverley for 25,000 pounds of tobacco. Beverley accepted the order, and afterwards gave his bond to Stubblefield for the amount. Stubblefield assigned the bond to Graham, and Graham to Dixon, each paying for the same a valuable consideration. Upon an action brought by Dixon upon the bond, Beverley confessed a judgment. He afterwards conveyed his estate to the appellants in trust, to pay his debts, and to apply the residue, towards the support of his family.—The trustees understanding the real nature of this demand, filed their bill in the High Court of Chancery praying an injunction to this judgment, and charging that Stubblefield, Graham, and Dixon, had full notice that the bond in question was given for a gaming consideration, before they respectively acquired an interest in it. Stubblefield in his answer, denies that he had notice of the consideration for which the bond was given.—Dixon, just previous to his death, drew up the heads of an answer, and swore to it, denying notice, and stating that he was induced to accept of an assignment of the bond, by Beverley, who assured him that the bond should be punctually paid. His executor's answer refers to those heads, as part thereof. The answer also refers to a letter from Beverley to Dixon, after he had come to full age, giving assurances of payment. The only deposition in the cause is that of Smith, one of the defendants, who does not answer, nor is his deposition excepted to. He proves the consideration of the order upon which the bond was given, to have been for tobacco lost at gaming by Beverley, and that Stubblefield had notice of it, at the time the order was given, and agreed, that if Beverley should accept the order, he would discharge Smith from all responsibility.

WARDEN

WARDEN for the appellants. The infancy of Beverley is proven, as also notice to Stubblefield, who does not positively deny it, but only says that he was not concerned in the gaming transaction. It is also fairly to be presumed, that the other defendants knew of it. But whether this were the case or not, Dixon ought not to have recovered; for tho' an assignee *without notice*, might in some cases be a sufferer, by considering him as standing in no better situation than the assignor, yet, this individual inconvenience is very far short of the public mischief, which would be produced by giving validity to a bond of this sort, because it had got into the hands of an assignee. For if the winner could pay his own debts, or make a valuable use of bonds acquired by gaming, it would be easy for him at any time to evade the statute, and to derive every advantage which he could desire, by a violation of the law. The case of Bowyer and Bampton 2 *Str.* 1155 is conclusive upon this subject. It is absurd to contend, that a bond, which the law has declared *void ab initio*, can by any thing subsequent thereto be made effectual.

CAMPBELL for Stubblefield. The appellant's counsel, has not, in the course of his argument, touched the only point in the cause; and that is, will a Court of Equity, after a judgment fairly obtained at law, and where the defendant has waved any legal advantage which he might have had, interfere to set aside that judgment without some special circumstances to warrant it? The case before the court, is not one of those, wherein Chancery can claim jurisdiction. It is not a case of trust, fraud, or accident. It is not a bill for a discovery, even if such a bill in a case like this could be sustained. The plaintiff does not pretend, that he is destitute of other evidence, than what he can draw from the defendants, and if he had stated such a charge in his bill, it would have been contradicted by the record, wherein a deposition appears, which completely proves the fact. Neither is this application warranted by the act of 22 *Geo.* II, C. 25, § 3, which authorises a bill of discovery only where *actual payment hath been made*, and upon a discovery and re-payment by the winner, excuses him from the forfeiture imposed by the law. So that, upon no principle whatever, are the plaintiffs (who stand in no better situation than Beverley did) proper in this Court.

WICKHAM for Dixon's executors. I shall in the first place object, that the bond in question, is not proved to have been given upon a gaming consideration. It is positively denied by the answers fwers, and thofe anfwers are contradicted only by the depofition of one of the defendants, whofe evidence can have no greater weight, than his anfwer would have had, which could not have operated againft a co-defendant. But paffing over this, want of notice is pofitively denied by Dixon; and it is a well known principle in this court, that if the plaintiff and defendant are both equally innocent, equity will not interfere, but will leave them to the law. That Dixon was entirely innocent is not denied: no imputation can lie againft him. But is Beverley fo? No. In the firft place, he violated a pofitive law. He then gave a negotiable paper, importing upon its face, the evidence of a juft debt. This is fent into circulation, to deceive and injure thofe, who might unfortunately become its poffeffors. But above all, he induces Dixon to throw away his money in the purchafe of that bond, under affurances of its being paid. Shall he then, who hath been guilty of a fraud, find countenance in a Court of Equity againft the perfon, upon whom that fraud hath been practifed, and who was thereby induced to throw away his money? It is a rule, that he who acquires a legal title without notice of an equitable claim oppofed to it, fhall not have it queftioned in a court of equity. Thus a purchafer for valuable confideration, without notice of a prior equitable claim, may in this court, defend himfelf by relying upon fuch a purchafe.—Suppofe in this cafe, the money had been paid by Beverley, (and the principle will be the fame after a judgment) could he have recovered it back at law? He might have done it perhaps under the act of 22 *Geo.* II *C.* 25 if he had brought his action within three months.—But otherwife he could not, as the law itfelf proves, by affording a remedy, and prefcribing a time within which it fhould be afferted. And if he could not recover it back at law, in an action for money had and received, which is as liberal a remedy as a bill in Chancery, would equity affift him? I contend it would not.

Upon the whole, I truft, that the decree will be affirmed: but if it fhould be fuppofed, that the appellants are entitled to relief, I hope it will not be granted againft Dixon's executors, whofe teftator was entirely innocent, and who have the benefit of a judgment at law. For fince all proper parties are before the court, it would be moft confiftent with the principles of equity, in order to prevent circuity of action, to decree at once againft the perfon who ought ultimately to fuffer.

Mr. CAMPBELL obferved, that as the bill prayed for an injunction, the court muft either make it perpetual, or difmifs the bill. Mr.

Mr. WICKHAM, in anfwer faid, that the bill prayed for general relief, and therefore the court might make any decree which was thought equitable.

WARDEN in reply. Notice is not pofitively denied by Stublefield, and the anfwer of Smith, not having been excepted to, muft be confidered as proper evidence in the caufe. The court muft not only confider the bond, but alfo the judgment as being void, under the act of Affembly. This act gives this court exprefs jurifdiction in the prefent cafe, and the policy of it was to compel a difcovery at all events, that the ftatute might not by any device, or means whatever, be evaded. For if refort in fuch cafes could not be had to a Court of Equity, the confideration of fuch bonds could feldom be difcovered, nor could the mifchief arifing to the public, from fuch pernicious practices, be prevented. The confeffion of judgment in this cafe, cannot alter the rights of the parties; for the defendant may not always know, whether he can eftablifh the fact, and unlefs he could prove it, it would be unneceffary to plead, or even to defend the caufe. It was to obviate this inconvenience, that the remedy pointed out by the act was provided. He cited *Dougl.* 743, which recognizes the cafe of Bowyer & Bampton.

The PRESIDENT not fitting in the caufe, LYONS, J. delivered the opinion of the court.—After ftating the cafe, and that the affumpfit of Beverley to Dixon was after he came of age, he proceeded. It is not important to decide upon the propriety of admitting Mr. Smith's depofition. The principal objection is, that this was a gaming debt, contracted by an infant, which no fubfequent act of his, nor any transfer could make valid. It is in general true, that an affignee of a bond of this fort, can be in no better fituation than the obligee, and the cafes cited at the bar fufficiently eftablifh the point. But the prefent cafe is very different upon principle from thofe cafes, and that difference, is produced by the conduct of Beverley, who by his affurances of payment, induced Mr. Dixon to receive an affignment of it. He not only concealed from him the legal objections to the bond, but afterwards affumed to pay it, and when fued, voluntarily confeffed a judgment.

The privileges allowed to infants are intended to protect them from injury, not to furnifh them with the means of deceiving, and of defrauding others; and if negotiable papers, accepted by others, under all the caution ufed by Mr. Dixon in this cafe, were permitted to be fet afide, there would be an end put to the negotiability of fuch papers, and to all confidence between men and

and man. Why did not Beverley avail himself at law, of the supposed advantage, which he now relies upon in this court? But suppose he had pleaded it, and the plaintiff had replied the special matter, " that he had been induced by the defendant to receive the bond;" upon a demurrer, the law would have been decided in his favor. 2 *Mod.* 279. If he had pleaded infancy, he might have avoided *the bond*, but certainly in another action, the plaintiff upon proving his assumpsit after his attaining full age would have succeeded. If then, this would have been his fate at law, upon no principle can he expect, that a Court of Equity will assist him in imposing upon innocent third persons a loss produced by his own fraud.

Upon the whole the court affirm the decree.

MINNIS, Ex'r. of AYLETT and others,

against

PHILIP AYLETT.

THIS was an appeal from a decree of the High Court of Chancery, and the question depended upon a clause in the will of William Aylett the father of the appellee, wherein he devised to the appellee and his heirs, " the plantation on which " he then lived, and all his lands in the county of King Wil- " liam, also his land in Drummond's neck in James City coun- " ty." The testator at the time of making his will, and at his decease, was seised of an estate of inheritance, in a tract of land in the county of King William, upon a part of which he lived, the residue being in the possession of others, under leases. He was also entitled to a leasehold interest for the term of 999 years in another tract of land lying in the same county, but of this last he was not possessed. He commenced a suit for the recovery of it, which abated by his death. His executors revived the suit after his death, and recovered the land. The appellee filed his bill in the High Court of Chancery, against the executors and residuary devisees of the testator, claiming the leasehold as well as the freehold lands. The only question was, whether the leasehold land passed under the above clause to the appellee, or was comprehended in the residuary clause in the will. The Chancellor decreed in favor of the appellee, upon his giving

bond

bond with condition to pay the proportion of the debts due from the teftator, for which this land is liable; and alfo, an account of the rents and profits thereof, received by the executors. From this decree the executors appealed.

WARDEN for the appellants. The decifions, from the cafe of Rofe *vs* Bartlett, *Cro. Car.* 292, down to the prefent day, have been uniform upon the fubject; and they all eftablifh this difference, that if the teftator be entitled to both freehold and leafehold lands, and devife *all his lands*, the former only will pafs; but if he have leafehold lands only, then they will pafs; for in the firft cafe, the freeholds lands will fatisfy the words of the will. He cited *Swinb.* on wills 139, 318, devife of all his lands and tenements—only the freehold lands pafs. 1 *P. Wms.* 286—3 *P. Wms.* 26—2 *Atk.* 450—1 *Vern* 271.

MARSHALL for the appellee. If the weight of authorities were out of the way, there could be no queftion, in cafes of this fort, about the intention, which certainly is, to pafs all the teftator's land, whether freehold or leafehold. The cafes cited, do not apply. They have all of them been decided upon fome expreffion in the will, fhewing an intention to pafs only the freehold lands. In thofe cafes, the teftator either gives all his lands and *tenements*, or all his *freehold lands*. As for inftance, in the quotation from Swinburne, the author explains thofe cafes, and fhews, that by the word *tenement*, the teftator is confidered as meaning *frank tenement* or *freehold*, and thereby limiting the general meaning of the word *lands*. In this cafe the teftator had but one tract of land in King William, except the leafehold, and the devife being of *all his lands*, in the plural, it cannot be fatisfied unlefs the leafehold land fhall be confidered as paffing.

WARDEN in reply. The cafe of Rofe and Bartlett is a devife of all his lands; and the word *tenements* is not mentioned. It is true, that the court, in giving the opinion, put the cafe of a devife of all a man's lands and *tenements*, and this is conclufive to fhew, that the infertion of that word makes no difference, fince they would not have decided the cafe under confideration, and the cafe ftated in argument, in the fame manner, if there were any thing in the word *tenement*. But this cafe, upon intention, is ftronger than any of thofe cited, becaufe here, the teftator not being in *poffeffion* of the leafehold land, it is not prefumable that he meant to devife it,

FALL TERM

The PRESIDENT delivered the opinion of the Court.

In the case of Shermer and Shermer's executors, the court declared their opinion to be, that where the intention of a testator is apparent, cases to over-rule that intention must be strong, uniform, and apply directly to the case before the court, or else they would be disregarded. If in this case, the intention appeared clear, that the leasehold land should pass, the court would give a decision according to this principle, in support of the intention; but we can discover no such intention. The rule is laid down in Rose and Bartlett, by all the judges, that where a testator having both freehold and leasehold lands in a particular place, devises all his lands in that place, only the freehold lands shall pass. Subsequent Judges and Chancellors have stated the rule, and uniformly decided accordingly, altho' in one case, the Chancellor acknowledged, that the testator intended the leasehold land should pass.

Thus settled, it has become a rule of property, which the court cannot depart from, without disturbing perhaps many titles, enjoyed under this long established principle. In this will, there are no words or circumstances, to shew an intention, which do not appear in the case of Rose and Bartlett.

The court are therefore of opinion, that the leasehold land did not pass under the clause in question to the appellee, but is comprehended within the residuary clause to the wife and children of the testator, and they reverse the decree, and remit the cause for further proceedings.

BROWN'S Executors, *against* PUTNEY.

THIS was an action of assumpsit brought by Putney against the appellants in the District Court of Williamsburg. The defendant pleaded the act of limitations, upon which, issue was taken. The jury, by consent, found a verdict for the plaintiff, subject to the opinion of the court upon the following case, viz: that no assumpsit was proved after the 27th of March 1786, and that the writ in this suit issued the 23d of August 1791: that to avoid the act of limitations the plaintiff produced a writ which issued for the same cause of action from the Court of Hustings of Williamsburg, dated the 24th of October 1786, and which was not served upon Brown; but in November following

it

it abated and was difmiffed as to him, he being returned, *no inhabitant*: That the fame writ was ferved upon Eaton another defendant, and abated by his death in Auguft 1787. The verdict to ftand if the law be for the plaintiff, otherwife to be fet afide, and judgment entered for the defendant. The judgment of the Diftrict Court was in favor of the plaintiff, from which the defendant appealed.

WICKHAM for the appellant. It appears, that for four years no fuit was depending. The claufe in the act of limitations which allows the plaintiff one year to recommence his action, after the reverfal of his judgment &c. is, I acknowledge, extended, by an equitable conftruction, to all cafes' where the plaintiff *gets out of court*; but a perfon coming within the benefit of this liberal conftruction of the law, muft recommence his action within the fame time after the abatement or difmiffion, as he muft have done in cafes coming within the letter of the act, he cited Wilcocks *vs* Huggins 2 *Str.* 907.

MARSHALL for the appellee fubmitted the cafe.

The PRESIDENT. The plaintiff according to the decifion in the cafe of Wilcocks and Huggins, would have been entitled to the benefit of the provifo in the act of limitations, under the equity thereof, if he had recommenced his fuit within a year after the former fuit was abated. But as four years had nearly elapfed between the abatement of that fuit, and the bringing of the prefent, he cannot avail himfelf of the provifo, but is barred.

The judgment muft be reverfed, and entered for the defendant.

LEFTWITCH & Wife,
againft
STOVALL &c.

THE cafe was this:—Eight perfons who were the defendants in error, fued out a writ in the County Court againft Leftwitch and wife, in cafe; damage £300. No declaration was filed, but the defendants below pleaded that they did not affume; on which the parties were at iffue. Afterwards, by a rule of court, they fubmitted all matters in difference between

tween them to arbitrators, and agreed, that their award, should be made the judgment of the court. An award was made, that the defendants should pay to each of the plaintiffs 1,724½ lbs. of tobacco, and 31/3 in money, amounting in the whole to 13,812 lbs. of tobacco, and £12: 10, in money, and also the costs. Judgment was entered according to the award. An execution issued for the aggregate amount, and a replevy bond was taken. The judgment was affirmed by the District Court of New-London, upon a superfedeas, and execution issued *upon that judgment* and a replevy bond was taken, upon which a third execution issued. To the judgment of the District Court, a superfedeas was obtained from this Court.

MARSHALL for the plaintiffs in error. I object, 1st, to the original judgment, and 2dly, to the subsequent proceedings. The objections to the original judgment are: First, the want of a declaration. Tho' it has been determined in this court, in the case of Picket and Claiborne, that the want of a declaration is cured by a confession of judgment, yet no decision of this, or of any court in England, has ever gone so far, as to extend this rule to judgments entered in pursuance of awards.

Secondly, The arbitrators exceeded their power; for tho' the plaintiffs demand was in money, as appears from the writ, (the damages being laid in money) yet the award is for the payment of tobacco, which was improper, and not within the submission. Such a change from money, to an article so fluctuating in its value as tobacco, might be very material to the parties.

2d point. The judgment does not pursue the award, or the execution is variant from the judgment. The award is several, and the execution joint, so that tho' by the award, the receipt of one of the plaintiffs could extend no farther *than to his share* yet being made joint, he might receive *the whole,* and give a discharge, which proves the variance to be material.

Again; after the affirmance of the judgment by the District Court, the force of the *replevy bond* which is considered as a *judgment,* was revived; and consequently the last execution could not issue upon the *original* judgment which was *discharged* by the replevy bond. For suppose a motion had then been made upon the replevy bond, the court could not have refused to give a judgment upon it. He cited the case of Taylor and Dundass, (see ante p. 92) as decisive upon this point.

CAMPBELL for the defendants in error. There are two ways, by which men settle their differences; either by the regular

gular courfe of law, in which cafe they muft purfue the rigid forms and rules of law, and unlefs they do fo, a judgment irregularly obtained will not be fupported: or by agreement, and this may be, either by the acknowledgment of the parties abfolutely, or by an acknowledgment dependent upon the judgment of their friends. In the latter cafe, where the parties withdraw their difpute from the regular mode of decifion, and the defendant acknowledges the propriety of the plaintiff's demand *abfolutely*, or acknowledges as much to be due, as their mutual friends fhall decide to be due, the court will not notice thofe irregularities which might have been fatal, if they had not been thus tacitly waved by the conduct of the parties. And fince it is conceded, that a confeffion of judgment is a releafe of errors, there can be no difference in reafon between fuch an acknowledgment, and one which is dependent upon the opinion of arbitrators, who are appointed to decide for the parties.

As to the other objection made to the judgment, it is not fupported by the facts in the caufe. The writ ftates the damages in money, but the claim may have been in tobacco, the confequential injury arifing from the non-payment of it, might be properly eftimated in money. The parties underftood this— The arbitrators will be prefumed to have underftood it. It cannot be denied, but that the defendant might have confeffed judgment in tobacco, and it is the fame thing, if the perfons appointed to afcertain the claim, and to act for them, give their judgment in the fame commodity.

In anfwer to the objections made to the proceedings which fucceeded the judgment, I contend, that a Superior Court can only notice errors in the *judgments* of inferior tribunals, and muft affirm or reverfe them. As to acts *merely minifterial*, they are under the controul of the court, under whom the officers act, and may, and ought to be there corrected (if wrong) upon motion.

The PRESIDENT delivered the opinion of the court.

The objections to the judgment are, 1ft, The want of a declaration. 2dly, That the arbitrators exceeded their power, in awarding tobacco, when the demand was for money.

Firft, The great purpofes for which declarations, containing a regular ftatement of the plaintiff's claim, are required, are 1ft, That the defendant may know with certainty, the nature of the charge againft him, fo that he may not be embarraffed, nor enfnared at the trial.

2dly,

2dly, That the demand should appear upon record, so as that a recovery in that suit, may be a bar to any future action, for the same cause.

This court in the case of Picket and Claiborn, determined, that both these ends were answered by a confession of judgment which implies a knowledge in the defendant of the cause of action, and that being stated in the judgment, would bar a subsequent suit for the same thing.

So in this case, the submission to arbitration, rendered it unnecessary to state the cause of action to the court, in the regular mode of proceeding, since they were not to try it; and the award stating the ground of the demand, will enable the defendant to plead the judgment in bar to any future action, for the same cause. But the principal answer, and one which applies also to the 2d objection is, that the parties by withdrawing their case from the ordinary judges, and submitting it to those of their own chusing, have waved all objections to the want of legal forms, and have confined themselves to considerations arising out of the award itself; such as partiality, corruption, *ex parte* proceedings, or that they exceeded their power. The latter, is chiefly applicable to bonds, submitting particular specified disputes. Here, the submission is *of all matters in difference*.

The objection made to the award, as exceeding the power of the arbitrators, is founded upon a comparison of the award with the *writ*, and not with the *submission*.

The next objections relied upon, are to the execution and replevy bonds; but as these are merely *ministerial acts*, unconnected with the judgment, which is alone before the court, they cannot be regarded. Errors of this sort, can only be rectified by the court from whence the execution issued, subordinate perhaps to the controul of this court, but it must come by appeal from the opinion of that court, given upon motion, and cannot be taken up collaterally upon an appeal from the original judgment.

The judgment must be affirmed.

LEE Executor of DANIEL, *against* COOKE.

THIS was an action of covenant, brought by Cooke in the District Court of King and Queen, upon a warranty contained

tained in a deed poll, dated in 1779, by which, the testator, for a valuable consideration, conveyed to Cooke, a negro, and covenanted for himself and *his heirs* to warrant the title against all persons whatsoever. The declaration charges; that the negro had been recovered by Wm. Morgan by the judgment of the County Court of King and Queen, in an action of detinue, and so neither the testator nor the executor had kept the testator's covenant, but had broken the same &c. Upon the plea of covenants performed, the jury found a conditional verdict, subject to the opinion of the court. If upon the bill of sale, an action of covenant can be supported against the defendant as executor, and if evidence can be admitted, or is necessary, to prove, that notice was given to the defendant of the action of detinue having been brought, (the notice not having been stated in the declaration, and the defendant having pleaded conditions performed,) then they find for the plaintiff £94: 10: 5, damages, but if the court be of a different opinion, on both, or either of those points, then they find for the defendant.

The District Court determined in favor of the plaintiff, from which the defendant appealed.

WARDEN for the appellant. The plaintiff most certainly ought to have charged in his declaration and established by testimony, that he had given notice to the warrantor, or to those liable under the covenant, of the pendency of the suit brought to recover the negro conveyed by that deed, in order that proper attention and assistance might have been afforded by those, so deeply interested in the defence of that suit. Otherwise, the judgment might have been recovered by covin, or negligence in the party; in which case the warrantor surely ought not to be bound. But it is not clear that this action could be maintained against executors. Negroes, at the time when that deed was made, were by the law of this state *real* property, and this being a covenant real, it descended upon *the heir*, who alone could be liable to this action. The heirs are specially named, and if this had been a deed for land, there could be no question, but that the executor in such a case could not have been sued upon the covenant.

MARSHALL for the appellee. The doctrine of warranty, has nothing to do with this case. This is a covenant to warrant the title of a slave, and in all conveyances of such property, whether by deed, or by will, they are considered as personal, and not real estate. The executor tho' not named, is bound to compensate in damages for a breach of covenant by his testator, and as no particular form of words is necessary to make a covehant, the agreement to warrant in this cafe muft be confidered as a covenant, which certainly binds the executor.

The notice which, it is fuppofed, ought to have been given to the warrantor, is not required by the deed; and it is only neceffary for the plaintiff to lay the breach in the words of the deed, which he has done. If the judgment had been obtained by fraud, the defendant might, and ought to have pleaded it, that it might have been put in iffue; and then the parties might have gone into the title.

The PRESIDENT. The objection, that a fuit will not lie againft the executor upon this warranty, becaufe the teftator bound only himfelf and his *heirs*, is novel and unfounded. Without inquiring, whether the executor is bound by fuch a covenant in a conveyance of real eftate, wherein he is not named, (which the court forbear, it being hinted at the bar, that there is another cafe in court where that is to be a queftion) it is admitted and clear, that in perfonal contracts, if the teftator be bound, the executor is alfo bound, tho' not named. This is fuch a perfonal contract; for in the fale of flaves, and in all transfers of them by deed, or will, they have ever paffed as chattles, and were only confidered as real eftate in the cafe of defcents.

The objection, as to the want of notice of the pendency of the action of detinue, ftands curioufly upon the ftatement in the verdict. It would feem, that the plaintiff was ready to prove fuch notice to the executor, if it were neceffary. The objection comes from the defendant, that fuch was improper, becaufe the notice was not charged in the declaration.

The court however are of opinion, that it was not neceffary to charge fuch notice in the declaration, nor to prove it. Every judgment of a court is prefumed to be fair, 'till the contrary appears, and if there were any collufion between Morgan and Cooke in that action, it fhould have been pleaded, and proven on the part of the defendant.

Judgment affirmed.

BURNLEY *againft* LAMBERT.

THIS was an action of detinue for flaves, brought in the Diftrict Court of Frederickfburg. On the plea of *non detinet*, a verdict was found for the plaintiff, and an appeal prayed to this court, upon exceptions taken to the inftruction given

to the jury by the District Court. The bill states. " That
" the defendant's counsel moved the court to instruct the jury,
" that the possession of the slaves in question not being proved to
" have been in the defendant at the date, or service of the writ,
" the law was for the defendant: That it was proved by the
" defendant, he was out of possession of the slaves before the
" date or service of the writ; and at all times since; and that
" the only evidence of a demand, was the writ. But the court
" instructed the jury that it was not necessary to maintain the
" issue on the part of the plaintiff, to prove possession in the de-
" fendant at the date, or service of the writ, but that proof of
" possession at a day anterior thereto, namely, on the day men-
" tioned in the declaration was sufficient.

" That it was proved, that the defendant purchased the slaves
" in question, belonging to the estate of John Jones, at a coroner's
" sale, under an execution against the executors of the said John
" Jones, altho' the defendant was warned by the plaintiff of
" his title to the property. That the plaintiff (who intermar-
" ried with one of the legatees of the said John Jones) had re-
" ceived from the executors (upon a division of the said estate)
" the negroes in question, the same having been devised to his
" wife, by the will of the said Jones. That the personal estate
" of the testator (independent of the negroes in question) was
" fully sufficient to have satisfied the execution, but that the
" same had been distributed by the executors amongst the dif-
" ferent legatees. That the defendant moved the court to
" instruct the jury, that the sale was a compleat transfer of the
" property to the defendant. But the court instructed the jury,
" that such sale was not a transfer of the property to the defen-
" dant, to which opinions the defendant excepted."

WARDEN for the appellant. Detinue will not lie, where the defendant has parted with the possession of the property, before the commencement of the suit. There can be no stronger evidence of this, than the judgment in such action, which is to recover the *property itself*, and damages for the detention, which could not be, if the defendant had not the property to deliver. He cited Southcotes case 4 *Rep.* 83—*Bull.* 49—51; the latter, to prove that the detainer is the gist of the action.

But 2dly, The title of a vendee under a sheriff's sale, cannot be questioned in any instance; for if it could, the inconvenience to the public would be infinite, since no person would purchase from a sheriff, and thus executions, which are the life of the law, would be rendered entirely ineffectual . 3 *Wills.* 309, 1 *Barr.* 20—8 *Co.* 96—*Cro. El.* 278—*Cro. Jac.* 246—5 *Co.* 90 *b.*

Duval on the same side, insisted, that in an action of detinue, it was incumbent upon the plaintiff to prove a demand, and that the record in this case, shewed that none had been made.

Washington for the appellee. I will consider the last point made in the bill of exceptions first; and that is, whether the assent of the executor to a specific legacy, does not so compleatly vest the property in the legatee, and divest the executor of any legal right thereto, that it is not liable to be seised in execution to satisfy a judgment against the executor? This point has not been argued by the counsel on the other side, from a conviction I presume, that it is too well settled to be now controverted. The creditor does not lose his remedy by this conduct in the executor; for he may either pursue the executor at law upon a devastavit, or follow the assets in equity against the legatees; and in this latter case, it would be essentially necessary to make them all parties, in order that they may all equally contribute to bear the burthen. But if the summary mode pursued by Burnley were permitted, suits in equity against legatees would never be heard of.

It is contended that a sale by a sheriff of A's property, taken under an execution against B, so compleatly divests the right out of A, that he cannot recover it in an action against the vendee. The case of Cooper and others *vs* Chitty and Backiston, 1 *Burr* 20, cited by the appellant's counsel, strikes me to be an authority as expressly against the doctrine, as could possibly have been brought forward. It would be monstrous if the law were otherwise. That case, as well as the others which have been cited, lay it down, that if the sheriff seize and sell, *by authority*, (as under a judgment which is afterwards reversed) the rightful owner is bound: but surely in the case just mentioned, or in the present, the sheriff does not sell *by authority*; because the writ, which is his warrant, directs him to levy the debt *of the property of the testator in the hands of the executors.*

As to the first point, there is more difficulty in it. But it will be sufficient for me to contend, that the defendant does not state upon the record a case sufficiently strong to bar the plaintiff, and of course the judgment ought not to be reversed. For tho' there may be a case, where detinue will not lie against a person out of possession, yet there are many cases, where it may lie. Thus, it *will not* lie where the defendant *is lawfully dispossessed* before action brought. But it will lie as Southcote's case proves, against a bailee, who is robbed before action brought, and in other

other instances there mentioned. So if the defendant make a fraudulent conveyance, or with a view to a secret trust, or indeed if he be dispossessed in any manner, *unless by a legal recovery*, I am inclined to think that this action will lie. Since therefore the case stated in the exceptions for the opinion of the judge, is not such an one, as will *in all instances* render this action improper (and such a case I contend ought to have been made out, not a doubtful, or uncertain one,) I submit it, whether the direction was not proper and legal. The verdict in detinue being in the alternative, is evidence of the law being so.

MARSHALL in reply. The pleadings are in general the best evidence of the law. Let us examine them. The declaration states a *present possession and detention*: the plea denies it in the *present tense also*, upon which issue the verdict is taken. Consequently, if the defendant be not in possession, or does not detain at that time, viz. at the time when the suit is brought, it is evident that this form of action is not sustainable. I admit that trespass or trover might lie. The direction of the judge is not such as is supposed by Mr. Washington. The exceptions do not state an uncertain case for the defendant, but the judge has, even upon Mr. Washington's own ground, given an opinion clearly wrong. For he lays it down generally in his instruction to the jury, " that it is not necessary for the plaintiff to prove possession in the defendant when the suit is brought, *but that proof of an anterior possession is sufficient.*" He does not qualify the opinion by speaking of a fraudulent dispossession, or of such an one as, it is contended, will not preclude this form of action, but he lays down the principle generally, which is unquestionably erroneous, since it would even apply to a case of dispossession produced by a *legal recovery*, in which case, it is admitted, this action would not lie. It is true, the verdict is in the alternative; but this does not arise from the possibility that the defendant may have parted with the property, and therefore cannot deliver it specifically. There are other sufficient reasons for that; for the property might perish, or be disposed of after action brought; and in such a case, it would be hard if the plaintiff could not get the alternative.

THE PRESIDENT. The question is, whether the judge misdirected the jury upon both, or either of the points submitted to his opinion. If he did, then the verdict must be set aside, and a new trial awarded. A majority of the court are of opinion, that it was not a misdirection. Mr. Marshall's argument,

drawn

drawn from a critical examination of the declaration, plea, and verdict, would prove too much, and that gentleman knows the consequence. For it goes to shew, that the defendant must not only be in possession at the time of the writ issued, but that it must continue in him to the time of the plea, and indeed to the time of the verdict, all of them being in the present tense. The plea is the general issue, and leaves the whole merits of the case to be brought forward upon the trial.

We come next to inquire what is necessary for the plaintiff to prove in this action? The books agree that he must prove a title in himself, and possession in the defendant; but *as to the time* at which the possession should appear to have been in him, whether at the date of the writ, or whether an anterior possession would be sufficient, the cases are totally silent.— This court agrees with the District Judge in declaring that the latter is sufficient, for otherwise the plaintiff might by contrivance be kept in a perpetual round of suits without effect. Thus A. finds B. in possession of his slaves which are refused to be delivered; he sets off to the clerk's office perhaps at a considerable distance for a writ. B. knowing of this, takes a witness to prove the delivery of possession to C. before the writ can issue; upon the trial, and after a tedious prosecution of the suit, this fact is made to appear, and A is defeated. He then sues C. who plays the same game, and so on, as often as persons can be found to take part in the fraud. This can never be right, and proof of possession prior to the suit ought to charge the defendant, unless he be *legally evicted*, which it is incumbent upon him to shew.

As to the next question which arises from an objection to the plaintiff's title, it requires very little consideration. It is true, that a testator should be just before he is bountiful; but if he can be both, who is to restrain him? And who is the proper judge of this ability, but his legal representatives, who by delivering up a specific legacy, acknowledge that ability in their testator.—After the assent of the executor, the legal property is completely vested in the legatee, and cannot at law be divested by the creditors. The creditors have a double remedy 1st, against the executors at law, in which case the executors have their remedy in equity against the legatees, to compel them to refund; or 2dly, the creditors may in equity pursue the estate in the hands of the legatees; and in either case, all the legatees must be made parties, that the charge may not fall upon one, but may be equally borne by the whole. But if this direct mode against a particular legatee were permitted, it would

would put it in the power of the creditor, to mark out the person who should in the first instance sustain the whole weight.

But a doctrine still more extraordinary was contended for at the bar: That the owner of the slaves in question lost his right thereto, by the seisure and sale of the coroner. Some of the cases, which were cited in support of this position, directly contradict it, and the others, such as Mathew Manning's case, only state, that where a judgment is reversed, the execution and sale under it, shall not be avoided, having been *lawfully made, under authority*; but that the party aggrieved shall be restored, not to the property, but to the money arising from the sale. But if an exucution issue against the goods of A. and the sheriff seize and sell the property of B, will it be said that this is done by *lawful authority*, as in the other case? Surely not.

Judgment affirmed.

COOKE *against* BEALE'S Executors.

THE case was as follows: In April 1785 Beale recovered a judgment against Willis, for whom Cooke was special bail. Upon the return of a *ca. fa.* "not found," a *fci. fa.* issued against Cooke on the 18th of May following, who pleaded in bar, that on the 2d of November 1784, he rendered the body of the said Willis to the jail of the county of Frederick (where the writ was served) according to the act of Assembly in that case made and provided, and took a receipt, for the body of the said Willis, from the sheriff, in the following words: viz, received &c. *and this &c.*—To this plea the plaintiff demurred specially, stating for a cause thereof 1st, that the defendant doth not set forth in his plea, that he returned the receipt *forthwith* to the clerk of the court where the suit was depending: 2dly, because the defendant in his plea neither tenders an issue to the country, nor offers to verify his plea by the record. The County Court gave judgment for the plaintiff upon the demurrer. The defendant then moved to amend his plea on payment of costs by inserting these words: " That he *forthwith lodged the receipt* with the clerk of the
" court, agreeably to the act of Assembly in that case made
" and provided, and this he is ready to verify" which motion was over-ruled by the court. He then moved to have leave to put in a new plea which was likewise over-ruled. In the record

cord is a certificate of the clerk of Frederick court, that the receipt mentioned in the plea was filed in his office on the 6th of May 1785.

Upon an appeal to the District Court, the judgment of the County Court was affirmed, from which the defendant appealed to this court.

MARSHALL for the appellant. The judgment againſt Willis was entered up in April 1785, and the *fci. fa.* iſſued in May of the ſame year. The ſurrender of the principal was in November 1784, and the receipt appears, from the record, to have been lodged with the clerk on the 6th of May 1785. The 1ſt queſtion is, whether the appellant, was diſcharged, tho' the receipt was not lodged immediately with the clerk? And this will depend upon the conſtruction of the act of Aſſembly, 5th *Geo.* III, C. 6. Upon the literal conſtruction of the act, it is evident, that if the ſheriff refuſe to give the receipt, or if the receipt be not returned to the clerk, ſtill the bail is diſcharged. The latter part of the 4th ſection, which ſays, " that the re-" ceipt ſhall be by the bail forthwith delivered to the clerk of " the court where the ſuit is depending," is merely *directory* to the bail, who is diſcharged by the act of ſurrendering the principal, tho' he ſhould fail to return the receipt. But if there be a doubt upon this clauſe, it is completely explained and removed by the 5th ſection which ſpeaks of the right of a ſpecial bail to diſcharge himſelf by *ſurrendering the principal*, without qualifying that right by any condition whatever. The words are, " that where the ſpecial bail, in any action or ſuit, where " judgment hath been, or ſhall be given, are or ſhall be entitled " to diſcharge themſelves by ſurrendering the principal, it ſhall " and may be lawful for ſuch bail to make ſuch ſurrender, " either before the court where judgment was obtained, or to " the ſheriff of the county, where the original writ in ſuch ſuit " was returned, *and thereupon the bail ſhall be diſcharged:*" So that the bail is diſcharged *upon the ſurrender.*

If I am right in giving to the act its literal expoſition, I feel great confidence in ſaying that it is founded upon good reaſon. For it would be ſtrange, if the ſheriff, by refuſing to give the receipt, ſhould prevent the bail from relieving himſelf. If then the returning of the receipt *forthwith* is not a prerequiſite to the bail's diſcharge, it was unneceſſary to aver it in the declaration. But if I am wrong in my conſtruction of the law, I then contend that the court ſhould have permitted the defendant to amend his plea. He cited 1 *Burr.* 317—322. I admit that the court poſſeſſes a diſcretionary power in allowing amendments, but this is a legal discretion, and if it be improperly exercised, a superior court will correct their judgment in this respect. It is to advance the justice of the case, that the defendant should be permitted to try the cause upon its merits.

As to the 2d cause of demurrer, I answer that the *et cætera* is tantamount to the tendering of an issue, for it will be construed to supply what the defendant ought to have added—the case of Sayer *vs* Pocock.—*Cow. Rep.* 407 is a strong authority as to this point.

WICKHAM for the appellee. There is an essential difference in reason, between a surrender *before* and *after* judgment. In the first case, the sheriff is not authorised to keep the body a moment after the judgment is rendered, unless the plaintiff pray him in custody. But in the latter case, the sheriff is to keep the body in the same manner, as he must have done, if he had been prayed in custody in the former case. This distinction will enable us the more clearly to give the law in question its true exposition. It is to be observed that the fourth section relates to a surrender *before* judgment; the 5th and 6th sections to a surrender *after*. If it be before judgment, and made *in court*, nothing farther is necessary for the bail to do; for this reason, because the plaintiff, who is supposed to be always in court, having notice of the surrender, may, if he chuse, pray the principal in custody, and therefore he cannot suffer but from his own neglect. But if the surrender be *before* judgment, and to the sheriff *out of court*, as the plaintiff is not presumed to have notice of what is done in *pais*, it is reasonable, and by this law, it is made an essential part of the duty of the bail, as a *condition* of his discharge, that he *forthwith return the receipt to the clerk*, that the plaintiff may have notice of it, so as to pray the principal in custody. So much for the 4th section. But if the surrender be made *after* judgment, then the 5th section does not require a receipt to be returned; for this reason; because, by the 6th clause, the sheriff is directed in such case to keep the principal in his custody, in the same manner, and subject to the like rules, as are provided for debtors committed in execution during the space of 20 days, &c. This, which I conceive to be the fair and liberal construction of the law, seems to be strongly supported by the reason and justice of the case. For were i otherwise, the sheriff and the debtor might, by collusion, defea the plaintiff of his security by a surrender made out of court, an by keeping out of sight that sort of notice, which is required b the law to be given him, and which, if given, would enable hir

to

to claim the body of the principal. Nay, this might happen without collusion. For the sheriff, not being bound to give the creditor notice of the surrender, the creditor would most frequently be ignorant of the fact till judgment was given, and the body discharged. It has been argued as a hardship on the other side, that the sheriff might refuse to give a receipt. To this I answer, 1st that the sheriff, in such case, would be liable to the bail, and 2dly the bail might avail himself of such refusal by pleading it, and would be excused; for it is a rule, that if an officer be *bound* and is *required* to do a particular act, his refusal shall not place the party for whose benefit it was to be done, in a worse situation, than if he had done it.

As to the 2d objection, the case relied upon from Cowper is not apposite to the present in any respect. The omission, there, was of words merely formal, and the question was made after a *trial* and verdict. The defect in this case is in a substantial part of the plea, and is specially demurred to. So that the statute of Jeofails, which might cure a great deal after verdict, cannot help even formal defects, if stated as cause of demurrer. But it is contended, that the *et cætera* must necessarily mean " and this he is ready to verify." But may it not as well mean a conclusion to the country?

As to the amendment: The motion was made after demurrer, argument and judgment thereon. I admit, that the discretion of the court in allowing amendments, is a legal one, and subject to the correction of a Superior Court, if improperly exercised. Yet I ask, will this court permit an amendment against the justice of the case. If the defendant in this case could claim it upon Mr. Marshall's principle, namely, that the cause might be tried upon its merits, then it might be always claimed as of right; and if so, a defendant who wished for delay, would always put in a frivolous plea, so as to force the plaintiff to demur, and, after taking that chance, claim the privilege of amending. If it be quite indifferent, whether the justice of the case favored the amendment asked for, (the reverse of which I think appears in the record) this court will presume that the Inferior Court did right, unless the party seeking to impeach their judgment, had stated enough upon the record to destroy this presumption. Besides, will this court do a vain thing? For if I am right upon first point, what good purpose could it answer to allow the amendment, since by correcting the plea according to the facts appearing in the record, the defendant could not succeed.

MARSHALL

MARSHALL in reply. The 4th section of the law relates to surrenders both before and after judgment. Mr. Wickham contends for his expofition of the law, becaufe otherwife the creditor might be entirely defeated of his fecurity by not having it in his power to pray the principal in cuftody. But if I can fhew, that even *his* conftruction would not in every inftance remedy the fuppofed inconvenience, then there can be no neceffity, for giving the law that conftruction. Now it is to be recollected, that when that law was made, there was a General Court in Virginia, embracing the whole ftate within its jurifdiction. Of courfe, the furrender might be made in fome remote county, far diftant from the court, a day or two before the judgment was rendered. So that it would be impoffible to return the receipt in time for the plaintiff to pray the principal in cuftody. In this cafe, therefore, the fuppofed inconvenience, which it is contended was meant to be prevented, would happen even upon Mr. Wickham's conftruction, and, fince it is not prefumable that the legiflature would attempt a vain thing, fo it is not to be fuppofed they meant it. The 6th fection fuppofes that the creditor will in 20 days obtain notice of what is doing in *pais*, and therefore compels him to do fo, under pain of lofing his fecurity. And why may he not alfo get notice by the fame means, where the furrender is made before judgment? As to collufion, this may as well happen between the fheriff and the creditor, to prevent the furrender, as between the fheriff and the principal, or bail, in order to deprive the creditor of his fecurity. So that we muft at laft refort to the literal meaning of the words, which feems plainly with the appellant.

This plea, if wrong, was moft probably entered by the clerk, and is his miftake; for there appears in the record a letter from the defendant's attorney to the clerk, defiring him to plead a furrender generally, and the formal defect arifes from his want of fkill, and therefore ought to be amended.

The PRESIDENT delivered the opinon of the court.

The queftion upon the firft point, depends upon the law, which has been fo fully commented upon at the bar; and is this, whether the fpecial bail be difcharged by the furrender to the fheriff, without his alfo *returning forthwith to the clerk* the receipt obtained from the fheriff. The 4th fection of the law upon which this queftion refts, points out two kinds of furrender; the firft in court, upon which the bail is difcharged, whether

whether the directory part of the clause (which says that the defendant shall be committed to the custody of the sheriff) be complied with, or not. The other alternative is, " that such spe" cial bail may discharge themselves, by surrendering the prin" cipal to the sheriff of the county, where the original writ was " served." The discharge of the bail therefore is compleat by the surrender, and the following parts of the clause are *directory* only, and do not impose a *condition,* the non-compliance with which can prevent the discharge. This appears the stronger since it begins with a direction *to the sheriff* what he is to do with the prisoner, and then goes on to direct what the bail shall do with the receipt. And this construction is farther enforced by a view of the 5th and 6th sections, respecting surrender after judgment. The 5th makes no distinction between a surrender in court, and a surrender to the sheriff out of court, a to the discharge of the bail. The 6th, without taking notice of the discharge of the bail, proceeds to direct what shall be done in the case of a surrender in the country. The sheriff is to keep the prisoner in custody for 20 days; and the bail is to give immediate notice to the creditor. So that in both cases of a surrender in the country, either before, or after judgment, the discharge of the bail is compleat, and the plaintiff has a new remedy, if the directory part be not complied with, either against the sheriff, if he fail in his duty, or against the bail, if he neglect to do what the law requires of him. The difference in these remedies is important; since in an action founded upon the directory part, the sheriff or bail would be let in to shew a reasonable excuse for not complying with the law, or to shew that no damage thereby arose to the creditor. But they might be precluded from these advantages upon the *sci. fa.* if the bail were considered as not being discharged.

The court have given their opinion upon this point for the satisfaction of the parties, and as it may prevent further litigation. As to the second cause of demurrer, we think that the plea is insufficient for want of a proper conclusion An *et cæter.* may be allowed to supply what must necessarily be inferred from what is expressed. But in this plea the words inserted will equally admit of a conclusion to the court or jury, and therefor the court cannot supply the words omitted by any necessary implication; besides this defect is specially demurred to.

But the court are clearly of opinion that the defendant ought to have been permitted to amend his plea upon payment of costs and upon this point, the judgment is to be reversed, and the cause remanded

remanded to the District Court, with directions to admit such amendment. The parties will consider whether it worth be their while to profecute the fuit farther, after the decifion of the court upon the firft point in which the Judges are unanimous.

TURNER *againft* STIP.

THIS was an ejectment, brought by Stip in the County Court of Berkeley. The plaintiff at the trial, offered in evidence in fupport of his title, a deed from Benjamin Halfey and wife and Margaret Halfey to him, dated in June 1785; to which deed is annexed a certificate of two perfons who ftile themfelves juftices of the peace for the diftrict of Camden in South Carolina, ftating that the three fubfcribing witneffes to the deed had declared upon oath, made before them as juftices aforefaid, that they faw the grantors fign feal and deliver the faid deed to the faid Stip as and for their act and deed.

That upon this certificate, the deed was admitted to record in Berkeley County Court, where the land was fituated on the 19th of July in the year 1785. The plaintiff alfo produced upon the trial, a witnefs to prove the execution of the deed. The defendant objected to the evidence of the deed, becaufe it had not been theretofore legally proved and legally recorded? and to the teftimony of the witnefs, becaufe it was improper to prove the execution of the deed by *one witnefs only* at that time. The court rejected the evidence of the deed, as well as of the witnefs, to which the plaintiff excepted. A verdict and judgment was given for the defendant from which the plaintiff appealed; the Diftrict Court reverfed the judgment of the County Court from which the defendant appealed to this court.

LEE for the appellant. 1ft, I fhall infift that the deed in queftion, not having been *legally* recorded, is void. The act of 1748, 1ft *Geo.* II. c. 1, declares, that no eftate of inheritance fhall pafs, alter, or change, from one to another, unlefs by deed indented fealed and recorded, within a particular time, upon the acknowlegment of the parties to the deed, or upon proof of the execution thereof, by three witneffes. By the 4th fection of the law, the deed is declared to be void as to all creditors and fubfequent purchafers, unlefs the fame be recorded according to the directions of the act. As to perfons refiding out of this

ftate,

state, that law provides no mode for proving deeds made by them, different from that which is prescribed as to residents But the act of October 1776. *Ch.* 16 permits the deeds of non-residents to be recorded, upon a certificate of two magistrates that the deed was acknowleged before them, or proved by the oaths of three witnesses, with the testimonial of the governor of the state where the deed is so proved, that the persons giving the certificate, are magistrates.—Now in this case, their being no such certificate by the governor, the deed ought not to have been admitted to record, and therefore is now to be considered as an unrecorded deed, and therefore void. For the act of 1748 declares all deeds, not recorded according to the directions of the act, void, except as between the parties, or those claiming under them, and the parties to this suit do not appear to be within the exception.

But 2dly, If the deed be not void, still the evidence produced at the trial to prove its execution was insufficient. The certificate of the probate in Carolina is not to be regarded as evidence at all, as the persons receiving the probate do not appear judicially to this court to have been magistrates agreeably to the act of Assembly, and consequently the deed has obtained no additional authenticity by having been admitted to record in Berkley Court. To obviate this difficulty, the plaintiff produced *one* witness to prove the execution of the deed; to which there are two objections.—1st, that one witness was not sufficient the law of 1748 above referred to requiring three,—2d, if one witness were sufficient, yet he ought to have been a *subscribing witness*, and from this record it does not appear that he was, or if a subscribing witness could be dispensed with, it could only be by proving that they were all dead, or could not be procured, and this should have been stated upon the record.

WASHINGTON for the the appellee. The first point in this cause depends upon the true exposition of the act of 1748, which has been read. The first and 4th clauses must be considered together. The first declares, that " no estate of inheritance, or any estate for life shall pass, alter, or change from one to another, by deed, unless the same be made in writing, indented, sealed and recorded in manner following," &c. And then it goes on to limit the time of recording the deeds of residents and of non-residents, and concludes with declaring, that " no such deed shall be admitted to record unless the same be acknowleged in court by the grantor, to be by his act and deed, or else that proof thereof be made in open court by the oath of three witnesses." The

The 4th clause declares, that "all such deeds shall be void as to all creditors and subsequent purchasers, unless they be acknowleged, or proved and recorded *according to the directions of this act*, but the same, as between the parties; shall nevertheless be valid and binding."

Now the true construction of the clauses taken together seems to be this. To pass a freehold interest, the deed must be *recorded*, and to give it validity against creditors and subsequent purchasers, the deed must also be recorded *according to the directions of the act*; that is to say, upon the acknowlegment of the grantor or proof by three witnesses, within eight months, in the cases of residents, and within two years, in those of non-residents. But in all cases except where creditors and subsequent purchasers are concerned, tho' the deed must be recorded, it need not be recorded *according to the directions of the act*. The reason of the distinction is apparent. As between the parties or those claiming under them, it is of little consequence, how, or when the deed be recorded; but it is highly important as to creditors and purchasers, who may be affected *by relation* to the date of a deed, tho' it be not recorded until after they had given credit or made the purchase.

In this case then, the deed in question was recorded, tho' not according to the directions of the act, and is valid under the 4th clause, the defendant below not appearing to be a subsequent purchaser or creditor.

"If this be the true exposition of the law, the deed must be considered as valid; and if so, the second objection cannot be maintained. Three witnesses are necessary to prove a deed, to entitle it *to be recorded*, and therefore I admit that the deed itself, or a copy *certified to have been proved by less than* that number of witnesses, could not be received as evidence in any court; because if this sort of evidence, which the statute authorises, be resorted to, the statute must be pursued. But surely *the proof of the deed at the trial* by one witness, is as good as if it had been proved by twenty. For at common law, one witness would be sufficient to prove the execution of a deed, and the act of 1748, which requires three, relates entirely to the proof necessary to *admit the deed to record*, and not to the evidence necessary in legal trials. As to the objection to the witness himself, it admits of two answers. 1st, That if he were not a subscribing witness, yet it is no good objection to his testimony, the law not requiring the witnesses to a deed to subscribe their names, as the statute respecting wills does; and this will

account

account for the necessity of producing the subscribing witnesses to prove a will. 2dly, It is not sufficient to suggest *possible exceptions* to the witnesses, but they should appear to be stated upon the record. It is the business of the appellant to state, and also to prove the ground of his objections, and it is not incumbent upon us, to shew that the witness was properly admitted; since this will be presumed until the contrary appears.

THE PRESIDENT. Upon the first point, the court are of opinion, that the deed offered in evidence was neither legally proved, nor legally recorded under the act of 1776, C. 16, because it wanted the governor's testimonial, that the persons who certified the probate were magistrates. The court below would therefore have done right in rejecting this as a *recorded deed*, in support of the plaintiff's title. But since by the act of Assembly passed in the year 1748, such deeds, though not recorded, are valid between the parties, though void as to creditors and subsequent purchasers, (neither of which the defendant is stated to have been,) the actual execution of the deed was a fact which the plaintiff was at liberty to prove, as in other cases by evidence satisfactory to the jury, whether it were by one or more witnesses. As to the objection, that the witness does not appear to have been a subscribing witness, and that none other could properly be admitted, the answer is, that the act does not require the three witnesses to a deed to subscribe their names, as in the case of wills. But another sufficient answer to the objection is, that it does not appear that he was not a subscribing witness, nor that the subscribing witnesses might not have been proved to be dead. The court improperly stopped the examination, and therefore the District Court rightly reversed the judgment.

Judgment of the District Court affirmed.

BOSWELL & JOHNSON,

against

JONES.

THIS was an action of trespass, brought by Jones against the appellants, in the District Court, *who pleaded jointly, ly*, not guilty. A verdict was rendered against Johnson for £15, and the defendant Boswell was found *not guilty*. Upon the motion of *Johnson alone*, a new trial was awarded, and a verdict was afterwards found, for £60, against both defendants. A motion in arrest of judgment being made by Boswell, and over-ruled, both defendants applied for, and obtained a supersedeas to the judgment of the court, rendered upon the last verdict.

The plaintiff's in error, being both dead, it was submitted to the court, whether a new supersedeas, or writ of error, should be awarded, or whether a *sci fa.* to revive the former ought to issue; and, in the latter case, whether it should be revived in the names of the executors of both plaintiffs, or of the survivor only. The court being of opinion, that a *sci. fa.* should issue in the names of the executors of both the plaintiffs, the counsel for the defendant consented to revive without a *sci. fa.* actually issuing, and now the cause came on to be argued upon the objections to the judgment of the District Court.

WASHINGTON for the plaintiffs, insisted, that where one defendant is acquitted by the verdict, the court cannot grant a new trial upon the motion of the other defendant, and referred to the following authorities, 2 *Str.* 813—12 *Mod.* 275—2 *Blac. Rep.* 1030—3 *Salk.* 362.

WICKHAM for the defendant. The rule contended for, considered as a general one, cannot upon principle be found. It is possible, that the jury may erroneously find a verdict against the wrong defendant. They may in writing their verdict, by mistake, convict the defendant, whom they intended to acquit.

In such a case it would neither be just nor reasonable, that the court should not have a power of setting aside the verdict. And if there be *a possible case*, where it would be proper to set aside such a verdict, it is enough for my purpose, because this court presuming, as they ought, every thing in favor of the judgment of the Inferior Court, will not reverse that judgment, unless the record exhibit such a case, as to authorise them in saying, that the Inferior Court decided erroneously. If the Inferior Court might, or might not award a new trial, according to the circumstances of the case, the party attempting to impeach their decision in granting it, ought to have spread upon the record those circumstances, which might satisfy this court, that this was a case in which the verdict ought not to have been set aside.

As to the authorities which have been cited, I would premise my observations upon them with this remark: That upon no subject have the adjudications varied so materially, as upon that of new trials. It is considered as a part of practice, and to be controuled by the court in such a manner, as best to answer the ends of substantial justice; and if the English courts have considerably changed the doctrine of new trials, so as to render it more perfect, and more consistent with the real principles of justice, why may not this court exercise the same power over the subject, if they are satisfied, that the rule now contended for be unreasonable? The cases from Strange and Blackstone, are merely obiter opinions. 3 *Salk.* is not authority—in the case from 12 *Mod.* the court say, they cannot grant a new trial *except against all*, which rather proves, that they might grant it against all, if the justice of the case required it.

WASHINGTON in reply. It is to be observed, that the motion for a new trial in this case was not made by the plaintiff, but by one of the defendants. If this were permitted, the acquitted defendant being out of court, it would be in the power of the other, without any authority, to put the successful defendant into jeopardy again, by stating a hardship as to himself, when the other defendant might not be present, nor have it in his power to shew that the verdict as to him was proper. I hold it to be sound law, that the court cannot set aside a verdict but upon motion, and this motion was not made by the plaintiff, nor by Boswell, but by Johnson, who had no more authority to make it for Boswell, than a stranger would have had; and surely it would have been as much an error to set aside the verdict upon the motion of a stranger, having no authority, as if the court had done it without any motion at all. So that the authorities cited, which stand uncontradicted, are fortified by the strongest reason. But if they were not, I trust that law is bottomed upon more solid and certain grounds, than the mere opinion of the judge, upon what is right, or wrong; reasonable, or otherwise; and known only when that opinion is pronounced.

If the rule, which is so firmly settled by the authorities before referred to, can be varied or destroyed, according to the opinions of different Judges who may decide upon it; with equal propriety may they unsettle every other rule of law, which does not meet their approbation. A position big with mischief! The principle decided in the case from *Salk.* tho' not directly determined in *Str.* and *Black.* is fully recognized, and admitted to be well founded. The

The PRESIDENT. The cases cited prove, that in trespass against two defendants, if one be found guilty, and the other be acquitted, a new trial cannot be granted on the motion of the convicted defendant, and a majority of the court are of opinion, that the rule is not without reason, since the plaintiff being satisfied, it ought not to be in the power of the convicted defendant to bring his co-defendant into jeopardy again, by obtaining a new trial. Upon authority, the rule is fixed. One judge doubted as to the reason of it, since the ground of new trials being to attain real justice, if the court perceive that injustice has been done in the acquital of one defendant, upon principle it would seem right to grant a new trial, from whomsoever the motion might come. And as to authority, the same judge is of opinion, that tho' uniform decisions which establish the rules of *property* ought to be adhered to, yet he does not view them as sacred in points of *practice*, which may be varied as experience shall evince their convenience or inconvenience. But the court are unanimously of opinion, that tho' in general, the subordinate courts need not state the facts on which they ground their opinion for a new trial, yet in this case, where they granted it, against an established rule of practice, they ought to have disclosed the circumstances which induced them to depart from that rule. We are also of opinion, that the District Court erred in awarding a new trial without payment of costs.

The judgment, and all proceedings from the granting of the new trial inclusive, is to be reversed with costs. Judgment to be entered against Johnson for the damages assessed by the first verdict and costs, and to be entered for Boswell for his costs.

ARMISTEAD,

against

MARKS & SAUNDERS.

THE defendants in error brought an action of debt upon a bond with a collateral condition against Herbert Claiborne, William Claiborne and others, in the District Court. The appellant, a deputy sheriff, arrested the defendant Herbert Claiborne and made return thereof, signing his name as *deputy sheriff*, but failed to return a bond for appearance. A common order

order was confirmed, and a writ of enquiry executed against the plaintiff in error, and the two Claibornes, and judgment was entered thereupon. The other defendants having pleaded *non est factum*, a verdict was found in their favor. The deputy sheriff alone applied for, and obtained a supersedeas.

The questions made were, 1st, whether the common order ought to have been confirmed against the *deputy sheriff*, and 2dly, whether Armistead alone could obtain a *supersedeas*.

WICKHAM for the plaintiff in error as to the first point, relied upon the case of White and Johnson (see ante p. 159) as being expressly in point.

THE PRESIDENT. On the first point the court have no difficulty in reversing the judgment, being of opinion that the law does not warrant a judgment against an *under sheriff* for failing to take appearance bail upon mesne process.

As to the other point (which was suggested by the court) we are of opinion, that as the deputy sheriff was in no respect concerned in the merits of the cause, he alone, might obtain a supersedeas.

The enquiry of damages must therefore, be set aside, as to all the defendants, as must the proceedings subsequent to the declaration, and the cause is to be proceeded in anew upon the sheriff's return, made upon the writs issued against the two Claibornes.

DANDRIDGE *against* HARRIS.

THIS was an appeal from a decree of the High Court of Chancery, dismissing the plaintiff's bill, which was, to be let into a specific performance of a contract between the parties, by which the defendant Harris was to repair a mill for the plaintiff, and to receive payment for it, either in money, or in property at a valuation to be made by two honest men, to be chosen, *one* by each party; and also to be relieved against a judgment at law obtained by the defendant, in consequence of his fraud in not inserting the alternative of payment in the written agreement, nor endorsing it on the back, as he agreed to do at the time of executing that agreement. The answer is a flat denial of every material allegation in the bill. The Chancellor conceiving the answer not to be disproved, dismissed the bill with costs.

The

The PRESIDENT delivered the opinion of the court.

However it might appear to the Chancellor, this court have no doubt, but that the anſwer is fully diſproved by more than two witneſſes, who make it evident, that by the original agreement, before the work was begun, Mr. Dandridge was to have the alternative, and that at the time of ſigning the agreement, he refuſed his ſignature until Harris promiſed to make the endorſement allowing him that privilege. The alternative is an important part of the contract, ſince it might make a conſiderable difference to the appellant, whether he ſhould give up his property at a fair valuation, or be obliged to part from it under an execution at three fourths of its value, or, if he replevied, to have it finally ſold, perhaps at a much greater loſs.

It appears, that in the action at common law, brought by Harris upon the agreement, the jury found a ſpecial verdict, ſtating the above facts, as ſet forth in the bill. The appellant excepted to the opinion of the court, permitting the appellee to give parol evidence of thoſe facts, and the judgment which was in favor of the appellee was reverſed in the diſtrict court on account of the parol evidence having been admitted. Whatever might be the deciſion of a court of law upon the propriety of admitting ſuch proof to contradict a written agreement, there can be no doubt in equity, but that the appellee refuſing to make that endorſement, upon his promiſe to do which the agreement was ſigned, and availing himſelf of that agreement as an abſolute one, which in fact was only conditionally executed, he was guilty of a fraud, againſt which the court will relieve, by conſidering the endorſement *as made*, and incorporated into the agreement. The caſe of Walker *vs* Walker in 2d *Atk.* 98, which was read at the bar, does not apply; there was no written agreement in that caſe, and the queſtion was, whether the parol evidence of it could be admitted, under the ſtatute of frauds and perjuries. But there is a caſe there put by the Chancellor, which does apply. He ſuppoſes a perſon, advancing money, and taking an abſolute conveyance, to which, by agreement, there was to be a defeaſance, ſhould refuſe to execute the defeaſance. He puts the queſtion; will not this court relieve againſt ſuch a fraud? A ſtrong manner of declaring his opinion that it would, and it is very much like the caſe before the court. Conſidering the endorſements then as made, the court proceed to conſider what would have been the effect of it, at law. The defendant at law might have pleaded the ſpecial matter, that he was always ready to deliver property;

that

that the plaintiff had neglected to name a person to value it, tho' he had promised to do so, and had refused to receive the property; which plea would have been supported by the proofs in the cause. But for want of this endorsement, the defendant was probably advised that he could not plead this matter, it being *dehors* the agreement, and therefore he pleaded conditions performed. It is true, the court permitted him at the trial, to give evidence of those facts; and if the jury had upon that evidence decided against him, it would be reasonable that he should be bound thereby, since he would have had a fair trial upon the merits, as much so, as if the endorsement had been made. But that is not the case. The jury found matter sufficient to excuse him, and the County Court gave judgment in his favor, which the District Court reversed, the ground of which reversal appears in the exceptions to have been, the admission of the parol evidence: so that the appellee has committed a fraud in withholding the endorsement, and has then availed himself of it, by a legal objection, founded upon the want of that endorsement. If this be not a proper case for relief in equity, we are at a loss to know how one can exist.

It was then objected, that suppose the endorsement made, it was the duty of Mr. Dandridge to tender property immediately, or else he lost the benefit of the alternative. This case from its nature is very different from the common one of a debtor, owing money, who is obliged to seek his creditor in order to pay the debt. Here property was to be delivered, which could not so easily be conveyed from place to place as money, and it would be natural to suppose, that it was to be valued and received at the defendant's house; and the rather so, as being more convenient to him, in the selection of property which might have taken place. That an actual tender of property was made prior to that made at Johnson's in November 1787, after the suit was brought, does not appear. And if it had stood upon that alone, the court would have considered Mr. Dandridge as having failed in performing his part of the agreement and consequently that he had forfeited the alternative. But the fact appears to be, that on the 16th of December 1786 (the very day the work was finished,) they settled their accounts, and fixed the balance at £48. Mr. Harris called upon Mr. Dandridge to sign the account, which he refused to do, unless Harris would state that property was to be paid; a circumstance which he constantly adhered to as a part of the original agreement. He then desired Harris to come to to him with the writing, and to join in naming persons to value the

property,

property, and to receive it, which Harris promised to do the next day, or the day after, but did not. Mr. Dandridge then wrote a letter to the father and son, requesting them to come and have the property valued. They did not object, that the property should be carried to them, but declared they would not receive property, and in February 1787, only 41 days from the time the work was finished, and before Mr. Dandridge could probably have time to make a legal tender, Harris brought his suit.

Upon this view of the case, although Mr. Harris appears to have done his work honestly, and is entitled to his stipulated reward, yet since he has been delayed by what this court calls a fraud in him, and by his endeavours to use that fraud to the disadvantage of the other party, he stands in a very different point of view in equity, from Mr. Dandridge, whose conduct through the whole transaction appears to have been fair and upright, at all times willing to perform his real agreement.

The court have to lament the expences which have been incurred on the occasion, but are of opinion, that they ought to fall upon Mr. Harris, the party in fault, who is adjudged to pay the whole costs at law and in equity.

It is objected that the court cannot decree a specific execution in this case, because the valuers were to be named by the parties, and as they did not name them, it is contended that the court cannot do it for them. In the cases of Pleasants Shore & company, and Anderson *vs.* Ross, (ante p. 156,) and Smallwood *vs* Hansborough, (ante p. 290,) the parties named the valuers in their agreement, and it was decided that others could not be substituted in their stead, upon their refusing in the one case to act, and in the other not having perfected what they were to do. In this case, no persons were named, so as to shew a personal confidence, but a description of their character only; they were to be honest men; and it is supposed, that if the parties should refuse to name, the Chancellor might easily find two men in the state to answer the description. The court are also of opinion, that the Chancellor might appoint a day, before which the parties should name the valuers, or in case either refused, might direct it to be done by two honest men appointed by himself, to value the property, (negroes excepted) and upon delivering, or tendering the property so valued, to the amount of £ 48, the injunction to be perpetual.

But as there is difficulty in such a decree, which may be delayed, if not defeated, by the valuers, whether chosen, or appointed, refusing to act; and since the appellant coming into equity, must do equity, and it appearing, that he has parted with the property in the mare, which in his bill he suggests to have been accepted by Harris, at £45, and to have been kept for him by the appellant; and the appellant having declared before bringing this suit, that he intended to pay the money, and only contended for the costs, the court is of opinion that the judgment at law ought to remain in force as to the £48, and be injoined as to the costs.

We therefore reverse the Chancellor's decree with costs. The injunction to be made perpetual as to all the costs at law: and to be dissolved as to the balance of the £48, if any shall remain after deducting therefrom the appellant's costs at law and in equity, as well as in this court: and if upon the adjustment of the account of the said £48 against the said costs, any balance shall remain due to the appellant, in that case the injunction to be perpetual as to the £48, and the appellee decreed to pay such balance.

Duval and Marshall for the plaintiff in error.
Cambell for the defendant.

N. B. The arguments at the bar are omitted being noticed much at large by the court.

NICOLAS *against* FLETCHER.

THIS was an appeal from a judgment of the District Court of Petersburg, affirming a judgment of the County Court of Amelia, rendered in favor of the appellee, upon a forthcoming bond, endorsed by the sheriff, "that the property therein "mentioned, had not been delivered on the day appointed for "the sale, to be dealt with according to law."

An exception was taken by the defendant below, that the plaintiff did not prove a non-performance of the condition, by good and sufficient testimony.

Marshall for the appellee. It was not necessary for the plaintiff below to prove a forfeiture, or breach of the condition, but it was incumbent on the defendant to prove performance. On the contrary, the sheriff has returned upon the bond, that the property was not delivered.

The court affirmed the judgment.
SCOTT

STOTT & DONALDSON,
againſt
ALEXANDER & Co.

THIS was an action of debt, brought by the appellants against the appellees, as endorſers of a proteſted bill of exchange drawn by Robert Morris of Philadelphia, in the ſtate of Penſylvania, which was endorſed to the appellants in this ſtate. The declaration is upon the act of Aſſembly. On the plea of *nil debet*, the jury found a ſpecial verdict, "that the bill, with three endorſments thereon, two of which are eraſed, was duly proteſted in London on the 10th of September 1787, and that notice thereof was given to the defendants, on, or about the latter end of June 1788. If this be a reaſonable notice, then they find for the plaintiffs, otherwiſe for the defendants."

The judgment of the County Court, which was in favor of the appellants, was reverſed in the Diſtrict Court, becauſe the verdict was defective, in not finding facts ſufficient to enable the court to judge of the reaſonableneſs of the notice of the proteſt therein mentioned. The verdict was ſet aſide, and the cauſe by conſent of parties retained for a new trial; from which judgment, Stott and Donaldſon appealed.

RONOLD for the appellants. There is but a ſingle queſtion in this cauſe, which ariſes upon the conſtruction of the act of Aſſembly, of the 22d *Geo.* II, C. 27.* The firſt branch of the law would give the holder of a proteſted bill of exchange a right to recover intereſt at the rate of 10 per cent per annum for any unlimited time, if it were not reſtrained, by the ſecond branch of the ſection, to 18 months; and from this it is evident, that

---

* The words of the law are, "That where any bill of exchange is or ſhall be drawn for the payment of any ſum of money, in which the value is, or ſhall be expreſſed to be received, and ſuch bill is or ſhall be proteſted for non-acceptance or non-payment, the ſame ſhall carry intereſt from the date thereof, after the rate of 10 per centum per annum until the money, therein drawn for, ſhall be fully ſatisfied and paid; but leſt any perſon, having ſuch bill, ſhould, for the ſake o the ſaid intereſt, delay negociating the ſame, or if after it ſhall be proteſted, ſhall not demand payment of the drawer or endorſer thereof *It is hereby declared* that no perſon whatſoever ſhall pay more than 18 months intereſt from the date of any bill to the time it *ſhall be preſent ed proteſted to the drawer or endorſer or endorſers thereof.*

that the object of the legiflature was merely to regulate the intereft to be paid upon protefted bills, and to fix it at 10 per cent per annum for 18 months, tho' notice be not given of the proteft within that time; and yet it is contended, that for the want of notice, during a period far fhort of that time, the holder is to forfeit both principal and intereft. This conftruction feems to be repugnant to the plain meaning of the law, and involves a contradiction not fairly to be attributed to the legiflature. If the expofition, for which I contend, be right, then it follows, that the jury having exprefsly found, that notice was given within 18 months, the appellants ought to recover under this act. But if notice fhort of that time be neceflary, ftill the judgment of the Diftrict Court is erroneous, becaufe, what is reafonable notice, is a point of law, and is properly to be decided by the court. This is clearly fettled by the modern decifions in England, and from hence, I draw an additional argument to prove, that the act of Affembly was intended to change the law of merchants upon the fubject of giving notice. For would it not be abfurd, that in this country, it fhould be necefsary to give notice of a proteft by the following poft, as the practice is in England. Such a regulation might be proper and convenient in that country, the communication from place to place being uniform and conftant. But our fituation, at the time when this law pafsed, and long after, and when too our commerce was confined to England, was very different. Our intercourfe with that country, was not only confined in a great meafure to particular times of the year, but various accidents might happen, to prevent fo prompt a notice from being given, and the adoption of fuch a rule here, would have proved fo mifchievous, that it would have put an entire ftop to the negociation of bills of exchange, which the legiflature (in the preamble to the law) declare it was their intention to " render equal to cafh in the payment of debts."

WICKHAM for the appellees. We all agree as to the rule eftablifhed by the law of merchants, but it is contended that the act of Affembly was made to change that rule, and the necefsity of that change is ftated and relied upon to prove fuch an intention. On the contrary I fhould conceive, that the inconvenience which would refult from fuch an innovation in the cuftom of merchants would be fufficient to induce the court to explode fuch a conftruction, unlefs the law be too clear and exprefs to be got over. The drawer of a bill tacitly agrees to pay the bill, if difhonoured, provided he has timely notice of the proteft and the holder tacitly agrees to give him that notice.

The custom of merchants having established this principle, such an implied contract is always understood between the parties, as certainly, as if it were expressed. The inconvenience resulting from a contrary principle, is as strongly exemplified in this case, as in any which could be thought of. The drawer lives in a state, where this rule prevails. If the plaintiffs in this cause can, without regarding that rule, recover against the indorser,—the indorser, in an action against the drawer, will be told, that for want of due notice the drawer is discharged. Who would be mad enough to draw bills, if at any distance of time, they might be returned upon him protested, after all accounts were settled between him and the drawee, and after he had otherwise applied those funds, which as a prudent man, he would retain so long as the fate of his bill was in suspence.

There is a great difference between *giving notice of the protest of a bill*, and *demanding payment*. The first is necessary by the *custom of merchants*, to entitle the holder to the *principal sum*; the latter, to entitle him to the *extraordinary interest* given by the act of Assembly, which last (beyond 18 months,) he loses unless by *presenting the bill protested to the drawer or indorser* within that time, he affords them an opportunity of taking it up. It may so happen, that the drawer may have *notice* of a protested bill circulating in some part of the world, and yet, if it be not shewn to him, so that he may pay it off, he will be excused the 10 per cent for a longer period than 18 months. The object of the law was to fix the interest which the holder should receive, and to lay him under a certain condition to entitle him to that interest. That condition is, that within a certain time he *present the bill protested to the drawer*. But as to *notice of protest* required by the custom of merchants, it is left unaffected by the act of Assembly, which never could have intended to alter a general law prevailing in a country with which we principally traded.

The rule in England, as to the time of giving notice, is not as Mr. Ronold has stated it; it is regulated by the circumstances of each particular case, and is a subject which the jury must decide. I admit, that a different rule prevails in cases of *inland* bills of exchange.

CAMPBELL on the same side. I admit that in England, what is due notice in the case of *inland* bills of exchange is a point of law, because the certainty of communication from one place to another, and the uniform decisions of juries upon that point, have so fully ascertained and settled it, that the judges are as competent

petent as the jury to decide upon it. The adoption of a similar practice in this country would be unjust and preposterous even in the cases of inland bills.

As to the main question, there is one reason to be given for the custom of merchants, which has not been much relied upon, and which has always had considerable weight with me, independently of those stated in the books. It is this: a merchant who draws a bill, must, if he mean to be punctual, and to preserve his credit, keep unemployed such a portion of his capital, as will enable him to take it up, should it return protested. If he may be kept in suspence as to its fate, for any length of time, (even 18 months) he must either retain that capital unemployed, during all that time, which would be very injurious to commerce, or he must part with it, and run the risk of being called upon unexpectedly to pay a protested bill, at a time when he may be unprepared to do so. It can hardly be believed, that the legislature could have intended to fetter commerce by the establishment of a principle unknown in any trading country, and particularly in that, with which we were solely connected. The law requires a *presentation* of the bill to the drawer or endorser, not as being necessary to authorise the holder to recover the amount of the bill, but to entitle him to 10 per cent per annum beyond 18 months. As to *notice of the protest*, the act is entirely silent, leaving that subject as it stood under the general law of merchants.

RONOLD in reply. The legislature certainly intended to alter the custom of merchants upon this subject, and to adapt it to the situation of this country, by declaring that 18 months should be considered as the time within which notice of protest should be given. Those persons whose recollection will carry them back to the period when this law was made, will remember, that protested bills passed from hand to hand as cash, and formed a circulating medium of commerce. The endorsements were never dated, and the bills sometimes remained in circulation here, for many months before they were remitted. This practice the legislature meant to regulate, having a view to the interest of all parties, and to limit the damages to a certain amount.

Mr. WICKHAM submitted another question to the court, which was; whether an action of debt upon this bill, (which was drawn out of this state) could be supported under the act of Assembly?

Mr.

Mr RONOLD anfwered, that it might lie againft the prefent appellees, who made the indorfement in this ftate, upon the principle, that every indorfer is confidered as a new drawer.

The PRESIDENT delivered the opinion of the Court.

Some general queftions have been difcuffed at the bar, upon the law refpecting protefted bills of exchange, fuch as; whether the act of Affembly has not done away the whole cuftom of merchants on the fubject of notice, and whether the holder may not, upon notice at any time however remote, recover his principal money, although he may lofe his damages. With thefe points, the court think it unneceffary to meddle, except fo far as they may concern the prefent cafe.

The act of Affembly does not feem to interfere with the negociation of bills, but taking them up as negociated, and protefted, proceeds to give the remedy for recovering their amount, leaving the point of their negociation to be decided upon the particular circumftances of each cafe. As to the diligence neceffary to be ufed by the holder in giving notice of the proteft, fince that depended upon the fituation of the parties, and of the countries between which the exchange was made, the legiflature, contemplating thofe circumftances, feem to have thought 18 months a reafonable time for the whole negociation, and for the giving of notice, by allowing full damages in cafe the notice be given within that time.

There may be particular circumftances, which would render a departure from this *general rule* reafonable and proper; and when they occur, the general rule may not be adhered to; but no fuch circumftances are ftated in the prefent cafe. The bill is dated in Philadelphia on the 15th of March 1787,—endorfed in Virginia, but at what time does not appear. It was prefented for acceptance about the 10th of June, and protefted in September in the fame year. Notice was given to the defendant in the latter end of June 1788, all within 15 months from the date of the bill, and the queftion fubmitted by the jury is, whether this be reafonable notice. No facts being ftated to take this cafe out of the general rule before mentioned, and eftablifhed by the act of Affembly, we are of opinion that the notice is reafonable.

As to the opinion of the Diftrict Court, refpecting the infufficiency of the finding, it is no objection to a verdict, that enough is not found to anfwer the purpofe of one of the parties, provided

provided what is found, be clearly stated, which is the case in the present verdict.

Judgment of the District Court reversed, And that of the County Court affirmed.

SOUTHALL,
against
M'KEAND, MAYO, &c.

THIS was an appeal from a decree of the High Court of Chancery, affirming a decree of the County Court, which dismissed the bill of the appellant Southall.

The PRESIDENT stated the case and the opinion of the court as follows. The ground of the appellant's equity is, that colonel Byrd, in the year 1767, published a scheme for disposing of his lots in the city of Richmond, and of his lands in the neighbourhood, by way of lottery, in which scheme, he described the *improved* lots as *tenements in the occupation of the several tenants*. The *unimproved* lots were to be laid off and to contain half an acre each. Under this scheme, the appellant and others became purchasers of tickets in the lottery. Some time after, and before drawing the lottery, colonel Byrd proceeded to survey and lay out the lots, and was about to reduce the improved tenements (which had been occupied by the tenants to various extents more or less,) to half an acre each, which being objected to, he desisted, and consented that they should stand agreeably to the occupation of the tenants, and most of them were laid out accordingly. But the tenement, called M'Keand's was laid, off, as for half an acre, narrowing (as the appellant suggests) that tenement from its usual occupation; to this circumstance however the appellant was a stranger, and having become the fortunate adventurer as to that tenement, he insists he was entitled to it, to the extent of its *occupation*, which included the land in dispute; but that colonel Byrd, confining him to the bounds of the lot, including only the houses on the tenement, had sold and conveyed the residue of the occupied ground to M'Keand, whom the appellant charges to have had full notice of his title thereto: that M' Keand had sold to Powell, and he to Mayo, who are also made defendants to the bill.

Mr.

M'Keand admits the scheme of the lottery, colonel Byrd's survey, and his desisting from reducing the improved tenements to half an acre, and agreeing to let them stand upon their occupation. But he denies that there was any additional ground possessed by him, or inclosed on either side of the said tenement, although he understood that colonel Byrd had given up an old kitchen, and nearly half an acre of ground on the east side of the said tenement, and annexed the same thereto, as part of the prize lot. He denies that the appellant ever forwarned him from purchasing; and does not recollect that he offered to purchase the ground in dispute from the appellant. That he erected buildings on the ground in dispute to the value of £1000, & then sold it to Powell.

The appellee, Mayo, in his answer, alledges that he holds the land under a deed from his father without notice of the appellant's title, and believes that his father had no notice at the time of his purchase from Powell.

The father in his answer had expressly denied such notice, and there being no proof to the contrary as it respects either Powell or Mayo, they must be considered as purchasers without notice.

Several depositions being taken, the Chancellor directed an issue to be made up, and tried by a jury, to ascertain the boundaries of M'Keand's tenement; also a survey to be made of the ground in dispute and returned, with the examination of witnesses, to the District Court, where the issue was to be tried, and also directed the scheme of the lottery and the plan of the city of Richmond to be given in evidence to avail so much only as the jury should think they ought; the former was objected to by the appellees, and the latter by the appellant.

On the trial of the issue, the first jury could not agree. A second, determined the bounds in favor of the appellees, and the District Court certified that the weight of evidence was in favor of the appellant. The Chancellor declared the verdict satisfactory, and affirmed the decree of the County Court, dismissing the bill with costs, from which decree, the appeal comes to this court.

It is agreed by the parties, and the court think rightly, that the verdict in the District Court ought not to stand, upon the certificate of the judges, that the weight of evidence was against it: Since it is unusual for the Chancellor to be satisfied with such a verdict; and tho' the Chancellor was to judge whether his conscience was satisfied, this court, exercising their legal discretion on the same subject, see no reason to depart from the general rule, and therefore they take up the case upon its original merits.

The queftion, how far the plot in the record is to be confidered as evidence, may become all-important to perfons interefted in the town property; and therefore it is left undecided till cafes fhall arife, and that queftion fhall be neceffary to be decided, when probably it may be brought forth with fuller proof than appears in this record. In this cafe, it feems of no confequence, fince neither Mr. Southall, nor Mr. M'Keand (the tenant at the time,) appear to have been prefent when Mr. Watkins made the original furvey, fo as to imply their confent that the occupied bounds of the tenement in queftion fhould be changed into the figure then laid down. Nor does it appear to the court, that fuch confent ought to be inferred from the expofure of the plan in the room where the lottery was drawn, even if the plaintiff had read it, which does not appear, fince he could not from thence difcover whether the lot was defcribed according to the occupied bounds or not.

The appellant had a right to confider himfelf as entitled to the occupied bounds of Mr. M'Keand's tenement, (whatever thofe were) under the fcheme, and under colonel Byrd's agreement that the tenements fhould go according to the occupation, and not be governed by the quantity, of which the unimproved lots were to confift.

The proofs upon the whole, amount to this: that during the occupation of the tenants, fome part of the ground in difpute was ufed as parcel of the tenement, for a garden, which was fomewhat extended by one of the tenants, beyond what it had been before, and the vacant ground, between that and the ftreet, was ufed as a cockpit, and fometimes by the planters, for picking their tobacco on. When M'Keand came to be the tenant, the garden was generally fuppofed to be part of the tenement, but as he did not want it, no ufe was made of it by him.

But fince that circumftance might be unknown to adventurers at a diftance, who might have received an impreffion of M'Keand's tenement from obfervations on the actual occupation of former tenants, and fince it appears that the neighbors acquainted with that circumftance, did not confider it as altering the extent of the tenement, but a number of them fwear, that if they had been fortunate, they fhould have confidered themfelves as intitled to the land in difpute, as part of the tenement, a majority of the court are of opinion, that the appellant was entitled to all the ground occupied as part of the tenement.

M'Keand purchafed with full notice, and if the tenement had remained in his hands, and the appellant had commenced his
fuit

fuit immediately, and M'Keand had, notwithſtanding, proceeded in his improvements, he would probably have loſt them with the ground itſelf. But ſince Mr. Southall tho' he made his claim known, did not commence any ſuit to enforce it, till M'Keand had placed improvements on it to the amount of £1000, (more than ten times the value of the lot,) it would be unreaſonable, that he ſhould in equity avail himſelf of the increaſed value produced by his own delay, ſince M'Keand had a right to ſuppoſe from that circumſtance, that he had deſerted his claim. All he can therefore expect in equity, is to be reſtored to the value of the ground at the time M'Keand purchaſed it, and which the court now think him entitled to.

The next queſtion is, againſt whom, this relief is to be granted? If the ground had remained in M'Keand's poſſeſſion, or were now in the poſſeſſion of a purchaſer with notice, the court would have no difficulty in determining, that it would have been charged with the payment of ſuch value. But ſince it was a latent equitable charge only, and the appellee, Mayo, holds under his father who was a purchaſer without notice of the appellant's title, the court are of opinion, that the ground in his hand is not charged or liable to make ſatisfaction for ſuch value, and that the decree is therefore right in diſmiſſing the bill as to Mr. Mayo with coſts.

But the appellant has a right to reſort for ſatisfaction to the eſtate of M'Keand, and therefore, the decree is wrong ſo far as it diſmiſſes the bill as to him, who ought to have been decreed to pay the value as before ſtated. That part of the decree muſt therefore be reverſed with coſts.

The period at which the value ſhould be fixed, ought to be the time when M'Keand parted with the property to a purchaſer without notice, and an iſſue ought to be made up by direction of the Court of Chancery, and tried to aſcertain what was the value of the ground in diſpute on the 26th of July 1779, independent of any improvement made thereon ſubſequent to the 8th of October 1769, which being aſcertained, the amount is to be paid to the appellant with intereſt from July 1779, and his coſts in the High Court of Chancery and the County Court, out of Mr. M'Keand's eſtate. But as M'Keand has died ſince the pendency of this appeal, tho' it has been revived, by conſent of parties, as to his heirs and repreſentatives in their general character without naming them, we think it proper that they ſhould reſpectively be made ſpecific parties, that they may diſcover a ſtate of M'Keand's aſſets, real and perſonal, in caſe there ſhould

not

not be sufficient of the latter to satisfy this demand. For this purpose, the cause is to be remanded to the High Court of Chancery, that the suit may be revived against the executors or administrators, as well as the heirs or devisees of the real estate, and for further proceedings therein.

WATSON & HARTSHORNE,

against

ALEXANDER.

THIS was an action of covenant brought by the appellee against the appellants in the District Court of Dumfries. The case was as follows: John Alexander, by his will devised to the appellee, his son, in fee simple, a tract of land lying in and adjoining to the town of Alexandria part whereof was laid off into lots. He further devised, that if his executors *therein after named*, should think it conducive to the interest of his said son, to lease out the whole, or any part of the said land, reserving ground rents for ever; that they, or the survivors might lay the same off into lots, and give leases therefor in fee simple, reserving an annual ground rent to his son, and his heirs: and he appointed *four persons his executors.*—In August 1779 a deed was executed purporting to be made by the *four* executors of the first part, the appellants of the second part, and the appellee of the third part, (who was then an infant) conveying the lots in question to the appellants in fee, reserving an annual rent of £78 : 10, *current money of Virginia*, payable to the appellee and his heirs, with a covenant on the part of the appellants to pay the said rent annually to the appellee and his heirs. The deed of which a *profert* was made, and upon which this action is founded, is made part of the record, and appears to be signed *by three of the executors*, and the appellants, and by no one else. The action was brought for 9 years rent in arrear and unpaid, and the declaration states the lease to be made by the *four* executors, of the first part, the appellants of the second part, *and the appellee of the third part*. The appellants after taking an imparlance, pleaded covenants performed. The jury found a verdict for the plaintiff, and assessed his damages at £626,

" subject

"subject to the opinion of the court, whether the rents in the declaration mentioned and granted by the deed therein set forth be within the operation of the act of Assembly, entitled an act directing the mode of adjusting and settling the payment of certain debts and contracts, and for other purposes."

"And if they be, by what rule the same ought to be reduced into specie value, if they ought to be reduced at all, and that the said damages may be reduced according to the same rule that shall be applicable to the said rents."

The District Court examined witnesses, and being satisfied (as the record states,) that the rents for which the action was brought, were expected to be paid in the money current at the time they should become due, gave judgment for the damages found due by the jury in specie. To the examination of the witnesses the appellant filed a bill of exceptions, and appealed to this court.

LEE for the appellants. The first question which arises in this cause is, whether the deed upon which the action is founded, be within the operation of the act of November 1781, Ch. 22;* and I contend that it is. The legislature, when they passed this law, had put a period to the existence of paper money, by calling the whole of it out of circulation. During its circulation, it had from its constant depreciation, united with the exertions

---

* The second section of the law is as follows: "And whereas the good people of this state will labor under many inconveniences for want of some rule, whereby to settle and adjust the payment of debts and contracts entered into and made between the first day of January, one thousand seven hundred and seventy-seven, and the 1st day of January, one thousand seven hundred and eighty-two, 'unless some rule shall be by law established, for liquidating and adjusting the same so as to do justice as well to the debtors as to the creditors. Be it therefore enacted, by the General Assembly, that from and after the passing of this act, all debts and contracts entered into or made in the current money of this state or of the United States, excepting at all times contracts entered into for gold and silver coin, tobacco, or any other specific property, within the period aforesaid, now remaining due and unfulfilled, or which may become due at any future day or days, for the payment of any sum or sums of money, shall be liquidated, settled and adjusted, agreeably to a scale of depreciation herein after mentioned and contained, that is to say, by reducing the amount of all such debts and contracts to the true value in specie at the days or times the same were incurred or entered into, and upon payment of said value so found in specie, or other money equivalent thereto, the debtors or contractors shall be forever discharged of and from the said debts or contracts, any law, custom, or usage to the contrary in any wise notwithstanding. *Provided always nevertheless*, that in all cases where actual payments have been made, by any person or persons, of any "sum

tions of the legislature to support its credit, and to re-assure the confidence of the public mind, given birth to a multitude of contracts, which depended for their performance upon its continuing to exist. It had also given rise to innumerable speculations, founded in a difference of opinion between those, whose confidence in the public assurances led them to expect specie in lieu of it, at par, and those, who calculated upon its progressive depreciation, and its ultimate destruction. In this situation of things, when the legislature at one stroke dispelled the delusion, it became an indispensable duty with them to establish some *general* and *fixed rule*, for the discharge of those contracts, to prevent the injustice which might otherwise have ensued, if debtors should have been compelled to pay specie, where they only calculated upon paying depreciated paper money. This rule then became necessary in all cases, where money was contracted to be paid, and the words of the law are sufficiently general to comprehend every possible contract. The cases which are within the letter of the law are, *all debts* and *contracts* entered into in *current money*, between *the 1st of January 1777, and the 1st of January 1782*. This case then is *strictly within it*, and is equally within the mischief, meant to be provided

_____

" sum or sums of the aforesaid paper currency, at any time or times,
" either to the full amount or in part, payment of any debt, contract or
" obligation whatsoever, the party paying the same, or upon whose ac-
" count such sum or sums have been actually paid, shall have full cre-
" dit for the nominal amount of such payments, and such payments
" shall not be reduced, any thing in this act, or any other act or acts,
" to the contrary in any manner notwithstanding.
 " V. *And be it enacted*, that where a suit shall be brought for the re-
" covery of a debt, and it shall appear that the value thereof hath been
" tendered and refused, or where it shall appear that the non-payment
" thereof is owing to the creditor, or where other circumstances arise
" which in the opinion of the court before whom the cause is brought to
" issue, would render a determination according to the above table un-
" just; in either case it shall and may be lawful for the court to award
" such judgment as to them shall appear just and equitable. And
" where any verdict hath been given for damages between the first day
" of January one thousand seven hundred and seventy-seven, and the
" first day of January one thousand seven hundred and eighty-two, and
" the judgment remains unsatisfied, it shall be lawful for the several
" courts within this commonwealth, in a summary way, by motion to
" them made, either before any execution issues, or at the return day
" of such execution, to fix, settle and direct at what depreciation the said
" damages shall be discharged, having regard to the original injury or
" contract on which the damages are founded, and any other proof or
" circumstances that the nature of the case will admit."

provided againſt. It cannot be otherwiſe conſidered, becauſe it is a contract always continuing, unleſs the law be rendered a dead letter. For where will the court draw the line? Would debts payable by inſtallments in one, two, fifty or a thouſand years, come within the law? Would rents reſerved upon a leaſe of an hundred years? If all of them would, this would. If ſome of them would not, I aſk which they are, and upon what principle the diſcrimination can be made? I think then there is no doubt, but that this caſe comes within the general rule eſtabliſhed by this law, and that the rents ought to be reduced according to the ſcale, unleſs the next queſtion to be conſidered be againſt me, and that is,

2dly, Whether this caſe be within the benefit of the 5th ſection of that law? That ſection was intended to reach the caſe of *debtors* only, and not that of *creditors*. The two inſtances ſpecified in the firſt part of the clauſe, are clearly intended for the benefit of the former, namely, 1ſt, where the debt has been tendered and refuſed; and 2dly, " where the non-payment is owing to the creditor." The third branch of the ſection, which provides for caſes in " which other circumſtances ariſe, which in " the opinion of the court, before whom the cauſe is brought to " iſſue, would render a determination, agreeable to the above " table, unjuſt"—was intended to comprehend caſes not within thoſe ſpecified, which could not then be foreſeen, and where from other cauſes the debtor might be injured, if the ſcale were ſtrictly to be applied. On the other hand, if the court conſider both the creditor and debtor as coming within the operation of this clauſe, the conſequence will be, that the law will furniſh no rule at all, and the legiſlature might as well have left all caſes to be decided by the court under the 5th ſection of the law; becauſe the conſtruction which will be contended for by the counſel on the other ſide, will produce the very ſame effect, and will render the rule a mere nullity. But admit that this caſe is within the operation of the 5th ſection, I inſiſt,

3dly, That it does not warrant the court in a departure from the general rules of evidence, or of judicial proceeding. One of thoſe general rules is, that parol evidence is inadmiſſible to contradict a written agreement; another is, that the jury are to decide upon facts; and the court upon the law ariſing out of thoſe facts. There is nothing in this act, which authoriſes the adoption of a different rule. The evidence, if it could properly have been admitted, ſhould have been heard and decided upon, pending the trial, or ſhould have been brought before the court by regular

regular pleading. The case of Pleasants and Bibb in this court and that of Loudon and Stotsdale in the General Court were de-decisions favorable to the appellant.

But if all these points be against me, I ask what can this court do, or how are they to decide; they should have the same means of judging upon the evidence, that the District Court had, else they cannot say whether the opinion of that court be right or wrong. It is the business of the appellee to produce the testimony relied upon to support that judgment; and if it be not offered to this court, the judgment must be reversed.

There is another objection which arises out of the pleadings, and which I conceive will be fatal to the judgment below. The deed set forth in the declaration, is substantially variant from that offered in evidence. It is stated in the declaration, to be made by the *four* executors on the first part, and by the appellee on the third, whereas it appears to be executed by only three of the executors, and not at all by the appellee. This error is not cured by a special verdict, such as this is, however it might have been considered after a general verdict.

WASHINGTON for the appellee. As to the first point, Mr. Lee's concessions respecting the motives which induced the legislature to pass the law in question, will warrant me in saying, that either the case before the court was not intended to be affected by the scale, or if it were, that it is also within the operation of the 5th clause. For surely, if the inconvenience and injustice, which were intended to be prevented, be as general as Mr. Lee admits, the legislature could never be so unjust as to provide a partial remedy, to fit the case of a particular class of men only. Whether this case be within the spirit, or within the letter of the law, I submit to the court upon the following considerations: 1st, the spirit of the law. During the existence of paper money, it was well understood by all men, that the nominal rise of property was produced by the fall in the value of the circulating currency. The confidence of one class of men in the public assurances, and the want of it in another, begot innumerable speculations founded upon this diversity in the sentiments of men; and therefore, in all *temporary* contracts, the duration of which was limited, and which *might* be complied with whilst paper money circulated, the debtor calculated upon further depreciation, and the creditor upon the appreciation of the money before the time of performance should arrive. Consequently, *paper money* was with both, the standard by which they estimated their expected gain. But when the legislature put an end to this ftandard, juftice compelled them to provide fome other, by which to adjuft fuch contracts. But in *continuing contracts* like the prefent, which from their nature were to extend far beyond the poffible exiftence of depreciated paper currency and which could never be fulfilled, the parties would naturally look beyond this period, and of courfe make fome thing more permanent in its value, than depreciated money, the ftandard by which to eftimate the property contracted for. They could never conjecture, that the legiflature would at a future period pafs a law for fcaling fuch debts, nor indeed any other, and of courfe would provide for themfelves a rule which would be juft, whatever might be the fate of paper money. This being the difference between *temporary* and *perpetual contracts*, that is, one, which *might*, the other which *could not* be fulfilled whilft paper money circulated, it follows, that fince the latter never could require legiflative interpofition, fo that interpofition never would be exerted. The cafe put by Mr. Lee, of a debt payable by inftallments, is that of a temporary contract, and tho' poffibly it might extend beyond the period, in fuch a cafe and therefore, it is poffible that the parties may have had paper money in view, yet it might terminate before. In this cafe, the fulfillment of the contract could not poffibly happen before, and therefore paper money could not have been contemplated by the parties.—Again, the act declares, that where payments are made, in fatisfaction of fuch debts or contracts, according to the reduced value, the payer fhall be *for ever difcharged of and from fuch debts or contracts*; which can never be conftrued to extend to contracts, incapable of being difcharged fo long as time fhall laft. If then this cafe be not within the fpirit, I fubmit it 2dly, whether it be within the ftrict letter of the law. The act fpeaks of "debts and contracts now remaining due and unfulfilled, or which may hereafter become due." Now this may well apply to *common debts*, payable either at one, or at different periods, for they are literally *debts*, immediately that the contracts are made, tho' to be difcharged at a future day. But a rent, is not a debt until the time of payment arrives, infomuch, that if the leafe by any means expire before the rent become due, the rent for the laft year could not at common law be demanded, becaufe it being a retribution made by the tenant out of the profits of the thing leafed, unlefs he have the full enjoyment thereof, he is not bound to make the retribution. The act therefore feems literally to apply to debts *due*, or to *become due*.

2dly,

2dly, If this case be within the law, then I contend with confidence that it is within the letter, as well as the spirit, of the 5th clause. The words are general enough to comprehend it, and surely neither reason nor common justice can warrant an idea, that the legislature would apply a partial remedy to a general mischief, and permit one class of men to suffer, who struggled equally in the general cause, and who were equally injured, with the other, by the delusion created by paper money.

It is insisted 3dly, That the mode of decision in this case was improper. The words of the law expressly give to *the court*, the power to render such a judgment as the principles of equity require, if *they be satisfied*, that the circumstances of the case would render the general rule unjust. If *the court* are to decide this question, *upon the circumstances of each case*, the *court*, must necessarily examine the witnesses, and any other testimony produced to establish the facts upon which this decision is to be given. It is perhaps immaterial, whether this be done, pending the trial, or after verdict; tho' I rather think it most proper after verdict, because until the jury have found whether any thing and what is due, it would be unnecessary, if not improper, for the court to decide the other point. But it is contended, that the admission of parol testimony in this case was improper. I cannot admit the position either upon common law principles, or upon the construction of *this* law. As to the first the rule is, that parol evidence may be admitted *to explain doubtful expressions* in a written agreement, though not to *contradict plain expressions*. Now the rent in this case is made payable if *current money*. But the question is, what sort of money was meant? For *specie* was *current*, tho' not as plentiful in 1779 as paper money. Evidence was resorted to, and it appeared to the satisfaction of the District Court, that *specie* was the sort of *current money* intended. Proof of the value of property in 1779 and at this day, was probably the evidence upon which this conclusion was formed. But however this may be upon the common rules of evidence, *the act* warrants such proof, since the court in all cases where there are circumstances to authorise a departure from the scale, are to decide upon equitable principles which they could not do, if prevented from hearing testimony to prove those circumstances.

It is then objected, that this court should possess the same means of judging, which the District Court had. I admit it and since the judgment of that court is in our favor, and every thing transacted in a court of justice is presumed to be rightly

done,

done, till the contrary appears, this court must affirm the judgment. The appellant's counsel thought it necessary to state in his bill of exceptions, the general weight of the testimony: why was it not as necessary to spread the whole evidence upon the record? For if he meant to impeach the judgment, he would have done so, or summoned the witnesses to attend this court.

As to the objection respecting the variance, it is easily answered. The deed is no part of the record, oyer of it not having been taken; so that this court cannot say there is a variance between the declaration and the proof. If the deed actually produced in evidence, was different from that declared upon, the appellant should have excepted to the deed going in evidence to the jury, and spread it upon the record, so as to enable this court judicially to notice the variance.

The court will presume, after this verdict, that sufficient, and proper evidence was produced to the jury, or else that they would not have found that the defendant had not performed his covenants, and was indebted in a particular sum for rent arrear. As to this point the verdict is general, and carries with it all the presumption in its favor, which arises out of general verdicts. The jury doubting upon a single point of law, the court are only to settle that doubt.

MARSHALL on the same side. In the exposition of a statute, we should attend to the mischief meant to be prevented; and the remedy should be made commensurate with it: it should never be extended beyond the mischief, unless the expressions made use of, are so strong, as to render such a construction absolutely necessary. The difference which has been stated between *temporary* and *perpetual* contracts is a striking one. In the former, the parties calculated the value of paper money at the day of making the contract, as well as the probable value of it, on the day of payment. If it continued to depreciate more rapidly than was expected, the debtor gained; otherwise he lost. The legislature put an end to the delusion; and rendered a performance of the contract impossible, by taking out of circulation that medium, upon which both parties calculated; and of course, it became necessary to provide a remedy to the evil, which the situation of this country had rendered inevitable. But in contracts, which, from their nature were calculated to continue long beyond the time when depreciated paper money could exist, or could furnish a standard by which to estimate the value of property, the parties would naturally look beyond that time for a standard, by which to estimate the present value of property, and

and would therefore make specie that standard. In the first case then, there existed a mischief, and the law is satisfied, by applying the remedy to that case, in the latter, no such mischief could happen, and therefore there was no necessity to provide a remedy. It is a strained, rather than a necessary construction to extend the law to such a case.

Second point. It is contended, that the benefit of the 5th clause must be confined to debtors. The words of a law must be express and clear beyond doubt, which can warrant a construction so manifestly at variance with the fundamental principles of justice. On the contrary, the words are so general, that nothing could justify an exception, but to prevent the gross partiality, which the construction on the other side tends to produce. It is said, that the two cases, which are specially provided for, point to the benefit of the *debtors* only. I do not think that the first case is intended to benefit the debtors, since the creditor who would, without this provision, have been obliged to accept of the identical money tendered and refused, is to receive in lieu thereof, an equitable payment. Tender and refusal are technical words, and will be construed to mean a *legal* tender, and not a mere *offer to pay*. But I rely upon the latter part of the 5th clause, to prove, that creditors were as much the objects of justice with the legislature as the debtors. Suppose the clause in question had been left out of the law, then I think it clear, that a judgment rendered within the period during which the scale operates, (being undeniably a debt) would also have been scaled. But the court, by this clause, are to fix at what depreciation the damages are to be paid, having regard to *the original injury or contract*, which by referring to a period antecedent to the judgment, must operate against the debtor. If then, in the latter branch of the clause, creditors were intended to be benefited, upon what principle can it be said, that they were intended to be excluded in the former part of it. Again; in the former part of the clause, (let it be, that the two specified cases are in favor of debtors only,) what can the words which follow mean? Namely, " in *either case* it shall be lawful for the court to award such judgment as to them shall appear just and equitable." I might with more propriety contend, that the general part of the section, viz: *other circumstances* &c. relate exclusively to *creditors*, if the former part related to debtors.

As to the propriety of admitting parol testimony, it is to be remarked, that in the latter branch of the 5th clause, this sort of of testimony is clearly to be heard and decided upon by the court, without bringing it before them by special pleading, and why is it to be excluded in the former part of the clause? But it is contended, that by our construction, there would be no general rule at all. In ordinary cases, men may settle their differences by referring to the scale, without the necessity of a suit, and this *extraordinary* remedy is provided only for *extraordinary* cases.

As to the objection, that all the evidence which was laid before the District Court, should appear before this, it is to be observed that the bill of exceptions renders it unnecessary; for it admits, as does also the judgment of the court, that there were circumstances proved to the court sufficient to except this case from the general rule, and the only objection relied upon, is the impropriety of the court's hearing and deciding upon such testimony; so that, if we be right in contending that the court below were authorised to hear parol evidence, there is an end of this question. But if it should be determined, that the evidence ought to have been spread upon the record by the plaintiff, the court will then send back the cause for that purpose; since in cases like this, (as in appeals from decisions respecting mills, wills and roads,) the practice as to this subject remains yet unsettled.

LEE in reply. If the act of Assembly does not apply to cases of rents which have become due since 1781, it does not apply to antecedent rents; and if this action had been brought for the rent due in 1780, could it have been contended that it should not be scaled? For it seems to be admitted, that this would have been a debt *due* when the law passed, and of course, literally within it. And if such a rent would have been subject to the scale, the rents which afterwards became due were, because the law is general, and I know no rule by which to limit its operation. It is said, that the 5th clause forms an exception, only in *extraordinary* cases. But I ask, how are these to be distinguished from *ordinary* cases, until they are all brought before the court and examined? So that the consequence would be, what I before stated; that the law forms no general rule at all, but is a mere nullity, if we apply it to creditors as well as debtors.

As to the argument, that this is no doubt till it become due, it is surely as much a debt before the time of payment, as where money is payable on a precedent condition, which, it is not contended, would not be within this law.

I differ very widely from Mr. Marshall in the construction of the last branch of the 5th section. It seems intended *exclusively*

sively for debtors; for if a judgment had been rendered for damages before 1781, execution might have iſſued for the *nominal* amount againſt the debtor, who would have been without remedy (unleſs perhaps in equity,) but for this proviſion in his favor, authoriſing the court, on motion of the debtor, to adjuſt the damages, which ought to be paid in ſpecie.

The COURT took time to conſider, and afterwards mentioned to the bar a doubt, which had occurred as to the plaintiff's title, which they deſired might be argued. It was, that only three of the executors appear to have executed the leaſe.

LEE. The teſtator deviſes the land in queſtion to the appellee, and the executors have a mere power uncoupled with an intereſt: and the law is well ſettled, that in ſuch a caſe all the executors muſt join in executing the power. The power is given to the executors not in their *capacity* as executors, in which caſe perhaps thoſe only who qualified might execute it, but it is a confidential truſt repoſed in them by name, becauſe he ſpeaks of them as his executors *thereafter named*, and it is therefore the ſame, as if he had given the power to thoſe four perſons, (naming them,) without ſtiling them his executors.

The deed therefore is void, and of courſe it cannot be the foundation of an action. The court cannot preſume the other executor to be dead. He cited *Pow.* on *Dev.* 292—294. *Co. Littl.* 446.

WASHINGTON. I ſhall contend 1ſt, That it was not neceſſary for all the executors to join in the deed. 2dly, If it were neceſſary, that it appears judicially to the court, that all of them did join. 3dly, If both points be againſt me, yet that we are entitled to recover.

1ſt, There is an obvious diſtinction, between a power given to executors in their *official capacities*, and one which is confined to them as *individuals*. In the former, if all the executors do not qualify, ſtill thoſe who do, anſwer the deſcription, and being executors, may as ſuch, execute the power. But if the power be given to A, B and C, who are alſo named executors, A and B cannot act, becauſe the confidence was not placed in them unleſs united with the other executor. Now the deviſe in this caſe is of the former ſort, that is, to his executors, whoſe names are afterwards mentioned, and the court will not preſume that more qualified than have executed the deed, unleſs the contrary appear.

But 2dly, the court muſt take notice, that all the four joined in the deed. The declaration ſtates it expreſsly. The defendants *without demanding oyer*, ſo as to enable the court to take advantage

vantage of the variance, if it exifted, plead, that they have performed the covenants contained in *the deed declared upon.* On the trial, no variance is difcovered, or excepted to, and the jury find, that the defendants have not performed the covenants, but that the plaintiff has fuftained damages by the breach of them, fubmitting to the court a fingle point of law, which is not *that* now under debate. As to every material fact in the caufe, this is a general verdict, and every thing neceffary to induce fuch a finding, without the proving of which it ought not to have been found, will be prefumed. This court therefore muft take it, that fuch a deed as is declared upon was produced in evidence to the jury, and tho' a different one appears in the record, yet it cannot be noticed as being that deed, fince it is neither made a part of the record by oyer, nor by a bill of exceptions.

3dly, This deed which appears in the record, and which for the fake of argument may be confidered as that declared upon, is executed by the *appellants*, who grant a rent—charge to the appellee. The declaration ftates, that the appellants *entered by virtue thereof*, *and were and ftill are feifed and poffeffed.* The jury have found in favor of the plaintiff. This fact then muft be confidered as eftablifhed, that the appellants have *enjoyed the land* ever fince the conveyance to them. They are therefore eftopped by *their deed*, to fay, that the grantors had no right to convey, but, are bound to make the ftipulated retribution during the period that they have enjoyed the poffeffion, whatever latent right the appellee may have to recover the poffeffion on account of a defect in the conveyance. When the appellee does this, then and not before his right to rent will ceafe.

The PRESIDENT. The firft point which merits our attention, is the objection to the plaintiff's title, to which two fufficient anfwers are given, 1ft, The non-execution of the deed by the fourth executor, does not appear judicially to the court. The declaration ftates, that all the executors made the deed. The plea (if it do not admit the fact,) does not deny it, and the verdict which as to this point is to be confidered as a general one, confirms it; nor can we confider this fact as being contradicted by the deed which appears in the record. 2dly, The declaration charges enjoyment of the property by the appellants, during the term for which the rent is claimed, which is fufficient to maintain the action, without deciding how far the doctrine of eftopples applies to the cafe.

We come next to the merits. The 1ft queftion is, if this contract for rent be fubject to be fcaled at all, under the 2d

fection

section of the act of 1781: and if it be, then, 2dly, whether it be within the 5th section of that law, so as to warrant the court in adjusting it upon equitable principles. 3dly, Whether the mode of adjustment be a proper and legal one.

1st, It may be premised, that the law in question, tho' rendered necessary by the peculiar situation of this country, at that time, was certainly retrospective in its operation, and the subject was of an extremely delicate nature.

The objection is, that the act meant only to respect *temporary contracts*, which might probably be fulfilled during the existence of paper money, and which the parties could not contemplate to continue forever: that of course, the legislature did not mean to scale rents payable annually, and for an interminable course of time, when even the remembrance of paper money might be retained. There is certainly considerable weight in the argument. On the other side it is contended with much strength, that the legislature in fixing the scale *at the time of the contract*, and not *at the time or times of future payments*, seem to have supposed, that the price was fixed by the idea, which the parties *then entertained* of the relative value of paper to specie. To govern our enquiries upon this subject by a loose comparison of the rent, with the thing for which it is to be paid, would prove quite unsatisfactory—£78 for three quarters of an acre of naked ground, may appear as high in specie, as that sum in paper money, reduced by the scale to £3 : 10, is unreasonably low. Our safest and only guide is to pursue the words of the law, which plainly include this case, being a contract for payment of *current money* at *future days*. The act is general, and not limited as to portions of time, nor can the court draw a line between a contract for payment at the end of two days or of twenty years or more. The act *excepts* the cases of contracts for gold or silver coin, tobacco, or other specific property, and if it be true, that an exception proves the rule, we must decide that all other contracts are within the law. The objection that one payment would discharge the whole contract, was well answered by the appellant's counsel, when he observed, that the discharge, was meant to be co-extensive with the payment only, and not to effect demands becoming due at future days, by the same contracts.

2dly, Although the second clause has established a general rule for adjusting contracts, where no particular circumstances intervene, yet the 5th section has allowed the equitable interposition of courts, in cases of particular hardship as,

1st, Where it shall appear that the value of the debt hath been tendered and refused.

2dly, Where it shall appear that the non-payment is owing to the creditor. Or 3dly, where other circumstances occur which, in the opinion of the court before whom the cause is brought to issue, would render a determination according to the scale unjust. In either case, the law authorises the court to award such judgment, as to *them* shall appear just and equitable.

It is objected 1st, that the application for this equitable interposition of the court, can come from the debtors only; that the clause under consideration was intended exclusively for their benefit, and not for that of the creditors, and that this was so decided in the General Court. I do not know the cases alluded to, but am persuaded they must have arisen from one of the two branches of the clause, which are clearly intended for the benefit of debtors only; for it would seem strange for any court to determine under the 3d branch of the clause, if circumstances appear which would render the application of the general rule unjust to the creditor, that the court were not at liberty to give a just and equitable judgment for him, as well as for the debtor, in a similar situation. Such partiality cannot fairly be imputed to the legislature, and it would require strong words to induce such a construction. In this law there is not the slightest ground for it.

Another objection contended for is, that this clause, if construed to apply to creditors, as well as to debtors, would render the second section a mere nullity, and would entirely destroy the effect of the general rule, by leaving the whole subject at large, and to depend upon the various opinions of the different courts. If this would be the case, are the court at liberty to reject a positive law, because its effects may be inconvenient? But how does this differ from the common case of exceptions from a general law? The latter is to prevail in all general contracts, unattended by any particular circumstances, and is to be departed from only when such circumstances occur. Again; does it not fall within the general system of jurisprudence, which although it fixes rules of decision governing courts of law, allows a departure from them in equity, upon circumstances of fraud or accident; yet different chancellors entertain different opinions as to the application of those circumstances, and courts of law differ daily in the construction of statutes, deeds and wills. So likewise, juries frequently, in the same cause, and on the same evidence, not to say on the same point, in different courts, give contrary verdicts. Yet this does not furnish a sufficient reason for restraining the different courts and juries from proceeding to try all cases before them.

Upon the whole, we must decide, that the District Court had a power, under this clause, to enquire into the circumstances of this contract, and from a view of them, to determine whether an adherence to the scale in this case would be unjust, either as to the plaintiff, or as to the defendant, and to substitute such other rule, as to them might seem more just and equitable.

But 3dly, How are those circumstances to be brought before the court, and to be decided upon? This is a question of some difficulty.

The 1st method is by a special verdict, stating the facts and circumstances, and leaving it to the court to decide upon them, whether the scale should be applied, and if so, whether by the legal rule, or by any other? This seems to be the most proper method as complying strictly with the words of the law, and according with the ordinary modes of trial. Indeed in this case, which is not an action of debt for rent certain, but of covenant for damages to be ascertained by the jury, the jury might upon evidence of the intention of the parties, encrease, or diminish the damages, and these they might find in specie, and so determine the question by a general verdict.

Another method would be, for the court to hear the evidence of those circumstances, on the trial, and to instruct the jury as to the point of scaling, subject to the controul of the court as in other cases, in setting aside the verdict, if their opinion be disregarded; or perhaps, if the evidence be heard at the trial, and a general verdict given, the words of the law might justify the court in entering a judgment for a sum different from that found by the jury, assigning as a reason for this departure, that circumstances required a deviation from the legal scale, and the adoption of another for the purposes of justice. But in either case, it would be the business of the party who is dissatisfied with the opinion of the court, to state the evidence in a bill of exceptions, that so the question might properly be brought before a Superior Court. Whether this mode, or that by way of special verdict, be adopted, the influential circumstances may be proved by parol evidence, and the parties, as to those, are not confined by the written contract. If it were otherwise, the clause would be vain and nugatory; since I cannot conceive, what circumstances could appear in the contract itself, to induce a departure from the scale, unless the payment is stipulated to be made in specie, or in some specific property, which would at once take the case out of the law altogether.

The scale, it is to be observed, was formed subsequent to the destruction of paper money, and on conjecture only; and that drawn from the ideas of mercantile men, not of the bulk of society. The contracts of men should be governed by the comparative value of paper to specie, as they understood it when those contracts were entered into; and if that be more, or less than the rate at which the scale afterwards settled it, the latter ought not to be a rule for them. Circumstances therefore tending to illucidate their ideas upon this subject, collected from their expressions in the treaty, the general opinion of the parties, and of others in the neighborhood at the time, and such like, seem to be what the law contemplates, and can only be collected from parol testimony. It is loose indeed; but it rests with the judges as in other cases of evidence, to say whether it produces conviction on their minds or not.

The objection therefore is not to the court's having (in this case) admitted parol proof of the circumstances, but the doubt arises as to the *time* and *manner* of that admission. For neither of the modes, before stated as proper, have been pursued; but one wholly new, and in my mind irreconcileable with every idea of propriety. A jury are sworn, who find a verdict for the plaintiff, subject to the opinion of the court, whether the money ought to be scaled, and in what manner, under the act of Assembly, without stating a single fact, or circumstance, to enable the court to decide upon the question. If the court were right in proceeding to judgment on this verdict, they were bound to decide as the case appeared upon the contract itself. And if they judged it to be within the second section, which they appear to have done, they should have scaled it, since no circumstances were disclosed to shew the legal scale to be unjust. Instead of this, after deciding that the contract was within the law, they examine witnesses, and upon their testimony, enter judgment for the whole sum in specie, saying " that it appeared the rent was expected to be paid in specie."

This, it is contended, is warranted by the law, which gives to the court, the power of hearing, and of judging of the circumstances, exclusive of the jury, and that at the time of entering their judgment.

But

But 1st, I doubt whether the act does any more than give the court jurisdiction over the enquiry, and whether the trial is not to proceed as in ordinary cases, in which the jury, if they please, may decide. For 1st, the words are, "the court before whom the cause is *brought to issue*", which are proper words to give jurisdiction. 2dly, A jury must be, and was sworn to try the issue, and surely, that was the time to bring forward the evidence as to this collateral point, for which both parties ought to be prepared. 3dly, The constitution declares, "that the trial by jury is preferable to all others, and ought to be held sacred." To go no farther, it may be affirmed, that this mode of trial is never to be taken away by implication, or without positive words in an act of Assembly. Laws for this purpose sometimes give the court an express power to proceed, without the solemnity of a jury; most usually to proceed upon motion in a summary way, by which, the same thing is understood. Of this, there is an instance in this clause, where a power is given to the courts to regulate judgments entered up during the existence of paper money. The different expressions in that, and the part under consideration, operate strongly against the exclusion of the jury from a part in this decision, and against the taking of it out of the ordinary mode of trial.

But 2dly, Suppose the court have the exclusive power of decision, surely it must come before them in a regular manner, and at a proper time; that is to say, by way of direction to the jury in case a general verdict be found, or by a judgment given upon a special verdict: or the point might be reserved on a proper state of facts, entered upon the record: none of which have been observed in this case.

I said, that if the court could give judgment on this verdict, it should have been for the money legally reduced, since the contract was within the law, and no circumstances are disclosed to take the case out of the general rule. And strictly speaking, such judgment might perhaps be proper, since enough is found to enable the court to decide upon the face of the contract; and it would seem to be no good reason for awarding a *venire facias de novo*, that such circumstances are not stated, since it may from thence be presumed that none such were proved to the jury.

However, since the record discovers, that there are circumstances which induced the district judges, to depart from the scale, though now determined to have been improperly brought forth; the party ought not to be precluded from the benefit of those circumstances

cumstances if disclosed in a regular way, and the justice of the case will be best attained, by awarding a *venire facias de novo*.

Judgment reversed, and a new trial directed.

WROE,

against

WASHINGTON, BUTLER & NEVISON.

THIS was a special action on the case, brought by the appellant against the appellees in the County Court of Westmoreland. The declaration stated an agreement between the appellant and the appellees; that the former *should rent and furnish a house in Leeds Town*, and entertain one of the appellees, two of their store keepers, and a servant, with meat and drink for one year, for which, the appellees agreed to pay him, for the three first, £ 15 each, and for the last £ 8; and that, in consideration of the appellant's having undertaken to *rent and furnish a house*, and to entertain the said four persons as aforesaid, the appellees promised to pay &c. and avers performance on his part &c. The breach assigned is in the non-payment of the stipulated sums. Plea, *non assumpsit*. The appellees at the trial, moved for a nonsuit, because the evidence did not correspond with the declaration, which being over-ruled, they filed a bill of exceptions, stating, "that the plaintiff *did not prove* that any contract had been made between the plaintiff and defendants respecting the *renting of a house* in Leeds Town as mentioned in the declaration, on the contrary it appeared by a witness, that the *plaintiff had applied to the defendants* upon this subject, informing them, that he *had rented a house* in Leeds Town for the purpose of taking boarders, and requested the defendants to board their assistants with him : that there was no proof of any application having been made by the defendants to the plaintiff touching the board of the said assistants in the town of Leeds, before the offer was made as aforesaid by the plaintiff to the defendants, nor did it appear in evidence, that any other contract had been made between the parties except such as is above stated. Whereupon the defendants did object, that no such contract as that laid in the declaration had been proved, and moved

moved for a nonsuit." The court refused to nonsuit the plaintiff, because it appeared that the price at which the assistants were to be boarded by the plaintiff was £83 per annum. The jury, found a verdict for the appellant, and upon an appeal to the District Court, the judgment was reversed, and a nonsuit awarded, from which the plaintiff below appealed to this court.

MARSHALL for the appellant. The 1st question is, if the variance between the declaration and the evidence be material. 2dly, If material, whether the Inferior Court erred in the judgment which they gave.

1st, The variance is certainly not a substantial one, since, whether the agreement was to *board*, or to *rent and furnish a house* and board, the appellant in either case, was entitled to the stipulated sum, and no more is claimed. The renting and furnishing of a house were circumstances entirely unconnected with the services to be performed by the appellant, and for which alone, he was to be paid.

2dly, The motion made was for a nonsuit. It has been so repeatedly decided in this place, that a plaintiff cannot be compelled to suffer a nonsuit, that the judgment below will surely not be reversed, because that was refused which this court has declared ought not to have been directed. If the court had given an improper direction, or opinion to the jury, it would be subject to the correction of this court? But that was not done. The Inferior Court decided properly upon the point submitted to them, and their judgment was therefore improperly reversed.

WASHINGTON for the appellee. If the contract laid, be proved to be made upon a *different consideration*, from that stated in the declaration, or on that and some other, the variance is fatal. *Bull. Ni. Pri.* 147. In *Gilb. Law of Evid.* 183, it is laid down " that in all special actions on the case, the *allegata* and the *probata* must correspond; for since in verbal contracts where the identity is not clearly ascertained in the declaration, and where it cannot be otherwise known till the trial, if a latitude were allowed that contracts might be considered as the same, which did not *substantially* differ, no man by the allegation could prepare for his defence."

These rules of law are in strict conformity with the real and substantial purposes of a declaration; which are, 1st, to apprize the defendant of the nature of the charge, and 2dly, to enable him by a reference *to the record itself*, to plead the judgment in
bar

bar to a second action, for the same cause. To discover whether the variance in this case be material or not, let me suppose that there had been at one time such a contract as is stated, and at another, such a contract as is proved, and this is at least a possible case. Suppose a judgment obtained upon the contract as stated, and another action brought some years after upon the contract as proved; could the former judgment be pleaded in bar? surely not. Again; suppose the defendants had had a witness material for them as to the first contract, and another as to the second: when the plaintiff found the defendants prepared to meet him upon the contract as laid, he had only to shift his ground *at the trial*, and prove the second contract, upon which he discovered the defendants were unprepared. By strictly requiring a close correspondence between the allegation and the proof, the plaintiff can never be injured, because knowing his own case, it must be his own fault if he mistate it. But infinite mischief will ensue from breaking in upon the rule, since we are then at sea, at the mercy of nice and capricious distinctions, without any certain guide to direct us.

The variance is said not to be material, because in either case, the appellant was entitled to £83, and for this he has brought his action. But if the plaintiff state what he might with propriety have omitted, yet having stated it, he must prove it, for otherwise the cases are not the same. The case of Bristow against Wright and Pugh. *Dougl.* 665, is a complete answer to this argument, and the doctrine is fully and ably stated by lord Mansfield. That was an action by a landlord against a sheriff under the statute, for levying an execution on his tenant, without paying him a year's rent, which in the declaration was stated to be payable *annually*. On evidence it turned out, to be payable *quarterly*, and the variance was considered as fatal. Now this variance was quite unimportant to the sheriff, since the action was brought for the year's rent, and more could not have been recovered, whether it were payable in one way, or in the other. It was agreed, that the mode of payment was unnecessarily set forth, but being stated, it should have been proved.

Should it be argued, that in the case at bar, the declaration is broader than the proof, and therefore the variance favourable to the appellees, I answer, so it was in the case reported in 1. *Ld. Ray.* 735 where the promise laid, was to deliver good merchantable wheat, and that proved, was to deliver good second sort of wheat which was decided to be a fatal variance.

Another variance equally material is, that the agreement laid, is to pay £25 for 3 persons each, and £8 for a servant, and that proved, is to pay *a gross sum of* £83.

I consider the second point as being more difficult and more important.—The decisions of this court are relied upon, and it is contended, that however the case might have been, if the motion had been more regular, yet in the shape in which it was made, the judgment must be affirmed. But if the court perceive from this record, that the appellant ought not to recover upon the principal point, it is strange to say, that he shall have the benefit of the judgment, because the appellees happened to make a *collateral motion* which was irregular.

Suppose for a moment, that this motion had not been made; how would the case have stood, if the appellees instead of proceeding as they did, had demurred to the evidence? If the variance be material they must have prevailed. I then submit it whether in substance this be not a demurrer to evidence, whatever it may be in form? An attention to the distinction between a bill of exceptions, and a demurrer to evidence will be important. The first is founded upon an objection to the *admission of improper testimony*; The judgment of the court is, that the evidence is, or is not, proper, and if it be improper a new trial is awarded. The latter admits the competency of the evidence, as well as the verity of it, but objects, that it is *insufficient to maintain the issue*; and in this case, the whole evidence must be stated, in order that the court may decide whether it be sufficient or not. The judgment is *final*, either for the plaintiff or defendant, and the verdict, which is a conditional one, stands or falls with that judgment. Now apply this definition to the present case. All the evidence which was given is spread upon the record, and it is further stated, that certain other facts were not proved. But the fact not proved was the very thing essentially necessary to have been established in support of the issue. This court then have it in their power to give a final judgment and to say, either that the issue was, or was not supported by the evidence. In the case of Keel and Herbert *vs* Roberts in this court, where the plea was non-assumpsit *within five years*, a bill of exceptions was filed, stating three depositions verbatim, from which it appeared that *those deponents* did not prove an assumpsit within five years. It was contended at the bar that this, though a bill of exceptions in form, might be considered as a demurrer to evidence, since it stated the whole evidence. Your honor in delivering the opinion of the court, observed that the question was, whether this was to be considered as a demurrer to evidence; which could never have been a question if the form was material to give the name. The cause was sent back for a new trial, and I presume for this reason, that the whole case

case was not stated, for notwithstanding three witnesses might not have heard an assumpsit within 5 years, there *might have been* other witnesses examined who did. If then the motion for a nonsuit had not been made, and this court have found enough stated in the record to satisfy them, that judgment ought to be given for the appellees, what alteration will that motion make? The motion was merely *collateral*, and the appeal is not from that, but from the *final judgment*, which I have endeavored to shew was erroneous, and which is either to be affirmed, or corrected here. And if the final judgment be wrong, will this court affirm it, because the counsel propounded an improper question to the court? This would be sacrificing substantial justice to considerations of mere form. But what is this court now to do? They must either give judgment for the appellant, award a new trial, or give judgment for the appellees. The first cannot be done, because it appears upon the face of the record that the appellant ought not to recover. Will they do the second? If they do, it will be a vain thing, since it is evident that the appellant upon this declaration cannot ultimately succeed. But the court may reverse the judgment of the District Court because it awarded a nonsuit; also the judgment of the County Court, and direct it to be entered for the appellees, upon the ground that the appellant ought not to have recovered upon the evidence.

MARSHALL in reply. The case from *Ld. Ray*, is not like the present. The variance there was material, since the price of the wheat not being fixed, it would depend upon the quality of it, and therefore it was essential in fixing the quantum of damages which the plaintiff was entitled to recover, whether it were of the first, or of the second quality. But in this case, whether the agreement was as it is stated in the declaration, or as it turned out in proof, still the appellant was entitled to £83, and to no more, nor less. If this action had been for damages, on account of the appellees refusal to *board* the four persons with the appellant, the variance might have been material, since those damages ought in that case to have been proportioned to the inconvenience and loss which the appellant sustained by providing himself with the means of accomodating the boarders.

Upon the second point, I would ask, whether it be possible to liken a bill of exceptions, to a demurrer to evidence? They are different in form, in their consequences, and in the conduct of the parties. In the former, the parties still proceed to a trial of the issue; in the latter, the jury are discharged immediately, or find a conditional verdict only. In the former, the question is brought before the court upon the motion of the objecting party only; in the latter, by the act of both parties, since the demurrer offered by the one, is joined by the other. In the former, either party has a right to the benefit of his exceptions before a Superior Court; in the latter, the court, if the case be clear, may refuse to compel the other party to join the demurrer, and leave the whole question to the jury. The judgment upon reversal in the one case is for a new trial, in the other, it is final and conclusive. But the order of nonsuit is not conclusive; the plaintiff is not obliged to submit to it, and if he do, he may re-inftitute his suit, and recover upon better evidence. But the final judgment is a perpetual bar. As to awarding a new trial, the court is not bound to do it against the justice of the case; for if in this cause, the appellant should fail, it must be, not because the justice of the case is against him, but because of a mere slip in his attorney in stating it.

The PRESIDENT delivered the opinon of the court.

This court having decided, that the plaintiff cannot be compelled to suffer a nonsuit, the counsel for the appellees acknowledged that the judgment of the District Court must be reversed, but he has insisted, that the bill of exceptions should be considered as a demurrer to evidence, and that the variance between the case stated and that proved, being material, the court ought to reverse the judgment of the County County.

In the case of Keel and Herbert *vs* Roberts, this court decided against the doctrine of taking a bill of exceptions for a demurrer to evidence; but the counsel endeavored to distinguish that case from this, on account of the whole evidence being stated in this, whereas there was in that only a partial recital of the evidence, and says that the reason which governed the court in that case was founded upon this distinction. Whether this was the only reason *assigned* by the court, I cannot ascertain, not having my notes with me; but the Judges recollect that their discussion went farther, and that they considered the two modes of proceeding as being so totally dissimilar, that the one could not be considered as answering the purposes of the other. On a demurrer to evidence, the court may refuse to compel the other party to join, and may either direct the jury as to the sufficiency of the evidence, or in a clear case, may leave it to the jury to decide upon, as the court seem to have done in this case. We cannot therefore consider this as a demurrer to evidence. The counsel for the appellees then insists, that the variance between the declaration and the proof is so material,

that

that this court cannot give judgment for the appellant, or affirm the judgment of the County Court; since in all special actions, the plaintiff must prove his case precisely as he has stated it; that if he fail to do so, he cannot recover, although he should prove another contract entitling him to the same relief, because such recovery would be no bar to a new suit founded upon such other contract. The cases cited for this purpose do not apply to the present. In those, the two contracts are entirely different from each other; such as good wheat, stated, and good wheat of a second quality proved—a lease reserving rent *annually* stated, and reserving it *quarterly* proved. These were *different contracts*, and the substance of the one, was not comprehended in the other. We are not inclined to meddle with these decisions, nor by any means to extend them beyond their principles. But in this case, the proof extends to all the substantial parts of the contract as laid, and what it does not reach was wholly immaterial, and might as well have been omitted as inserted. But if it could be material, yet the evidence being stated in the bill of exceptions, and a general verdict found for the appellant, he would be barred from a future action, and the appellees would have it completely in their power to avail themselves of this recovery, by referring to the record. The appellant was to find the store keepers meat and drink for £83; to do this, he must have a house, and whether he then had one, or was to procure one, or whether they solicited him, or he them for the contract, was wholly unimportant.

The judgment of the District Court must be reversed, and that of the County Court affirmed.

BREWER *against* TARPLEY.

THIS was an appeal from the District Court of Northumberland, and the only question was, whether an issue was properly joined. It was an action on the case upon an assumpsit. Plea non-assumpsit, concluding as usual to the country, but no *similiter* appears in the record.

WARDEN for the appellant contended, that the omission of the *similiter* was fatal, and could not be amended by an appellate court. He cited 1 *Str.* 641 in point.

There being other cases in the court of a similar nature, the counsel who were interested in the general question, argued the point.

WASHINGTON

WASHINGTON on the same side contended, that the case from *Stra.* cited by Mr. Warden, was expressly in point, and was unimpeached by any subsequent adjudication.—Those which come the nearest to it, are Sayer *vs* Pocock *Cowp. Rep.* 407. and Harvey *vs* Peak 3 *Burr.* 1793.—In the first, there was an *et cætera* which the court construed to mean a *similiter*, since nothing else could be inferred from it. That at farthest it could be considered only as an issue *misjoined*, and (being in the same court) amendable by the statute of Jeofails, which however does not cure the *want of an issue*. In the other case, the plaintiff replied " and the *defendant* likewise" instead of the *plaintiff*. In that case it was no more than the misjoining of the issue. But no case can be produced where the total want of an issue has been aided by verdict.

WARDEN; in the case of Sayer *vs* Pocock, the amendment was made in the same court, and to prevent a writ of error.

CAMPBELL for the appellee.—It would be mischievous as well as a disgrace to justice, if such captious objections were permitted after a trial. The issue is completely formed by an affirmation on the one side, and a negation on the other, and the adding of the *similiter*, is either done by the clerk, or by the party who tenders the issue. It is always understood that the one or the other will do it, and it would be a palpable fraud to permit the party to avail himself of a mistake, which it is understood and expected he will prevent. The case of Cooper *vs* Spencer *1 Str.* 641 is not in point, for the replication did not tender an issue.

WASHINGTON in reply. The replication in the case of Cooper and Spencer was *de injuria sua propria*, &c. which was a complete negation of the plea of son assault *demesne*, and concludes to the country as the plea now under consideration does.

The PRESIDENT delivered the opinion of the court.

The mere omission of a similiter in a plea importing the general issue, if it be a fault at all, is the misprision of the clerk, and therefore amendable. In this case, the parties considered it as joined; the jury were sworn to try the issue joined—the parties go to trial upon the merits, and the verdict is that the defendant did assume. After this, it is too late to object.

Judgment affirmed.

COSBY

COSBY Executor of LOUDON,
against
HITE.

THIS was an action on the case brought by the appellant against the appellee in the County Court. The declaration was upon an assumpsit, and the general issue was pleaded. Afterwards, the plaintiff moved the court for leave to amend, by filing a new declaration in trover, which was permitted, and to this the defendant pleaded not guilty. The latter declaration being in many parts of it blank, when the issue was joined, was afterwards filled up by the plaintiff in *material parts*. The defendant moved that the words thus inserted should be stricken out, which was refused by the court. He then moved, that he might have leave to plead *de novo*, in which he was also overruled, it appearing (as the record states) that he intended to plead the act of limitations. Verdict and judgment was given for the plaintiff, which was reversed in the District Court, from which the plaintiff below appealed.

WICKHAM for the appellant. The first objection to the judgment of the County Court will probably be, their refusing to permit the appellee to plead *de novo* to the new declaration. In answer to this I shall insist that wherever the defendant pleads to a blank declaration, he waves all objection to it on that account, and tacitly consents, that the plaintiff may fill up the blanks as he pleases.

I shall admit, that in general, where either party has leave to amend their pleadings, the opposite party should also be permitted to plead *de novo*. But it does not follow as a necessary consequence, that this must happen in all cases. There may be, and certainly are, exceptions from the general rule, as for instance, if the amendment be in form only, and not in substance; if the pleading *de novo* be unnecessary; if it should be (as it often is) the practice of the court to permit amendments of this sort at any time. In short, if a possible case can happen where an exception from the rule can be warranted, it will be presumed in support of the judgment, unless the facts stated in the record are sufficient to over-rule the presumption, and to bring the case within the general rule. Now in this case, the appellee could not possibly be injured by the rejection of his motion, because upon not guilty he might have given any thing in evidence, which could afford him a defence. It is laid down generally, that the only pleas in trover are not guilty and a releafe; but it is alfo faid by lord Holt, that a releafe may be given in evidence upon the general iffue. Of courfe, the appellee's only view was to produce delay by the amendment afked for, fince he might have defended himfelf upon the plea of not guilty, as completely after, as before the blanks were filled up; and furely, if the motion made by him, was merely for the purpofe of delay, the court were not bound to grant it.

MARSHALL for the appellee. I fhall not differ this cafe from what it would have been, if the motion had been originally made by the appellant to amend his declaration, but I hold it to be a rule without an exception, that where one party is permitted to amend, it is the unqueftionable right of the other party to plead *de novo*. The amendments made in the declaration in this cafe were material, fince they ftated the appellant's title, and defcribed the thing in difpute. The appellant ftakes his right to recover upon the declaration, the defendant his defence upon the plea. It is unequal and unjuft to permit one of them to fhift his ground, and to hold the other bound by his firft plea. The appellee might think the plea firft put in a fufficient anfwer to a blank declaration, knowing that the plaintiff could not recover upon it; otherwife he might have pleaded a releafe, which I do not agree could be given in evidence on the general iffue. I do not pofitively fay that the appellee was injured by the court's refufing him the liberty of pleading *de novo*. It is fufficient for me, if it were barely poffible that he might have been. Now it appears, that the appellee wifhed to plead the act of limitations, from which I conjecture that his attorney thought it neceffary. I admit it might have been given in evidence, but if the attorney was impreffed with a different opinion, it is probable that this ground of defence was entirely loft to the appellee, by the court's refufing the amendment afked for on his part. It is faid, that the amendment was unimportant; if it were, then no good reafon can be given for its being refufed.

WICKHAM in reply. Mr. Marfhall's argument might have been proper, before the Inferior Court, where the materiality of the amendment might have been difcuffed and confidered. But fince there are exceptions to the general rule, and this record does not ftate fuch facts as can enable the court to decide upon the materiality or immateriality of the propofed change in the plea, this court prefuming the Inferior Court to have done right,

right, until satisfied of the contrary, must conclude that the change was unimportant and intended merely for delay.

The PRESIDENT delivered the opinion of the court.

Whatever terms the court might have imposed on the appellee, had he moved to amend, or to plead *de novo*, the case is quite altered when the motion came from the other side. Equal justice required in that case, that the appellee should be allowed to change his plea, or even to demur if he thought proper, without being subjected to terms. The appellant having amended his declaration without leave, it can only be sustained upon the ground, that if he had moved the court, they would have permitted the amendment to be made. It is therefore to be considered in the same point of view as if the amendment had been made at his motion, and this bring it within the principle above stated.

HEWLETT *against* CHAMBERLAYNE,

THIS was an action of debt brought by the appellee in the District Court of Williamsburg, upon a forthcoming bond, the condition of which upon oyer appeared to be in common form, except that it did not recite the amount of the debt due by the execution—the pleas were, 1st, Conditions performed. 2dly, That the plaintiff had in pursuance of the act of Assembly moved the court at a former term for judgment upon the bond which was over-ruled, the court being of opinion that the bond was insufficient. 3dly, That the bond was taken by the sheriff under colour of his office and contrary to the statute &c. To the 1st plea, the appellee replied generally. To the 2d, that the motion was made under the act of Assembly of 1769 entitled " an act to amend an act entitled an act declaring the law concerning executions and for relief of insolvent debtors" which said act being construed strictly in motions, an award of execution upon the said forthcoming bond was refused for some inaccuracy in the condition of it. To the 3d plea, the appellee replied, that the bond was taken in pursuance of the act of 1769 upon an execution &c.

The parties agreed the following case; that the bond in the declaration mentioned was taken by the sheriff upon an execution issued at the suit of the appellee, conditioned for the forthcoming of property seized by the said sheriff under that execution. That the property was not delivered according to the condition of the bond, nor the money paid. That a motion was made for an award of execution upon the said bond, which was over-ruled and the motion dismissed with costs, on account of the insufficiency of the bond. That afterwards another motion was made by the appellee to quash the execution which was also rejected. Judgment was entered below for the appellee.

WICKHAM for the appellant. This bond was taken under the act of 1769, but not pursuing that act in reciting the execution, and the amount of it, it is utterly void. The law requires forthcoming bonds to be returned to the clerk's office and to have the force of judgments; but if the bond be not made in conformity with the law, it can have no greater force than a defective judgment or recognizance, upon which no recovery could be had. An irregular judgment may be set aside upon motion, and if this be considered as such, the appellee could not elect to take it as a thing in *pais* and bring an action upon it. But if he had such an election, he has made it, and a regular judgment has passed against him upon his motion.

MARSHALL for the appellee. This question has been fully settled by this court, in the case of Meriweather and Johnson. In that case the objection to the bond was: that it was taken payable to the sheriff, instead of the creditor, as the law required; but the principal decided in that case is strictly applicable to the present.

In that case, as in this, a motion for judgment upon the bond had also been made and overruled. In short, the very same objections were there stated and argued, which are now urged; and upon full consideration, the court determined, that an action of debt upon the bond might be sustained.

The PRESIDENT.—The case of Meriweather and Johnson is expressly in point.

The judgment must therefore be affirmed.

EDWARD M'GUIRE,

against

WARDER Executor of PARKER.

THE President stated the case, and delivered the opinion of the court to the following effect. In June 1764, the appellant

appellant mortgaged a tract of land lying in Virginia, to the testator of the appellee then a resident of Philadelphia for the purpose of securing the payment of £88 : 12 : 6½, Pensylvania currency, with lawful interest thereon from the 5th day of March preceeding. In 1773 the appellee instituted a suit in Chancery, in the County Court of Frederick, to foreclose the equity of redemption in the mortgaged premises, and for a sale thereof, towards satisfying the principal debt and interest. The appellant in his answer admitted the execution of the deed of mortgage, and that £88 : 12 : 6½ Pensylvania currency with interest thereon at the rate of *five* per centum per annum from the 6th day of March 1764, was due and unpaid; but that Peter Hogg the attorney of the appellee had agreed that the sale of the mortgaged premises should be respited until the first Tuesday in August 1775. The appellant consented that a decree conformably with this agreement should be pronounced. The cause was heard in September 1773, by consent of the parties, by their counsel upon the bill and answer, and a decree was made, that the appellant should on or before the 10th day of September 1775, pay to the appellee £70 : 18 : 5 Virginia currency, with interest thereon after the rate of six per centum per annum, from the 6th day of March 1764, and in case of failure, that the sheriff should sell the mortgaged premises, for the purpose of satisfying the principal, interest, and costs, mentioned in the decree.

It is probable that *this decree* was entered by the consent of parties, as it varies from the answer in two circumstances, 1st, in changing the rate of interest from *five* to *six* per cent. and 2dly in altering the time agreed upon for the sale of the property. If the change in the rate of interest were made from a consciousness in the parties, that the debt originated in a contract made in *Pensylvania*, it was lawful and just that the decree should be for six per cent. If on the contrary, the interest was increased with a view to procure the two years indulgence, it would have been usurious and void. This court presume the former for many reasons. 1st, The residence of the creditor usually fixes the place of the contract. Money-lenders or vendors of goods, do not generally travel to seek for borrowers, or purchasers, but the reverse. 2dly, The payment is stipulated to be made in Pensylvania money. But 3dly and principally, this court will never presume a contract to be usurious unless it be proved; especially in this case where such a presumption, would be at variance with the decree of a court, which it is not to be supposed would sanction such a contract. We therefore consider the decree for six per cent.

to have been entered by confent, upon the ground of the creditor being entitled to it, by his original contract.

The next point in the caufe which deferves attention, is a receipt given in May 1777 by Hogg (the attorney of the appellee tho' he does not ftile himfelf fuch) to the appellant, for £ 117 : 12, Virginia money, being the amount of principal and intereft due upon the mortgage. In September 1778, the appellant fent the money by Mr. Jones to Philadelphia, requefting him to pay it to the appellee, but it was not paid, in confequence of the abfence of the appellee, and the money was returned to the appellant. In October 1778 the appellant gave to Hogg a receipt in the following words, viz. "Received of Capt. Hogg £ 117 : 12, to be paid into the continental loan office, for the executors of Richard Parker of Philadelphia, by me Edward M'Guire." The appellant acknowledged to the executor of Hogg, that he had given fuch a receipt, and that he had paid into the treafury of Virginia in January 1780, the fum of 380 dollars for the executors of Richard Parker, for which payment, a receipt was given by the treafurer, as for fo much received from the appellee, without noticing by whom it was paid. In March 1789 a *fci. fa.* iffued at the fuit of the appellee to revive the decree, to which the plea of payment was filed and iffue taken upon it. The trial of the iffue being referred to a jury to be empannelled on the law fide of the fame court, Hogg's receipt of May 1777, was admitted as evidence, and the jury found for the appellant. An exception was taken to the admiffion of the receipt, becaufe Hogg had no authority, nor warrant of attorney from the appellee to inftitute, or to profecute that, or any other fuit for him, and becaufe no procefs had iffued to enforce the decree prior to the receipt given by Hogg. The County Court difmiffed the *fci. fa.* with cofts.

Upon an appeal, the High Court of Chancery reverfed the decree, and directed a new trial of the iffue, on which, the receipt was not to be admitted in evidence, unlefs the appellant could give other proof that Hogg was the attorney of the appellee, than what appeared in the record.

From this decree M'Guire has appealed to this court.

In both Courts, the caufe appears to have been difcuffed upon the queftion, whether Hogg, as attorney for the appellee, could properly receive the money, and difcharge the appellant. But we deem it unneceffary to decide that point. We are fatisfied from the record, that the receipt was either fictitious and without actual payment, or if genuine, that all its effects

fects were done away by the return of the money to the appellant in October 1778, (above ten years before the *sci. fa.* was sued out,) and therefore that the payment could not be confidered as obligatory upon the appellees at that time, although it fhould be admitted, that Hogg had authority to receive it. That the receipt was merely colourable, is highly probable from the general complexion of the evidence. We do not find Hogg in any inftance endeavoring to convey the money to the appellees, but on the contrary, it appears always to have remained in the poffeffion of the appellant; who delivered it to Mr. Jones in 1778 to carry to Philadelphia, and who paid it into the treafury for the ufe of the appellee. This indeed was after the date of the appellant's receipt to Hogg in October 1778. But that receipt, fo far from removing the fufpicion, ftrongly confirms it. If Hogg had really received the money as attorney for the executor, and in confequence of his refufal to accept it, he had intended to pay it into the treafury, under the act relating to debts due to Britifh fubjects; it was Hogg's bufinefs to have paid it in, and not to have returned it to the debtor for that purpofe. The money was not paid into the treafury for fifteen months after the date of the receipt, and from the evidence in the caufe it is clear that it was not entrufted to the appellant by Hogg, as an immediate bearer of it, but for fome other purpofe which it is not difficult to develope.

It is obfervable that M'Guire's receipt is dated the 9th of October 1778, immediately after Mr. Jones's return from Philadelphia, when Hogg probably fufpecting, that the appellee wifhed to avoid receiving the money, began to reflect upon the confequences which might refult to himfelf from his former fictitious receipt, and therefore fecured himfelf by a counter receipt equally fictitious, no money paffing at either time. In this view of the cafe, we are of opinion, that the receipt ought not to be admitted as evidence of a payment, altho' it fhould be proved, that Hogg had a legal authority to receive the money, and fo far we reverfe the Chancellor's decree. In all other refpects it is to be affirmed, and as the appellees have prevailed, they are to recover cofts.

BARNETT

BARNETT & WOOLFOLK,

againſt

WATSON & URQUHART.

THIS cauſe which was argued at the laſt court, and being continued to be re-argued, came on again, at the preſent term. It was an action on the caſe brought by the appellees in the County Court, againſt Barnett, Woolfolk & Co. The declaration ſtates, "that the defendants were indebted to the plaintiffs in the ſum of £ 171: 5: 4, ſterling money of Great Britain, worth in Virginia currency £228: 7, for ſo much advanced by the plaintiffs to Foreſt and Stoddart, at the ſpecial inſtance and requeſt of the ſaid Barnett, Woolfolk & Co. and being ſo indebted they aſſumed to pay &c. The damages are laid at £500. The writ being ſerved upon Woolfolk, he pleaded ſeparately the general iſſue; and an abatement of the ſuit was entered as to Barnett, who was returned "no inhabitant." An order was made for taking the depoſition of Benjamin Stoddart on the part of the appellees, and at a ſubſequent term, and after a jury had been ſworn upon the above iſſue, and withdrawn, Barnett, as the record ſtates, " came into court, and entered himſelf a *defendant* at the ſuit of Watſon and Urquhart, and the ſaid *defendants* acknowledged legal notice, as to the taking of the above depoſition, and on the motion of the *defendants,* the ſuit was continued at their coſts." At another day, (it is ſtated) " the parties aforeſaid came, as alſo a jury, who ſay upon their oaths, that the *defendants have not paid the debt in the declaration mentioned,* as in pleading they have alledged, and aſſeſs the plaintiff's damages, by occaſion of the non-performance of that aſſumption, to £294: 12, current money." Upon this verdict, judgment was entered for the apellees. Barnett and Woolfolk filed a bill of exceptions to the opinion of the court, which admitted the depoſition of Benjamin Stoddart to be read in evidence at the trial; the objection was made upon the ſcore of incompetency. The ſubſtance of the depoſition (which is ſpread at large upon the record) is, that Barnett, Woolfolk & Co. ſhipped to Foreſt and Stoddart 16 hogſheads of tobacco, and drew on them for £ 240 ſterling, in favor of the appellees, who remitted the bill, and requeſted that it might be honoured, though the tobacco ſhould not produce that ſum, agreeing to be anſwerable themſelves to the drawees for the

the deficiency, if any. In consequence of this request, Foreft and Stoddart paid the bill, although the tobacco netted only £68 : 14 : 8 fterling ; that Foreft and Stoddart have fince demanded and received from the plaintiffs the balance due from Barnett, Woolfolk & Co. The depofition was not figned by Stoddart and was excepted to, for this reafon alfo. The magiftrates who took the depofition certified, " that in purfuance of a commiffion, they had examined the faid Benjamin Stoddart, a witnefs, as well on the part of Watfon and Urquhart, as on behalf of *Jofeph Woolfolk*, in a fuit depending in Orange Court, the witnefs being firft duly fworn." The defendants Barnett and Woolfolk moved for a new trial, which being refufed, they excepted for that reafon likewife, ftating as the ground of it, that a material witnefs was abfent; that the damages were exceffive, being a few pounds more than the debt in the declaration mentioned, and that the court would not permit them to urge any other reafons for a new trial, except the two above ftated.

Upon an appeal to the Diftrict Court of Frederickfburg, the judgment of the County Court was affirmed; and a writ of fuperfedeas to this latter judgment was awarded by one of the judges of this court.

WARDEN for the appellants. I rely upon the following errors in the judgment of the County Court. 1ft, The plaintiff in his declaration claims a *fterling money* debt, of the value of fo much in *current money*, whereas the demand fhould have been made in *fterling* money only. In fupport of this objection, the cafe of Scott's executors *vs* Call, (ante 115) is fully in point.

2d, The declaration ftates a demand againft *Barnett*, *Woolfolk & Co*. and the judgment is againft *Barnett* and *Woolfolk* only, which is a fatal variance. The contract as ftated is a joint one, and the judgment fhould have alfo been joint, that the whole might affift in bearing the burthen.

3d. There is no iffue as to Barnett, and yet a verdict and judgment is rendered againft him. The plea of Woolfolk is feveral, that *he* did not affume, and Barnett, who was not bound to ftake his defence upon this iffue, might have chofen to put in a fpecial plea : but inftead of his having an opportunity to do fo, a verdict was rendered upon the plea of Woolfolk alone, againft *Barnett* as well as Woolfolk, tho' the former was in truth no party to the fuit, and probably was not, nay could not, be defended upon any fpecial ground, which he might have chofen, diftinct from that taken by Woolfolk.

4th,

4th, The deposition of Stoddart does not go to prove that the appellants assumed, or that the money was paid by Watson and Urquhart, at their request.

5th, Stoddart appears clearly to have been an interested witness. Barnett and Woolfolk considered their tobacco as having been either disposed of at an under value, or as having been sold at a higher price than that stated by Forest and Stoddart, and they would have been entitled, in case Forest and Stoddart had sued them on their bill, (and which was alone prevented by the officious interference of Watson and Urquhart) to oppose the demand by proofs of improper conduct in the sale of their tobacco. Stoddart therefore was a very improper witness, to prove the price at which the tobacco sold.

6th, The deposition not being signed by Stoddart, it ought not to have been read, since if perjury had been committed, a prosecution could not have been instituted against the witness in consequence of this omission. 1 *Morg. Ess.* 124.

DUVAL on the same side. For any thing which appears in the record, the bill drawn by Barnett, Woolfolk & Co. may yet be in circulation, and may at some future time rise up against the drawers, for it does not appear, that Watson and Urquhart took it up. Upon the third objection made by Mr. Warden, he cited 3 *Morg. Ess.* 10.

WASHINGTON for the appellees. The first objection is, that the current money value of the sterling debt ought not to have been stated, in the declaration; and in support of this, the case of Scott's executors *vs* Call, is relied upon. That was an action of *debt for a specific sum*, where the jury failed to ascertain the value of the money, tho' that subject was rendered by the pleadings an essential part of the matter in issue. This is an action on the case, founding entirely *in damages*, and the jury have assessed those damages in current money, leaving nothing for the court to do.

In answer to the second objection let it be premised, that contracts by partners are joint and several. If the action be not brought against all, those who are sued may plead in abatement, discovering the names of the other partners, so as to prevent the plaintiff from making more than one mistake. But if they do not plead in abatement, they cannot afterwards object that all are not joined. If there be any thing in the objection now insisted upon, a recovery can never be had upon a partnership contract, where some of the firm, are not named, but included under the general stile of the *company*, if the members
will

will only keep their own fecret. For if, as in this cafe, the fuit is brought againft Barnett, Woolfolk & Co. it is objected, that a judgment cannot be obtained againſt Barnet and Woolfolk only; and it is clear that it cannot be rendered againſt the whole if the unnamed partners be unknown, fince they cannot be made parties to the fuit. You cannot fue the known partners only, for then the contract muft be ftated to be made by them, and if this be done, then it would be variant from the real one, which would be clearly fatal. So that, if the prefent objection, be a good one, the plaintiff, in a cafe like this, would be without any remedy at all at law, whereas on the other hand, the defendants may difcover who are the concealed partners by a plea in abatement, and ought to do fo, if they mean to make it a joint burthen.

There is more difficulty in the next objection, than in any which has been mentioned. To underftand it, we muft confider the real nature and end of *pleading*. A plea confifts of two parts; the firſt is the *making of defence*, and the other is the extenfion of that defence, under all the various modifications of which the cafe admits. *Making defence*, is the denial of the plaintiff's demand as he has ftated it. 3 *Blac. Com.* 296. If the defendant mean not to rely upon a bare denial, but would go farther and oppofe the plaintiff's claim by fomething not neceffarily growing out of the defence, but quite collateral thereto, he muft ftate fuch other ground in the form of a plea. Thus in affumpfit, the defendant by making defence, and confequently denying the plaintiff's demand fet forth in the declaration, *fubſtantially* fays, that he did not affume; becaufe the affirmation being that he did affume, the negation muft be that he did not affume, which forms a compleat iffue: but if the defendant would go farther, and fay, for inftance, that he did not affume within five years, he muft *plead* that fpecial matter, (becaufe this is not neceffarily implied by a mere negation,) fo as to give the plaintiff notice of the real ground of defence, which is the primary and only end of pleading, In this cafe then, Barnett, by entering himfelf a *defendant* which is tantamount to *defending the force and injury*, denies the affumpfit charged, as much, as if he had faid fo, in a more regular plea. But what puts this queftion beyond doubt is, that his *co-defendant* had regularly pleaded non-affumpfit, to a joint demand, and therefore Barnett, by entering himfelf defendant, going to trial on the plea, and *actually defending the fuit* in all its ſtages, as the record fhews he did, made Woolfolk's plea his own, and after a verdict againſt him, ought not to be permitted to fet it afide, becaufe he had neglected to put in a formal plea. The want of a *similiter* appears from the case of Cooper *vs* Spencer, 1 *Sir.* 641 cited in 3 *Morg. essays*, p. 10, to have been considered as fatal, and not aided by the statute of Jeofails, yet *after defence made*, the objection is removed. 21 *Vin.* p. 480.

4th, This objection, as well as that made by Mr. Duval, may be answered together, by observing that the whole evidence is not stated. This is not a demurrer to evidence, where all the testimony is spread upon the record, but it is merely an exception to the admissibility of a particular deposition. So that this court cannot say that evidence was not produced of the assumpsit, or of the request, or that the bill was taken up by Watson and Urquhart. Besides, as to the first, the *law* creates the assumpsit, and as to the latter, the bill not having been protested never can charge the appellants.

5th, Stoddart can neither gain, nor lose by the event of this cause, and this is the touchstone by which to try the interest of a witness. The claim of Forest and Stoddart, against Watson and Urquhart, was independent of Barnett, Woolfolk & Co. It arose from their special undertaking, they did that without suit, which they might have been compelled to do. They could not defend themselves, by alledging an injury done by Forest and Stoddart, to Barnett, Woolfolk & Co. nor are they precluded by this judgment, nor by the payment made by the appellees from contesting that point with Forest and Soddart, who could not in such a suit avail themselves of any benefit from the evidence given in this cause. If Forest and Stoddart has injured the appellants, it is nothing to the appellees, who only claim the money advanced for them, and to prove the amount of that advance, the receiver is a proper and often the only witness.

6th, This objection is supported neither by authorities, nor by principle. 2 *Sir.* 920, which is referred to, does not warrant the doctrine contended for, and the reason assigned for it, is totally unfounded. The signing of the deposition cannot be necessary, even for the purpose of furnishing evidence of the oath, since upon a prosecution for perjury, it would be requisite to prove, that the evidence stated in the deposition and signed by the witness *was sworn to by him*. The certificate of the magistrate would not be sufficient. The signature, if proved, (for this too must be done,) might be evidence of his having deposed what is there written; but, that he deposed it upon *oath*, would still remain to be proved. So that after all, other evidence must be resorted to, in order to sustain the prosecution. If the false oath were not committed to writing, yet upon proving it, the witness might suffer for perjury, and surely it is not *less perjury* if it be committed to writing, because it is not signed.

CAMPBELL in reply. The objections upon which I rely, are 1st, That no plea is put in by Barnett, and yet judgment is entered against him. But it is contended that there is a plea. I ask what is it? Is it payment? Non assumpsit? The act of limitations, or what? For if there be a plea, it may be all or either of those which I have mentioned. The oath administered to the jurors is, that they shall well and truly try the *issue joined*. But if there be no plea, there can be no issue, and consequently the jury cannot answer to their charge. It is essential that the pleadings should be so far formal at least, as to submit some point or other to the consideration of the jury, for otherwise, the court cannot even presume, that the matters in difference between the parties have been settled by the verdict. We know, that whereever an immaterial point is put in issue, a repleader will be awarded, and for the very reason which I have mentioned, namely, that the rights of the parties were not involved in the issue, and therefore could not have been decided by the jury. There is certainly a great distinction between *making defence*, and *pleading*. The former is no more than an introduction to the latter, and although it imports a general denial of the plaintiff's right to recover, it does not disclose the ground upon which that right is opposed, so as that it may appear whether the question decided by the jury, was upon a point material to the merits of the cause or not. *Co. Lit.* 127, *b*. The truth is, that *no defence* in this case, according to the technical meaning of the word, was made, the appellant Barnett having done no more than enter his appearance to the suit, so as to dispense with the necessity of process being served upon him. But if any particular plea can be presumed to have been intended by Barnett, the probable one would be the general issue; and if so, it may properly be objected 2dly, that the verdict is totally immaterial, since it is neither for nor against the appellants. The jury have found " that the defendants have not paid the debt in the declaration mentioned;" now they may not have *paid* the debt claimed, and yet they may never have *assumed to pay it*. The former may be the consequence of the latter, and the jury have not found that he did assume. So that the very gist of the issue (if there be any) is still left undetermined. 3 *Salk.* 374.

3d, Stoddart was certainly an interested witness. If the tobacco sold for a price equal to the sum drawn for by the appellants, then

then Foreſt and Stoddart had no right to demand any thing from either the drawers, or endorſers of the bill, and an action, for money had and received, might have been maintained againſt them by the appellees, in caſe they had failed in this ſuit, upon the ground of the tobacco having ſold for a greater price than that credited by Foreſt and Stoddart. The ſucceſs of the appellees, was conſequently intereſting to Stoddart.

WASHINGTON in reply. The caſe from *Salk.* 374, was decided when the courts were much more rigid, than they now are, reſpecting the doctrine of verdicts. The rule now is, that after a fair trial, the court will not ſet aſide a verdict, merely becauſe it may be informal, but will mould it into form. And if this be the rule in England, it ſhould be very liberally adopted in this country, when it is recollected, that in the County Courts, a ſhort minute only is made of the proceedings by the clerk, during the ſitting of the court; the verdict is uſually drawn by the jury in general terms, and the extenſion of it ſo as to make it reſponſive to the iſſue, is always left to the clerk, who does it after the term is ended, when he makes out a complete record. So that errors of this ſort are the mere miſpriſions of the clerk. But in this caſe, the verdict ſtated in the record ſubſtantially correſponds with the iſſue; for the damages aſſeſſed, are for the plaintiff's *non-performance of his aſſumpſion:* which is clearly finding an aſſumpſit and a non-performance of it.

THE PRESIDENT. The firſt objection ſtated to the judgment of the County Court is, that the demand is for *ſterling money* of the value of ſo much in Virginia currency; in ſupport of which, the caſe of Scott's executors *vs* Call is relied upon. The principle of that caſe is a ſtrong one in ſupport of this judgment. The error in that was, that the jury left the value of the ſterling money to be aſcertained by the court, inſtead of ſettling it themſelves; the very reverſe of which has been done in the preſent caſe.

The next objection is, that the declaration is againſt *Barnett, Woolfolk & Co.* and the judgment is againſt *Barnett & Woolfolk only.* The anſwer to this is obvious. Barnett & Woolfork are ſued as the *oſtenſible partners* of the company, and have it completely in their power to make it a joint charge upon the whole company, by diſcloſing the names of the unknown partners by a plea in abatement. But inſtead of pleading this matter, they take the whole defence upon themſelves, and it is certainly too late after verdict, to complain that the judgment is not againſt all the members of the company.

But

But it is objected, that no plea was put in by Barnett, and consequently, that a verdict against him was improper. The declaration is against both; Woolfolk alone, pleaded, and an issue was made up. Barnett voluntarily appeared and desired to be made a defendant with Woolfolk. It is true, that he might have pleaded seperately if he had been inclined to do so: but not desiring it, his being made a defendant with the other, who was at issue, implies a consent to be united with him in his plea. This consent is sufficiently established by his subsequent conduct. He acknowledged notice of the taking of Stoddarts deposition; proceeded to the trial and defended the suit.

The 4th objection is, that no assumpsit was proven. To this there are two answers.—1st, That the deposition does not appear to have been the only evidence given at the trial. 2dly, The plaintiff having proved a debt to be due, the law implies an assumpsit to pay it.

The 5th objection is, to Stoddart's deposition on the score of interest. The only evidence as to this point is the deposition itself. From that it appears, that Forest and Stoddart paid the excess of the bill beyond the proceeds of the tobacco, at the request of Watson and Urquhart, and upon their special promise to be answerable for such payment. When that was ascertained, they applied to Watson and Urquhart, who performed their promise, without any agreement to refund, or to connect it in any manner with the fate of the present dispute. So that Stoddart could be in no wise interested in the event of this cause. But it has been contended that the sales of the tobacco were fraudulent, and that there was a combination between Forest and Stoddart, and Watson and Urquhart, to shift the demand for the balance into the hands of the latter, to deprive Barnett, Woolfolk & Co. of their defence on the ground of the fraudulent sales. Of this combination there is no proof. On the contrary, there is the strongest ground to presume otherwise. Watson and Urquhart appear to have been the friends of Barnett, Woolfolk & Co. and, as such, they endorsed their bill and gave it credit. They went further, and requested honor to the bill, tho' the funds upon which it was drawn should prove deficient: by which friendly interference they preserved the credit of the drawers, and saved them from the payment of damages which would have been the consequence of the bill's being protested. This conduct does not warrant a suspicion of combination to the prejudice of Barnett, Woolfolk & Co. But it was said that Watson and Urquhart ought not to have paid the money without the consent of Barnett, Woolfolk & Co. If they had been litigious, or inclined to evade a performance of their promise, they might have delayed payment under a pretext of this sort. But knowing that they had induced Forest and Stoddart to advance the money, they very properly and without delay repaid it with interest, having nothing to do with any dispute between them and the appellants; but leaving it to be litigated between them, when and how they pleased. This may still be done if the appellants are inclined, and nothing sworn by Stoddart in this suit, can avail him in that.

Another objection to this deposition is, that the witness has not subscribed it. Whether Stoddart could be prosecuted for perjury (in case he has taken a false oath,) in consequence of this omission, is a question which we leave to be determined by those before whom the prosecution shall be instituted. The deposition is certified, by two magistrates, to have been taken before them *upon oath*, which gives it sufficient authenticity.

The objection to the verdict applies meerly *to the form* of it. The damages assessed by the jury are *for the non-performance of the assumption, in the declaration mentioned*, and the irregularity, in the extension of the verdict, is apparently a clerical misprision and therefore amendable.

Judgment of the District Court affirmed.

BRAXTON *against* MORRIS.

THIS was an appeal from a decree of the High Court of Chancery. At the last term, a rule was obtained by the counsel for the appellee, that the appellant should shew cause, why this appeal should not be dismissed, unless bond and security in a penalty sufficient to cover the decree were given. The Chancellor allowed the appeal upon the appellants giving bond in a sum merely nominal. The question depended upon the construction of the acts of Assembly relating to this subject,

The PRESIDENT. The law constituting the Court of Appeals passed in 1792, refers (as to this point) to the law relating to appeals from the County Courts, to the High Court of Chancery and District Courts.

The County Court law, after referring to the Chancery law for the *manner* of exercising the right of appeal, declares that bond and security shall be given by the *plaintiff* if he appeal, but
totally

totally omits the clause in the old County Court law, which directed bond and security to be given by the *defendant,* if he appealed. The chancery law does not supply the defect in a case where the appeal is prayed for at the *time of pronouncing the decree,* although (where that has been neglected) it provides for the case of a petition of appeal *afterwards,* and in this latter case, requires bond and security to be given. It takes no further notice of an appeal prayed for at the time of a decree, as it respects the bond, than to declare it valid, if given by sureties of sufficient ability, tho' it should not be executed by the party himself. But this is not enough to warrant a County Court in demanding bond and security from a *defendant* praying an appeal, as the condition upon which it is granted; nor can the Chancellor require it. This was probably a mere omission in the legislature, but it belongs to them, not to this court to rectify it.

The court are therefore of opinion, that the Chancellor took the only bond which he was authorised to require: viz. a bond in the penalty of £20, from Mr. Braxton as a *plaintiff appealing.*

PENDLETON *against* VANDEVIER.

THIS was an ejectment brought upon the demise of *Jacobus* Vandevier the appellee, against the appellant, in the District Court of Winchester. The jury found a special verdict to the following effect viz: That John Vanmeter being seized in fee simple of a tract of land, of which the land in question was a part, departed this life at some time previous to September 1745, having first duly made and published his last will and testament, bearing date the 13th of August, in the same year, whereby he devised the land in question by the following clause viz: "Item, I
" give and bequeath to my daughter Magdalena, twenty shil-
" lings, as her full legacy, which when paid, is to bar her of a-
" ny title to my real or personal estate, and I do devise *unto her*
" *heirs lawfully begotten on her body,* a certain tract of land
" part of that on which I now live, bounded as follows; [here
" follows a particular description of this parcel according to cer-
" tain courses and distances] containing by estimation 250 acres
" more or less, to be held by the heirs of my said daughter un-
" der the limitations and restrictions according to the devise made
" to my son *Abraham Vanmeter's heirs.*" That he devised to
Abraham

Abraham Vaumeter another parcel of the same tract particularly described by metes and bounds *to him and his heirs, lawfully begotten*; but if there should be no heirs male or female of his said son or sons (thereafter named) who should attain the age of 21 years, then after the death of his said son or sons, or their heirs, remainder to his surviving devisees equally to be divided. The residue of the tract he devised in the same manner to his other children describing accurately the courses and distances of each parcel. That at the time of making the will, Magdalena had one daughter named Prudence born in the year 1744. That she had also a son born about 20 months after the birth of Prudence who lived only a few days. That Prudence (who is still living) did in the year 1769, convey the land in question by deeds of lease and release to Jacob Vandevier, the father of the lessor of the plantiff.

The jury find a survey of the entire tract, as well as of the several parcels given to the respective devisees with the boundaries of the whole (except of the part bequeathed to the heirs of Magdalena) particularly laid off and described, and corresponding with the courses and distances mentioned in the will. The parcel devised to the heirs of Magdalena, is laid off in the plat referred to by the jury, in two ways, the one comprehending about 30 acres more than the other. The verdict then proceeds as follows: " If from the words of the will the testator's
" intention can be legally construed so as to convey unto the
" heirs begotten on the body of the said Magdalena, the lands
" contained between the lines and letters s, t and K,* then we
" find that the part of the land devised to the heirs lawfully be-
" gotten on the body of the said Magdalena, and which is the
" land in the declaration mentioned, is contained within the
" lines and letters, m, n, o, p, q, r, s, t, E, D, C, B and m. But
" if from the words of the will, the intention cannot be legal-
" ly construed so as to convey the lands between the lines and
" letters s, t and E, to the heirs begotten on the body of the said
" Magdalena, then we find that the part of the lands devised to
" the heirs lawfully begotten of the body of the said Magdalena
" (which is in that case the land in the declaration mentioned) is
" described in the plat aforesaid by the letters m, n, o, p, q,
" r, s, E, D, C, B and m." They further find that Jacob Vandevier the father of the plaintiff, being seised &c. departed this life having by his will devised the land in question to his son *James the lessor of the plaintiff.* To

---

* This is a mistake, it should have been E, as it is apparent from the plat.

To several of his children he devises ("after his wife's thirds of his moveable estate, and legacies are paid) an equal proportional child's part arising therefrom, *as well of lands to be disposed of, if any there be*, as of all things else."

The District Court gave judgment for the plaintiff according to the lines which included the smallest quantity of land, from which the defendant appealed.

WILLIAMS for the appellant. The first question is, whether Prudence took any estate at all or not? 2dly, If she did, then what estate she did take? 3dly, Whether the verdict be not so defective, as that no judgment can properly be rendered upon it?

First, the rule of law is well established, that no person can take by the name of *heir* during the life of the ancestor, for *nemo est hæres viventis*. From this general rule, a departure is sometimes permitted, in the case of last wills in favor of intention; but then, the person who is intended to take by that name, must be almost as accurately described, as if he were named. The word *heir*, unconnected with some other description, is a word of limitation, Cowp. Rep. 309, 313. In all the cases which form exceptions from this general rule, there will be found superadded words descriptive of the person intended to take: Thus in Long and Beaumont, 1 P. *Williams* 229, which was a devise to the heirs male of a person then living, there is not only a legacy given to the ancestor, by which the testator takes notice that he is alive, but legacies are also given to his three sons by name, who were of course known by the testator to be then living; and in that case it was resolved, that the eldest son should take *as heir thus described* So in Burchett & Durdant, 2 *Vent.* 311. The devise was to the heirs male of the body of R. D. *then living*. But in the case now under consideration, there are no words descriptive of the daughter of Magdalena. The testator takes no notice of her at all, nor does it appear that he knew she was in being; for she was born only in 1744, the year before the testator's death. It is also to be observed, throughout the will, that when the testator gives any thing to *grandchildren*, he mentions them by name.

2dly, If Prudence takes any thing, it cannot be a greater estate than for life, for the devise is to the heirs of the body of Magdalena without words of limitation superadded, and the reference to the devise, to Abraham Vanmeter's heirs does not enlarge the estate; for the words in that clause are not (as in this) to the *heirs of Abraham*, but to *Abraham and the heirs of his body*.

So

So that there is no such devise in the will, as that to which the reference is made.

If then Prudence only took an estate for life, her conveyance being by *lease and release* amounts to a forfeiture of her estate. I admit, that if this had been a conveyance operating under the statute of uses, it would have been otherwise; but a lease and release like the present is a common law conveyance. The consequence is, that the heir at law was the only person entitled to enter for the forfeiture.

3dly, It may be very seriously questioned, whether as *Jacobus* the lessor of the plaintiff must recover by deducing a clear title to himself, he can succeed upon this verdict which finds that the devise from Jacob Vandevier was to his son *James*.

As to the conclusion of the jury, it seems too vague for the court to decide upon, since there is nothing but the will itself from which the intention of the testator can be discovered.

Whether the testator in describing the parcel of land in question meant to confine, or to extend its limits, according to either of the two lines stated in the verdict is a question, which must depend entirely upon evidence. The courses mentioned in the will do in no respect fit either of them, but might have been explained to the satisfaction of the jury by a variety of circumstances of which they were, as I conceive, the only proper judges.

LEE for the appellee. In this case, both parties may be considered as appellants. Pendleton complains because a judgment is rendered against him for any thing, and Vandevier contends that he is entitled to a judgment for the whole of the land.

As to the first point, I shall admit the general rule, *nemo est hæres viventis*. But it is equally clear, that to favor the intention of a testator, the word *heir* may be as descriptive of the person to take, as if he were particularly named. In this case, it is evident from the misspelling, and from other inaccuracies in the will, that it was written by an illiterate man. The testator was about to divide a large tract of land between his children and grand-children, and intended to describe each parcel by certain metes and bounds. He then *gives all the residue of his estate* to be divided amongst several of his children, which proves that he did not intend to die intestate as to any part, or to leave any thing to descend to his heir at law. He takes notice that Magdalena is living, and of course, that she could not have *heirs* in the legal sense of the word. Prudence is also found to have been born before the will was made,

with

with which it is prefumed he was acquainted, tho' fhe is not noticed in the will. All thefe circumftances are as ftrong as can occur in any cafe, to fhew an intent in the teftator, to defcribe Prudence by the words which he ufed. The cafe of Doe and Lamming, 2 *Burr.* 1100, was that of a prefent devife, unattended by any particular defcription of the perfons meant to take as heirs, other than may be drawn from the manner in which they were directed to take. The cafe of Brooking *vs* White 2 *Blac. Rep.* 1010, is a very ftrong and pointed authority.

As to the fecond point, it is immaterial whether Prudence took an eftate for life, or intail, for as fhe is found to be ftill living, the conveyance to Jacob Vandevier is fufficient to enable the appellee to recover in this action, and the conveyance does not produce a forfeiture, as is fuppofed. If it were neceffary to contend that fhe took an eftate of inheritance, the reference to the devife to Abraham Vanmeter might without violence to the words be conftrued to mean " to Abraham Vanmeter and the heirs of his body," fince the devife in that claufe is not to *the heirs* of Abraham Vanmeter &c. but to " *Abraham Vanmeter, and the heirs of his body.*"

The third objection does not feem to be much relied upon. The jury having found that the devife was to the *leffor of the plaintiff* (whofe name is Jacobus) and the devife being to Jacobus, the court will at once perceive that it is a miftake of the jury, and will reject the word Jacobus in the verdict as furplufage.

The laft objection is, that the jury ought to have found the boundaries of the land in queftion and not to have fubmitted that queftion to the court.

The court being the proper tribunal to decide upon the conftruction of deeds and wills, and of the intention of the makers thereof, the jury did right in fubmitting to them the queftion refpecting the difputed lines, as they depended entirely upon a comparifon of the courfes and diftances mentioned in the will, with thofe laid down and defcribed in the plat of the land found by the verdict. From that it appears, that the teftator intended to parcel out one entire tract amongft the different members of his family, according to certain metes and bounds. There is a perfect correfpondence between the will, and the plat, as to every fubdivifion, except that in queftion. It is clear therefore that he meant to devife the whole, and not to leave a remnant of 30 acres in a tract of 1700 undifpofed of, which will be the cafe, if the judgment below be right. Now it is plain, that the teftator

tor had the plat found by the jury before him, at the time he was writing his will, and after purfuing the boundaries of this parcel of land to a particular point, by miftake he left out a courfe, and confequently if the will be literally purfued, the lines of the furvey could never be made to unite. This would be abfurd and repugnant. To effectuate the intention of the teftator therefore, the court will fupply the line which was omitted, fo as to produce a compleat difpofition of the whole tract. If then the court is of opinion that the teftator meant to difpofe of the whole tract, the judgment below will be reverfed and entered for the whole; if otherwife, the judgment will be affirmed.

WASHINGTON on the fame fide. The rule of law, as a general one, is truly ftated by Mr. Williams. The doctrine formerly prevailed in all its rigor, but it has long fince been mitigated, and it is now as well fettled, as any principle whatever, that *heirs* in a will may take *eo nomine* by purchafe, if the court be fatisfied that fuch was the intention of the teftator. • The cafe of Long and Beaumont, cited by Mr. Williams, proves it, and is much like the prefent. In this, as in that cafe, the heir was living when the will was made, and the teftator took notice that the *anceftor alfo was living*, a circumftance much relied upon in that cafe. In this cafe, as in that of Brooking and White, the teftator has made a provifion for his heir at law, which proves that he could not intend to leave any thing to defcend. But, what renders this cafe ftill ftronger is, that there was an evident intention to make an equal divifion of this tract of land amongft the children, and to prevent the poffibility of an inteftacy as to any part, the refiduum of the real eftate is difpofed of.

2d point. Independent of the ftrong argument to be derived from the reference to the devife to the heirs of Abraham Vanmeter, it is clear that the heirs of Magdalena took an eftate tail. It is not true, I conceive, that where *heirs* or *iffue* take by purchafe, they take only an eftate for life. If they be defcribed by the former name, they take the abfolute property and dominion; if by the latter, a limited fee. Trevor and Trevor 1 *Eq. Ca. Ab.* 387.

But fuppofe only an eftate for life paffed, ftill that is fufficient to entitle the leffor of the plaintiff to recover. And in that cafe the deed from Prudence to Vandevier could not produce a forfeiture as Mr. Williams fuppofes, becaufe the conveyance has its operation under the ftatute of ufes. The leafe is a deed of *bargain and fale*, which by the operation of the ftatute, vefts
the

the poſſeſſion, ſo as enable the leſſee to receive a releaſe. The only difference between this mode of conveyance before, and ſince the ſtatute is, that in the one caſe, *actual entry* by the leſſee was neceſſary for the releaſe to operate upon; in the other, the bargain and ſale paſſes the uſe, and the ſtatute executes the poſſeſſion, which enables the leſſee to receive a releaſe. Now the leaſe in queſtion is made by a deed of *bargain and ſale*, and recites the intent of it to be, *to put the leſſee in poſſeſſion, ſo as to enable him by virtue of the ſtatute of uſes to receive a releaſe.*

MARSHALL for the appellant. We do not contend, that *heirs* or *iſſue*, ſo named, are incapable of taking by purchaſe, but that the general rule as ſtated by us, and admitted on the other ſide, is never departed from, but in favor of a clear intention, plainly deſcribing the *perſon* who by that name is to take. Is Prudence ſo deſcribed? There is not a circumſtance in the caſe to prove that ſhe was meant. It does not appear that the teſtator knew that ſhe exiſted; for if he had, it is probable he would have named her, in the ſame manner as he has done others of his grand children; and if he knew ſhe was living, then it would ſeem that he rather meant to exclude her. The deſcription is too vague for the court to ſay who was intended, and therefore the deviſe is void for uncertainty. Suppoſe there had been a ſon who had lived;—could the court ſay that Prudence ſhould take in excluſion of that ſon? Or is it not more probable, that the teſtator would prefer the male to the female iſſue?—If the caſe ſuppoſed had happened, and the ſon would have been entitled, then it cannot be ſaid that *Prudence was intended to be deſcribed.* The argument that no perſon can be ſuppoſed to intend a partial inteſtacy, if admitted in the latitude contended for, would entirely defeat the general rule, becauſe it would apply in all the caſes which have been cited, where the heir not being properly deſcribed, it has been determined, that he could not take as a purchaſer. Long and Lamming is not like this caſe; the deviſe there, is to A. C. and to her heirs *male* and *female* equally to be divided, as well thoſe *begotten* as to be begotten. So that there was no uncertainty who was to take. In this caſe it might mean a ſon, or a daughter. The caſe of Brooking *vs* White, comes within the exception, as the teſtator took notice that the anceſtor had children living. The deviſe in queſtion is therefore void, being an *immediate one*, which could not take effect upon the death of the teſtator.

As to the nature of the eſtate given to Prudence, (if ſhe be entitled to any thing) it cannot I conceive exceed an eſtate for life. I know of no caſe in which the heir takes by purchaſe, that he takes a greater eſtate than for life, unleſs words of inheritance are engrafted upon the deviſe, or a ſtrong intention appears to paſs a greater eſtate. As to the reference to the limitations to Abraham Vanmeter's heirs, the counſel aſk too much when they call upon the court to ſupply the words " to *Abraham Vanmeter* and his heirs" &c. inſtead of thoſe actually uſed by the teſtator.

As to the laſt point, I think it impoſſible for the court to ſupply a whole courſe, without a ſingle fact being ſtated by the jury. The teſtator may have blundered, but I cannot perceive upon what principle this court can correct it. It would be to *make* not to *interpret a will.*

LYONS J. delivered the opinion of the court.

The firſt queſtion made in this cauſe is, whether the deviſe to the heirs of the body of Magdalena be void or not. The argument to prove it void is, that no perſon can be the heir of an anceſtor whilſt living, and therefore, as ſuch, cannot take. But the court are of opinion that the word *heir* may mean *heir apparent,* and that ſuch was the intention in the preſent caſe. We are clear, that the teſtator meant to give the eſtate to the perſon *who ſhould be the heir apparent of Magdalena at the time of the teſtator's death,* and that he has uſed proper words to convey ſuch an intention. If the heir apparent at that period had been a ſon, he would certainly have taken, but being a daughter, ſhe took as ſuch by purchaſe.

The ſecond queſtion was, what eſtate ſhe took? It is unimportant for the court to decide, whether ſhe took an eſtate of inheritance or not, ſince as ſhe is found to be ſtill living, her grantee has a title to recover in this action, though ſhe only took an eſtate for life.

But it was contended, that if ſhe took only an eſtate for life, the deeds of leaſe and releaſe produced a forfeiture of it. We are of opinion that there is nothing in this objection. The conveyance has its operation under the ſtatute of uſes, and therefore the grantor could paſs no greater eſtate than ſhe might lawfully part with.

The next objection is that the verdict finds the land in queſtion to have been deviſed to *James* inſtead of *Jacobus* who is the leſſor. This is clearly a miſtake in the jury, and ought not

not to be regarded, since the description of the devise is sufficiently plain when he is called *the lessor of the plaintiff.*

The last point is attended with more difficulty. It respects the boundaries of the land upon the special statements in the verdict. There is some inconsistency in the finding, which might be important, if the court doubted about the true boundaries of the land intended to be devised. It is evident that the testator had surveyed this land, and marked down by specified boundaries, the part intended for each of the devisees, and that he must have had the plat before him when he made his will. The boundaries of the other devisees are right; when he comes to describe the parcel in question, he begins right and continues so, with little variation in course or distance, till he gets to s; then by mistake in transcribing the courses, from the plat, into the will, he appears to have overlooked one line viz. s, t, which creates the difficulty. If it be omittted altogether, none of the subsequent lines are right; if it be supplied from the plat, then they are all right and the disposion of the whole tract is compleat. The court has no hesitation in saying, that the testator's intention was to pursue the lines which comprehends the 30 acres not included in the judgment of the District Court, and therefore, that their judgment though right as to the plaintiff's title, is erroneous in not comprehending the land contained within the lines of the survey described by the letters s, t, E, and to s again.

But as that error was in favor of the appellant, the costs of this court ought to be paid by him to the appellee as the party prevailing, although the judgment be reversed.

The judgment must therefore be reversed and entered for the appellee, for the land contained within the survey taken in this cause and described by the small letters m, n, o, p, q, r, s, t, and the large letters E, D, C, B, and to little m, together with his costs in this court. Judgment reversed.

HOOMES Executor of ELLIOTT,

against

SMOCK.

ELLIOTT having brought a suit at law against Stanard upon a bond, Smock, the appellee, became Stanard's appearance

ance bail. Stanard having failed to give special bail, judgment was rendered against Smock in the County Court. On the chancery side of that court, Smock filed a bill, stating, that Beverley being possessed of Stanard's bond, given for a sum of money lost at unlawful gaming, assigned it to Elliott, who afterwards understanding the nature of the consideration for which it had been given, delivered up that bond to Stanard and obtained from him another in lieu thereof, upon which the judgment was obtained. The bill seeks a discovery of those circumstances and prays for an injunction. Elliott by his answer insists that the assignment to him was made for a valuable consideration. That he is ignorant of the consideration for which Stanard gave his bond to Beverley, but that the whole transaction relative to his obtaining the bond, was on his part fair and *bona fide*, and as far as he knows and believes in strict conformity with the laws of the land. He further states that Stanard acknowledged that the debt was justly due, and promised that he would pay it. That he applied to Stanard for payment, which not being made, he proposed to him to take in the bond and an order drawn by Beverley, and to give a new obligation for the whole, to which Stanard readily consented. Beverley, who was also made a defendant, states in his answer, that a bond was given by Stanard to him for money won at gaming, amounting to £80 — that he owed 35 barrels of corn to Elliott, which not being able to pay when it was demanded, he assigned the above bond to him, and also drew an order for £10: 10, (making together the exact amount of the bond for which this judgment was recovered) in discharge of the corn debt, which Elliott accepted; that Elliott knew those sums were due on account of money won at gaming. Only one witness was examined, who proves the bond for £80 to have been given for a gaming debt, and that *after the assignment* but before the execution of the new bond he informed Elliott of this fact.

The County Court perpetuated the injunction, from which Elliott appealed to the High Court of Chancery, and pending the appeal died. The suit being revived by his administrator the decree was affirmed, from which an appeal was prayed to this court.

Wickham for the appellant. I contend 1st, that the decree in this cause was not warranted by the proofs exhibited, and 2dly, That a court of equity ought not to relieve in such a case as this, but leave the parties as the law had placed them.

1st,

1st, It is a rule, that the anfwer of one defendant is not evidence againſt another; and therefore, Beverley's anfwer muſt be put out of the cafe; if fo, there is no proof at all of notice to Elliott *prior to the affignment*, and therefore he is not liable to the original equity attached to the bond. The cafe of Buckner and others *vs* Smith &c. (ante 296) is a ſtrong authority for the appellant.

2dly, But if notice were proved, the appellee is not I conceive entitled to the relief prayed for. Smock can be in no better fituation than Stanard would have been, had he been plaintiff in equity. The matter relied upon in equity, to defeat the legal advantage obtained by the appellant, might at law have furniſhed a compleat defence; but after a judgment obtained there, a Court of Equity will not relieve againſt an innocent aſſignee, without notice of the illegal confideration, fo as to deprive him of the advantage which that judgment has given him. The equity of an innocent aſſignee who has fairly paid his money for this bond, is at leaſt equal with that of the obligor, and therefore the law muſt prevail.

LEE for the appellee. I admit that in general, the anfwer of one defendant cannot be read for, or againſt another; but there are exceptions to the rule, and this cafe furniſhes an example. For Beverly having aſſigned this debt to Elliott, there is a privity between them, and the latter, deriving his right under the former, is bound by his acts. Beverley's anfwer therefore, which acknowledges that the bond was given upon an illegal confideration, ought, as againſt Elliott, to be taken as evidence of that fact.

2dly, Whether Elliott had notice or not before the aſſignment of the bond, that it was given upon a gaming confideration, is immaterial, becaufe the bond is by the law abfolutely void, and can never be made valid by aſſignment. The ſtatute confiders it as being fo tainted, that no ſhift or change whatever can purge it of its original fin. It is the duty of all courts to arreſt the money before it is paid, though the parties may confederate to elude the law, and therefore a court of equity is bound to interpofe, though a judgment has been obtained. The cafe of Buckner and others, *vs* Smith &c. is entirely unlike to the prefent, for the ground upon which that decifion was made, was the fraud practifed by Beverley upon Dixon, by inducing him to purchafe the bond.

The bill having expreſſly charged notice, and Elliott having declined anfwering it, the facts proved in the cafe and ſtated in his

his anfwer, furnifh ftrong prefumption that the charge is true. It is a rule, that where a man defends himfelf on the ground of want of notice, he muft in direct terms admit or deny it, if it be charged. A perfon claiming a gaming debt in a court of juftice, can never be confidered as having equal equity with the oppofite party; becaufe fuch a claim is in itfelf iniquitous.

LYONS J. delivered the opinion of the court. It has been rightly contended by the counfel for the appellee, that all bonds given for a gaming confideration are void as between the parties; and it is equaly true that the affignee cannot ftand in a better fituation than the obligee, unlefs there be fome particular circumftances in his favor independent of the mere affignment. But if an innocent man fhall be induced by the obligor to become a purchafer of fuch a bond, it is a deceit upon him, and he ought not to be fubject to the fame equity to which the obligor was entitled againft the obligee. In this cafe, Elliot was induced by the debtor to take the bond, who renewed it without difclofing his objection; afterwards fuffered a judgment to pafs at law, and then reforts to a Court of Equity for relief. The province of that court is to relieve againft frand, and not to fanction it, and in general it will leave the parties to the law even if their equity were equal; much lefs will that court interfere, where the equity is altogether on the fide of him who has obtained a legal advantage. As to the facts in the cafe, they are with the plaintiff at law; his anfwer is contradicted by one witnefs only, without circumftances to ftrengthen the teftimony, for the anfwer of the other defendant as it could not benefit his co-defendant, cannot injure him.

The COURT entered a decree to the following effect, viz: William Elliott by his anfwer having denied notice of the illegal confideration, upon which, it is fuggefted by the bill, the bond from Beverley Stanard was given, and there appearing but one witnefs to contradict the anfwer in this refpect, without fufficient circumftances to corroborate his teftimony, Elliot ought to be confidered as an innocent affignee of the faid bond, and the fubfequent bond taken by him of Stanard upon which the judgment was obtained was not tainted or effected by the illegal confideration of the firft bond. That the decree which injoins the plaintiff below from proceeding to execute his judgment is erroneous. The decree of the High Court of Chancery and County Court, muft be reverfed with cofts, the injunction obtained is to be diffolved, and the bill difmiffed.

END OF THE FIRST VOLUME.

A
TABLE
OF THE PRINCIPAL MATTERS.

A
ABATEMENT.

1. Declaration, that A. the defendant, together with B. affumed. The writ as to B. having been returned "no inhabitant," it was abated as to him. The verdict and judgment may be entered against A. only. Brown *vs* Belches. 9.

2. In detinue, the jury found a virdict for the plaintiff, if the law upon the facts *agreed to be stated* be for him, otherwise for the defendant. Before they were agreed, the defendant died, and a *sci fa.* issued to his executors, to shew cause why the facts should not be agreed. The executors appeared and agreed a case. This will be binding upon them, tho' they might have refused to agree to them, and in that case, they might have insisted upon the abatement of the suit. Hooe & Harrison *vs* Pierce. 212

ACTION.

1. An action may be maintained by a creditor upon the bond given by the executor for performing the duties of his office, but the plaintiff must first fix a devastavit against the executor, before he can resort to this remedy against the securities. Braxton &c. *vs* Winslow. 31.

2. The defendant *as Treasurer* of the *Jockey Club*, agreed to rent from the plaintiff a piece of ground, for the use of the club, and by an agreement in writing, bound himself to pay the rent. He is individuably liable. M'Williams *vs* Willis. 199.

3. An action of *debt* will not lie against a sheriff, for levying an execution upon the property of the plaintiff's tenant without paying him a year's rent. It should be an action on the *case* for consequential damages. Bird *vs* Cocke. 232.

4. An action of trespass *for freedom*, is *in form* an action for a personal tort; *in substance*, it is a remedy to try the question of freedom or slavery, and therefore, *two or more* may join in it. Coleman *vs* Dick. 238.

5. An action of debt may be brought upon a defective forthcoming bond, even after an unsuccessful motion has been made upon it. Hewlett *vs* Chamberlayne. 367.

ACTS

A TABLE OF THE PRINCIPAL MATTERS.

ACTS OF ASSEMBLY.

1. Under the act of 1758, intituled "An act for preventing fraudulent gifts of slaves;" a gift not by deed or will, tho' possession were delivered, is void. Turner *vs* Turner. 139.

2. The act passed in 1787, entituled "An act to explain and amend the acts for preventing fraudulent gifts of slaves;" is *prospective* in its operation, and cannot affect gifts of slaves made prior to its passage. Turner *vs* Turner. 139.

3. The act of October 1779 C. 3, "For discouraging extensive credit, and repealing the law prescribing the method of proving book debts; applies only to the store accounts of retail merchants. Tomlin *vs* Kelly 190.

4. The two first branches of the 5th section of the law for scaling debts, was intended for the benefit of debtors, the 3d, is equally intended to benefit the creditors, as the debtors. Watson *vs* Alexander. 353.

5. The proper mode of bringing before the court the equity claimed under the 5th sect. of the above law, is by a special verdict finding the facts; or for the court to receive evidence of the equitable circumstances and so instruct the jury; or to hear the evidence at the trial, and correct the verdict according to the extent of the equity proved. But it is improper for the court, after the verdict, to examine testimony, and so to vary the verdict. Watson *vs* Alexander. 354.

ADMIRALTY.

1. A negro who went by the name of *Taliver*, the property of the defendant, ran off to the enemy, and was afterwards recaptured by an American vessel of war. He was libelled and condemned by the name of *Jack Robinson*, and being sold under the sentence of the court of Admiralty, was purchased by the plaintiff. The defendant procured a warrant under the act of 1782. ch. 8. and retook him. The sentence and sale was not binding upon the former proprietor, as he was no party, and the negro was not libelled by the name he usually bore. *Aliter* if the condemnation had been by a foreign court. Hoe & Harrison *vs* Pierce. 212.

2. The slave in the above case was not lawful prize, the jury not having found, that he belonged to an inhabitant of Great Britain, or that he was taken in war. 216.

ADVANCEMENT.

1. Where a child is advanced with money, or negroes, the donee need not bring into hotchpot the increase of the one, or account for the interest upon the other. Beckwith *vs* Butler. 225.

2. In general, equity will not aid a volunteer, in *supplying legal defects* in a prior deed, against

gainſt a ſubſequent volunteer. The caſes of advancements for younger children otherwiſe unprovided for, forms an exception to this rule. Ward *vs* Webber. 274.

AGENT.

1. Agents,—Their powers, and how far they may bind their principals. Hoe & Harriſon *vs* Oxley &c. 23.

2. The defendant, *as Treaſurer* of the *Jockey Club*, agreed to rent from the plaintiff a piece of ground for the uſe of the club and by an agreement in writing bound himſelf to pay the rent. He is individuably liable. M'Williams *vs* Willis. 199.

3. If in conſequence of a notorious agency, the agent is in the habit of drawing bills, which the principal has regularly paid, this is ſuch an affirmance of his power to draw, that the principal will be bound to pay other bills, tho' the agent ſhould *miſapply the money* raiſed by the bills. Hoe & Harriſon *vs* Oxley 23.

AGREED CASE.

See ABATEMENT, No. 2.

AGREEMENT.

1. An agreement between the children of a family, in the life time of their parent, to divide his eſtate equally between them at his death, let him make amongſt them whatever diſtribution he might think proper, will be enforced in equity, if made out clearly by proof. Nelſon *vs* Nelſon. 136.

2. A private, domeſtic converſation between a huſband and his wife, wherein the former ſpeaks of an intention once formed, (but then relinquiſhed,) of giving a certain portion to his daughter, ſhall not bind the father to give that portion to the future huſband of the daughter, Baniſter's Ex. *vs* Shore. 173.

3. A. agrees to ſell his right to land in poſſeſſion of B. if 3 perſons (then named) ſhall by ſuch a day decide, that he has a title, and ſhall fix the price which B ſhall pay for it. No award was made. C. a purchaſer from B. (but with notice of this agreement) cannot compel A. to make a conveyance, nor to ſubmit thoſe points to any other mode of adjuſtment. Smallwood *vs* Hanſborough 290

4. The parties agreed to endorſe upon the written contract, a memorandum permitting the debtor to pay in money, or in property, at a valuation to be made by two honeſt men to be choſen by the parties. If the creditor refuſe to make the endorſement, chancery will relieve, and will conſider the memorandum as endorſed. Dandridge *vs* Harris. 326.

4. In the above caſe, if the creditor refuſe to join in nominating the valuer, the debtor might plead the ſpecial matter, & avail himſelf of it at law; or the Court

A TABLE OF THE PRINCIPAL MATTERS.

Court of Chancery might name valuers, unless the parties will do it by a certain day. *ibid* 6. See Contract, No. 1, 2, 3

AMENDMENT.

1 The court reversed the judgment of the inferior court, because that court (after judgment upon a special demurrer) refused to permit the defendant to amend his plea. Cooke *vs* Beale's Executor. 313.

2. Where one party is permitted to amend, or amends without leave, the other has a right to plead *de novo*, whether the new plea be material to his defence or not. Cosby &c. *vs* Hite. 365.

3. Verdict that the land in question was devised to *James* (instead of *Jacobus*,) the lessor of the plaintiff. This is an evident mistake in the jury, and amendable. Pendleton *vs* Vandevier. 388

APPEAL.

1. Upon a bond with a penalty, the jury may make their verdict of the aggregate of principal and interest, and if they do, the defendant cannot appeal, for it is for his benefit. Smith *vs* Harmanson. 7

2. The appellant dies, and the appeal being revived against his executor, the judgment is affirmed. Damages ought not to be awarded against the proper estate of the executor, in case of deficiency in that of the testator. Hudson *vs* Ross. 74.

3. The appellee being dead, an appearance was entered for the executors, and on the motion of their counsel, the cause was tried without waiting for a *sci fa*. Daniel *vs* Robinson's executor. 154

Contra. Wood *vs* Webb [note to page 154.]

4. Upon an appeal from the judgment of an Inferior Court, errors in the execution, or replevy bond, issued, or taken after the judgment, will not be noticed. They are merely *ministerial acts*, and must be corrected in the same court upon motion; and if the court give an erroneous opinion on that motion, the party injured may then appeal and have it corrected. Leftwich *vs* Stoval. 306

5. Security given upon an appeal from the High Court of Chancery — What? Braxton *vs* Morris. 380

6. If judgment be in part favorable to the appellant, and it is reversed as to that part, the appellant shall pay costs. Pendleton *vs* Vandevier. 389

APPLICATION.

See PAYMENT.

APPOINTMENT.

1. See AGREEMENT No. 5

ARBITRAMENT and AWARD.

1. Reasons for setting aside awards, are either for some illegality,

A TABLE OF THE PRINCIPAL MATTERS.

legality, or injustice apparent on the face of them, or for misbehavior in the arbitrators. Shermer vs Beal. 14

2. The Court of Chancery having directed an issue, the parties waved the trial by jury, and submitted the question to five persons mutually chosen by them, and agreed that their report should be certified in lieu of a verdict. The court must consider the report of the arbitrators as *an award*, and to be governed by the same rules and principles which prevail in cases of awards. Pleasants &c. vs Ross. 156

3. To set aside an award for *mistake* in the arbitrators, either as to law, or fact, the mistake must appear on the face of it. Or if the arbitrators will certify the principles on which they proceeded, the court will set aside the award, if improperly decided. Affidavits may be introduced, but they must go to prove partiality, or misbehavior, and not mistakes in law or fact. 158

4. When an issue is tried, it is under the superintendance of the court, who will prevent the introduction of improper testimony, and if the verdict be against evidence, the court will certify this, and the Chancellor will not be satisfied. If no certificate be given, still the Chancellor may direct a new trial on affidavits, tending to prove *misbehavior in the jury*, but not that their verdict is *against evidence.* Ibid.

5. Where an award is for the performance of a special thing, as to make a conveyance, equity will decree it. Smallwood vs Mercer. 290

6. See AGREEMENT No. 3

7. An award made *for tobacco,* upon a reference by rule of court, in an action where no declaration was filed, but the damages laid in the writ were *in money*; determined to be good. Leftwich vs Stoval. 303

8. If the arbitrators be made parties to a suit for setting aside an award, they may demur to the bill. Shermer vs Beal. 14

ASSIGNMENT.

1. The assignee of a gaming bond, stands in no better situation than the obligee would have done; but it is otherwise, both at law and in equity, if he be induced by assurances of payment from the obligor, to become the purchaser of it. Buckner vs Smith &c. 299

2. If a man be induced to purchase a bond given for a gaming consideration, (not knowing that circumstance) by the obligor, equity will not relieve against a judgment obtained upon it. Hoomes vs Smock. 389

ASSUMPSIT.

1. Declaration, that the plaintiff having obtained a judgment against I. G. and being willing to give the said I. G. an opportunity

A TABLE OF THE PRINCIPAL MATTERS.

portunity of selling his property to advantage, an agreement was entered into, (which is set forth verbatim) between the plaintiff, the defendant, and the said I. G. whereby, the defendant bound himself to see the balance of the debt, (which should remain unsatisfied by the sale of the property) paid by such a day. That the intention was to favor the said I. G. in consideration whereof, defendant assumed to pay such balance; avers a sale made, and that a balance still remained unsatisfied. To the agreement are three scrolls annexed, but it is not said to be sealed in the agreement itself, nor in the attestation.

The agreement is the only inducement to the action, and the foundation of the action is the subsequent assumpsit, and therefore it is sustainable. Baird &c. vs Blaigrove. 170

2. A parol agreement made subsequent to one under seal, may be declared upon, tho' it should alter the terms of the written agreement. *Ibid*

3. D. carried a letter to the defendant upon the subject of the defendant's prior promise to indemnify F, and the defendant after reading the letter promised that he would indemnify F. F. may recover upon this promise. Field *vs* Spotswood. 280

4. Promise to indemnify against an act then performed—where good? Field *vs* Spotswood. 280

ATTORNEY.

1. Payment to an attorney at law is good, on the custom of the country, particularly if he have possession of the specialty. Under particular circumstances it might be otherwise, as if notice were given that no such power was vested in the attorney. Hudson *vs* Johnson. 10

BAIL.

1. If an office judgment be entered against the sheriff for not having taken or returned a bail bond, in a case where bail is not demandable, the court ought to set it aside as to the sheriff. Williams *vs* Campbell. 153

2. It is no objection to a bail piece given by one defendant, that it takes no notice of the other defendant. Smith *vs* Wallace. 254

3. If the special bail before or after judgment, surrender the principal to the *sheriff*, his discharge is compleat by the surrender, whether he return the receipt *forthwith* to the clerk or not, and if any injury result to the plaintiff on that account, his action is against the bail. Cooke *vs* Beal's executor. 313

B

BAR.

See CHANCERY No. 6

BILL OF EXCHANGE

1. See AGENT No. 3

A TABLE OF THE PRINCIPAL MATTERS.

2. If notice of the protest of a foreign bill be given within 18 months, it will suffice under the act of Assembly, unless there be particular circumstances to warrant an exception from the general rule. Stott *vs* Alexander. 335

BILL of EXCEPTIONS.

1. A bill of exceptions cannot be considered in the light of a demurrer to evidence. In the latter, the court may (if the case be clear) refuse to compel the other party to join, and may instruct the jury, or leave the question with them. Wroe *vs* Washington &c. 362

BOND.

1. See APPEAL No. 1.

2. An endorsement on a bond, made by consent of parties, tho' at a future day, is to be considered as part of the bond, as much so as if it had been incorporated with it. Shermer *vs* Beale. 14

3. Upon a motion against a deputy sheriff and his securities upon a joint bond, if the principle plead *non est factum*, this must be first tried and decided against the plea, before judgment can be rendered against the securities. Asberry *vs* Calloway. 72

4. See ASSIGNMENT No. 1 and 2.

5. In a joint bond, the charge will survive against the surviving obligor, but the fact of the survivorship must be pleaded. Bentley *vs* Harmanson. 273

BREACH.

1. Bond with condition, that the defendant would faithfully collect certain debts due to the obligee, and would pay the amount so collected, and return an account of his collections, and surrender up all bonds not fully paid, except such as might be lodged with lawyer's and clerks. Declaration lays the breach in the defendant's *neglecting to bring suits for the recovery of the debts*—variance not material. Hawkins's Executors *vs* Berkley. 204

2. In a motion upon a forthcoming bond, it is the business of the defendant to prove performance, and not of the plaintiff to shew a breach. Nicolas *vs* Fletcher. 330

3. In a joint bond, the charge will survive against the surviving obligor but the fact of the survivorship must be pleaded. Bentley *vs* Harminson. 273

C

CAVEAT.

1. The effect of a caveat is to prevent the emanation of a grant, not to set one aside. Wilcox *vs* Calloway. 40

CHANCERY.

1. A court of Equity may set aside a verdict improperly obtained, and award a new trial Cochran *vs* Street. 79

2. Where a man fraudulently obtains a patent in preference to

to one having a prior equitable title, if this be proved, a court of equity has competent jurisdiction, and can afford the most ample relief.

White *vs* Jones. 118.

3. In what cafe a court of equity has jurisdiction? See Thornton & Spotswood. 142.

Hunter *vs* Spotswood. 145.

4. If a caufe come on upon bill and anfwer, the latter muft be confidered as true in all its parts. Kennedy *vs* Baylor. 163

5. Bill to fore-close.—The county court appointed *Commiffioners* to afcertain the damages which the land had fuftained whilft in the poffeffion of the mortgagee, and deducted the amount reported, from the payments made by the mortgagor. Decree affirmed. Kennedy *vs* Baylor. 162.

6. The plaintiff went to trial, in a cafe where he might have fued in equity, and a verdict by furprife was rendered againft him. He fhall not afterwards refort to a Court of Chancery. Tarpley *vs* Dobyns. 185

7. The value and profits of land being in the nature of damages, ought to be afcertained by *a jury* upon an iffue to be directed by the Court of Chancery, and not *by commiffioners*. Euftace *vs* Gafkins 190

8. If after anfwer filed, and depofitions taken, the plaintiff makes new parties, and files a new bill, the depofitions previoufly taken, cannot be read againft the new defendants. Jones *vs* Williams. 230

9. If the judge before whom the iffue is tried, certifies the verdict to be againft evidence, the Chancellor ought not to be fatisfied with it, but fhould fet it afide. Southall *vs* M'-Keand. 337

10. See ARBITRAMENT and AWARD, No. 2, 3, 4, 5.

AGREEMENT No. 5.

EQUITY No. 1, 3, 4, 5.

CLERK.

1. Quere, If a fheriff may levy a diftrefs for fees due the *deputy* clerk of a court. Anderfon *vs* Bernard. 186

COMMISSION.

1. An executor, who is alfo a *nephew* to the teftator, and to whom a legacy is given, is entitled to his commiffion alfo, and that, by cuftom, is generally fixed at 5 per cent. Granberry *vs* Granberry. 250

COMPENSATION.

See CONTRACT No. 3.

CONDITION.

1. Devife of land to A. upon condition, that fo foon as he arrives at full age, he *joins* the executors in a conveyance of certain flaves to fuch perfons as they may fell them to. Upon A's arrival at age, he makes a declaration in writing which is recorded,

A TABLE OF THE PRINCIPAL MATTERS.

recorded, that he will perform the conditions in the will. He afterwards fells and conveys the land to I S. and then fettles the flaves upon his family. This is no breach of the condition. Keene *vs* Lee, 239

2. The declaration paffed away all his right to the flaves. *ibid*

3d. He was not bound to convey, until the executors had fold and *applied to him to join in a conveyance*. Ibid.

4. The fettlement was a fraud upon I S. and void as to all the world but the grantor. *Ibid*.

5. See BREACH, No 2.

CONSIDERATION.

1. What is a fufficient confideration to give validity to a promife to fave harmlefs. Carr *vs* Gooch. 260

2. See ASSUMPSIT No 1, 4.

CONTRACT.

1. A. contracts to deliver to B. £260 current money in final fettlements, at the rate of 20/. fuch fettlements, for each 13 d. current money, *on the 1ft of Dec.* But B, agrees, that the fame may be difcharged by the payment of a like fum in faid fettlements at any time *on or before the 1ft of Nov. preceding*, at the rate of 20/. fuch fettlements, for each 26 d. current money. The contract is not ufurious, but the 13 d. is to be confidered as a penalty, and the time of delivery is the 1ft of November. Groves *vs* Graves. 1

2. The rule for eftimating the damages in this cafe, is the value of the certificates at the time when they ought to have been delivered, and not that at which the caufe was tried. 3

3. A contract to pay a larger fum at a future day upon non-payment of the fum agreed upon at a prior day, is not ufurious, but the encreafed fum will be confidered as a penalty, and relievable againft in a court of equity upon compenfation being made, and that compenfation is legal intereft, unlefs fome fpecific damage can be fhewn. Winflow *vs* Dawfon. 119

4. See DAMAGES, No. 2.

COSTS.

1. Cofts by whom payable. Thompfon *vs* Davenport. 128

2. If an executor lay an affumpfit to himfelf and fails in his fuit, he fhall pay cofts. Thornton *vs* Jett. 139

3. See APPEAL No. 6

NEW TRIAL, No 3.

COURT.

1. The court muft decide upon the admiffibility of evidence, but cannot give a direction refpecting the weight of it. Rofs *vs* Gill. 90

2. The court have no right to inftruct the jury as to the weight of evidence, this being a fubject proper only for the jury to decide upon, unlefs it be brought before the court by a demurrer to evidence. Keel &c. *vs* Herbert. 203

3. Upon a motion for a nonfuit, the court may give their opinion that the plaintiff has no caufe

B 3

A TABLE OF THE PRINCIPAL MATTERS.

cause of action, and may direct him to be called, but he may appear and refuse to be nonsuited. So, the court may declare the action not maintainable; or may refuse to give any opinion, and so leave the whole to the jury. Thweat &c. *vs* Finch. 219

4. Though in *general*, the court need not state the facts which induced them to grant a new trial, yet if it be awarded against *an established rule of practice*, the ground for doing so ought to be disclosed. Boswell &c. *vs* Jones. 325

COVENANT.

1. Upon a covenant to warrant the title of a slave in which the heirs only are bound, an action will lie against the executors. Lee *vs* Cooke. 306

D

DAMAGES.

1. What interest judgment shall be entered for, upon a motion of the sheriff against his deputy, where a judgment has been obtained against the sheriff for taxes. Alberry *vs* Calloway. 72

2. If a man fraudulently purchase certificates, by taking an improper advantage of the person from whom he purchases, a court of equity in setting aside the contract will decree the defendant, in case he has parted with the original certificates, to purchase others, or to pay in specie the value they are of, *at the* time the cause is tried. Reynolds *vs* Waller. 164

3. See CONTRACT No. 1, 2.

APPEAL No. 2.

CHANCERY No. 5, 7.

DEBT.

1. See APPEAL No. 1.

DECLARATION.

1. Action of debt on a protested bill of exchange for £187: 15, *sterling money*, of the value of £250: 6: 8, *current money*. The declaration ought not to have demanded the current money value of a debt due in sterling money. Scott's executor *vs* Call. 115

2. A parol agreement reduced to writing does not change the nature of the contract; the writing is merely evidence of the agreement, and it ought to be produced, though not specially declared upon. M'Williams *vs* Willis. 202

3. Case against 2 inspectors of tobacco at *Robert Bolling's warehouse*, for that they having inspected a hogshead of tobacco, the property of the plaintiff, they refused to deliver the notes, as by law and the *duty of their office*, they were bound to do, but had *delivered the notes* and the tobacco to another, having no authority to receive it, *contrary to law, and the duty of their office*. Objections to the declaration for being multifarious, and for not stating the warehouse

A TABLE OF THE PRINCIPAL MATTERS.

house to be a *public one* over-ruled. Thweat and Hinton *vs* Finch. 217

4. Quere, If in an action against A, upon a bond given by A and B, it is necessary to alledge non-repayment by B? Peter *vs* Cocke. 257

5. *Indeb. assump.* for £ 171 : 5 : 4, sterling, of the value of £228 . 7 currency, for so much advanced by the plaintiff's to F and S. at the request of the defendant &c. laying the damages in current mony. Verdict in current money. The jury were right in finding the value of the sterling money, instead of leaving it to the court, as in the case of Scott's executor's *vs* Call. Barnett &c. *vs* Watson &c. 378

6. See BREACH No. 1.

PLEADING No. 2.

INTEREST No. 1.

JURISDICTION No. 1.

7. Reference by rule of court. After judgment entered upon the award, defendant cannot object to the want of a declaration. Leftwich *vs* Stovall. 303

8. In an action by the vendee of a slave, against the vendor, upon a covenant of warranty, he need not state in the declaration, nor prove, that he gave notice to the vendor, of the pendency of the suit in which the possession was recovered from him. Lee &c. *vs* Cooke. 306

DEED.

1. In what court a mortgage of personal property may be recorded? Clayborn *vs* Hill. 177

2. A father by deed executed, conveyed to his daughter several tracts of land with many slaves &c. After this, the father got possession of the deed surreptitiously, and cancelled it, upon a bill brought by the daughter, the court restored the deed to its legal force. Ward *vs* Webber. 274

3. If the proof, or acknowledgment of a deed, made by a *non resident*, for land lying in Virginia, be not certified according to law, tho' it should be admitted to record, it cannot be read in evidence as a *recorded deed*. But it will be sufficient at the trial to prove the execution by one witness, tho' he be not the subscribing witness, if the subscribing witnesses be dead, or cannot be procured. Turner *vs* Stip. 319

4. A deed tho' not recorded, is valid between the parties. Turner *vs* Stip. 319

5. If tenant for life, by deeds of lease and release under the statute of uses, conveys the fee, it creates no forfeiture. Pendleton *vs* Vandevier. 388

6. See ADVANCEMENT No. 2.

AGREEMENT No. 4.

EQUITY No. 4.

DEMURRER.

A TABLE OF THE PRINCIPAL MATTERS.

DEMURRER TO EVIDENCE.

1. A demurrer to evidence may be allowed at any time before the jury retire, altho' the party offering the demurrer may have examined witnesses, the whole evidence on both sides being stated, (which ought always to be done) unless the court think the case clear against the party, in which case, the court may refuse to receive the demurrer. Hoyle *vs* Young. 151
2. If one of the parties offer a demurrer to the evidence, the court (if the evidence be clearly against him) may refuse to compel the other party to join. Thweat &c. *vs* Finch. 220
3. See BILL of EXCEPTIONS No. 1.

COURT No. 2.

DEPOSITION.

See WITNESS No. 2.

DEPRECIATION.

1. Bond dated 1st of February 1780, payable on or before the 17th of December 1781, *with interest from the 16th of February 1779*. These latter words, with other circumstances, will fix the period at which the scale of depreciation ought to be applied, to *February* 1779. Pleasants *vs* Bibb. 8
2. An account for goods not delivered, nor accepted as a payment, nor liquidated between the parties, ought not to be taken as a payment in paper money, so as to stand at the nominal value, according to the strict words of the act, but should be received as an off-sett, and adjusted (especially in equity) upon just principles. Hill *vs* Southerland's executor. 133
3. The legal scale of 1777, and 1778, is not a just rule in itself, not corresponding with the general opinion of the citizens at the time it was made, as to depreciation; nor does the scale *at any time*, give a proper rule for fixing the price of *imported goods*. 134
4. In April 1778, a sum of paper money was lent, not to be repaid in less than 12 months thereafter. The money was tendered shortly after the 12 months, (but not on the very day) and was refused. A mortgage having been given to secure the debt, the mortgagee brought an ejectment and recovered the possession, but the judgment was injoined. The mortgagee shall receive the money according to the scale of the day it was borrowed (notwithstanding he had received the identical money in discharge of a *specie* debt and notwithstanding the mortgagor made use of it to discharge a specie debt) without interest, from the time of the tender, to that of new demand. Wilton *vs* Keeling. 194
5. To make an executor answerable for paper money, at the scale of the day on which he received

received it, is in general wrong, but if he hath charged himself fo, and pointed out no other mode of adjusting it, he shall be bound by his own act.
Granberry *vs* Granberry. 246
                            · 248

6. A conveyance of land in 1779 in fee simple, upon a ground rent payable for ever in *current money*, the rent is subject to the scale of depreciation. Watson *vs* Alexander. 353

7. See Acts of Assembly, No. 4, 5.

8. See Executors &c No 5

GUARDIAN, No. 2.

DETINUE.

1. In an action of detinue, for five slaves, if the jury find for the plaintiff as to four of them, without also finding for the plaintiff or defendant as to the fifth, the verdict will be set aside. Butler *vs* Parks. 76

2. In detinue, the plaintiff must prove *property* in himself, and *possession* in the defendant; but proof of a possession *anterior* to the bringing of the action is sufficient, unless he has been *legally dispossessed*, and this the defendant is to shew. Bumley *vs* Lambert. 308

DEVISE.

1. The testator devises to five persons being his brothers and nephews, to each a tract of land by name, with all the cattle &c. and appurtenances thereto belonging in fee. Then gives all his negroes young and old, at all his plantations before named, to be equally divided between his three brothers before mentioned: After some pecuniary legacies he directs, that if his two nephews should either of them die before marriage, or without issue, the legacies left to one, to go to the other, and if both die before marriage, or without issue, their legacies to go to the testator's three brothers. The testator when he made his will, had no lands but those devised, nor any slaves, but those who were on the plantations. He afterwards purchased another plantation called W. & 8 slaves, only 3 of whom were at W. at his death: the others were at the devised plantations from whence others were removed to W. & some were out at nurse for their maintenance. The words *all my negroes, young and old, at all my plantations, above named*, form a specific restrictive devise of the slaves on the devised plantations at the time of the testators death, and not a devise of all his slaves; nor is there any difference between the after purchased slaves and the others, for in this respect, they are to be considered as personal property. But their settled habitations, as fixed by the testator, ought to give the rule and not any casual absence therefrom at his death. P. 58, 59, 60.

A TABLE OF THE PRINCIPAL MATTERS.

3. The negroes found on the plantation at W. at the time of the testator's death, do not pass under this clause, but descend to the heir at law. 60

4. The crops growing at the time of the testator's death (he having died in September) do not pass under the word appurtenances, to the devisees of the respective plantations, but go into the surplus, 61, 62, 63.

5. The residuary estate in this case goes to the executors, as is always the case where there are many executors, and unequal legacies are given to them. 64

6. Devise in 1764 to A. for life, and after her decease to the testator's nephew and the heirs of his body lawfully begotten, for ever; but in case he die without such issue, then to T. H. the brother of the testator in fee. The nephew died in 1780 under age, in estate and without issue. A. died in 1786, the remainder over cannot take effect, but the estate will descend to the heir at law of the first remainder-man.
Hunter vs. Haynes, 71

7. R. M. seized of three tracts of land, and entitled to the equity of redemption in a fourth, made his will in 1743, and after declaring " that as touching his temporal estate he desires the same may be employed as follows." in the first place directs that all his just debts be paid. He then devises to his eldest son all his lands at O & F with some negroes and stocks. To his other son all his lands at C with some negroes and stocks. To his wife and daughter he gives *all the rest of his estate real and personal* (saving one negro by name which he gives to his second son;) but no words of inheritance are annexed to any of the devises. The inheritance in the land devised to the heir at law descended upon him, and did not pass under the residuary clause to the wife and daughter. Kennon vs M'-Robert & wife. 96

8. In a *general* devise of lands *without limitation* or *restriction*, the reversion will not pass under a general residuary clause, but will descend to the heir at law.
Ibid.

9. A reversion in slaves after an estate for life given by the same will, will pass under a general devise of " all the rest and residue of my slaves."
Cole vs Claiborne, 262

10. The testator devises the whole of his estate to his wife during her natural life, and after that is ended, then to be equally divided between whoever his wife should think proper to make *her heir or heirs*, and his brother R S. The wife died without making any appointment. She took a fee simple in the moiety which will descend to *her heir* at law. Shermer vs Shermer, 266

A TABLE OF THE PRINCIPAL MATTERS.

11. If a man having both freehold and leasehold lands in the same county, devise *all his lands in that county*; only the *freehold lands* will pass. Minnis *vs* Aylett. 300

12. The testator devises to his daughter M. 20*l.* as her full legacy, and in bar of any claim she might have on his estate. He then gives a tract of land to her heirs lawfully begotten on her body, to be held by them under the limitations contained in the devise to *the heirs of A V.* He devises to *A V. and his heirs* lawfully begotten, a tract of land with sundry limitations over. At the time the will was made, M. had a daughter, and afterwards a son who immediately after his birth died. The daughter of M. took by purchase as *heir apparent* at the death of the testator. Pendleton *vs* Van devier. 381

13. See CONDITION, No. 1
    VERDICT, No. 5.
    SLAVES, No. 1.
    DISTRESS.
    ↲. See CLERKS.

E

EQUITY.

1. Courts of equity, never interfere to deprive the plaintiff at law of a legal advantage, which he may have gained, unless the party seeking relief, will do compleat justice by paying what is really due. Upon the same principle, that court has refused its aid in relieving against a judgment obtained by fraud. Payne *vs* Dudley. 199

2. Though *equitable* rights, may in favor of a fair *bona fide* purchaser for valuable consideration, and without notice, be lost by a sale; *legal* rights never can, unless there be fraud. Hoe and Harrison *vs* Pierce 217

3. A Judgment entered against a sheriff under a false idea in the clerk, that the bail piece was insufficient, where the counsel had agreed that it might be filed, relieved against in equity. Smith *vs* Wallace. 254

4. The grand father who had promised before mariage, to give his daughter a negro, made a deed of the negro to *the children of his daughter* begotten or to be begotten, (with the consent of the husband.) The next day, the grand father and father agreed to exchange the above negro for another, which was done. Bill to set up the first deed which was lost, and for a decree for the negro conveyed by that deed,—dismissed. Applebury *vs* Anthony. 287

5. If a man purchase land with notice of anothers equitable title, but that other neglects to assert his right for a long time, during which, valuable improvements are made, he ought not in equity to lose the value of those improvements, *aliter* if after the right is asserted, the improvements are made. Southall *vs* M'Keand. 336

6. In this case, the lawful proprietor

A TABLE OF THE PRINCIPAL MATTERS.

proprietor is entitled as againſt the purchaſer, or one claiming under him with notice, to the value of the land at the time it was purchaſed, for which he would have a lien on the land. But he would have no lien on the land in the hands of a purchaſer without notice, or againſt one who claimed under ſuch a purchaſer. *Ibid.*

ERROR.

1. See DECLARATION No. 7.

SUPERSEDEAS & WRIT of ERROR throughout.

APPEAL No. 4.

AMENDMENT No. 1.

ESCAPE.

1. In an action for an eſcape, the actual eſcape forms the *giſt* of the action, and therefore, muſt be proved by the plaintiff, but he is not bound to prove that it was with the conſent, or through the negligence of the officer, for this is to be preſumed, unleſs a tortious eſcape be ſhewn, and that freſh purſuit was made. Johnſon *vs* Maſon. 5

ESTATE TAIL.

1. See DEVISE No. 6.

EVIDENCE.

1. Parol proof may be admitted to prove, that an abſolute deed was intended to operate as a mortgage. Roſs *vs* Norvell. 15

2. It cannot be laid down as a general rule, that parol proof to contradict a deed, is not to be admitted *in any caſe*, or that it is to be admitted *in all caſes*. 15

3. A book of accounts in the hand writing of, and kept by a clerk who is ſince dead, is proper evidence, upon thoſe facts being proved. Lewis *vs* Norton. 76

4. The execution book kept by a clerk, will be *prima facie* evidence of the truth of the entries made in it, but it may be contradicted by other evidence. Taylor *vs* Dundaſs. 94

5. Hearſay evidence, in what caſe to be admitted? Jenkins *vs* Tom 123

6. If ſeperate actions be brot' againſt two for a joint treſpaſs, one defendant may be a witneſs for the other. Johnſon *vs* Bourn. 187

7. Upon a charge of fraud in obtaining a deed, witneſſes were examined, who proved an incapacity in the donor, both before and after the execution of it. But the evidence of the atteſting witneſſes, as to his capacity *at the time of execution*, overcame all the reſt of the teſtimony. Beckwith *vs* Butler. 225

8. If the defendant without taking oyer of the bond, plead to iſſue, the plaintiff may offer a copy in evidence, if the original be proved to be loſt or deſtroyed. Taylor's adminiſtratrix *vs* Peyton's adminiſtratrix. 253

9.

A TABLE OF THE PRINCIPAL MATTERS.

9. See ESCAPE No 1.

COURT No. 1.

CHANCERY No. 4, 8.

ACTS of ASSEMBLY No. 3.

DECLARATION No 2, 8.

DEED No. 3.

EXECUTORS &c. No. 4.

EXECUTION.

1. An execution being levied upon the property of one defendant, and a replevy bond taken, a second execution against the other defendant cannot iſſue, ſo long as the replevy bond is in force, it being a ſatisfaction of the original judgment. Taylor *vs* Dundaſs. 94

2. If a debtor in execution obtain an injunction, the ſheriff muſt diſcharge him out of cuſtody. Roſs *vs* Poythreſs. 120

3. Quere, If an injunction be obtained *after ſeizure of property* under a *fi. fa.* if the officer may reſtore the property? *Ibid.*

4. After the aſſent of an executor to a ſpecific legacy, the property is changed, and a creditor obtaining a judgment againſt the executor, cannot levy an execution upon the property in the hands of the legatee. He may purſue the executor, or follow the property in equity, making all the legatees parties. Burnly *vs* Lambert. 308

5. If a judgment be obtained againſt an executor, and the execution be levied upon a ſpecific legacy in poſſeſſion of the legatee, (with the aſſent of the executor) a purchaſer at the ſheriff's ſale acquires no title thereto. *Ibid.*

6. A purchaſer under a judgment and execution which is afterwards reverſed, ſhall not have his title impeached, but the injured party ſhall be reſtored to the money ariſing from the ſale. Burnley *vs* Lambert. 313

EXECUTORS and ADMINISTRATORS.

1. Tho' a judgment againſt an executor, amounts to an admiſſion of aſſets, and a court of equity would not relieve againſt the conſequences of the judgment, yet it would not by an original decree charge an executor on that ground. White Whittle & Co. *vs* Banniſter's executors. 168

2. There is no general rule as to an executor's liability to pay intereſt on money in his hands. In this caſe, he was charged with it from the end of *each year*, for the balance then reſting in his hands, but ſuch intereſt, not to be carried to the balance of the ſucceeding years. Granberry *vs* Granberry. 249

3. A legacy is given to an executor *as nephew* to the teſtator. He will be entitled to the legacy tho' he renounce the executorſhip. 250 *Ibid.*

4. An executor by the will is allowed the uſe of £500 for

A TABLE OF THE PRINCIPAL MATTERS.

for 5 years, without intereſt. He may pay it in depreciated paper money, and the entry of the payment in his account, will be evidence of his having paid it. Granberry vs Granberry. 251

5. A debtor by becoming an executor, not precluded from paying a debt due the teſtator in depreciated paper money. Ibid.

6. See ACTION No. 1.

DEVISE No. 5.

APPEAL No. 2.

COSTS No. 2.

DEPRECIATION No. 5.

COMMISSION No. 1.

COVENANT No. 1.

7. A legacy to executors, which ſhall exclude them from taking the ſurplus, muſt always be of a perſonal nature. Shelton vs Shelton. 67

EXTINGUISHMENT.

1. An annuity extinguiſhed in equity, (under the circumſtances of the caſe) by a bill of exchange and bond. Thornton vs Spotſwood. 142

F

FACTOR.

1. See AGENT No. 1. 3.

FAIRFAX Lord.

1. The maxim, " *nullum tempus occurrit regi*" never did apply to lord Fairfax. Birch vs Alexander. 37

FEES.

1. See CLERK No. 1.

FORFEITURE.

1. If land he forfeited for non-payment of quitrents &c. ſtill if they be paid, or the conditions performed, before the land is petitioned for, it is ſaved. Wilcox vs Calloway. 39

2. See DEED No. 5.

FORTHCOMING BOND.

1. In a bond for the forthcoming of property taken under execution, it is not neceſſary that the *time* appointed for the delivery ſhould be ſtated to be *that, at which the ſale is to take place.* Wood vs Davis. 69

2. The condition of a forthcoming bond ought to be certain as to the *time* and *place* of ſale, but need not ſtate, that *the day* mentioned is that appointed for *the ſale.* Irvin, &c. vs Eldridge. 161

3. A forthcoming bond appoints no *place* at which the delivery is to be made, yet good. Burwell vs Court. 254

4 The condition ought to recite, *againſt* whom the execution iſſued, and upon *whoſe property* it was levied. Hubbard vs Taylor. 259

5. A partial delivery is not a performance; but if the ſheriff receive and ſell what is ſo delivered,

A TABLE OF THE PRINCIPAL MATTERS.

livered, the amount is to be credited in the judgment on the bond. Pleafants, &c. *vs* Lewis. 273
6. See BREACH No. 2.

ACTION No. 5.

FRAUD.

1. A mortgagor of perfonal property continuing in poffeffion, is not an evidence of fraud, if the mortgage be upon a *bona fida* confideration, and be duly recorded. Claiborne *vs* Hill 177
2. See CHANCERY No. 2.

DAMAGE No. 2.

CONDITION No. 1, & 4.

DEED No 2.

AGREEMENT No. 4.

FREIGHT.

1. A merchantman being alfo a letter of marque, having taken in goods on freight, may *chafe* an enemy in fight, but cannot *cruize* out of her courfe to look for one. If therefore fhe be injured in an action with an enemy, in fight when fhe chafed, by which fhe is forced into a port different from that of her deftination, fhe is entitled to freight. But if the goods be not afterwards fent to the port of delivery, fhe is entitled only to freight *pro rata itineris*, unlefs prevented from doing fo by the freighter. Hooe & Harrifon *vs* Mafon. 211.

G.

GAMING.

1. See ASSIGNMENT No. 1, 2.

GRANT.

1. A lapfe patent relates back to the original grant, fo as to avoid all *mefne* grants from the crown. Wilcox *vs* Calloway. 39

GUARDIAN and WARD.

1. A guardian may leafe the lands of his ward during infancy, if the guardianfhip fo long continue, and may referve the rents to the ward, or to himfelf; and payment of the rent in either cafe to the guardian would be good. Rofs *vs* Gill. 90
2. A legacy paid in 1778 to the guardian, in depreciated paper money, is good, and will be a difcharge at the nominal amount. And the guardian, having lent out part of the money, and received it in depreciated paper which he at laft funded, he is not liable for the lofs by depreciation. Sallee *vs* Yates. 226

H.

HEIR.

1. See DEVISE No. 12.

HOTCHPOT.

1. See ADVANCEMENT No. 1.

HUSBAND and WIFE.

1. A feme fole entitled to flaves in remainder, or reverfion,

A TABLE OF THE PRINCIPAL MATTERS.

sion, and afterwards marrying and dying before the determination of the particular estate, the right vests in the husband. Dade *vs* Alexander. 30

J.

JEOFAIL and AMENDMENT.

1. See PLEADING No. 2.

JUDGMENT No. 1.

IMPROVEMENT.

1. See EQUITY No. 5. 6.

INDIANS.

1. When Indians might be made slaves, and when they could not, and what Indians they were which could be made slaves? Jenkins *vs* Tom. 123
2. Since the year 1705, no *American Indian* could be made a slave. But foreign Indians coming within the description of that act might he made slaves. Dick *vs* Coleman. 239
3. The jury having found that the plaintiffs were brought into this state *generally*, without saying *from whence*, is a sufficient finding for the plaintiffs. *Ibid.*

INDORSEMENT.

1. See BOND No. 2.

INFANT.

1. The priviledges allowed to infants are for their protection, and not to furnish them with the means of defrauding others. A man tho' not bound by a bond given during infancy, may after full age bind himself by his assumpsit to pay it. Buckner *vs* Smith. 499

INJUNCTION.

1. See EXECUTION No. 2, 3.

INSOLVENT.

1. The *property* of an insolvent debtor afterwards acquired, is not exempted from the payment of prior debts; it is his *person* only which is protected. Payne *vs* Dudley. 198

INSPECTOR.

1. If an inspector deliver tobacco to a forged order, he is liable. Thweat *vs* Finch. 217

INTEREST.

1. Debt upon a note for the payment of a certain sum *with interest from the date.* If the declaration do not claim *interest*, judgment upon *non sum informatus*, must be entered for the *principal only.* Hubbard *vs* Blow 70
2. See DAMAGES No. 1. EXECUTORS No. 2.
3. An officer of a court having in his possession money raised by the sale of attached effects, which the court had forbid him to pay over, shall pay interest, unless he kept the principal by him. Hunter *vs* Spotswood. 145

ISSUE.

1. The omission of a *similiter* after a trial, shall not vitiate the

the verdict. Brewer *vs* Tarpley. 363
2. Judgment reversed for want of an issue. Stevens *vs* Taliaferro. 155
3. A special plea concludes thus " and this &c." This is bad if specially demurred to. Cooke *vs* Beale's executors 312
4. Where one defendant entering himself a defendant, shall after a trial and verdict, be confined to the issue made up by the other defendant. Barnet *vs* Watson. 379
5. See ARBITRAMENT, &c. No. 2, 4.
CHANCERY No. 7, 9.
PLEADING No. 2, 5, 6.

JUDGMENT.

1. In debt for rent, the verdict was for £490 the debt in the declaration mentioned, and £130 : 16 : 3 dam. Judgment was entered for the same, *to be discharged by the payment of £420.* The latter part is no part of the judgment, and will be considered as a release of the difference. Ross *vs* Gill. 90
2. The judgment in an action upon a bond brought in the name of the commonwealth, for the benefit of an *individual* injured by a breach of the condition, ought not to *attach* the recovery *to that individual as to future injuries,* but should leave *other persons* who may be so injured, to sue out a *sci. fa.* upon it. Bibb *vs* Cauthorne. 91
3. See APPEAL No. 4.

JURISDICTION.

1. Where a suit is brought in a *Corporation Court,* the cause of action must be laid to have arisen *within the jurisdiction of the court* Thornton *vs* Smith, 81
Winder *vs* Eddy, 87
2. See CHANCERY No. 3, 6.

JURY.

1. The trial by jury is not to be taken away, without positive words in an act of Assembly. Watson *vs* Alexander, 356
2. See COURT No. 2.

L.

LAND.

1. A right by settlement in the crown lands, could not be acquired until the act of 1779, and this act only gives to settlers a preference, in lands at that time *waste and unappropriated,* and which had not before that time been located under *warrants.* Jones *vs* Williams 231.
2. See FORFEITURE No. 1.

LANDLORD & TENANT

1. If the tenant has enjoyed the land, he cannot repel the landlord's claim for rent, by saying he had nothing in the land, or that the conveyance was void. Watson *vs* Alexander. 355
Aliter if he be evicted. Ross *vs* Gill. 90
2. See action No. 3.

LAW.

1. See ACTS of ASSEMBLY No. 2.

LEGACY.

A TABLE OF THE PRINCIPAL MATTERS.

LEGACY.

1. See DEVISE, No. 5.
EXECUTORS, &c. No. 7, 3.
EXECUTION, No. 4, 5.

LETTER OF MARQUE.

1. See FREIGHT No. 1.

LIABILITY.

1. See ACTION, No. 2.

LIEN.

1. See EQUITY No. 6.

LIMITATIONS, act of.

1. In what cases, the act of limitations will not bar a right in equity. Hunter *vs* Spotswood, 145
2. If the action be commenced within 5 years, and that time runs out, and then the suit abates, the plaintiff is within the equity of the proviso in the act, if he recommence his action within a year after the abatement. Brown's exec. *vs* Putney. 302

M.

MARRIAGE agreements.

1. Construction of—Roane's ex. *vs* Hearne. 47
2. AGREEMENT, No. 2.

MAXIMS.

1. See FAIRFAX Lord, No. 1
PURCHASER, No. 1.

MEMORANDUM.

1. See AGREEMENT, No. 4

MISTAKE.

1. See EQUITY, No. 3.

MONEY.

See DECLARATION, No. 1, 5.
DEPRECIATION No. 2, 3, 4, 5, 6. GUARDIAN No. 2.
TENDER & REFUSAL, No. 2

MORTGAGE.

1. The reason why 20 years is generally fixed upon as the time, within which an application for redemption must be made, is not because the entry is taken away after that period, but because the right of redeeming after such a length of time, is presumed to have been abandoned. Ross *vs* Norvell. 18
2. Slaves may be redeemed after 5 years, and within 20. *Ibid.*
3. What is a mortgage, and what a defeasable purchase. Thompson *vs* Davenport. 125
4. See EVIDENCE No. 1.
CHANCERY No. 5
FRAUD No. 1.
DEED No. 1.

MOTION.

See BOND No. 3.

N.

NEW TRIAL.

1. Where some of the jury are persuaded by the others, that a majority agreeing to the verdict must prevail, in consequence of which they do not object, this being proved by the testimony of many of the jurors, will set aside the verdict

A TABLE OF THE PRINCIPAL MATTERS.

dict. Cochran *vs* Street. 79

2. In trespass against 2, if one be found guilty, and the other be acquitted, a new trial ought not (upon the motion of the former) to be awarded. Boswell *vs* Jones. 325

3. It is error to award a new trial without costs. *Ibid.*

4. See CHANCERY No. 1, 9. COURT No. 4.

5. It is irregular and improper to move for a new trial upon the ground of misdirection. Johnson *vs* Macon. 5

NONSUIT.

1. The court cannot compel the plaintiff to suffer a nonsuit; they may advise it, and order the plaintiff to be called, but if he will appear, the court can no otherwise protect its opinion, in case the jury find against the direction, but by granting a new trial. Ross *vs* Gill. 87

2. If the court direct a nonsuit, and the plaintiff submit to it, he deserts his cause, and cannot avail himself (by a bill of exceptions) of an erroneous opinion delivered by the court. Thornton *vs* Jett. 138

3. See COURT No. 3.

NOTICE.

See DECLARATION No. 8.
EQUITY No. 5.
PURCHASER No. 1.

O.
OBLIGATION.

See BOND.

OYER.

See EVIDENCE No. 8.

P.

PARENT and CHILD.

See EQUITY No. 4.

PARTNERS.

1. One partner may be sued alone, and he can help himself only by a plea in abatement. Brown *vs* Belches. 9

2. A debt due from an individual partner cannot be set off against a partnership demand. But a payment to one partner is a payment to all, unless perhaps where it is forbidden by the company. Scot *vs* Trent. 79

3. See ABATEMENT No. 1. PLEADING No. 8, 9.

PAYMENT.

1. In what manner payments are to be applied. Thompson *vs* Davenport. 127

2. See ATTORNEY No. 1.
PARTNERS No. 2.
DEPRECIATION No. 2.
GUARDIAN No. 2.
EXECUTORS &c. No. 4, 5.
AGREEMENT No. 4.

PENALTY.

See CONTRACT No. 1, 3
PLEADING.

A TABLE OF THE PRINCIPAL MATTERS.

PLEADING.

1. See ABATEMENT No. 1.
PARTNERS No. 1.
INTEREST No. 1.
BOND No. 3, 5.
JURISDICTION No. 1.
ASSUMPSIT No. 1, 2.
BREACH No. 1.
EVIDENCE No. 8.
ISSUE No. 1, 3.
AGREEMENT No. 5.
AMENDMENT No. 2.

2. Declaration upon a marriage promise, by which the defendant agreed to give to the plaintiff, as much of his estate as he should give to any of his own children. The plaintiff should have avered the *quantity* and *quality* of the estate given to the defendant's own children. This might have been cured by verdict, if rendered upon the trial of a proper issue. Smith *vs* Walker. 135

3. The plea of non-assumpsit within 5 years, if general, will refer to the *time of the plea*, whereas it ought to refer to the *institution of the suit*, and ought to conclude with an averment. 155

4. If all the pleadings including the declaration be faulty, the court will dismiss the suit, and will not award a repleader, tho' in a case, where otherwise a repleader would have been proper. *Ibid.*

5. Debt upon a bond. Plea " that I. S. was jointly bound with the testator of the defendant in the bond, and survived him." Replication, " that it " is not *expressed* in the bond, " that the said I. S. was *jointly* " bound with the defendant's " testator, and if it were, by " the act of 1786 intituled an " act &c. it is declared, that the " representative of one jointly " bound with another, may be " sued, as well as the surviving " obligor, and insists therefore, " that the action does not sur- " vive &c. and this he is ready " to verify &c." The record states " and thereupon an issue was joined by the parties." The plea is good, and the replication vicious, and a repleader from the plea awarded. Stevens *vs* Taliaferro. 155

6. The judgment in this case also erroneous, because no issue joined. *Ibid.*

7. Power given to 4 executors to make a conveyance, which is executed by 3 only, but the declaratoin states that all of them joined in the deed, and the defendant without craving oyer, pleads covenants performed. After verdict, it cannot be objected, that all the executors did not execute the deed. Watson *vs* Alexander, 340, 351

8. Declaration *vs* B W & co. W appears and pleads non-assumpsit. Aterwards B against whom the suit had abated by the return, *entered himself a defendant*, and without filing a plea, entered into the trial and defended the suit. Judgment against B & W only. The judgment is

A TABLE OF THE PRINCIPAL MATTERS.

is proper against those two, as they did not discover by a proper plea, that there were other partners. Barnet *vs.* Watson. 372

9. In the above case, B by entering himself a defendant and going to trial, without putting in a seperate plea, bound himself to abide by the plea of his partner. Barnet *vs* Watson 379

10. See TENDER & REFUSAL, No. 1, 2.

POWER.

See DEVISE, No 10.
PLEADING, No. 7.

PRACTICE.

1. After office judgment, the court has a discretionary power to admit any plea, which appears necessary for the defendant's defence, tho' not issuable, and should refuse it only, where delay appears to be intended. Downman *vs* Downman's ex. 28

2 The court will not permit the clerk to give out a copy of any judgment during the term, without a special order, which will never be given but for strong reasons; as if the delay would endanger the debt. Hudson *vs* Ross. 75

3. If after a supersedeas obtained, the defendant, in error die, a *sci. fa.* must be awarded against his executors or administrators, and not a *new writ of superfedeas,* because the latter, could not be considered as *a continuing process,* and therefore the executor could not sue upon the supersedeas bond first given. Keel and Roberts *vs* Herbert. 138

4. If in trover, the true nature if the action be not endorsed, the court may upon *inspection of the writ,* dismiss the suit, if the motion be made *at* or *before the term,* next after an office judgment has been entered, but not after. Williams *vs* Campbell. 152

5. Where both of the plaintiffs in error die, a *sci. fa.* must issue in the name of both of their executors. Boswell *vs* Jones. 325

6. See APPEAL No 3.
CHANCERY No. 8.
COURT No. 4.
ACTS of ASSEMBLY No. 5.
AMENDMENT No. 2.
TENDER and REFUSAL No 2.

PRESUMPTION.

1. The Presumption arising from length of time, may be repelled by accounting for the delay. Eustace *vs* Gaskins. 188.

2. See ESCAPE No. 1.

PRETENSED TITLES.

1. The act for preventing the purchasing of pretensed titles does not extend to a person in *possession,* so as to prevent him from confirming that possession by purchasing the rights of others. Wilcox *vs* Calloway 39.

PRIZE.

See ADMIRALTY, No. 1.

PROFITS

A TABLE OF THE PRINCIPAL MATTERS.

PROFITS.

See CHANCERY, No. 7.

PROMISE.

See AGREEMENT No. 2.
CONSIDERATION, No. 1.
ASSUMPSIT, No. 4.

PROPERTY.

See ADMIRALTY No. 1.
EQUITY, No. 4.
EXECUTION, No. 4, 5, 6.

PURCHASER.

1. The rule *caveat emptor*, applies only to the purchasers of defective *legal* titles. The purchaser of the legal title, is not to be affected by a latent equity, of which he had no notice, actual or constructive. Wilcox *vs* Colloway. 41
2. See EQUITY No. 2, 5, 6.
EXECUTION No. 5, 6.
DEVISE No. 12.

R.

RECORD.

See DEED No. 1, 3.

RELATION.

1. See GRANT No. 1.
2. Priority of title will draw to it priority of relation. Wilcox *vs* Calloway. 40

RELEASE.

See JUDGMENT No. 1.

REMAINDER.

See DEVISE No. 6.

RENT.

See LANDLORD &c. No. 1.

REPLEADER.

See PLEADING No. 4, 5.

REPLEVY BOND.

See EXECUTION No. 1.

S.

SALE.

See ADMIRALTY No. 1.
EQUITY No. 2.

SATISFACTION.

See EXECUTION No. 1.

SCIREFACIAS.

1. See JUDGMENT No. 2.
PRACTICE No. 3, 5.
APPEAL No. 3.

SEAL.

1. A scroll is a seal. Jones *vs* Logwood. 42

SEISIN.

1. In tracing a title in a special verdict it is not necessary to find a *seisin in the crown*, because that is the ultimate point, beyond which the party is not bound to go. Birch *vs* Alexander. 36

SENTENCE.

See ADMIRALTY No. 1.

SETTLEMENT RIGHT.

See LAND No. 1.

SETT-OFF.

A TABLE OF THE PRINCIPAL MATTERS.

SET-T-OFF.

1. A tenant having leafed land from an executor, cannot purchafe in judgments againft the teftator and fet them off againft the rent. It might be otherwife, if the executor fhould have *acknowledged* that he had a fufficiency of affets. White, Whittle & Co. *vs* Bannifter's executors. 167

2. An executrix having advertifed the fale of the property of her teftator, and agreed that *creditors* purchafing at the fale fhould be entitled to a difcount of 5 per cent, the defendant (who was not a creditor) purchafed at the fale and gave his bond. Upon the plea of payment, the defendant offered to fett-off 2 bonds due from the teftator, which were affigned to him fince the inftitution of the fuit. The *advertifement* extended only to *purchafing creditors*, and the bonds were not a proper off-fett. Brown's adminiftratix *vs* Garland. 221

3. See PARTNERS No. 2.
DEPRECIATION No. 2.

SHERIFF.

1. The high fheriff alone is liable for the official acts of his deputy, unlefs in thofe cafes, where the law provides a fpecial remedy againft the latter. White *vs* Johnfon. 159

2. The law requires a deputy fheriff to add the name of his principal, as well as his own to all mefne procefs executed by him. But if he fail to do fo, it does not authorife the entering a judgment againft him for failing to take a bail bond, tho' individually he is liable to a penalty for the omiffion. *Ibid.*

3. A judgment cannot be entered againft a *deputy* fheriff, for failing to take a bail bond. Armiftead *vs* Marks. 326

4. If a judgment be entered againft the defendant and *deputy* fheriff, the latter may alone obtain a fuperfedeas. *Ibid.*

See DAMAGES, No. 1.

BAIL, No 1.

SLANDER.

1. Declaration; that the defendant *with intention to injure the reputation of the plaintiff as a merchant, falfely and malicioufly* fpoke of him (then being a merchant) the following words, " Mr. Y. I muft tell you, that you have received more tobacco than you have accounted for to the Houfe," (meaning the mercantile houfe of which the plaintiff and defendant were partners) but no *colloquum* is laid. After verdict, the judgment ought not to be arrefted. Hoyle *vs* Young. 150

SLAVES.

1. Money directed by will to be laid out in flaves and annexed to lands devifed in tail by the fame will, are to be confidered as flaves, and will go with the land in tail. Dade *vs* Alexander

A TABLE OF THE PRINCIPAL MATTERS.

2. See HUSBAND and WIFE. No. 1.
INDIANS, No. 1, 2, 3.
ACTS of ASSEMBLY, No. 1.
ACTION, No. 4.
CONDITION, No. 2.
SPECIFIC PERFORMANCE.

See AGREEMENT, No 3.
ARBITRAMENT and AWARD, No. 5.

STORE ACCOUNT.
See ACTS of ASSEMBLY No. 3

SUPERSEDEAS and writ of ERROR.

1. A superfedeas is sometimes an auxiliary process, but most commonly it is a mean, by which the record of an inferior court may be removed before a superior one for revision. In the former case, it can have no effect after the decree or judgment is *executed*, tho' the suit may still go on, and if a reversal take place, a writ of restitution will be awarded. White *vs* Jones 118
2. See PRACTICE No. 3, 5.
EXECUTION, No. 6.
SHERIFF, No. 4.

SURETY.
See ACTION, No. 1.

SURVIVORSHIP.
See BOND, No. 5.

T.

TENDER & REFUSAL.
1. Plea of tender—what

good one. Downman *vs* Downman's Ex. 28
2. Where paper money was tendered, the plea ought to state specially the *sort of money*, which was offered, "and that the defendant was always ready to pay *that very money*." But if it alledge a tender of money generally, the defendant must bring into court, that which *is money at the time of the plea pleaded*. If he do not, the plaintiff may sign judgment, or the plea, if offered upon setting aside an office judgment, ought not to be received. Downman *vs* Dawnman's Ex. 29.
2. Where a man is to pay money, or to deliver property at a valuation, he is not bound to carry the property to the creditor, but the latter should receive it at the debtor's house. Danlride *vs* Harris. 326
See DEPRECIATION, No 4.
BOND, No. 3.

U.

USURY.
1. The court will never presume a contract to be usurious, unless it be proved. Upon a contract payable in Pennsylvania currency, reserving interest *generally*, if a decree be entered by consent, for 6 per cent. it will be considered as a Pennsylvania contract and not usurious. *Aliter* if the decree were entered for 6 per cent. in consideration of indulgence as to the time of payment. M'Guire *vs* Warler. 368
See

A TABLE OF THE PRINCIPAL MATTERS.

See CONTRACT, No. 1, 3.

VALUER.

See AGREEMENT, No. 5.

VARIANCE.

1. The obligor is stated in the bond to be *of the county of E* which is omitted in the declaration. This not a material variance. Evans *vs* Smith, 72
2. Agreement by one *as treasurer of a jockey club*. Declaration against him without this description. Determined not to be a material variance. M'Williams *vs* Willis. 199
3. Declaration upon a bond given to W. P. *of the county of S. on account of Mess.* G & P. *merchants in Glasgow*. The declaration is in the name of W. P. without stating for whose use. variance immaterial. Peter *vs* Cock. 257
4. Declaration stating an agreement that defendant *would rent and furnish a house at L.* and board the defendant. Proof of an agreement *to board the defendant*.—variance immaterial. Wroe *vs* Washington, 357

See BREACH, No. 1.

VERDICT.

1. What is a sufficient finding of such a length of seizin as to give a title. Birch *v.* Alexander.

2. Verdict set aside as being uncertain and contradictory. Murra *vs* Northern. 282
3. Ind. ass. Plea non assumpsit. Verdict that the defendant has not paid the debt, and assess the damages by occasion of the non-performance of that assumption to 2941. The verdict substantially pursues the issue. Barnett, &c. *vs* Watson. 380.
4. See APEAL No. 1.
 NEW TRIAL No. 1.
 DETINUE No. 1.
 JUDGMENT No. 1.
 PLEADING No. 2.
 SLANDER No. 1.
 ABATEMENT No. 2.
 INDIANS No. 3.
 DECLARATION No. 5
 AMENDMENT No. 3.
5. The testator in attempting to describe the boundaries of a tract of land he is disposing of, leaves out a course, which throws the whole into confusion. The jury in a special verdict say " that if the testator intended to convey by such boundaries as they describe, then they find that to be the land in question; if by certain other bounds, then they find that the land devised was according to those bounds."
The court upon such finding, may decide which are the true boundaries. Pendleton *vs* Vanlevier. 381

W

WARRANTY.

See DECLARATION No. 8.

WILLS.

A TABLE OF THE PRINCIPAL MATTERS.

WILLS.

1. A will made since the 1st of January 1787, may pass lands acquired after the making of the will. Turpin *vs* Turpin. 75

2. A subsequent marriage and having of a child is an implied revocation of a will, and in such a case, the will ought not to be proved or admitted to record. Wilcox *vs* Rootes.

WITNESS.

1. See EVIDENCE No. 6.

DEED No. 3.

2. It is no objection to a deposition, that it is not signed by the witness. Barnett *vs* Watson. 380

3. What degree of interest disqualifies a witness. Barnett *vs* Watson. 140

ERRATA.

The Reader's attention is requested to the following corrections.

PAGE.	LINE.	
19	21	*for* of *read* or.
23	42	*for* refuse *read* refused.
25	17	*for* required *read* acquired.
28	16	*for* it *read* is.
29	17	*for* 1796, *read* 1790.
36	20	*after* grant *insert* to Robertson.
38	9	*for* appellee *read* appellant.
39	23 & 24	*for* to prevent *read* against.
	24	*for* pretensio *read* pretensed.
	40	*after* taken *insert* a.
40	30	*after* court *read* in.
45	2	*for* argued *read* agreed.
48	4	*after* death *strike out* also.
	19	*after* not *insert* to.
51	16	*for* statement *read* agreement.
	24	*for* maritial *read* marital.
	40	*after* be *insert* the.
	43	*after* gifts *strike out* of *and insert* made to.
52	15	*for* doubted *read* doubtful.
56	22	*for* Intention. The *read* intention, the.
57	8	*after* 2 P. Williams *read* 28.
59	15	*for* doubts *read* doubt.
60	33	*after* 2d *read* The.
	37	*for* in *read* on.
61	2	Horse-shoe to be enclosed within ( ).
62	23	*for* restrain *read* retain.
	27	*for* cas. in eq. anb. *read* Cas. Eq. Abr.
68	42	*for* go *read* goes.
85	9	*for* unresistible *read* irresistible.
102	42	*for* Burn. *read* Burr.
106	4	*for* 234. *read* 236.
122	12	*for* or *read* nor.
127	15	*for* purchase *read* re-purchase.
133	40	*for* or *read* nor.
140	33	*for* was *read* were.
144	28	*for* or *read* nor.
151	25	*for* frofessional *read* professional.
160	30	*for* County *read* Country.
191	36	*for* monts *read* months.
192	15	*for* to prevent *read* for discouraging.

ERRATA.

ERRATA.

P.	L.	
219	23	*for* his *read* their.
251	16	*for* that *read* than.
272	18	*strike out* to.

345   19 20 & 21, *for* in such a case and therefore it is possible that the parties may have had paper money in view, *read* (and therefore it is possible, that in such a case the parties may have had paper money in view.)

349   38   *for* doubt *read* debt.

INDEX TO REPORTS OF CASES ARGUED AND DETERMINED IN THE COURT OF APPEALS OF VIRGINIA

The following all-inclusive index referencing the individual, company, geographic, county, court jurisdiction and ship names setforth in the civil, probate and criminal cases on pages 1 through 392, inclusive, of <u>Reports of Cases Argued and Determined in the Court of Appeals of Virginia</u> by Bushrod Washington Vol. I. Richmond printed by Thomas Nicolson, M,DCC,XCVIII, was prepared and compiled by Carol E. Chafin Copyright © 2000. All rights are reserved under International and Pan-American Copyright Conventions. This Index may not be reproduced, in whole or in part, in any form, without written permission of Carol E. Chafin.

----, Henry 105
----, Nathan 105
----, Prudence 382-388
----, William 105
A.C., 387
A.R., 91
ABOTT, 110
ACCOMACK COUNTY, Court of 6 District Court of 273
ALBERMARLE COUNTY, 69 Court of 135
ALEXANDER & CO., 331
ALEXANDER, 30 34 37 77 285 340 Charles 35 36 Gerard 35 36 John 34-37 340 Parthenia 35 Philip 34 35 Robert 34-36 Sarah 35
ALEXANDRIA, Va. 207 209 211 340
AMBROSE, 100 102
AMELIA COUNTY, Court of 330
AMSTERDAM, 207
ANDERSON, 6 156 158 186 294 329 Nathaniel 260 Thomas 186 William 5
ANTHONY, 287 289 James 287 288
APPAMATOX, 97

APPLEBURY, 287-289 Elizabeth 287 Thomas 287
ARMISTEAD, 325 326
ARSCOTT, 259
ASBERRY, 72 73 George 72 73
ATKINSON, 108 253
AYLESBURY, 85 86
AYLETT, 300 Philip 300 William 300
BACHE, 206
BACHELLOR, 66
BACKISTON, 310
BADDELEY, 102
BAILEY, 13
BAIRD, 170
BAKER, 78
BALDWIN, 267-269
BALTIMORE, 23 208
BAMPTON, 297 299
BANKS, Mrs. 240
BANNISTER, 166 173-176 John 174 176 177 Mr. 173 174 176
BARKSDALE, 70
BARNETT, WOOLFOLK & CO., 372-376 378-380
BARNETT, 372-375 377-379
BARTLETT, 301 302
BATES, 75

REPORTS OF CASES ARGUED AND DETERMINED IN THE COURT OF
APPEALS OF VIRGINIA

BATTERSEA mills, 166-169
BAYLOR, 162
BEACHCROFT, 106 108 109 Joseph
  109 Sir Robert 109
BEALE, 11-13 192 313
BEAUMONT, 383 386
BECKWITH, 107 108, Sir Jonathan
  224 Sir Marmaduke 224 226 Mary
  107
BEDFORD COUNTY, Court of 72
BELCHES, 9
BELL TAVERN, 106
BENNET, 247 248
BENTLEY, 273 William 4
BERKELEY COUNTY, Court of 162
  193 319 320
BERKLEY, 206 Nelson 204 Sir
  William 34
BERNARD, 85 86 186
BERRIGE, 63
BEVERLEY, 296-300 390-392
BIBB, 8 91 344 Richard 91 William 91
BIRCH, 34 36 285 Jenet 36
BISHOP (ship), 212
BLACKBOURN, 267
BLACKET, 103
BLAIGROVE, 170
BLAND, Theoderick 97
BLIGHT, 103 104
BLOW, 70
BLOWE, 78
BLUMFIELD, 95
BOLLING(S), 218 219 Robert 217 218
  220
BOLTON, Duke of 104
BOROUGHS, 202
BOSTON, city of 208
BOSWELL, 322-325
BOURN, 187
BOWKER, 66

BOWS, 103
BOWYER, 297 299
BRACKENRIDGE, 161
BRASBRIDGE, 66
BRAXTON, 31 128-130 132-134 178
  179 181 380 C. 179 Carter 130 177
  Mr. 129 131-133 381
BREWER, 363
BRIDGES, 284
BRIDGEWATER, Countess of 104
BRIGGS, 170
BRISTOL, Lord 62
BRISTOW, 359
BROOKING, 385-387
BROOKMAN, 253
BROOMAN, 47
BROWN, 9 56 221 302 W.B. 221
BROWNS, 66
BRUNSWICK, District Court of 98
BUCHANAN, Andrew 291
BUCKINGHAM COURTHOUSE, 161
BUCKNER, 296 391
BULLER, Judge 103
BURCHETT, 383
BURNLEY, 308 310
BURWELL, 254
BUSHER, 258
BUTLER, 76 132 225 357 Beckwith
  224 Lawrence 224 Mr. 132
  Thomas 129
BYRD, 232 Colonel 336-338
CALL, 115 373 374 378 attorney 218
  219
CALLOWAY, 38 39 41 42 72
CAMDEN South Carolina, District of
  319
CAMERON, Baron of 34
CAMPBELL, 145-150 153 attorney
  151 183 186 191 195 197 198 226

INDEX

CAMPBELL (Cont.)
  235 241 248 256 276-278 293 297
  298 304 330 333 364 377 John 145
CANTERBURY, 86
CARGILLS (tract of land), 96 97 104
CARR, 260 John 260
CARRINGTON, George 45 Joseph 45
  Mayo 45 Nathaniel 45 Paul 45 Paul
  Court of Appeals Judge opposite
  page 1 116 223
CAUTHORNE, 91 Catherine 92 Mrs.
  91
CHAMBERLAYNE, 367
CHAMP, 138
CHANCERY, High Court of 2-4 11 12
  14 18 19 22 38 46 47 49 53 54 55
  79 93 116-118 120 125 126 128
  129 136 143 145 150 156 157 163-
  165 169 172 173 177 186 189 194-
  196 224 226 227 229 230 232 246
  251 253 254 255 266 274 275 287
  290 296 300 326 336 339 340 370
  380 390 392
CHANDOS, Duke of 284
CHARLOTTE COUNTY, Court of 259
CHARLOTTE COURTHOUSE, 259
CHARLOTTESVILLE, District Court
  of 10 69 70 77 187 259 260 273
CHESAPEAKE, 20 25
CHESELY, 13
CHILD, 16
CHINN, John 26 27
CHITTY, 310
CLAIBORN, 31 83 306
CLAIBORNE, 129 130 133 134 304
  326 Herbert 325 Mr. 132 William
  325
CLARK, 112
CLAYBORN, 179 262 A. 177-179
  Augustine 177-179 184 185 H. 177-
  179 184 Herbert 177-179 181 184

427

CLAYBORN (Cont.)
  185 John 177 Mary 263 William
  263 William P. 184
COCHRAN, 79
COCKE, 232 Henry 257 258 Richard
  258 Samuel 257
COGHILL, 108
COKE, Lord 44
COLE, 106 262 Mary 263 William
  262-264
COLEMAN, 233 237 239 Francis 234
COOK, Mrs. 47 51
COOKE, 306-308 313
COOPER, 86 310 364 376
COP(E)LAND, attorney 258 288
CORRIE, 153
COSBY, 365
COTTEREL, Mrs. 279 280
COWPER, Lord 109
COX, 39 40 John 38
CRAIG, Adam 128 186
CRENSHAW, 128
CREW, 107
CUBECK, estate of 107
CULLEN, 202
CUMBERLAND COUNTY, 93
CURRIE, 98 Mr. 98
CUSTICE, 76
DADE, 18 30 T. 35
DANDRIDGE, 326-329 N.W. 31
DANIEL, 154 306
DARTMOUTH, New England 208 209
  211
DAVENPORT, 126 127 D. 125 David
  125 126 J. 125 James 125
DAVIS, 69 112 162 H. 112 Humphrey
  112 J. 69
DAWSON, 118 120
DEAN, 109
DeGREY, Judge 105 108
DERBY, 109 Lord 144

DILLON, 280-282
DINWIDDIE, Governor 116
DIXON, 296-299 391 Mr. 299
DOBYNS, 185
DODSON, Thomas 107
DOE, 282 385
DONALDSON, 38-42 331
DOWNMAN, 26
DRUMMOND, 30
DRUMMOND'S NECK, 300
DRY, John 34
DUDLEY, William 196
DUMFRIES, District Court of 34 207 340
DUNCOMBE, 253
DUNDASS, 92-95 304
DURDANT, 383
DUVAL(L), attorney 80 160 179 223 264 310 330 374 376
DYGHTON, 267-270
DYKES, 95
EATON, 66 206 303 Mr. 66 William 9
EDDY, 87
EDGLEY, 267
EDMUNDSON, 192
ELDRIDGE, 161
ELLIOTT, 389-392 William 392
ESSEX COUNTY, 72 Court of 50 51 91
EUSTACE, 188 John 188-190 Mrs. 188 190 William 188 189
EVANS, 72
FAIRFAX, 144 County of 240 Court of 22 Lord 227-229 Thomas Lord 34
FARRINGTON, 65
FEARNE, Mr. 99
FIELD, 280-282 Theophilus 97
FINCH, Adam 217 John 217 218
FINNEY WOOD, 96 97 104
FLEET, 196-198

FLEMING, William Court of Appeals Judge opposite page 1
FLETCHER, 330
FOREST, 372-374 376 378-380
FORTESCUE, 110
FOSTER, 64 66
FREDERICK COUNTY, 313 Court of 314 369
FREDERICKSBURG, Corporation Court of 87 District Court of 155 199 281 308 373
FREEMAN, Sir John 106
FRESHWATER, 206 Thomas 282
GALT, 161
GANT, 271 272
GARDINER, 113
GARLAND, 221 224
GARRET, 118 120
GASCOIN, 16
GASKINS, 109 188
GENERAL WASHINGTON (ship), 207-209 210 212
GILES, 111
GILL, Erasmus 87 88 Sarah 87 88 90
GLEN, 257 258
GLENN, Jeremiah 170
GOFTON, 233
GOOCH, 260
GOOCHLAND COUNTY PLANTATION, 62 68
GOODRIGHT, 114
GORDON, 75
GORE, 233
GRAHAM, 296
GRANBERRY, 246 James 246 Josiah 246
GRAVES, 1-3 119 120 165 246 Francis 1
GRAY, 143 George 142 143 Mrs. 142-144

INDEX

GRAYSON, 108
GRIFFIN, 179
GROVES, 1-3 119 120 165 John 1-3
HALDIMAND, 200
HALSEY, Benjamin 319 Margaret 319
HALSTEAD, 108
HAMILTON, 189
HAMPSHIRE COUNTY, Court of 229
HANCOCK, 19-23 25 26
HANOVER COUNTY, 4 Court of 125 126 128
HANOVER PLANTATON, 53
HANSBOROUGH, 290-295 329 J. 291 Lettice 290
HARDWICKE, Lord 108 109 189
HARMANSON, 6 273
HARRIS, 326-330 Benjamin 226
HARRISON, 19 179 184 207 212 C. 178 Charles 185
HARTSHORNE, 340
HARVEY, 111 364
HATCHER, 117 H. 116 Henry 117
HATCHERS RUN, 173
HAWKINS, 204 206 John 204
HAXALL, 21 23
HAYLING, 96
HAYNES, 71 Thomas 71 72
HEALE, 259
HENDRICKS, 92-94
HENL(E)Y, Colonel 208 210 212
HERBERT, 138 203 360 362
HERN, 47 49 Ann 49 50 Mrs. 47
HERNDON, 145-149
HEWLET, 367
HILL, 16 83 128 129 134 177 Mr. 132
HINTON, 217
HITE, 365
HITHER DALE, 107
HODGSON, 100 102
HOGAN, 47
HOGG, 370 371 Capt. 370 Peter 369

HOLT, Lord 27 104 105 366
HOOE, 19 207 212
HOOMES, 389 Elizabeth 34
HORD, 30
HORNE, 114
HORSE-SHOE, 61
HOW, 152 190
HOWSEN, 34 36 37 Robert 34
HOYLE, 150
HUBBARD, 70 259
HUDSON, 10 70 71 74 Charles 74 Christopher 74 75
HUGGINS, 303
HULL BRIDGE, 85
HUNGERFORD, 62
HUNTER, 66 145-149 Elizabeth 71 James 146 Mr. 66 Thomas 71 72 William 71 145
HUNTERS, 71
HUXTEP, 47
I.L., 70
IBBETSON, 107 108
INDIANS (as slaves), Bess 123 124 Judith 234-239 Mary 123 124
IRHAM, Lord 16 17
IRVIN, GALT, AND COMPANY, 161
JACKSON, 128 Rowland 47
JACOBS, John J. 230
JAMES CITY COUNTY, 300
JEFFEREYS, 103
JENKINS, 123 237
JETT, 138 254
JOCKEY CLUB, 199-201
JOHNSON, 4 10 159 187 322-326 328 368 Mr. 18
JONES, 42 116 230 231 322 John 309 Joseph 88 89 291 Mr. 370 371 Peter 88 Sir Thomas 110 Wood 117 118
KEEL, 138 203 360 362
KEELING, 194-196

KEENE, 239 John 240 Newton 240-242 244 245 Robert 241 Thomas 240 William 239-245
KELLY, 190
KENNEDY, 162
KENNON, 96 265
KERR & CO., 172
KERR, George 173
KING, 267
KING AND QUEEN COUNTY, Court of 307 District Court of 42 72 153 306
KING WILLIAM COUNTY, 177 178 300 301 Court of 128 180
KNIGHTLY, 65
KNOTSFORD, 113
LADY JOHNSON (ship), 20-22 25
LAMBERT, 308
LAMMING, 385 387
LANCASTER, 86
LANCASTER COUNTY, Court of 188
LANGLY, 267-269
LAWSON, 67
LEAKE, 23
LEE, 239 306 attorney 209-211 213 215 319 341 344 345 349 350 384 391
LEEDS, 105
LEEDS TOWN, 357
LEFTWITCH, 303
LEIGH, 263 265 Martha 263
LEPPINGWELL, 102
LEWIS, 76 125 273 John 10
LICKING HOLE CREEK, 53 68
LOGWOOD, 42
LONG, 383 386 387
LOUDON, 344 365
LOUDOUN, 240
LOUGHBOROUGH, Lord 66-68
LOUISA COUNTY, 159 Court of 10

LOUISA PLANTATION, 53
LOVE, 172
LOVELACE, 86
LUTTEREL, Mr. 16
LYONS, Peter Court of Appeals Judge opposite page 1 180 196 198 202 206 253 257-259 261 265 299 388 392
MacBEATH, 200
MACON, 4 5
M'ALISTER, James 193 194 John 193 194 Sarah 194
MANCHESTER, 157
MANNING, Mathew 313
MANSFIELD, Lord 67 68 81 103 104 111 113 359
MARKS, 325
MARSHALL, attorney 76 80 86 122 148 149 155 163 171 175 180 182 187-189 196 198 205 206 209 219 222 223 230 236 238 253 256 261 264 267 269 275 277 278 288 292 293 295 301 303 304 307 311 314 316 317 330 347 349 358 361 366 368 387 William following dedication page
MARTIN, Bryant 227
MASON, George 207
MATISON, 253
MAYO, 336 337 339 Daniel 45 Joseph 45 Mr. 339 Wm. 45
MEATH COUNTY, 112
MEDTARD, 82 83
MELLING, 267
MERCER, 95 290-295 James Court of Appeals Judge opposite page 1 154 223 John 291
MERIWEATHER, 368
MERVYN, 112 Audl(e)y 112 Henry 112 113 Olivia 113

INDEX

M'GUIRE, 370 371 Edward 368 370
MICKIE, 135
MIDDLE-ROW, 85
MINNIS, 300
MITCHEL, 109 190
M'KEAND, 336-339 Mr. 338 339
MOOR, B. 146-148 Bernard 145 146
MOORE, 31 33 260 Bernard 31 John 260
MORETON, 254
MORGAN, Wm. 307 308
MORRIS, 70 71 380 Robert 331
M'RAE, 194-196
M'ROBERTS, 96 265 Mrs. 98
MUDGE, 103 104
MULLHALL, 96
MUMFORD, Ann 97 Elizabeth 97 Robert 96-99 104 111 Theoderick 97 98 104 111
MUNT, 64 66
MURRA, Tobias P. 282
MURRAY, 106
M'WILLIAMS, William 199 201
NASH, John 178
NELSON, 136
NEVISON, 357
NEW KENT COUNTY, 178 Court of 178 179
NEW LONDON, District Court of 170 304
NEWSUM, Lucy 87 88
NEWTON, 247 248
NICOLAS, 330
NICOLSON, Thomas title page
NOEL, 108
NORFOLK distillery, 172
NORTH-CLOSE estate, 107
NORTHERN, 282 284-286 E. 283 Edmund 283
NORTHERN NECK, 34 36 37 227
NORTHUMBERLAND, District Court of 26 123 138 191 237 239 252 282 363
NORTHWITH-CLOSE estate, 107
NORTON, 76
NORVELL, 14 15 17 18 Mr. 18
OCHANEACHY ISLAND, 96 97 99 104
OPIE, 114
ORANGE, Court of 373
OSBORN, John 78
OWENS CREEK, 53
OXLEY, 19-23 25 26
P.D., 70 71
PAGE, 157
PALGRAVE, 233
PALMER, 103
PANKY, 196
PARKER, 368 Lord 65-67 Richard 370
PARKS, 76
PATTIE, John 155
PAYNE, 197-199 John 196 William 196
PEACE AND PLENTY (ship), 20
PEAK, 364
PEAL, 111
PENDLETON, 381 384 Edmund Court of Appeals Judge Dedication Page, opposite page 1 3 5 7-10 13 15 23 27 36 39 43 46 51 55 73 74 77 78 80 82 89 92 93 98 117 119 123 126 131 135 136 138 139 141 151 153 156 158 160 162-164 167 171 172 176 182 184 186 188 190 192 198 211 215 219 225 226 228 231 233 238 244 248 271 273 274 278 282 286 288 294 299 302 303 305 308 311 317 322 325-327 335 336 351 362 364 367 368 378 380
PETER, 93 257 258 Walter 257 258

PETERSBURG, 157 Borough Court of 83 District Court of 87 120 150 217 233 330
PEYTON, 252
PHILADELPHIA, 208 331 335 369-371
PHILIPS, 258
PICKET, 83 304 306
PIERCE, 1 213 214 216 217 Thomas 212
PIPER, Benjamin 254 William 254
PLEASANTS & CO., 273
PLEASANTS, 8 344
PLE(A)SANTS SHORE & CO., 156 158 329
POCOCK, 315 364
POFEY, 76
POLLEXSEN, 110
PONSONBY, Richard 19-26
POTOMACK, 208
POTOWMACK RIVER, 19
POWELL, 111 336 337
POYNTZ, 103
POYTHRESS, 120
PRIDE, 83
PRINCE EDWARD COUNTY, Court of 8 District Court of 8 140 161 186
PRINNE, 152
PROCTOR, 206
PUERED, 253
PUGH, 359
PURCELL, 284-286 Tobias 283
PUTNEY, 302
QUEBECK, 20
QUEENSBERRY, Duke of 202
RADLEY, 189
RAPPAHANOCK RIVER, 208
RATCLIFF, 246
READ, 253

REYNOLDS, 164
RICE, 9
RICHARDS, 103
RICHMOND, 157 Borough Court of 82 City of 81 82 336 337 County Court of 185 District Court of 4 157 205 221 Hustings Court of 81
ROANE, 47 Ann 49 Mr. 51 52 Spencer 50 Spencer Court of Appeals Judge opposite page 1 Thomas 50 William 47-49 52
ROANOKE RIVER, 97
ROBERTS, 22 24 138 203 360 362
ROBERTSON, 36 37 James 36 Jenet 36
ROBINSON, 154 Jack 212 213 216
RODES, Matt 69
RODGERS, 230-232 David 230
RONALD, 273 attorney 121-123 159 160 170 175 186-188 206 246 254-256 266 331 333-335
ROOMER (farm), 107
ROOTES, 140 Philip 140
ROSE, 301 302 Alexander 291
ROSS & CO., 74
ROSS, 14 15 18 88 120 125 156 294 329 David 87 88 Mr. 17-19
ROWANTY, 97
ROWLINSON, 106
ROY, 153
ST. MARY'S, 20 25
ST. PETER'S CLOSE, 109
SALLEE, 226
SAUNDERS, 112 325
SAYER, 315 364
SCOTT, 77-79 115 373 374 378 James 78 John 78
SCRUGGS, G. 72
SEACROFT, 105
SEARLE, 66

INDEX

SEEKRIGHT, 45
SELWIN, 56
SEMPLE, 197 198 John 197
SHELLEY, 268
SHELLY, 187
SHELTON, 250 David 53 54 58 62 68
   John 53 54 58 68 Joseph 53-55
   Samuel 53 54 58 68 William 53 54
   58 68 69
SHERMER, 11 13 14 266 302 John
   266 Mrs. 266 267 271 Richard 266
SHIPMAN, 222
SHORE, 173-175 Mr. 174 175 Mrs.
   177
SHUTE, 9
SIDEBOTTOM, 109
SINGLETON, John 227 229 Thomas
   229
SISSON, 280 281 283-285 George 283
   286 Robert 282
SKIPWORTH, 82 83
SLAVES (given name only), Bess
   (Indian) 123 Bridget 263 Cudjo 61
   Dick 233 Dinah 287 289 Fanny 69
   Jack (at Rowanty) 97 Judith
   (Indian) 234-239 Lucy 287-289
   Mark 61 Mary (Indian) 123 Pat 233
   Rachel 61 Sam (at Roanoke) 97
   Sampson 61 Sarah 262 Taliver 212
   213 Tom 61 123 237 Will 262
SMALLMAN, 189
SMALLWOOD, 290 292-295 329
SMITH, 4-7 25 72 81 109 135 254 296
   299 391 Ballard 1 Mr. 299 Parke 4
SMOCK, 389-391
SNEED, 30
SNOW LADY JOHNSON (ship), 20
SOUTH BRANCH, 228
SOUTHALL, 336 Mr. 338 339
SOUTHCOTE, 309 310

SOUTHERLAND, 128-130 132-134
   Fendall 130 Mr. 131 132
SPENCER, 364 376
SPOTSWOOD, 144 147 148 280 281
   A. 142 Alexander 142 145 John 31
   142-145 mine tract 142 143
SPOTSYLVANIA COUNTY, Court of
   142 Justices of 31
STAFFORD COURT, 34
STANARD, 389-392
STANDISH, 189
STARK, attorney 148
STEVENS, Edward 155
STIP, 319
STITH, J. 232
STOCKDELL, John 1 2 4
STODDART, 372-374 376-380
   Benjamin 372 373
STOTSDALE, 344
STOTT, 331
STOVALL, 303
STREET, 79
STRONG, 112
STUBBLEFIELD, 296 297 299
SUFFOLK, District Court of 71 139
   212
SUMNER, Joseph 291
SURREY COUNTY, 258
SUSSEX COUNTY, Court of 178
SUTTON, 267 269
TABB, John 45
TALBOT, Lord 107-109
TALIAFERRO, John 155
TANNER, 106 108
TARGET, 271 272
TARPLEY, 185 363
TAYLOE, Col. 224 225
TAYLOR, 92-95 252 259 304 John 259
TAZEWELL, Henry Court of Appeals
   Judge opposite page 1
TEMPLE, 42

THOMAS, 222 Michael 69
THOMPSON, 125-127 142-144 Mr.
  126 142 143
THORNTON, 81 138 142 156 John
  155
THRUSTON, 76 77
THURLOW, Lord 66-68
THWEAT, 217
THWING, 16
TODD, Mr. 63
TOMKIES, 259
TOMLIN, 190
TOMLINSON, 230 267-270
TORRINGTON, Lord 77
TOTOPOTOMOY HANOVER, 53
TRAFFORD, 63
TRENT, 73 O. 72 73 P. 78 79
  PETERFIELD 77 78
TREVOR, 386
TRIGGS, 109
TRUEHEART, Mary 53 54 58 61
TURNER, 319 Benjamin 139
  Catharine 139 Clear 139 Joseph
  139 Sampson 139
TURPIN, 75
TWINE, 179 181 183 184
TYRONE COUNTY, 112
UPSHAW, 30
URQUHART, 372-374 376 379
URRY, 111
VALENTINE, 164 Edward 165
VANDERPOOL, 227 228
VANDEVIER, 381 384 386 Jacob 382
  384 385 Jacobus 381 384 385 388
  James 382 384 388
VANMETER, Abraham 381-383 385
  386 388 John 381 Magdalena 381-
  384 386 388 Prudence
  (granddaughter of Abraham) 382-
  388

WADE, 30
WALDOCK, 86
WALKER, 135 144 327 Mr. 142
WALLACE, 254 Henry 47
WALLER, 31 32 164 Benjamin 31
  Edward 165 Mr. 33
WARD, 274 277 280 289
WARDEN, attorney 143 148 154 181
  192 200 222 226 242 276 284 285
  297 299 301 307 309 363 364 373
  374
WARDER, 368
WASHINGTON, 357 attorney 143 146
  156 189 201 221 223 226 242 252
  253 260 268 281 283 285 310 311
  320 323 324 344 350 358 364 374
  378 386
WATKINS, Mr. 338
WATSON, 159 187 340 372-374 376
  379 John 91
WEAVER, 202
WEBB, 154
WEBBER, 274 277 289 Mrs. 274
WEST, 21 23 Mr. 23
WESTFALL, Abel 227-229 Cornelius
  227-229 Isaac 228 Jacob 227 228
  John 227-229 Zachariah 228
WESTMORELAND COUNTY, Court
  of 357
WHITE, WHITTLE & COMPANY,
  166
WHITE, 116 159 160 326 385-387
  Samuel 259 W. 159 William 159
WHITEHALL (tract of land), 97 98
WHITTLE, 166
WICKHAM, attorney 151 174 176 203
  213 215 233 234 237 238 258 259
  297 299 303 315 317 323 326 332
  334 365 366 368 390
WIGGETT, 16

INDEX

WILCOCKS, 303
WILCOX, 38-41 140 Edmund 140
   Mrs. 140 Susannah 140
WILD-BOAR CREEK, 53 62
WILLIAMS, 153 230 231 attorney 281
   383 386
WILLIAMSBURG, Borough Court of
   9 District Court of 9 76 254 257
   302 367 Husings Court of 302
WILLIAMSONS (tract), 54 55 60 61
WILLIS, 313 314 Colonel 199 Lewis
   199
WILMOT, Judge 102
WILSON, 194 195
WILY, 196
WINCHESTER, District Court of 194
   381
WINDER, 87
WINDHAM, 233
WINSLOW, 30 118-120
WISE, 106 108
WOOD, 69 154 162 D. 69 David 69 70
   J. 69 John 69 Josiah 69
WOODBRIDGE, John 240 241
WOODROFFE, 66
WOODSON, Mrs. 280
WOOLFOLK, 372-375 378 379 Joseph
   373
WRIGHT, 99 105 109 114 359
WROE, 357
YATES, 226
YERBY, George 241
YOUNG, 150

www.ingramcontent.com/pod-product-compliance
Lightning Source LLC
Chambersburg PA
CBHW050325230426
43663CB00010B/1749